The Anchor Guide to Orchestral Masterpieces

MELVIN BERGER

The Anchor Guide to Orchestral Masterpieces

ANCHOR BOOKS
DOUBLEDAY
New York London Toronto Sydney Auckland

AN ANCHOR BOOK
PUBLISHED BY DOUBLEDAY
a division of Bantam Doubleday Dell Publishing Group, Inc.
1540 Broadway, New York, New York 10036

ANCHOR BOOKS, DOUBLEDAY, and the portrayal of an anchor
are trademarks of Doubleday, a division of
Bantam Doubleday Dell Publishing Group, Inc.

Library of Congress Cataloging-in-Publication Data

Berger, Melvin.
The Anchor guide to orchestral masterpieces/by Melvin Berger.—
1st Anchor Books ed.
p.   cm.
Discography: p.
1. Orchestral music—Analysis, appreciation. I. Title.
MT125.B44   1995
784.2'015—dc20   94-41050
CIP   MN

ISBN 0-385-47200-5
Copyright © 1995 by Melvin Berger
All Rights Reserved
Printed in the United States of America
First Anchor Books Edition: September 1995

1 3 5 7 9 10 8 6 4 2

Once more, for Gilda, with all my love

Contents

SIR EDWARD ELGAR

CÉSAR FRANCK

GEORGE GERSHWIN

EDVARD GRIEG

GEORGE FRIDERIC HANDEL

ROY HARRIS

FRANZ JOSEPH HAYDN

Preface

THIS BOOK is for music lovers, for those eager to become familiar with the treasures of our musical heritage as well as for seasoned concertgoers. Although not designed primarily for professionals, it can also provide practicing musicians with a compact, basic guide to the symphonic repertoire.

In this *Guide* I cover over 300 of the world's greatest orchestral masterpieces, fully discussing about 230 compositions and offering capsule comments on the others. Underlying all is the premise that the more you know about a piece of music, the greater will be the gratification and joy you get from your listening experience—be it a live concert, CD, radio broadcast, or telecast.

My motivation in writing this book is to share with others the immense satisfaction and stimulation I derive from music. For background I draw on the many years I served as a violist in orchestras under the batons of such eminent conductors as Leonard Bernstein, Leopold Stokowski, Leonard Slatkin, James Levine, Michael Tilson Thomas, Erich Leinsdorf, and Fritz Reiner, to name just a few. Always interested in sharing my observations and perceptions, I have written program notes for concerts at Carnegie Hall, Lincoln Center, and many other concert halls, have prepared liner notes for several recording companies, have taught at the City University of New York, have lectured widely, and, of course, have always been a devoted and avid music listener. While I genuinely value the primacy of each person's emotional response to music, I am also aware of the extent to which an informed understanding of musical language can enhance and deepen the listening experience.

Each entry in this book begins with a brief biography of the composer. Then, depending on the particular piece, the discussion focuses on the social and philosophical conditions of the time, the purpose for which the composition was written, its place in the history of music, or the composer's own comments on the work.

A movement-by-movement analysis of the individual composition follows, emphasizing the actual language of the music and how the composer assembles the themes and other musical elements to create the work. I consider the composers in alphabetical order, with their works alphabetically arranged by title, to allow the reader easy access to the material.

The "75 More Masterpieces" section includes very brief remarks on works of high quality that were precluded from fuller discussion because of space limitations. Generally, I avoid technical language, but I have included a Glossary that defines the few less familiar words and explains sonata allegro form and other structural organizations frequently found in orchestral masterpieces. Readers seeking to build their CD collections may consult the Discography. As an extra convenience I have listed the approximate playing time for each title.

The process I followed in selecting the orchestral masterpieces for this book was both objective and subjective. To find which works are most often performed and recorded, I studied orchestral programs, CD catalogs, and the program booklets of music radio stations. I also spoke to any number of conductors, instrumentalists, critics, and composers to get their views. Only then did I make the final selections, based on my background in playing, listening, teaching, and presenting music to others.

The compositions vary widely. They date from the 18th to the 20th century and range from massive works lasting more than an hour to miniature gems that are over in a few minutes. Yet all the pieces are the same in one important way: they have the power to touch, move, excite, comfort, stimulate, challenge, or amuse listeners. And it is this special quality, for which words can only be a very poor substitute compared to the music itself, that establishes each work as a "masterpiece."

Of course, this book is not an end in itself. Rather, it is a means, a way, to help the reader get the maximum pleasure from every exposure to music. My most fervent hope is that this book succeeds in bringing to others the delights and deep satisfaction that symphonic music has always brought to me.

MELVIN BERGER

The Anchor Guide to Orchestral Masterpieces

Johann Sebastian Bach

Born March 21, 1685, in Eisenach, Germany
Died July 28, 1750, in Leipzig

SOME GREAT COMPOSERS act as beacons, guiding others toward new styles and methods of musical expression, while others, equally noteworthy, serve as summarizers; their summaries come at the end of a period, elevating its accomplishments to the highest level. Johann Sebastian Bach, who died around the close of the Baroque era, belongs in that category. Although generally accepted as the most outstanding composer of the period, having written outstanding masterpieces in every form except opera, Bach sustained criticism common to composers who appear at the very end of an epoch. To many of his contemporaries, his music was hopelessly old-fashioned.

Bach began his career with an apprenticeship in various minor German courts before receiving his first significant post as court musician in Weimar in 1708, where he wrote most of his major organ works. In his next appointment, at Cöthen in 1717, Bach's patron was Prince Leopold, an avid amateur performer on the viola da gamba and other instruments. It was during his six years here, therefore, that Bach turned out most of his instrumental compositions, including the six "Brandenburg" Concertos and probably two of his four orchestral suites. While holding his final position as Cantor of St. Thomas' Church in Leipzig, from 1723 until his death in 1750, Bach produced most of his great choral masterpieces and the other two orchestral suites.

The role of the composer in Bach's time was very different from what it is today. Bach wrote the vast bulk of his music for specific functions or occasions and for the particular performing forces that were available. It is a tribute to his genius that virtually none of his compositions betray their written-on-demand origins. And just as he discarded the compositions of his predecessor on becoming *Kapellmeister* in Leipzig, so he had every reason to expect that his successor would do the same to his music. While a few of his compositions were published and occasionally performed over the next century, Bach could hardly have imagined that his creations would endure far into the future. Nevertheless, it was in the 1830s, largely through the efforts of Felix Mendelssohn, that Bach's music took its preeminent place in the musical repertoire.

An important element in the music of Bach, and most Baroque composers, was the use of a technique variously known as continuo, basso continuo, thorough bass, or figured bass. Characteristically, this largely polyphonic music was supported by a keyboard instrument, such as a harpsichord or organ, with a bass instrument, such as cello, double bass, or bassoon, doubling the bass line of the keyboard. Beneath the bass line the composer wrote numbers (the figures of figured bass) that told the keyboard player which harmonies should be improvised above the bass line. Modern editions of Baroque music usually have the harmonies written out and printed on the score.

The most accurate way of identifying Bach's compositions is by their BWV *(Bach Werke Verzeichnis)* number, a reference to Wolfgang Schmieder's thematic catalog of all of Bach's music.

BRANDENBURG CONCERTOS

The so-called Brandenburg Concertos date from 1717, when Bach took up employ as *Kapellmeister* at the court of Prince Leopold of Cöthen. The Prince belonged to the Reformed Calvinist Church, in which music played but a small part. Since the Prince was an avid and excellent amateur performer on the violin, viola da gamba, and harpsichord, Bach composed mostly instrumental music during his service in Prince Leopold's court.

The year after taking up his position at Cöthen, Bach traveled to Berlin, probably to order a new harpsichord. While there, Bach had a chance to perform for Christian Ludwig, Margrave of Brandenburg, and brother of King Friedrich Wilhelm I of Prussia. The Margrave, an enthusiastic patron of music who was particularly interested in collecting the scores of concertos, asked the composer to write some works in that form.

Bach took over two years to prepare a special presentation copy of six concertos, the usual number in such a grouping, which he entitled "Six Concertos with Diverse Instruments." He sent off the manuscripts on March 24, 1721, with an obsequious letter, which included such phrases as ". . . begging Your Highness most humbly not to judge their imperfection with the rigor of the fine and delicate taste that the whole world knows Your Highness has for musical pieces." Scholars assume that Bach originally wrote these compositions for the use of the extensive musical establishment at the court of Cöthen, rather than for the very limited number of performers (believed to be no more than six) employed by the Margrave.

Astounding as it may seem, the Margrave probably never heard any of the six concertos. Perhaps he lacked the required performing forces, or had more interest in collecting manuscripts than in hearing music, or found the pieces unworthy of performance. Nevertheless, on the Margrave's death in 1734, archivists combined the concertos with a number of "concertos by various masters," and appraised them at four groschen each—about eight cents in today's money! The manuscripts remained in the Margrave's archives until the 19th century when they were rediscovered and subtitled "Brandenburg Concertos."

Bach cast the Brandenburg Concertos, not as the more familiar concertos for solo piano or solo violin and orchestra, but as concerti grossi. Each one has a small group of instruments, the *concertino,* that functions as a contrast to the larger mass of string instruments, the *ripieno.* Generally speaking, Bach structures the concertos into three separate movements—a fast, vigorous opening, a slow, lyrical middle, and a fast, happy conclusion.

Another way in which the Brandenburg Concertos differ from the solo concertos of the following Classical and Romantic period is in their lack of contrasting themes within each movement. In these, and in most of his compositions, Bach was guided by a principle known as *Affekt,* which is related to the English word "affection." Today the word refers to fond feelings; but during the 18th century it connoted strong emotions, any feeling short of passion. Simply put, Bach tried to express a particular *Affekt* in each movement—be it noble or joyful, tragic or exuberant—and to explore aspects of that feeling, without setting it off against a theme or section of contrasting character.

The Brandenburg Concertos are considered masterpieces for many reasons. Perhaps most striking are the vigor and vitality of the writing and the fascinating interplay of the individual voices, which brings to mind nothing so much as animated conversations between friends.

Brandenburg Concerto No. 1 in F major, BWV 1046
(20 minutes)

Composed for a *concertino* of *violino piccolo* (small violin), two hunting horns (*corni di caccia*), three oboes, and bassoon, with a *ripieno* of strings and continuo (usually played by cello and harpsichord), the first Brandenburg is perhaps the most "orchestral" of the six, yet is programmed less often than the others. The reason may be the difficulty in finding a performer for the prominent *violino piccolo* part, which Bach wrote for a now obsolete instrument that was tuned a fourth (or third) higher than the modern violin. Rather than have the part played on a traditional instrument, many conductors, unfortunately, merely avoid the work.

I. {*Allegro.*} Although there is no tempo marking in the score, the first movement is obviously an Allegro, vigorous, propulsive, and highly rhythmic. Bach makes no effort to separate the *concertino* from the *ripieno*, but combines the instruments in a rich tapestry of string, woodwind, and brass timbres, with only occasional solo bits for one or more *concertino* instruments.

II. *Adagio.* The short, simple Adagio passes a melody of ineffable sadness from the oboe to the *violino piccolo,* to the instruments of the continuo.

III. *Allegro.* Hewing more to traditional concerto grosso structure, Bach alternates the full *ripieno* sound with solos, duets, and trios of *concertino* instruments in this dancelike movement. The Allegro includes several recurrences of the opening melody with its repeated-note motif.

IV. *Menuetto.* Unexpectedly, Bach adds another movement at this point, a series of related dances that provide an opportunity for a dazzling display of varying tone colors. Within the single Menuetto movement are the Menuetto (full orchestra), Trio (two oboes and bassoon), repeat of the Menuetto (full orchestra), Polacca (strings), repeat of the Menuetto (full orchestra), new Trio (horns and oboes), and repeat of the Menuetto (full orchestra). Scholars speculate that Bach included the polacca, a stylized dance of Polish origin, because in 1697, Friedrich August, Elector of Saxony, also became King of Poland and there were extensive cultural exchanges between the two countries.

Brandenburg Concerto No. 2 in F major, BWV 1047
(14 minutes)

The Second Brandenburg Concerto is one of the most popular and appealing of the group of six. It is so highly regarded that space scientists placed a recording of part of the first movement into the Voyager spacecraft, which was launched in 1977. They hope that intelligent beings in outer space will somehow be able to hear this glorious piece and recognize it as one of the outstanding achievements of humankind.

Bach composed the concerto for a *concertino* of flute (recorder), oboe, trumpet (more properly, clarin trumpet), and violin. (The clarin trumpet is a long-tubed, valveless instrument on which performers in Bach's time were able to play fast passages in a very high range; today the part is most often played on the short-tubed, valved "Bach" trumpet.) The *ripieno* is a string orchestra and a continuo of harpsichord and cello.

I. *{Allegro.}* The first movement lacks a tempo indication, but seems clearly to be a lively Allegro. The section essentially alternates between the *ripieno* and *concertino,* which are presented in ever-changing patterns and combinations. Bach succeeds in transforming the fanfarelike theme, which seems particularly suited to the trumpet, so that it fits each of the solo instruments. Although the trumpet is the last of the solo instruments to be introduced, its burnished, refulgent tone comes to dominate the entire movement.

II. *Andante.* The theme of the slow second movement projects great gloom and melancholy as it passes from instrument to instrument. The trumpet and the string orchestra stay mute throughout this tender, moving section.

III. *Allegro assai.* The high good spirits of the opening movement return with the sparkling trumpet statement of the theme in this brilliant, fugal finale. Theorists can marvel at Bach's skill in creating what is, in effect, an intricate double fugue, which never betrays the complexity of its writing. Listeners, though, have only to delight in the youthful vitality and irresistible drive of this splendid movement.

Brandenburg Concerto No. 3 in G major, BWV 1048
(10 minutes)

Bach does not allow any one instrument to eclipse the others in the Third Brandenburg Concerto, which he wrote for three violins, three violas, and three cellos, along with a continuo of harpsichord and bass. (In modern performances conductors often divide the orchestral violins into three groups and do the same with the violas and cellos.) The composer does, however, adhere to the concerto grosso concept of contrasting the full group with smaller numbers of instruments.

I. *{Allegro.}* After presenting the principal theme of the first movement, which lacks a tempo indication, Bach focuses on various elements—rhythmical and melodic—of the theme. He uses them to fashion a surging movement that sometimes treats each instrumental group as a unit and other times divides the group into individual players.

Instead of a traditional slow movement, Bach merely wrote two chords. Musicologists speculate that Bach composed the concerto for his own performance use and that, when performing, he improvised a slow movement on the harpsichord, ending with the two chords shown in the score.

II. *Allegro.* Relentless and propulsive, the final movement is propelled forward without restraint. The torrent of notes continues virtually without interruption until the rather abrupt ending.

Brandenburg Concerto No. 4 in G major, BWV 1049
(17 minutes)

Bach called for a solo violin and two *flauti d'echo* as the *concertino* for this piece. Since scholars have not been able to trace the latter instrument (some suspect it was a high-pitched whistle flute used to teach songs to canaries!), the parts are usually played on recorders. The *ripieno* is the traditional string orchestra, plus harpsichord.

I. *{Allegro.}* Playing as a pair—as they do most of the time in the first two movements—the two flutes set the light and graceful tone of the first movement, a presumed Allegro, even though not so marked. The violin soon enters and, in the course of the movement, displays such dazzling outbursts of virtuosity that many consider the work essentially a solo violin concerto.

II. *Andante.* Moderate in tempo, the Andante projects a quiet, reflective mood that makes much use of echo effects. A notable separation of the flutes comes with the brief cadenza for one flute near the end of the movement.

III. *Presto.* The Presto offers a brilliant fugue based on a rhythmic, good-humored little tune that gives the violin another opportunity for bravura playing. After the intricate interweaving of voices throughout the movement, the instrumentalists unite for a brief passage just before the conclusion.

Brandenburg Concerto No. 5 in D major, BWV 1050
(22 minutes)

The Fifth Brandenburg Concerto includes *concertino* parts for flute, violin, and harpsichord. Bach specified a modern-type transverse flute, instead of the recorder he used in the earlier concertos, probably because the florid writing for the harpsichord required the flute's greater power for the proper balance. The prominent harpsichord part was most likely inspired by the new instrument Bach bought in Berlin in 1719. This may have led the composer, who often played viola in his ensemble compositions, to play the challenging harpsichord in performances at Cöthen before sending the score off to the Margrave of Brandenburg. So dominant is the harpsichord that many consider this the first true solo keyboard concerto.

I. *Allegro.* The first movement opens with a bold, vigorous theme played forcefully by the *ripieno*. After the initial statement, the three soloists and the string orchestra alternately comment on the theme until the harpsichord comes to the fore. The keyboard instrument presents an extended cadenzalike solo passage, followed by the return of the opening *ripieno* section to end the movement.

II. *Affetuoso*. The slow movement, written for the solo instruments without *ripieno*, casts what Bach scholar Arnold Schering calls "a mood of oppressive melancholy." The composer features the harpsichord in a dual role—accompanist to the flute and violin and melodist on its own.

III. *Allegro*. The gay, giguelike theme of the concluding Allegro passes fugally from solo violin to solo flute, to harpsichord right hand, to harpsichord left hand, and finally to the full *ripieno*. Showing the influence of the younger composers of the time, Bach introduces a contrasting, more lyrical middle section, before ending the movement with a reprise of the first part.

Brandenburg Concerto No. 6 in B flat major, BWV 1051
(18 minutes)

The Sixth Brandenburg Concerto calls for two violas, two violas da gamba (fretted instruments with a distinctive delicate tone; similar to the cello in size and held between the knees), cello, and continuo, usually played by harpsichord and double bass. Scholars surmise that Bach wrote the first, challenging viola part for himself and the less demanding first gamba part for Prince Leopold of Cöthen. (Since gamba players are in short supply today, many modern performances have the gamba parts played on cellos.)

I. *{Allegro.}* The first movement creates the impression of a lively chase between the various instruments, particularly the two violas, who seem to be engaged in a never-ending game of catch-up. The first three notes of the theme—note, note below, original note—become a motif that runs throughout the briskly athletic movement.

II. *Adagio ma non tanto*. Poised and quiet, this movement is essentially a trio for the two violas and cello over the discrete continuo. Bach brings back the earlier three-note motif, but in the slower tempo of this movement.

III. *Allegro*. The theme of the rollicking finale grows from a variant of the motif, which was so important in the first movement and appeared again in the second. Between statements of the theme, or fragments of the theme, the two violas and cellos interject their spirited comments on the same material.

SUITES FOR ORCHESTRA

Bach originally titled his four suites "overtures," a reference to the French form developed by Jean-Baptiste Lully (1632–87), on which they are modeled. As used by Lully to introduce his operas and ballets, the overture consisted of a slow, solemn section with a repeated dotted rhythm (a pattern of long/short notes). He followed this with a much faster, lighter section that was fugal in texture, and ended with a shortened repeat of the opening. In French overtures, too, the composer often appended one or two dance movements at the end.

Bach added either four or six dance movements to his overtures, so that his were really a set of dances preceded by an extensive prelude—which is known as a suite. Hence, during the 19th century, when the four works were rediscovered, scholars began to call them suites instead of overtures.

No one is sure when and why Bach composed these four suites. Since each has a different instrumentation, however, we assume they were composed at different times for various purposes. Based on both internal and external evidence, many now believe that Suites 1 and 4 were composed while Bach was at Cöthen (1717–23) and that Suites 2 and 3, the more popular ones, were written at Leipzig (1723–50).

The ouverture in each suite makes up, by far, the longest and weightiest movement. The following movements—with the notable exception of the famous Air from Suite No. 3—are all dances; they are mostly of French origin and often in three-part form—the dance (A), a shorter, usually quieter dance of the same type (B), and a repeat of the first dance (A).

Suite for Orchestra No. 1 in C major, BWV 1066
(27 minutes)

I. *Ouverture.* Despite the great pomposity and majesty of the first part of the Ouverture, it moves forward with a propulsive energy to the lilting fugal middle section. This part scampers hastily along until a foreshortened repeat of the opening ends the movement.

II. *Courante.* This is a "running" dance in a fast tempo and triple meter.

III. *Gavotte.* Cast in three-part form, the movement offers a more legato Gavotte between two statements of the more sharply articulated original.

IV. *Forlane.* Associated with Venice, this joyful dance is commonly performed at carnival time.

V. *Menuet.* By using the French spelling of minuet, Bach makes apparent that his source of inspiration was the stately French court dance.

VI. *Bourrée.* This movement treats the Bourrée dance, which has simple, peasant roots, in a highly sophisticated manner.

VII. *Passepied.* A spirited dance and a favorite at the courts of Louis XIV and Louis XV, the Passepied brings the suite to a joyful conclusion.

Bach wrote Suite No. 1 for two oboes, bassoon, string orchestra, and harpsichord.

Suite for Orchestra No. 2 in B minor, BWV 1067
(23 minutes)

Composed for flute, string orchestra, and harpsichord, Suite No. 2 may well be considered a solo flute concerto. It is probably the best known of the four suites.

I. *Ouverture.* The slow opening of the Ouverture has the characteristic grandiose, but spiky melody of the form, replete with many trills and ornaments. The fast middle section starts with fugal imitations of the bouncy new theme before developing into a graceful, high-spirited discourse between the flute and the strings. A brief reminder of the slow section comes at the end.

II. *Rondeau.* The Rondeau (French spelling of rondo) presents a guileless, winsome principal theme that Bach repeats several times, with the repetitions separated by contrasting interludes.

III. *Sarabande.* The sarabande, a slow, stately dance in triple meter, originated in Persia and made its way to Europe through Spain.

IV. *Bourrée.* Written in three parts, the movement gives the flute a chance for virtuosic display in the middle section, before bringing back the opening part.

V. *Polonaise.* Inspired by a dignified dance from the courts of 16th century Poland, Bach creates a flute variation on the melody in the middle section.

VI. *Menuet.* This poised movement, "minuet" in English, recalls the small, mincing steps of the French aristocrats who made this dance their favorite.

VII. *Badinerie.* French for "bantering," the Badinerie charms and delights listeners with its happy jocularity.

Suite for Orchestra No. 3 in D major, BWV 1068
(23 minutes)

Bach composed Suite No. 3 for three trumpets and timpani—along with two oboes and the usual strings and harpsichord—indicating that he probably intended it for some unidentified festive or ceremonial occasion.

After about a century with only occasional performances, Bach's music was rediscovered in the 19th century, largely through the efforts of Felix Mendelssohn. In 1830, Mendelssohn played Suite No. 3 (one of the first pieces to be uncovered) on the piano for Johann Goethe; the poet was, in Mendelssohn's words, "delighted."

I. *Ouverture.* Of this movement, Goethe said, ". . . it sounds so distinguished and pompous, one really sees a crowd of elegantly attired people descending a broad staircase," an apt description of the slow part of the overture. As is traditional, the Ouverture continues with a fast, fugal middle section and a concluding short reprise of the opening.

II. *Air.* Air, French for "song," and related to aria, is not a dance, but one of the most beautiful and beloved of all melodies, that was made famous in a transcription for violin and piano by the German violinist August Wilhelmj, as *Air for the G String,* and in dozens of other transcriptions for all combinations of instruments.

III. *Gavotte.* After the muscular opening section, Bach introduces a more lyrical center portion, before ending with a return of the opening.

IV. *Bourrée.* In this movement, the strings carry most of the melodic burden, with punctuation by the trumpets and timpani.

V. *Gigue.* The movement sets the same character as the Bourrée, with the trumpets lending a special brilliance.

Suite for Orchestra No. 4 in D major, BWV 1069
(23 minutes)

I. *Ouverture.* Bach later reworked this Ouverture as the opening chorus of his Cantata 110: The slow opening section of the Ouverture became the instrumental prelude; the fast middle part was sung to a text from Psalm 126: "Then was our mouth filled with laughter and our tongue with singing"; and the short reprise of the first part became the instrumental postlude.

II. *Bourrée.* The sprightly movement appears in the usual three-part form, with a repeat of the opening after a contrasting central interlude.

III. *Gavotte.* Bach makes this dance somewhat slower and heavier than more typical examples of the form.

IV. *Menuet.* Here Bach also leans more toward a heavier, more sedate style.

V. *Réjouissance.* The "Rejoicing" movement starts with the same four notes as the Bourrée; although not properly a dance, it brings the entire suite to an exuberant, exhilarating culmination.

Bach wrote Suite No. 4 for three oboes, bassoon, three trumpets, timpani, strings, and harpsichord.

Béla Bartók

Born March 25, 1881, in Nagyszentmiklós, Hungary (now Romania)
Died September 26, 1945, in New York City

MOST CONSIDER Igor Stravinsky, Arnold Schoenberg, and Béla Bartók, the leading composers of the first half of the 20th century. Although different in many ways, the three composers shared the need to move music forward from 19th century Romanticism. As Bartók said: "The excesses of the romantics began to be unbearable to many." Stravinsky evolved from so-called Neoprimitive and Russian nationalist works to Neoclassical and 12-tone compositions. Schoenberg devised the system of 12-tone composition. And Bartók found his inspiration in the national, peasant music of Hungary. He called it "the ideal starting point for a musical renaissance, and a composer in search of new ways cannot be led by a better master."

Bartók started piano lessons with his mother at age five and began composing four years later. Over the following years he continued his studies of both piano and music theory, entering the Royal Academy of Music in Budapest in 1899. A significant turning point in his development came while on a summer holiday in 1904 when he heard a young girl singing a peasant melody in the Hungarian countryside. The composer was struck by the great beauty of her song and by its exotic, modal melody and strange, irregular rhythms, so different from the folk song arrangements that tended to smooth out or remove unconventional features.

This pivotal experience set the composer off on a quest that lasted several decades—traveling to rural areas in Hungary and other countries, recording the old songs, transcribing, codifying, and publishing the music he collected, and preparing research papers on his discoveries. In the process, Bartók completely assimilated this unique and unfamiliar musical vocabulary, eventually infusing the folk tradition into every note that he composed, not by direct quotation, but by coloring and shaping his own modes of expression.

Although Bartók was deeply involved with folk music research, he considered himself primarily a composer. A man of strict and forbidding principle, Bartók refused to ingratiate himself with publishers and those in musical authority to obtain performances and recognition. To earn money, he performed or taught piano, but refused to teach composition for fear that it might stem his flow of musical ideas.

Ironically, it was death that brought Bartók the acclaim and widespread acceptance that he had been denied in life. Orchestras around the world scheduled nearly 50 performances of his music within a few weeks of his passing. The royalty income derived from his compositions rose from a mere pittance to a substantial amount. Today, the vibrant voice of this innovative composer continues to enrich the orchestral repertoire.

Bartók made ample use of the most advanced techniques of 20th century music, including harsh dissonances, irregular rhythms, and striking effects. Yet, at the same time, his works are grounded in the melodies and rhythms of the folk music that he knew so well and had so completely assimilated into his own compositional style. These folk-music roots, which represent the end product of countless generations of singers and performers refining and improving the original folk creations, lend his own compositions an authenticity and atavistic appeal that modern audiences find particularly attractive.

Concerto for Orchestra
(38 minutes)

In late spring 1943, Bartók lay seriously ill with leukemia in a New York City hospital. Pale and weak, he had wasted away to a mere 87 pounds and believed he would never recover. At this point, Serge Koussevitzky, then the flamboyant conductor of the Boston Symphony, strode into Bartók's room. Draped in his flowing cape and carrying a highly decorated walking stick, he made Bartók an extraordinary proposition.

With a dramatic gesture, Koussevitzky flung a $500 check onto the bed of the frail composer, explaining that the money represented partial payment on a commission for an orchestral work to honor the conductor's late wife, Natalie. Unknown to Bartók, the commission actually came from two of Bartók's Hungarian-born friends, violinist Joseph Szigeti and conductor Fritz Reiner. They had decided to make the offer in this roundabout way for fear that Bartók would reject any commission that he suspected was motivated by pity.

Greatly flattered, Bartók demurred at first, believing that he was too ill to undertake the strain of preparing a major orchestral composition. But Koussevitzky persisted, urging the composer to start work on the piece as soon as he was well and pressing Bartók to keep the money in any event.

The commission proved to be the best tonic that Bartók could have received. The doctors were soon able to release him from the hospital and the composer retired to a cabin near Saranac Lake, New York, where he began composing on August 15, 1943. When he returned to New York City on October 8 he brought with him the completed manuscript of the Concerto for Orchestra.

The following year, the doctors allowed the now desperately ill composer to attend the premiere, given in Boston by Koussevitzky and the Boston Symphony on December 1, 1944. Bartók witnessed the audience's enthusiastic reception of a piece that has gone on to become one of the most popular and frequently performed of all 20th century scores.

In the program notes Bartók prepared for the first performance he clarified why he called the composition a concerto, instead of symphony: "The title of this symphonylike orchestral work is explained by its tendency to treat single instruments or instrumental groups in a 'concertante' or soloistic manner." Of the character of the music, he wrote: "The general mood of the work represents, apart from the jesting second movement, a gradual transition from the sternness of the first movement and lugubrious death-song of the third, to the life assertion of the last one."

Several of Bartók's signature stylistic elements appear in the Concerto for Orchestra: an overall arch shape (substantial outer movements in free sonata allegro form, scherzolike second and fourth movements, with the slow third movement forming the keystone of the entire work); frequent use of fugal textures; much development of short motifs; and many instances of thematic inversion. Despite the work's complex structure, the music is inviting and accessible, contributing to its enduring appeal.

I. *Introduction: Andante non troppo; Allegro vivace.* The slow beginning of the Introduction contrasts the dark tones of the cellos and basses with high-pitched responses in the violins and winds. An acceleration leads to the main part of the movement, which Bartók described as structured in "more or less regular sonata form," though handled with much greater freedom than was previously the norm. A high point of this endlessly fascinating movement is the brass fugato that occurs in the development section.

II. *Game of Pairs: Allegretto scherzando.* Bartók wrote that this movement "consists of a chain of independent short sections, by wind instruments consecutively introduced in five pairs (bassoons, oboes, clarinets, flutes, and muted trumpets). Thematically, the five sections have nothing in common. A kind of trio, that is, a short chorale for brass instruments and side drum [without snares], follows, after which the five sections are recapitulated in a more elaborate instrumentation."

III. *Elegy: Andante non troppo.* "The structure of the third movement is also chainlike; the three themes appear successively," Bartók wrote. "These constitute the core of the movement, which is enframed by a misty texture of rudimentary motifs. Most of the thematic material of this movement derives from the 'introduction' to the first movement."

IV. *Interrupted Intermezzo: Allegretto.* "The form of the fourth movement . . . could be rendered by the letter symbols A-B-A-Interruption-B-A." According to commentator Jonathan Kramer, the B theme is the song "Hungary, Gracious and Beautiful." Bartók's son, Péter, and conductor Antal Dorati also have provided some background details on the movement's composition. Apparently, while working on his Concerto for Orchestra, Bartók heard a radio broadcast of Shostakovich's Seventh Symphony. So ludicrous did he find the march theme that he decided to parody it, turning the vulgarized theme into the Interruption section of this movement.

V. *Presto.* After a brief brass fanfare, the strings launch into a fierce perpetual motion replete with bright bursts of orchestra sparks. In time, folk dance rhythms emerge from the onslaught of rushing notes. The development section includes an extremely intricate fugue. Bartók returns the perpetual motion and some of the dance melodies in the recapitulation, and we hear a grandiose version of the fugue melody in the concluding coda.

Concerto for Piano and Orchestra No. 1
(23 minutes)

Because the piano often plays sustained notes and smoothly connected melodies, few realize that the piano is basically a percussion instrument in which hammers strike strings to produce the sound. In his First Piano Concerto, the first of three, Bartók emphasizes the piano's percussive and rhythmic qualities. From the hammered piano notes that open the concerto to the piano dialogue with the orchestra battery and the crashing chords in the second movement, to the driving beat and tempo of the finale, Bartók continually downplays the piano's melodic qualities in favor of its percussive effects.

The themes of the First Piano Concerto are almost all scalar, extremely short, and fragmented with much repetition. They lend the work much visceral stimulation, what Bartók called "a strange, feverish excitement." Nonetheless, the concerto was slow to find favor. Composed between August and November 1926, the piece was originally intended by Bartók to serve a very personal and practical purpose. As a performing piano virtuoso, he needed an original composition for his appearances with orchestra. After the Frankfurt premiere on July 1, 1927, played by the composer with Wilhelm Furtwängler conducting, however, the work received few performances. The very difficult orchestra score made conductors reluctant to schedule it; the finger-breaking demands of the solo piano part dissuaded pianists, other than Bartók, from undertaking performances; and its harsh, uncompromising sounds discouraged audiences. Recently, however, perceptions have changed. Conductors, soloists, and audiences have grown more comfortable with the music and critics have come to appreciate its great worth. Now part of the repertoire, the concerto has won an estimable place on concert programs.

I. *Allegro moderato; Allegro.* The concerto opens with the timpani, piano, and brass instruments playing at the very bottom of their range. The tempo speeds up as the piano takes over with its pounding, repeated notes against the orchestral background. The orchestra furnishes the few moments of repose and quiet in the movement, while the piano remains largely restricted to the ferocious driving character of the opening.

II. *Andante.* The bulk of the slow movement consists of a dialogue between the solo piano and the percussion section of the orchestra—admittedly not an exchange between equals, since the piano clearly predominates. The wind instruments join in later, but the strings remain absent. Although quieter than in the first movement, the piano maintains its exclusive focus on rhythmic figures.

III. *Allegro molto.* The finale, which follows without pause, starts with an explosive outburst in the orchestra, from which the violins emerge with a short repeated figure. Bartók does allow some brief fragments of melody in this movement, but it is rhythm, not melody, that drives the proceedings.

Concerto for Piano and Orchestra No. 2
(25 minutes)

Bartók realized that his First Piano Concerto was "very difficult—both for the orchestra and for the audience." Consequently, he decided to write a Second Piano Concerto, "a kind of complementary piece to the First, with fewer difficulties for the orchestra and more attractive in its thematic material." Indeed much lighter in tone than the First, the Second Piano Concerto proved ideal for Bartók's appearances as piano soloist with orchestra.

Bartók began composing his Second Piano Concerto in October 1930 and finished exactly one year later. He gave the premiere with the Frankfurt Radio Orchestra under Hans Rosbaud on January 23, 1933. It was extremely well received by critics and public alike and led, within months, to invitations for Bartók to play the concerto with orchestras in Amsterdam, London, Stockholm, Strasbourg, Vienna, Winterthur, and Zurich. Since then, the Second Concerto has become one of the more popular and widely performed 20th century works for piano and orchestra.

Overall, Bartók structured the three-movement Second Piano Concerto in a symmetrical arch form: the two outer movements are fast in tempo and share the same melodic material; the slow middle movement has a fast middle section that constitutes the keystone of the entire work. The melodic and rhythmic character of the music very obviously springs from the composer's deep involvement with the peasant and national music of his native Hungary and the Magyar people, not by direct quotation, but by the integration of the folk music qualities into his own musical vocabulary.

I. *Allegro.* The sparkling and bravura first movement, which makes no use of the orchestral strings, bursts with vitality and motoric drive. It is organized in a comparatively traditional sonata allegro form: the first theme is a ringing call flung out by the trumpet; the piano states the quiet second subject, with the two hands rolling chords in opposite directions; the development of the themes follows and leads to the recapitulation, in which the composer inverts and reverses some of the thematic material; a cadenza and a coda conclude the movement.

II. *Adagio; Presto; Adagio.* The strings, heard for the first time, open the second movement with a slow, expressionless melody, which they play muted and without vibrato. The melody is an example of Bartók's "night music," the evocation of the ominous sounds heard on a dark night in the countryside. The soloist replies with a striking section for piano and timpani that captures the spirit of Hungarian *parlando rubato* ("spoken, not strictly in tempo") folk song style. Variations of these two episodes alternate and lead to the central section, which the piano leads by playing at breakneck speed. The initial section then returns for a shortened, varied repetition, along with echoes of the middle part.

III. *Allegro molto.* Bartók begins the last movement with a barbaric, highly rhythmic new theme in the piano, accompanied only by bass drum and timpani. He returns this melody three more times, preceding each repetition with an episode freely derived from themes heard in the first movement. At the end, Bartók recalls the trumpet melody that opened the concerto, heralding the symmetry of the arch and the conclusion of the concerto.

Concerto for Piano and Orchestra No. 3
(21 minutes)

"I'm working on a birthday present for your mother," Béla Bartók confided to his 20-year-old son, Péter, early in the summer of 1945 at their cabin near Saranac Lake in New York's Adirondack Mountains. "A piano concerto for her own use. It's a surprise and you mustn't say anything to her about it," he said, hoping to leave the concerto as a legacy for his wife, the outstanding pianist Ditta Pásztory-Bartók.

That summer Bartók was already very ill with leukemia, although only Ditta knew how far the disease had progressed. On the days when his strength allowed, he worked simultaneously· on the present for Ditta, a reworking of an earlier Concerto for Two Pianos, and a Viola Concerto, commissioned by the eminent viola virtuoso William Primrose. Péter Bartók reports that his father went to great lengths to keep the Piano Concerto a secret. Whenever Ditta or anyone else entered the room, Bartók would "slide the Piano Concerto under the Viola Concerto and just go on working on that one."

In September the composer and his family returned to their tiny apartment in New York City. Bartók asked Péter to draw bar lines for the final 17 measures of his Third Piano Concerto and, although he did not fill in those blank measures, after them he penned the word, *vége,* Hungarian for "the end," the first such marking on any of his manuscripts.

Soon after, Bartók's doctor recommended immediate hospitalization. "Can I go tomorrow?" the composer asked. "There is something I want to do here" —an obvious reference to the missing measures. But the doctor insisted, and Bartók entered the hospital on September 22, where he died four days later. Composer Tibor Serly, a close friend and disciple of Bartók, used the sketches that he found among Bartók's papers to complete the last pages. Sad to say, Ditta went into seclusion upon her husband's death, and György Sándor with the Philadelphia Orchestra under Eugene Ormandy gave the premiere on February 8, 1946. Ditta did not perform or record the concerto until well into the 1950s.

The Third Piano Concerto has an immediacy, lucidity, and simplicity not always found in his earlier piano concertos. With it, Bartók has refined and purified his writing to reach the emotional and expressive core of the music.

I. *Allegretto.* The piano begins by stating a straightforward, albeit highly rhythmic theme over a murmured accompaniment. Bartók biographer Halsey Stevens traces the theme's origins to the Romanian folk song of lament, the *doïna.* The composer then introduces a number of subsidiary subjects and organizes the entire movement into rather conventional sonata allegro form.

II. *Adagio religioso.* The spiritual string opening and the melodic piano response recall the third movement, the "Heiliger Dankgesang," of Beethoven's Op. 132 String Quartet, in which Beethoven gives thanks for his recovery from illness. Could Bartók have written this movement in the belief that somehow he had conquered his illness and wanted to express the same gratitude? The movement's middle section provides another exquisite example of Bartók's "night music," replete with a variety of birdcalls that he notated while on a 1944 stay in Asheville, North Carolina. The movement ends with a much altered return of the opening.

III. *Allegro vivace.* The finale, cast as a rondo, follows without pause. This bright, sparkling movement, with a spiky, syncopated principal subject and free-ranging episodes, includes a striking fugal section. The vitality and lightness of touch in the music belie the composer's condition, a man quite literally at death's door.

Concerto for Violin and Orchestra No. 2
(32 minutes)

After devoting much of his life to researching the folk music of his native Hungary, Béla Bartók sought to understand the impact of this experience on his music. He once asked the rhetorical question "What is the best way for a composer to reap the full benefits of his study in peasant music?" To which he replied: "It is to assimilate the idiom of the peasant music so completely that he is able to forget all about it and use it as his mother tongue." Bartók's Violin Concerto No. 2 demonstrates how the composer very successfully transmuted the characteristic melodies and rhythms of Hungarian national music into a unique and personal expression of his own musical creativity.

Early in 1937, Bartók's friend the eminent Hungarian violinist Zoltán Székely approached the composer with a commission for a violin concerto. Bartók suggested a large-scale work in variation form, an organizing principle that he favored. (In typical variation form a theme is stated and subjected to a number of changes that can range from merely adding decorations to the original theme to almost completely transforming the original.) Bartók held that variation "is characteristic of our folk music, [and] is at the same time the expression of my own nature." But Székely would have none of it; he wanted a traditional, virtuosic, three-movement concerto. Bartók agreed and began composing in August of that year, completing a preliminary draft for solo violin and piano by the end of the summer and finishing the orchestration on December 31, 1938.

Székely was very pleased with the concerto, but he objected to the twenty-two measures of rest in the solo part while the orchestra brought the concerto to a close. He asked for a conclusion "more like a concerto than a symphony," with prominent, rousing display passages for the soloist that continued to the end of the work. Bartók accommodated the violinist by rewriting the final pages, but insisted that both endings appear in the published edition. Today, most performers use the flashier ending favored by Székely.

Although Bartók seemed to give in to Székely on the matter of the form, he had the last laugh: in actual fact the work is a series of extended variations, just as Bartók had wanted. Thus, movement three is a variation of movement one, and movement two obviously consists of a theme and variations.

I. *Allegro non troppo.* The first movement starts with the solo violin presentation of the principal theme, one deeply rooted in Magyar folk melody. After some discourse, the composer offers a tender, lyrical second theme that contains all twelve notes of the chromatic scale. Bartók describes it as "a kind of 12-tone theme, yet with pronounced tonality." Many hear in this melody a satirical reference to Arnold Schoenberg's 12-tone method of composition, similar in intent to Bartók's parody of Dmitri Shostakovich in the *Interrupted Intermezzo* movement of the Concerto for Orchestra. The rest of the movement unfolds in sonata allegro pattern, with moments of delicate, shimmering tracery, contrasting both with passages of great strength and with sections of radiant warmth. Before the solo cadenza that closes the movement, Bartók has the violinist play in quarter tones, intervals smaller than the usual half tones, perhaps as a way of poking fun at the avant-garde music of the day. In the concluding coda he directs the orchestra string players to pluck their strings so that they snap down against the fingerboard.

II. *Andante tranquillo.* The slow movement consists of a melancholy theme, stated by the solo violin, and six variations, which at times sound like a Gypsy violinist improvising on the melody. The first variation simply embellishes the theme, with the notes of the melody embedded in the violin's decorative line, while the following variations go further and further afield until the final one, when the violin plays the now ethereal original melody an octave higher than before.

III. *Allegro molto.* The melodic material of the final movement closely resembles the first—but as though reflected in a distorting mirror. Similarly treated, the two principal themes have many of the same notes as appeared earlier, but in completely different rhythms and with much changed character.

Zoltán Székely gave the premiere of the concerto on April 23, 1939, with Willem Mengelberg conducting the Amsterdam Concertgebouw Orchestra. Believed to be Bartók's only essay in the form, the work was simply known as the Violin Concerto for many years. Then, in the 1950s, a violin concerto the composer wrote in 1908 but subsequently suppressed came to light, and the present work was then identified as Violin Concerto No. 2.

Ludwig van Beethoven

Born December 16, 1770, in Bonn
Died March 26, 1827, in Vienna

BEETHOVEN'S CAREER spans the years from the last quarter of the 18th century to the first quarter of the 19th century. Scholars usually group him with Haydn, Mozart, and other masters of the Viennese Classical school because his early music resembles theirs in style and conception. Yet, in the years after the turn of the century, Beethoven began to move in a new direction, adding more power and intensity to his music and vastly increasing the contrasts of mood and contrasts of pitch and dynamics. As he discovered innovative ways to express the music welling up within him, he became the herald of 19th century Romanticism.

Changes in society also impinged on Beethoven's creativity. The French Revolution, with its ideas of equality and freedom, encouraged him to strike out in new directions and to make the quest for liberty the subject of some compositions. The end of absolutism and the rise of the bourgeoisie turned Beethoven away from the more heroic qualities in his earlier music toward a warmer, more intimate style. The time when musicians were employed only in noble courts or churches was coming to an end and the era of public concerts and home music making were starting to flourish.

Born in Bonn, Beethoven received his first music instruction from his father, a dissolute court musician. At age 22 the young composer went to Vienna to complete his musical education, which included a short period of very stormy lessons with Haydn. Beethoven quickly won a reputation as a brilliant pianist and a very able composer. Within a few years, though, Beethoven became increasingly aware that he was losing his hearing, and the strong emotions brought on by his ever-deteriorating condition raged within him.

After several years of railing against the cruel fate that was robbing him of what he called his "most noble faculty," Beethoven entered a new phase of musical composition. Realizing that he could overcome his terrible loss and still compose music that went far beyond the strictures of the Classical style that he had inherited, Beethoven went on to create music of surging passion, deep expressivity, and vastly expanded scope. In a sketchbook he asked himself the rhetorical question "Can anything in the world prevent you from expressing your soul in music?" Beethoven's compositions from this middle period strongly affirm an extraordinary ability to transcend his profound disability.

But it was in Beethoven's final period, when he was completely cut off from the world by his deafness, that he achieved the greatest sublimity and universality of expression. Beethoven was, in the words of the great German poet Johann Goethe, "more concentrated, more energetic, more warmly and tenderly emotional" than any other artist, no matter the medium.

Beethoven is universally adjudged to be a leading figure in that select pantheon of the greatest of all creative spirits, along with Leonardo, Shakespeare, Rembrandt, Michelangelo, and few others. One can easily list his outstanding compositional strengths—the emotional, expressive quality of every note he wrote, his skill as melodist and orchestrator, his unerring instinct in devising logical, organic formal structures, the attractiveness of his harmonies and rhythms, and so on.

But, as Leonard Bernstein put it in his *Joy of Music,* all this is "mere dust." What Bernstein calls the "magic ingredient" is Beethoven's "inexplicable ability to know what the next note has to be." There is a rightness, an inevitability, that we all sense in every measure of Beethoven's music. And it is largely for this reason that virtually every piece by Beethoven is truly a masterpiece.

Concerto for Piano and Orchestra No. 1 in C major, Op. 15
(38 minutes)

In the years following Beethoven's arrival in Vienna from his home in Bonn, he was much better known as a pianist than as a composer. Scholars estimate that there were about 300 pianists in Vienna at the time, and Beethoven had to compete with them for performing and teaching opportunities—a contest in which he was remarkably successful. Many compositions from this period, including his C major Piano Concerto, were written to display his technical skill in public performances.

Specific details on the C major are missing beyond the fact that Beethoven composed it in 1798 and gave the premiere that year in Prague. Although now known as Concerto No. 1, it actually followed Concerto No. 2 in composition, but was the first to be published.

I. *Allegro con brio.* The first movement begins with an orchestral traversal of the thematic material, starting with an elegant, Rococo melody that Beethoven immediately transforms into a loud, forceful tutti statement. This is followed by a calm, quiet second theme; a marchlike concluding theme completes the orchestral exposition. The piano then nonchalantly wanders onto the scene, and proceeds to weave its roulades around another, free statement of the themes. The rest of the movement follows traditional organization—the development and return of the themes, a cadenza for solo piano, and a brief coda.

II. *Largo.* Beethoven favors this movement with one of his most touching and expressive melodies. He then treats the melody very freely, often as a gentle dialogue between piano and orchestra or between sections of the orchestra, taking the listeners on an exceptionally appealing and emotionally satisfying musical journey.

III. *Rondo: Allegro scherzando.* The Rondo presents a startling contrast to the soulful beauty of the Largo. The principal theme, a rollicking melody of great verve and exuberance, is followed by a truly comical episode with its hiccuplike accents. After a return of the principal theme, the sly and witty second episode comes along to increase the good humor, and another reprise of the opening, a short cadenza, and some echoes of the first episode bring the movement to a rousing conclusion.

Concerto for Piano and Orchestra No. 2 in B flat major, Op. 19
(31 minutes)

For several years after his arrival in Vienna in 1792, only a handful of Viennese music lovers were acquainted with Beethoven's extraordinary talent. But everything changed early in 1795 when he was asked to compose and perform a piano concerto at a charity concert for the widows and orphans of the Society of Musicians.

The concerto did not have a particularly promising genesis. As was his wont, Beethoven put off composing the piece until he had only two days to write the last movement. Increasing the pressure was a punishing attack of colic that required a doctor at his side to administer painkilling drugs. Four copyists in his apartment snatched each completed manuscript page from his hands to write out the orchestral parts. According to some accounts, a further complication arose at the first rehearsal, which was held in Beethoven's rooms the day before the performance. Beethoven had so abused his piano, neglecting to tune it and spilling water on the keys, that it was a full half step below the pitch to which the wind instruments could tune. Beethoven solved this problem by transposing the solo part a half step higher at sight—a formidable task under the very best of conditions!

Nevertheless, the March 29, 1795, premiere proved an overwhelming success. "Herr Beethoven gained the unanimous applause of the audience," wrote the *Wiener Zeitung*. Beethoven revised the concerto for a 1798 performance in Prague, and that version has come down to us today.

I. *Allegro con brio.* The orchestra states the basic premise of the movement at the very outset: a brief, bold, vigorous phrase, immediately answered by an equally short pleading, lyrical response. The appealingly melodic movement continues to juxtapose opposites in a highly dramatic way—forceful against pliant, loud against soft, staccato against legato.

II. *Adagio.* The Adagio grows from its opening—a broadly sung melody that maintains its arching structure despite several silences that the composer inserts into the melody. By adding embellishments and increasing intensity, Beethoven continues to build to the very end, when the orchestra offers a quiet, concise reminder of the original impetus for the movement.

III. *Rondo: Molto allegro.* Gay and cheerful in mien, the last movement is ordinary in all respects—but touched with genius. In Classical rondo form, the movement features a saucy, syncopated refrain that appears four times, the repetitions separated by felicitous, contrasting interludes.

Although this concerto was Beethoven's first mature orchestral work, we identify it as Concerto No. 2 because of publication order.

Concerto for Piano and Orchestra No. 3 in C minor, Op. 37
(37 minutes)

The key of C minor had special significance for Beethoven; he used this signature for his Fifth Symphony, Fourth String Quartet, piano sonatas Op. 13 ("Pathétique") and Op. 111, and this third Piano Concerto—all stormy, intensely emotional works.

Beethoven began preparing sketches for the concerto in 1797 and worked on it, with many interruptions, over the following six years. He played the solo part at the first performance on April 5, 1803, in Vienna, in a program that also included his First and Second symphonies and his oratorio *Christ on the Mount of Olives.*

A description of events preceding the first performance provides an interesting insight into musical practices of the time. The one and only rehearsal began early in the morning of the concert day. Since Vienna's best musicians were preparing for a performance of Haydn's *Creation* that same evening, Beethoven had to engage performers of lesser quality. The rehearsal went very badly and by midafternoon everyone was exhausted and disgusted. Prince Karl Lichnowsky sent for baskets of bread, cold meat, and wine. Everyone partook heartily and, reinvigorated, ran through the program once more in preparation for the six o'clock curtain.

Although the concerto had long since been completed, Beethoven continued to make revisions until the last minute. Consequently, he had no chance to copy out the final solo piano part. But since it was expected that the soloist would play from music, he made some shorthand scribbles on essentially blank pages and placed them on the music rack. "He gave me a secret glance whenever he was at the end of one of his invisible pages," the page turner later said. "My scarcely hidden anxiety amused him greatly."

I. *Allegro con brio.* The orchestra brings up the two main themes of the opening movement, the first spare and quiet but seething with inner tension, the second an amiable, gentle foil to the electricity generated by the first. The piano then flings out three loud, ascending scales before presenting its version of the thematic material. Led by the soloist, the two melodies are then developed and returned. A brilliant cadenza, supplied by Beethoven, goes directly into the coda, which quickly builds to a powerful conclusion.

II. *Largo.* A serene and stately melody dominates the slow movement. In the contrasting middle section the piano's rippling arpeggios serve as the accompaniment to a bassoon and flute duet. A reworking of the original melody then ends the movement.

III. *Rondo: Allegro.* The full-scaled, high-spirited finale combines rondo form with sonata allegro form. The piano sets the mood with the jaunty principal tune and shares in the many equally beguiling melodies that follow, either as the leading voice or providing the florid background. At the end, the meter changes (from 2/4 to 6/8) and the tempo picks up (from Allegro to Presto), bringing the concerto to a high-speed, happy finish.

Concerto for Piano and Orchestra No. 4 in G major, Op. 58
(37 minutes)

Even though Beethoven's sketches for this concerto date back to 1804, he did not complete the concerto until 1806, because he was simultaneously working on his Fourth and Fifth symphonies, the three "Rasoumowsky" quartets, his opera *Fidelio,* and other compositions. In those pre-copyright days, to prevent other pianists from performing the work Beethoven withheld publication until 1808.

The Fourth Concerto represents a giant advance in style over Beethoven's earlier concertos. While the composer wrote all four to be performed by himself at the keyboard, he designed the first three primarily to display the soloist's command of the instrument. In the fourth, though, the emphasis is obviously on the music's expressive qualities, despite an extremely demanding solo part.

For the first performance, Beethoven wanted his student Ferdinand Ries to learn the piece. But Ries demurred, saying that the solo part was too difficult to master quickly and suggested that he play the composer's Third Piano Concerto instead. Annoyed with Ries, Beethoven engaged another pianist, who agreed to prepare the Fourth Concerto but at the very last minute reneged and performed the Third Concerto instead.

Beethoven himself finally gave the premiere at a private concert in the Viennese palace of Prince Franz Joseph Lobkowitz in March 1807, and performed the work before the public on December 22, 1808, in Vienna.

I. *Allegro moderato.* Avoiding the Classical tradition of starting concertos with an orchestral exposition of the themes, which he followed in his first three concertos, Beethoven opens with a hushed piano statement of the principal theme; its repeated notes recall the openings of the Fifth Symphony and the Violin Concerto, which date from the same period. After its brief statement, the piano remains silent as the orchestra introduces the many melodic motifs of the movement. The soloist and orchestra then take this thematic material through many changes in mood—from light and tender to thundering and puissant. The movement ends with a very free restatement of the melodies with the piano proudly proclaiming the opening motif, not whispering it as before.

II. *Andante con moto.* Unison strings offer a bold, challenging statement, to which the piano responds warmly and soothingly. Again, the strings insist on their audacious musical point; once more the piano delivers its gentle, poetic answer. As the movement continues, the orchestra takes on more and more of the piano's expressive qualities until they come together for the final measure of this brief, magical movement.

III. *Rondo: Vivace.* Following without pause, the Rondo has the strings play the light, skittering main theme and thus sustain the quiet of the Andante ending. The piano enters with a graceful episode of its own before the tutti orchestra restates the theme, now in full voice. With brilliant writing for the soloist and scintillating orchestral comments, Beethoven makes this a joyous cap to a remarkable concerto.

Concerto for Piano and Orchestra No. 5 in E flat major, Op. 73, "Emperor"

(40 minutes)

On December 22, 1808, while giving the premieres of his Fourth Piano Concerto and Choral Fantasia for Piano, Orchestra, and Chorus, the pianist and orchestra fell apart, most likely because of the composer's ever-worsening deafness. Characteristically, Beethoven blamed the orchestra musicians. He later wrote: "The musicians, in particular, were enraged that when, from sheer carelessness, a mistake had been made, I suddenly made them stop playing and called out in a loud voice, 'Once more!' "

Despite his rage at the musicians, there is little doubt that Beethoven suspected the cause to be his deafness and that he knew that future appearances as a pianist were virtually impossible. The "Emperor" Concerto proved to be the only one he never played in public and his last effort in the form, although he had nearly 20 highly productive years remaining to him.

He began to compose the Fifth Concerto soon after the fateful 1808 concert and continued work during the summer of 1809, when Napoleon attacked Vienna, where the composer was then living. Contemporary accounts tell how Beethoven cowered in the cellar of his brother's house, pillows clapped over his head, trying to protect his little remaining hearing amidst the din of the bursting shells.

Completed late in 1809, the concerto was first performed in Leipzig on November 28, 1811; Friedrich Schneider was soloist and Johann Schulz conducted. The first program did not use the "Emperor" subtitle; no one knows who added the sobriquet or when it first appeared.

I. *Allegro.* Three powerful orchestral chords, each majestically calling forth a sweeping cadenzalike response from the piano, open the concerto. The first theme emerges immediately, stated by the violins and echoed by the clarinet. Other themes follow in profusion, including the second theme proper, initially in minor and played by the violins and then transformed into a lyrical, major-key melody sung by the French horns. The piano continues with its version of the thematic material, which leads to a development section, characterized by brilliant figurations for the soloist against fragments of melody in the orchestra. A return of forceful orchestral chords similar to those that opened the movement ushers in a restatement of both themes, but this time utilizing the piano as an active participant.

II. *Adagio un poco mosso.* Brief in length and simple in construction, the Adagio is sublime in inspiration. Muted violins state the tranquil, hymnlike theme until a series of rising trills announces a piano variation of the opening melody. After another variation, played by the woodwinds with a flowing accompaniment in the piano, the composer offers a slow, whispered preview of the next movement.

III. *Rondo: Allegro.* Suddenly, with untrammeled exuberance and exultation, the main theme of the Rondo erupts, its syncopated rhythms masking the underlying 6/8 meter. After the orchestra has a go at the theme and a subdued contrast, the composer develops the opening theme at some length. An echo of the transition passage from the second movement leads this time to a repetition of both themes. The coda features a duet for piano and timpani before a torrential flow of notes brings the concerto to a triumphant finish.

Concerto for Piano, Violin, Cello, and Orchestra in C major, Op. 56, "Triple Concerto"
(36 minutes)

Archduke Rudolph, son of the Emperor, was an important source of support for Beethoven, both moral and financial. The two first met when the Archduke was a young teenager and began piano lessons with the composer. And it was at the request of the 16-year-old Archduke for a concerto that he might play with two leading instrumentalists of Vienna—violinist Ignaz Seidler and cellist Anton Kraft—that Beethoven wrote his "Triple Concerto."

In developing his concept of the "Triple Concerto," Beethoven had to choose between treating the three players as a trio, essentially playing together, or three relatively independent players, performing individually as soloists. The composer opted for the latter course, though he often kept the piano on its own and paired the strings.

Beethoven composed most of the concerto in the remarkable winter of 1803–4, when he was also working on the "Eroica" Symphony, the "Waldstein" Sonata, and the opera *Fidelio.* He probably finished the concerto a few years later; the private premiere was given at the Archduke's palace in 1807 and the first public performance followed in May 1808.

I. *Allegro.* As in traditional Classical concertos, the orchestra states the several not dissimilar themes of the exposition before the three soloists enter with a free interpretation of the thematic material. The remainder of this spacious movement divides the melodic lead and the decorative arabesques among the three soloists, with the orchestra now accompanying, now in the lead.

II. *Largo.* Beethoven assigns the exquisite theme of the brief Largo to the muted orchestral strings, after which it is taken up by the solo cello. Instead of introducing a contrast, the composer fills the body of the movement with free variations on the original melody. He then moves to the coda, in which the cello's fast repeated notes act as a bridge to the Rondo, which ensues without pause.

III. *Rondo alla Polacca.* In this movement Beethoven skillfully captures the character of a polacca, or polonaise, a national Polish dance that is moderate in tempo but with a festive, sprightly quality. For many, the Rondo alla Polacca, with its wonderful themes, is the most gratifying part of the concerto. Structurally, Beethoven combines rondo form, with repetitions of the principal theme (which is first heard at the very opening played by the cello in its high register), and sonata allegro form, with some development of the principal theme and the contrasting episodes.

Concerto for Violin and Orchestra in D major, Op. 61
(40 minutes)

Early in 1806 Franz Clement, the 26-year-old concertmaster and conductor at the Theater-an-der-Wien, invited Beethoven to write a concerto for a performance on December 23 of that year. The composer was delighted to comply with the request since he was a great admirer of young Clement's accomplishments as a violinist.

It is said that Beethoven did not finish the score until two days before the concert and that the violinist read it at sight the evening of the performance. More certain is the fact that Clement inserted a Fantasia of his own composition between the first and second movements of the concerto, and played it on one string with the violin held upside down! It appears that, in addition to being a master of the violin, Clement must have been something of a musical clown. Surely Beethoven recognized the humorous facet of Clement's personality or why would he have made a punning plea for clemency when he wrote "Concerto par Clemenza pour Clement" on the score?

The concerto was not very well received at first. It languished until 1844, when the great virtuoso Joseph Joachim played the work and helped people recognize it as the first outstanding violin concerto of symphonic proportion.

I. *Allegro ma non troppo.* The audacious opening—four quiet strokes on the timpani—arrests the ear and suggests an amazing potential for expansion and development. Immediately after the fourth stroke Beethoven begins the principal theme of the movement, a calm, reflective woodwind melody. After working it through to a climax, the violins repeat the four-note phrase as the background to the subsidiary theme (not unlike the first theme), which is also introduced by the woodwinds. After presenting the closing theme of the exposition, Beethoven has the violin enter with an improvisatory-sounding passage. For the rest of the movement, the violin and orchestra participate as partners in working through the thematic material, with the four repeated notes never far from our attention.

II. *Larghetto.* The strings announce the simple but moving theme of the slow movement, which Beethoven then subjects to three variations, as the orchestra carries the melodic burden and the solo violin adds its comments and embellishments. The soloist then enters with a new theme, followed by one more variation on the opening theme and a variation on the new theme, leading to a brief cadenza that flows into the finale.

III. *Rondo: Allegro.* Playing on the violin's lowest string, the soloist states the soft but robust main theme of the movement. A repeat two octaves higher and a full-voiced orchestral statement complete the refrain. Two more times we hear this subject without change, separated by contrasting interludes, with the soloist sometimes carrying the melody and sometimes performing brilliant figurations around orchestral statements. Among the many delights of this movement is Beethoven's splendid surprise ending.

OVERTURES

Overtures fall into two broad groups: instrumental introductions to stage works, such as operas, ballets, or spoken dramas with incidental music; and concert overtures, which are orchestral compositions with some specific inspiration or program in mind. Beethoven wrote both kinds.

Coriolan, Op. 62
(9 minutes)

Beethoven's familiarity with Plutarch's *Lives,* Shakespeare's *Coriolanus,* and especially Viennese playwright Heinrich Josef von Collin's play *Coriolan* acquainted him thoroughly with the story of the legendary Roman general Coriolanus. The various accounts describe how the high-ranking Roman was forced into exile by the tribune. When he returns to attack his home city, the pleading of his mother and wife dissuade him from proceeding, and ultimately lead to his death.

Beethoven uses the music of the overture to depict the main points of the tale, while at the same time conforming to sonata allegro form. The opening (first theme) presents a tonal portrait of Coriolanus—proud, defiant, restless. In opposition Beethoven puts forth a tender, pleading melody (second theme), obviously his mother and wife begging him to spare his home and his people. Throughout the rest of the overture we experience Coriolanus' inner turmoil and indecisiveness (development and recapitulation), finally ending with his death (coda).

A private performance (on March 8, 1807) and a single public performance (April 24, 1807) of Collin's *Coriolan* were held in Vienna, with Beethoven conducting the overture.

The Creatures of Prometheus, Op. 43
(5 minutes)

In 1800, choreographer Salvatore Vigano encouraged Beethoven to write the score for a ballet. The composer, who was eager to write a major stage work, welcomed the opportunity and set to work. The subject was to be Prometheus, the mythological god who fashions statues of a man and a woman from clay, brings them to life with fire he steals from heaven, and then calls on the other gods to instruct the mortals in music, dance, reasoning, comedy, tragedy, and the pleasures of wine. Beethoven composed an overture and 16 separate numbers for the ballet, which received its premiere in Vienna on March 28, 1801, and had a highly successful run of 29 performances. While the overture has become a concert favorite, the ballet music has faded from the modern repertoire.

Beethoven's gem of an overture seems more a piece of abstract music than a depiction of the Prometheus legend. Organized in sonatina form, the work proceeds from a slow introduction to a perpetual motion string first theme, a playful woodwind second theme, and some new thematic material to end the exposition. Then, without a development section, Beethoven repeats the three subjects to conclude the overture.

Egmont, Op. 84
(10 minutes)

From October 1809 to June 1810 Beethoven composed incidental music for a revival of Goethe's play *Egmont* at Vienna's Hofburg Theater. The undertaking was a labor of love, partly because of Beethoven's great affection and respect for the playwright and partly because of the drama's main themes—the defiance of tyranny and the struggle for freedom—causes dear to the composer's heart. Regrettably, the very excellent incidental music currently receives very few performances today.

Goethe freely based the play on the real-life adventures of Count Egmont (1522–68), who was a patriot in the Netherlands when the Spanish army under the Duke of Alva tried to subjugate that area. In the end, Count Egmont fought against the Spaniards and was beheaded.

To some extent, the overture explicates the story of the play. The solemn opening chords, forcefully played in the rhythm of a very slow Spanish sarabande, introduce the evil Duke of Alva. The middle section conveys the spirit of battle and the rage of conflict. The concluding moments include a very somber few measures, perhaps signaling Egmont's death, followed by a jubilant, triumphant conclusion. Beethoven based this last section on the "Symphony of Victory" ending he wrote for the musical drama, leaving listeners with the distinct impression that Egmont did not die in vain; his death will inspire the people of the Netherlands to overthrow their Spanish conquerors.

Beethoven completed eight pieces of incidental music for *Egmont* in time for the opening of the play on May 24, 1810. He then finished the overture, which was added for the performances starting on June 15.

Fidelio
Leonore No. 1, Op. 138
Leonore No. 2, Op. 72a
Leonore No. 3, Op. 72b
(between 5 and 15 minutes)

Speaking of his sole opera, *Fidelio*—which was originally entitled *Leonore*—Beethoven said: "Of all my children, this is the one that caused me the worst birth pangs, the one that brought me the most sorrow; and for that reason, it is the one most dear to me." Beethoven's "pangs" in the creation of *Fidelio* lasted from 1803 to 1814, as he reworked the opera, completing no fewer than four overtures and preparing sketches for a fifth!

The plot of *Fidelio* is simply told: Florestan, an opponent of tyranny, is unjustly imprisoned and sentenced to die in a state prison. His wife, Leonora, disguised as a man named Fidelio, tries to rescue him. At the end, Don Fernando, the minister of state, arrives and grants Florestan his freedom.

Current scholarship now holds that *Leonore Overture No. 1,* which was believed to have been the first overture composed and discarded before the premiere of *Fidelio,* actually was written after *No. 3.* Beethoven prepared it in 1807 for a performance of the opera in Prague that never materialized; this overture did not receive its first performance until February 7, 1828, nearly a year after Beethoven's death. In some ways *Leonore Overture No. 1* is a simplification of *Leonore Overture No. 3*—though without the drama and tension of that version. It starts with a slow introduction before the fast body of the work. In the middle of the fast section, Beethoven stops and introduces a slow melody taken from a lamenting aria sung by Florestan in his dungeon cell. The fast tempo resumes with the return of previously heard themes to end the overture.

Beethoven wrote *Leonore Overture No. 2* in time for the premiere of *Fidelio* on November 20, 1805, in Vienna. This overture, the longest of all four, opens slowly with a falling line that some hear as the descent into Florestan's cell; it is succeeded by an extensive quotation of his dungeon aria melody. In the fast section, which includes Florestan's melody, Beethoven builds up to the offstage trumpet call that announces the arrival of Don Fernando in the opera. Another reminder of Florestan's lament comes after the call and precedes the high-speed, triumphant conclusion.

After the disappointing premiere of *Fidelio*, Beethoven undertook extensive revisions in the opera. Also, probably realizing that the overture was much too long and powerful, he completely reworked that music. Beethoven created the shorter, tighter *Leonore Overture No. 3*, which was premiered at the first performance of the revised opera in Vienna on March 29, 1806. A deliberate descending scale and a brief quotation of Florestan's aria are heard before some excited spasms of sound lead to the fast section, which is organized in sonata allegro form. The first theme is an upward-reaching melody; the warm, cantabile subsidiary contrast hints at Florestan's theme. Beethoven whips these melodies into crashing climaxes until everything is stilled by the distant trumpet call, which sounds again, closer this time. Now, instead of a quick, joyful wrap-up, Beethoven reviews the themes we have heard before and only then does he allow the music to burst forth in a happy celebration of freedom.

Leonore Overture No. 3, as an opera overture, satisfied neither Beethoven nor the audience. So once again the composer went to work on the score. One result was what we now call the *Fidelio Overture*, which is lighter and shorter than all the others, does not quote any of the opera melodies, and does not summarize the plot in any way. The *Fidelio Overture* opens in great exultation with a brief fast section built on a vibrant fanfarelike motif. A pensive slow episode follows and is soon interrupted by a return of the opening. Another, lengthier slow episode comes next, leading to the buoyant fast body of the overture, with its echoes of the initial fanfare figure. Beethoven introduces one final reminder of the slow melody before rushing toward an energetic conclusion.

Today, *Leonore Overture No. 3* and *Fidelio* are firmly ensconced in the orchestral repertoire; *Leonore No. 1* and *No. 2* are less frequently played. All performances of the opera use the *Fidelio Overture; Leonore Overture No. 3* often appears as an orchestral interlude between the scenes of Act II, after a practice initiated by Gustav Mahler.

Symphony No. 1 in C major, Op. 21
(30 minutes)

Imagine Beethoven's First Symphony as it must have sounded to audiences at the premiere almost 200 years ago. The dissonance with which the composer opened the symphony probably shocked listeners. The touches of humor in the third and fourth movements may have made them smile, or even chuckle aloud. Maybe they clucked their tongues at the degradation of symphonic form, raised to such high levels by the still-living Haydn and by Mozart, who had recently died. But the more prescient among them surely were thrilled to hear the exciting new sounds and the rugged vigor brought to music by the provincial from Bonn.

While we cannot forget all the music composed in the intervening 200 years, we can still delight in this symphony for its wondrous originality, wit, and strength.

I. *Adagio molto; Allegro con brio.* The movement starts with the notorious dissonance, given an extra bite by the string pizzicato beneath the sustained wind chord. The dissonance is not fully resolved until the arrival of the principal subject in C major, the home key of the symphony. A lyrical subsidiary theme is gently tossed back and forth by various instruments until a concluding group, which starts forcefully but soon quiets, brings the exposition to an end. The brief development section mostly focuses on the first theme, which the composer fragments in any number of ways before building to a climax and recapping all the themes.

II. *Andante cantabile con moto.* The second violins state the subdued, but elegant, melody of the contrapuntal slow movement. Although the movement falls into sonata allegro form, it all seems to grow from the main theme, in particular the first two notes of the melody. Of especial interest in this movement is the prominent role of the timpani.

III. *Menuetto: Allegro molto e vivace.* While Beethoven calls this movement a Minuet, the "very fast and lively" tempo indication and spirited writing clearly identify it as a Scherzo, the name Beethoven used in his later symphonies. The compact first section sparkles with sudden changes in dynamics; in the middle section we hear a dialogue between the sedate winds and the playful violins; a shortened return of the opening ends the movement.

IV. *Adagio; Allegro molto e vivace.* In the short humorous introduction to the finale, the violins struggle to ascend the scale that finally launches into the jolly main tune. Beethoven then keeps the good spirits percolating throughout this delightful concluding movement.

Beethoven conducted the premiere in Vienna on April 2, 1800, at an *Akademie,* a concert he himself organized and presented.

Symphony No. 2 in D major, Op. 36
(33 minutes)

In 1796, Beethoven first noticed his hearing difficulties; six years later he realized that he was growing deaf. He spent the summer and fall of 1802 in the tiny village of Heiligenstadt outside Vienna, where he had been sent by a doctor who thought the silence of the country might restore his hearing. While there Beethoven wrote the well-known Heiligenstadt Testament, a letter to his brothers about his desperate situation: "O you men who think or say I am morose, stubborn, or misanthropic, how you do me wrong! For six years past I have fallen into an incurable condition . . . my bad hearing! O how could I possibly admit an infirmity in the one sense which ought to be more perfect in me than in others, a sense that I once possessed in the greatest perfection. . . . I would have ended my life—only my art held me back."

It was also at Heiligenstadt that Beethoven composed his Second Symphony, one of the most radiant works in the entire symphonic repertoire. Given what we know of his state of mind, we can only marvel at his ability to transcend his unhappy circumstances and sing this song of unbounded joy.

I. *Adagio; Allegro con brio.* A long, dramatic introduction leads to the high-spirited first theme, given out by the lower strings, and the jaunty second theme, which Beethoven entrusts to the winds. With great energy and vigor, Beethoven develops and returns both themes and ends the movement with a substantial coda.

II. *Larghetto.* The outpouring of songlike melody and the cantabile quality of the slow movement stir many listeners with its intense spirituality. Other composers have created at least two church hymns by setting words with religious content to the melody of this movement. Beethoven provides an abundance of melodic phrases in place of longer, more complete themes, and he organizes them into traditional sonata allegro form.

III. *Scherzo: Allegro.* Scholars believe that this movement marks the first time a composer calls the traditional minuet movement of a symphony a Scherzo, Italian for "joke." Faster and more spirited than a minuet, the Scherzo keeps the three-part minuet form of opening section, contrast, and shortened return of the opening. The humor resides in the surprising changes and juxtapositions—loud/soft, treble/bass, solo/tutti.

IV. *Allegro molto.* Commentators have appropriately called the opening of this movement a somersault or a backflip. As different from a vocally conceived melodic line as can be imagined, it is nevertheless effective in setting the tone for this delightfully comic movement, which Berlioz called a "second scherzo." The wit and whimsy continue all the way through to the bombastic close.

Symphony No. 3 in E flat major, Op. 55, "Eroica"
(55 minutes)

Beethoven's student Ferdinand Ries furnished an account of the creation of the "Eroica" Symphony:

> In 1803 Beethoven composed his Third Symphony [with] Bonaparte in mind, but this was when he was First Consul. I myself had seen this symphony lying on his table; at the head of the title page was the word "Bonaparte" and at the foot was "Luigi van Beethoven."
>
> I brought him the news that Bonaparte had declared himself Emperor. Thereupon he flew into a rage and cried out, "He, too, is nothing but an ordinary man! Now he will trample underfoot all the rights of man and only indulge his ambition; he will set himself on high, like all the others, and become a tyrant!"
>
> Beethoven went to the table, seized the title page from the top, tore it up completely, and threw it on the floor. The first page was written out anew and it was now the symphony received the title "Sinfonia Eroica."

While historians generally accept this account, some scholars quarrel with the timing; there is some evidence that Beethoven substituted the title "Sinfonia Eroica" ("Heroic Symphony") two years later, when he added the words (in Italian): "Composed to Celebrate the Memory of a Great Man."

A few questions, however, persist about the symphony: Why did Beethoven dedicate this work to the man who invaded and defeated Austria two years earlier? Why should a symphony for Napoleon include a funeral march —since Napoleon was still alive? What is the significance of Beethoven using a melody from his ballet *The Creatures of Prometheus* as the theme of the final movement? And why, despite Beethoven's own subtitle, "Eroica," does the work have so few sections that bespeak true heroism?

Conjectures range from the belief that Beethoven was planning to move to Paris and hoped to ingratiate himself with the French, to speculation that the composer himself was the true hero of the "Eroica."

Shortly before beginning work on the piece, Beethoven announced to a friend: "I am not satisfied with my work up to the present time. I mean to take a new road." In the "Eroica," he realized his objective. Musicologist Paul Henry Lang calls it "the greatest single step made by an individual composer in the history of the symphony and in the history of music in general." The "Eroica" vastly deepened and extended the emotional range of the symphony, considerably increased the size of the orchestra, and nearly doubled the length of a symphonic work. The combination of dramatic intensity, personal involvement, monumental conception, and complexity of realization went so far beyond what had come before that many consider the "Eroica" the first Romantic symphony.

I. *Allegro con brio.* Two powerful chords mark the start of the symphony —an arresting signal that we are embarking on a musical journey of considerable import. The main theme follows immediately in the cellos; the melody, though simple and sedate, glows with intensity. Beethoven presents other themes, works them through, and brings them all back before moving on to the rousing conclusion.

II. *Marcia funebre.* The start of the slow movement evokes the solemn tread of a funeral procession, even re-creating the sound of muffled drums in the background. Starting on their very lowest note, the violins state the grief-laden theme. A middle section in the major mode lightens the mood somewhat, but the despair soon returns. At the end Beethoven fragments the melody, further adding to its poignancy, before ending the movement with a final shudder.

III. *Scherzo: Allegro vivace.* Like a distant buzzing, the Scherzo sneaks into the listeners' consciousness. For nearly 100 measures the barely audible chatter continues, followed by a glorious burst of sound—radiant and robust, and surging with vitality. The French horns take the lead in the contrasting fanfarelike middle section before the return of the Scherzo.

IV. *Finale: Allegro molto.* A short, furious introduction leads to the main body of the Finale, which is organized as free variations on two themes. The pizzicato strings present the first theme in bare, skeletal outline before offering two variations on this melody. Beethoven then transforms the first theme into the bass line of the melody he borrowed from his ballet *The Creatures of Prometheus.* Working his musical magic on the two themes, Beethoven builds inexorably to the brilliant coda, which recalls the movement's introduction.

A private performance of the "Eroica" took place in December 1804 at the palace of Prince Maximilian Lobkowitz, to whom the work is dedicated. The public premiere took place in Vienna on April 7, 1805, with Beethoven conducting.

Symphony No. 4 in B flat major, Op. 60
(33 minutes)

In September 1806, Beethoven left Vienna for the castle of his patron, Prince Lichnowsky, where he met another music-loving noble, Count Franz von Oppersdorf. Count Oppersdorf maintained a full orchestra at his castle in Oberglogau, which he staffed with servants who were good musicians as well as competent domestics.

The Count commissioned Beethoven to compose a symphony for this household orchestra, which the composer completed during his two-month residence with Prince Lichnowsky. The orchestra probably performed the Fourth Symphony at the Oberglogau castle during the following months; it was first heard in Vienna at a private subscription concert around the middle of March 1807.

Two well-known composers offered particularly felicitous comments on this symphony. Robert Schumann, struck by the graceful, melodious Fourth Symphony coming between the impassioned "Eroica" and the powerful Fifth Symphony, called the Fourth "a slender Grecian maiden between the two Nordic giants." Hector Berlioz described the Fourth as "lively, nimble, joyous, or of heavenly sweetness"; of the second movement he said that "such a marvel of inspiration" could not have been written by man, but "seems to have been sighed by the Archangel Michael."

Apparently cheerful and carefree, the Fourth Symphony is not without a substratum of pain, due, very likely, to Beethoven's overwhelming difficulties at the time. His deafness was quite far advanced; he was having tremendous difficulty in reworking his opera *Fidelio;* his brother had entered into a marriage that Beethoven unalterably opposed; and his homeland had come under the direct control of Napoleon.

I. *Adagio; Allegro vivace.* A slow introduction, serene and reflective in mood, opens the symphony. The principal theme of the movement appears —at times light and sparkling, at times hard and driving. After the excitement quiets, a new, playful theme emerges, passed gingerly from bassoon, to oboe, to flute. Beethoven mostly devotes the development section to an elaboration of the first subject. Dramatic rolls on the timpani signal the return of both themes and a forceful conclusion.

II. *Adagio.* The second movement starts with a disarmingly simple musical statement—a heartbeatlike rhythmic figure in the second violins. The pulsation continues as the first violins play a rhythmically free scale that descends and then heads up again. Seldom is the art of the composer better concealed than in the masterful construction of this movement, with the transformation of the accompanying figure into an independent melody, the variations of the theme, and the contrasting interludes.

III. *Allegro vivace.* The Allegro vivace, really a Scherzo, erupts in a riot of sound in which Beethoven superimposes a two-beat rhythmic pattern on the three-beat meter, and alternates raucous outbursts with more lyrical passages. The woodwinds dominate the slightly slower middle section as the strings chirp up at the phrase endings. A shortened return of the opening section follows and then, in a rare structural innovation, Beethoven brings back the middle section before ending the movement with a bravura coda.

IV. *Allegro ma non troppo.* Beethoven keeps the headlong flight of the finale—which Berlioz described as an "animated swarm of sparkling notes" —in check by inserting occasional lyrical passages. These interruptions serve the additional purpose of setting into stark relief the movement's powerful propulsive character. Some conductors consider Beethoven's high-speed metronome marking (half note equals 80) too fast in view of his tempo designation, which translates as "Fast, but not too fast," and prefer to get greater clarity and sense of structure from a slightly slower tempo. Either way, this surging movement provides a fitting conclusion to a highly inventive and delightful symphony.

Symphony No. 5 in C minor, Op. 67
(36 minutes)

From 1804 through 1808 Beethoven struggled to compose his Fifth Symphony while simultaneously working on his Fourth Symphony, Fourth Piano Concerto, and Violin Concerto.

This was a particularly difficult period in Beethoven's life. Squabbles with his brothers, disappointments in love, and despair over Napoleon's transformation from champion of the French Revolution to tyrannical emperor were most painful to bear. But worst of all, Beethoven realized that his deafness was growing worse and that he had to give up any hope of a cure. The machinations of fate threatened to rob him of all that he held dear—love, freedom, and the joy of hearing and making music.

Most people consider the C minor symphony Beethoven's most intensely personal and emotionally appealing work; it is surely the most popular of his nine symphonies. Concerning the opening motto of the symphony, he reputedly told his less than reliable biographer Anton Schindler: "So Fate knocks at the door!" Although some have questioned whether Beethoven actually made the remark, there can be little doubt that this symphony represents a fearsome struggle, a reflection of Beethoven's own heroic efforts to conquer and control his own destiny.

I. *Allegro con brio.* The symphony begins with the famous four-note motto—three shorts and a long—that dominates the first movement and reappears in each subsequent movement. Beethoven extends the motto and gives it thematic shape before presenting the lyrical second theme, introduced by a French horn statement of a variant on the opening figure. The following development section largely concerns itself with the motto theme in all its various guises. The traditional recapitulation is interrupted by a brief oboe cadenza before moving to the lengthy coda, which relentlessly pounds away at the four-note motto.

II. *Andante con moto.* The luminous second movement consists of a free set of variations on two similar themes, the first played by violas and cellos, the second by clarinets and bassoons. In the early part of the movement, Beethoven subtly recalls the rhythms of the motto theme from the first movement.

III. *Allegro.* The Scherzo starts with a quiet, somewhat ominous cello and bass melody. The mood is shattered, though, as the French horns loudly insist on the first movement motto. The two themes alternate until the middle section, when the cellos and basses start a lumbering canonic passage that moves up through the string sections. A free repeat of the opening follows and then, in a particularly enchanting moment of the symphony, the strings hold a soft, sustained note, while the timpani pulsates with hints of the motto rhythm in the background. Echoes and wisps of the Scherzo flit through the orchestra as the harmonies begin to shift, leading inexorably and without break to the glorious last movement theme.

IV. *Allegro.* Adding piccolo, contrabassoon, and three trombones to the orchestra for the first time, Beethoven pours forth a wealth of exuberant melody in the Finale. The propulsive forward motion continues until he suddenly recalls the first movement motto in a ghostlike quotation from the Scherzo. Using a transition not unlike the bridge from the Scherzo to the Finale, Beethoven plunges into a review of the themes of the movement and a lengthy, energetic coda that makes abundantly clear the triumph of his indomitable spirit.

Beethoven led the premiere of the Fifth Symphony in Vienna on December 22, 1808.

Symphony No. 6 in F major, Op. 68, "Pastoral"
(46 minutes)

Beethoven eschewed program music—music that describes a scene or event, tells a story, or conveys a meaning outside the pure music—and offered a stock response to anyone asking about the meaning of his music: "That can only be answered at the piano." Yet scholars often call his highly descriptive "Pastoral" Symphony, with its extramusical associations, the first modern example of program music.

In earlier program music, dating back to the 14th century or so, composers imitated such sounds as birdcalls, hunting horns, or the roar of battle. By the 17th century composers conveyed emotions, such as sorrow or happiness, and concepts of heaven or death, through so-called word painting. At the turn of the 18th century, composer Marin Marais went so far as to write *Tableau de l'opération de la taille,* a graphic description in sound of a surgical operation!

Beethoven's thoughts on his programmatic Sixth Symphony can be gleaned from individual sentences he wrote in his sketchbooks: *"Sinfonia caracteristica,* or a recollection of country life." "The hearers should be allowed to discover the situations." "People will not require titles to recognize the general intention to be more a matter of feeling than of painting in sounds." "Pastoral symphony: no picture, but something in which the emotions are expressed that are aroused in men by the pleasures of the country." "All painting in instrumental music, if pushed too far, is a failure." Finally, on the actual score he wrote: "Pastoral symphony or Recollections of rural life (more expression of feeling than tone painting)," and inserted a specific title for each movement.

I. *Awakening of Cheerful Thoughts on Arriving in the Country: Allegro ma non troppo.* It is now thought that Beethoven derived the opening theme from an old Slavonic folk song. The music convincingly evokes both a beautiful country setting (presumably near Heiligenstadt, a favorite country retreat for Beethoven) and his joyous reactions every time he came there. Beethoven introduces other themes, some of which spring from elements of the principal melody, creating the impression that the entire movement grows from that melody.

II. *Scene by the Brook: Andante molto mosso.* From the very beginning the strings set out a soft murmuring figure—the flowing brook—that continues virtually without stop throughout the movement. The first subject mostly contains little wisps of melody played by the first violins against the gently gliding accompaniment; the second presents a more sustained lyrical line, also given out by the first violins. Beethoven allows some turbulence to intrude as he works out these two themes, but soon returns the tranquil flow. Near the end Beethoven imitates three birdcalls—nightingale (flute), quail (oboe), and cuckoo (clarinet), an insertion that Beethoven later asserted was "nothing but a joke."

III. *Merry Gathering of Country Folk: Allegro.* About this movement, Beethoven's friend and pupil Anton Schindler wrote: "Beethoven asked me if I had noticed how village musicians often played in their sleep, occasionally letting their instruments fall and keeping quite still, then waking up with a start, getting in a few vigorous blows or strokes at a venture, although usually in the right key, and then dropping to sleep again. Apparently he had tried to portray these poor people in his 'Pastoral' Symphony."

After Beethoven introduces the two main themes of the movement, he gives the violins what Schindler calls a "stereotyped accompaniment," which so startles the oboe that it comes in on the wrong beat and takes four measures to get in step with the others. Soon the "sleep-drunken second bassoon [joins in] with his repetitions of a few tones," and after a while the violas and cellos awaken and start to imitate the bassoon's three-note motto. A faster robust peasant dance comes next, which gives way in turn to a truncated return of the opening section.

IV. *Thunderstorm, Tempest: Allegro.* This brief movement follows without pause, conjuring up images of a furious summer storm with deafening thunderclaps and flashing streaks of lightning.

V. *Shepherd's Hymn; Happy, Thankful Feelings After the Storm: Allegretto.* Beethoven offers no break before the final movement, which opens with a clarinet gently piping the bucolic melody, letting us know that the sun is again shining on the lovely scene. The entire movement glows with a luminous radiance, reflecting Beethoven's powerful regard for nature's grandeur. "No man can love the country so much as I," he said.

Beethoven began composing the "Pastoral" Symphony in his beloved Heiligenstadt during the summer of 1807, while also working on his Fifth Symphony. He led the premieres of the two symphonies in Vienna on December 22, 1808.

Symphony No. 7 in A major, Op. 92
(37 minutes)

Surely no other symphonic work elicited as many passionate—and diverse—reactions from well-known composers as did Beethoven's Seventh. Most often quoted is Richard Wagner's observation that the symphony is "the apotheosis of the dance," that "tables and benches, cans and cups, the grandmother, the blind and the lame, aye, the children in the cradle, fall to dancing."

The eminent French composer Vincent d'Indy, however, did not share Wagner's view, calling it "nothing else than a pastoral symphony. The rhythm of the piece has truly nothing of the dance about it; it would seem to come from the song of a bird."

On hearing the fast principal theme of the first movement, Hector Berlioz declared it was a "peasant round." Carl Maria von Weber reacted to the section near the end of that movement where the lower strings stubbornly persevere with a repeated five-note figure by stating that the composer was "quite ripe for the madhouse!" And Robert Schumann called the second movement a "rustic wedding."

Despite these widely divergent views, the symphony scored a huge success at its premiere, on December 8, 1813, in Vienna, and continues to be regarded by this commentator and most modern critics as one of Beethoven's truly great symphonies. The enthusiastic audience reaction impelled the performers to repeat the slow movement, an honor seldom bestowed on movements that create their effects without resorting to dazzling speed or brilliance.

Beethoven, whose hearing had by then so deteriorated that he could only catch the very loudest passages, led the concert. Violinist Ludwig Spohr attended the performance and has left us this firsthand account of the composer's conducting style:

> At this concert I first saw Beethoven conduct. As often as I had heard about it, it still surprised me very much. He was accustomed to convey the marks of expression to the orchestra by the most peculiar motions of his body. Thus at a *sforzando* [strong accent] he tore his arms, which until then had been crossed on his breast, violently apart. He crouched down at a *piano* [soft section], bending lower as the tone decreased. At a *crescendo* [gradual increase in loudness] he raised himself by degrees until at the *forte* [loud section] he leapt to his full height; and often, without being conscious of it, would shout aloud at the same time.

I. *Poco sostenuto; Vivace.* The symphony opens with a slow, extended introduction that contains two themes, both introduced by the oboe—the first poised and serene, the second warm and appealing. The movement's main portion follows without pause, the flute presenting the principal, frisky theme with its insistence on a continuous rhythm closely akin to the poetic dactyl (HEAVY/light/light). Here, and in the three subsequent movements as well, Beethoven seems to limit the melodic variety in order to focus more attention on the rhythmic patterns.

II. *Allegretto.* Although Beethoven marked the second movement Allegretto (moderately fast), it functions as the slow movement of the symphony. After an introductory chord, the lower strings present the somber melody, characterized more by its rhythm (long, short/short, long, long) than by the shape of its melodic line, which remains rooted on one note with but a few departures. Beethoven then subjects the theme to five continuous variations, but with the rhythmic pattern persisting throughout—either in the melody, as a countermelody, or as the underpinning in the cellos and basses.

III. *Presto.* The third movement, a Scherzo, even though not so titled, opens with great vigor and abounds with sharp distinctions—loud, ferocious outbursts alternating with soft, light responses. Following this first part,

Beethoven introduces the slightly slower Trio, a contrasting section of sighing, lyrical beauty that is thought to be based on an old Austrian pilgrim's hymn. Then once more he brings back the Scherzo, the Trio, and the Scherzo. Beethoven starts the Trio for a third time, but immediately interrupts with five imperious chords that bring the movement to a sudden halt.

IV. *Allegro con brio.* The whirlwind finale moves forward propelled by a raging demonic energy that only Beethoven could summon. Virtually without respite, the music hurtles onward, rising repeatedly to climax, until the brilliant culmination. How suitable is the statement Beethoven made around the time of the Seventh Symphony: "I am the Bacchus who presses out for men this glorious wine and intoxicates their souls!"

Symphony No. 8 in F major, Op. 93
(26 minutes)

Beethoven completed his Eighth Symphony in Linz in October 1812, four months after he had come there to break up the romance between his brother, Karl, and his brother's housekeeper. Apart from finishing the symphony, Beethoven accomplished little else; he alienated his brother and failed to prevent what proved to be a disastrous marriage. Little of this unpleasant business, nor the added bitterness over his increasing deafness, chronic stomach ailments, and failure in love, surfaces in this witty and humorous symphony. Like other even-numbered symphonies of Beethoven, the Eighth tends to be lighter and happier in spirit; his odd-numbered works tend to be more serious and intense.

I. *Allegro vivace e con brio.* The playful opening theme alternates loud and soft phrases, a feature of the entire symphony that contributes to its humorous character. The second theme is characterized by its flowing grace, despite the hesitation occasioned by the repeated first note at each statement of the ascending figure. The composer creates a comic touch in the development section by failing to allow each instrument to advance beyond the first measure of the principal theme. When the entire theme finally returns to begin the recapitulation, Beethoven marks it *fortissimo* ("very loud") and gives it to the cellos and basses instead of the violins. After the recapitulation he appends a lengthy coda that vanishes finally like a puff of smoke, ending with the opening theme's first measure.

II. *Allegretto scherzando.* Instead of a traditional slow movement, Beethoven inserts a movement with the tempo indication "Moderately fast, playful in style." He bases the melody on a little tune that he made up in the spring of 1812, when Johann Mälzel showed him his newly developed musical chronometer, a device that developed into the metronome. Over repeated metronomelike chords in the winds Beethoven introduces a delicate, bouncy theme in the violins, punctuated with sudden outbursts of sound. The more forceful second theme, played by the violins and violas, presents a marked contrast to the previous lightness. A third theme, more legato than the others, concludes this section and is followed immediately by a recapitulation of all three themes.

III. *Tempo di menuetto.* After marking the slow movement scherzando, one can understand why Beethoven made the third movement a Minuet instead of a Scherzo, as in most of his earlier symphonies. The rough and rude first section offers only occasional quiet moments in the midst of the predominantly heavily accented phrases. A most tender Trio, with its lovely French horn duet, precedes the return of the heavy-footed opening section.

IV. *Allegro vivace.* The brilliant, joyful finale rushes along at breakneck tempo—now whispering, now shouting, full of playful pranks, surprising turns of melody, and striking harmonic invention. At the end of the movement Beethoven adds an extremely lengthy coda that is, in effect, another development section.

Audiences first heard the Eighth Symphony at a private concert in Archduke Rudolph's palace in Vienna on April 20, 1813; the public premiere, also in Vienna, was on February 27, 1814, with Beethoven conducting.

Symphony No. 9 in D minor, Op. 125, "Choral Symphony"
(66 minutes)

A 1793 letter written by Beethoven's friend Fischenich tells us that when the composer was only 23 years old he was already proposing to set Friedrich Schiller's epic poem "An die Freude" ("Ode to Joy") to music. Beethoven's own notebooks show that over the following years he continued to search for a way to achieve his goal.

Finally, in 1822, Beethoven found a place for the "Ode"—as the last movement of his Ninth Symphony. He simply added four vocal soloists and choir to the orchestra that appeared in the first three movements.

Commentators debate the value of the choral finale. In the words of musical scholar Donald Tovey: is it a "crime or a crown"? Some critics of the finale say it is an artistic blunder and a major miscalculation. Others dismiss the significance of the lyrics in this abstract piece of music. After all, they point out, Beethoven used only about one-third of Schiller's 96-line poem and freely changed the order to suit his musical needs. And since Schiller suggested that it be read by friends "around the festive board," a few even hold that the "Ode" is simply a German student drinking song!

For most listeners, however, the "Ode" is the "crown" of the Ninth

Symphony. Viewed in this light, the first three movements of the symphony are but an extended preparation for the choral finale.

Richard Wagner, an enthusiastic admirer of the Ninth, set down his interpretation of the symphony:

I. A struggle, conceived in the greatest grandeur, of the soul contending for happiness against the oppression of that inimical power that places itself between us and the joys of earth. . . .

II. Wild delight seizes us at once. . . . It is a new world that we enter, one in which we are carried away to dizzy intoxication.

III. How differently these tones speak to our hearts! How pure, how celestially soothing they are as they melt the defiance, the wild impulse of the soul harassed by despair into a soft, melancholy feeling!

IV. A harsh outcry begins the transition from the third to the fourth movements, a cry of disappointment at not attaining the contentment so earnestly sought. Then, with the beginning of the Ode, we hear clearly expressed what must appear to the anxious seeker for happiness as the highest lasting pleasure.

I. *Allegro ma non troppo, un poco maestoso.* Beethoven forges the first movement's principal theme out of evanescent flickers of sound that build up to a rhythmically charged melody based on a descending D minor chord. After expanding this subject, Beethoven introduces a contrasting quiet, lyrical melody, along with a number of varied subsidiary ideas. The remainder of the movement works through the different melodies and brings them back for a condensed, but complete recapitulation before summarizing the entire movement with a climactic coda.

II. *Molto vivace.* Instead of placing the slow movement second, Beethoven introduces a Scherzo, even though it is not so named. Several groups of vigorous hammerlike blows announce the movement's arresting, rhythmic motto, which quickly evolves into a light, tripping tune that passes fugally through the strings. (The premiere audience was so taken with this movement that it burst into applause and demanded a repetition.) Beethoven bases the central contrasting Trio on a flowing cantilena melody, after which he repeats the Scherzo and concludes the movement with a coda.

III. *Adagio molto e cantabile.* For the slow movement, Beethoven creates two themes with such perfection of line, deep emotion, and sublime nobility that they seem to transcend human invention. He treats these melodies in free, leisurely variation form, giving the movement a profound, spiritual quality that few composers, including Beethoven, ever surpassed.

IV. *Presto; Allegro assai.* The finale opens with two ferocious outbursts in the winds, answered by brief recitativelike passages in the cellos and double basses. The remainder of the strings then enter and recall the first movement theme, which is interrupted by another recitative in the lower strings. Fragments of the second and third movement themes also present themselves, each time cut short by a recitative. Finally the cellos and basses state the fourth movement theme, a disarmingly simple folk-songlike melody that Beethoven arrived at after creating and discarding about 200 preliminary versions!

Beethoven varies the melody, adding more instruments and increasing the complexity and volume until the full orchestra bursts into an enormous, raging dissonance. At this point, the baritone soloist enters with the only words by Beethoven (the rest of the text is from Schiller's "Ode"): "O Freunde, nicht diese Töne! Sondern lasst uns angenehmere anstimmen, und freudenvollere!" ("O friends, not these tones! Let us raise our voices together in more pleasant and cheerful tones!") This is followed by Beethoven's setting of the "Ode" as a gigantic set of free and wide-ranging variations involving soloists, choir, and orchestra.

Beethoven completed the symphony in February 1824, after about a year and a half of concentrated work. The Vienna premiere took place on May 7, 1824, with Michael Umlauf conducting and Beethoven seated on the stage, back to the audience, to help with the tempos. The composer, now totally deaf, could not hear the audience's tumultuous applause at the end, but thanks to a singer who turned him around, was able to see the fervid response his music had evoked.

Hector Berlioz

Born December 11, 1803, in La Côte-Saint-André, Isère, France
Died March 8, 1869, in Paris

THE EARLY YEARS of the 19th century witnessed a cataclysmic up-
heaval in the role of music in society. No longer were most composers in
the employ of nobles, many of whom had disappeared as a result of the
French Revolution and the Napoleonic Wars. The pervasive changes in the
social order were accelerated by such factors as the Industrial Revolution, the
rise of the middle class, and the growth of cities, all of which helped to move
the focus of musical activity from aristocratic salons to public concert halls.
Composers no longer wrote to fulfill the needs of their patrons; their work
was now largely concerned with satisfying their own need for self-expression.

Along with the new role of music in society, musical style also underwent
a dramatic transformation. The clarity, poise, and control of the Classical
period, as heard particularly in the works of Haydn and Mozart, gave way to
a variety of highly intense, emotional, and individualistic styles. This shift
ushered in the Romantic period of music, which lasted for most of the 19th
century.

Critics regard Hector Berlioz as one of the seminal figures in the development of the Romantic style. To the task of writing music he brought a fertile
imagination, an incredible grasp of the tonal possibilities of the orchestra as
well as each instrument, and a burning desire to stretch the limits of self-
expression. So innovative was his approach to orchestral composition that
many consider him the father of the modern symphony.

Berlioz scrutinized every cherished canon of music, including melodic
construction, harmonic manipulations, rhythmic patterns, formal structures,
and use of instruments, to decide whether or not it suited his expressive
needs. Thus, his compositions were among the first to furnish psychological
insights into the mind of the creative artist. Also, they displayed so stunning

a command of the orchestra that they served as models of music writing for future generations. As he wrote in a 1856 letter: "I am for the music that you yourself call *free*. Yes, free and wild and sovereign; I want it to conquer everything, to assimilate everything to itself."

While still a very young man, Berlioz reluctantly agreed to follow in his physician father's footsteps—that is, until he was asked to perform his first dissection. The procedure so horrified him that he fled the laboratory and soon after, at age 20, entered the Paris Conservatory. At the Conservatory he composed his best-known work, the *Fantastic Symphony*.

For the rest of his career, Berlioz had a small but loyal public following, and was either greatly venerated or soundly disparaged by other musicians. Unable to support himself by composing alone, he wrote musical criticism and a book on orchestration that show a very strong literary talent married to keen musical understanding. New ways of communicating through music, a very high quality of musical composition, and several major contributions to the repertoire rank Berlioz high in the annals of music history.

Fantastic Symphony (Symphonie Fantastique): *Episode in the Life of an Artist,* Op. 14
(60 minutes)

Three artistic events profoundly affected the impressionable Berlioz at the age of 24: he read Goethe's *Faust* and discovered the hero, which the young composer saw as "genius in all its greatness"; he heard Beethoven's "Eroica" Symphony and recognized the work as a major step forward in orchestral composition; and he attended excellent productions of Shakespeare's *Hamlet* and *Romeo and Juliet,* and fell in love with the leading Irish actress Harriet (called Henrietta in France) Smithson.

After watching Smithson perform in *Romeo and Juliet,* Berlioz averred: "I shall marry that woman and on that drama I will write my greatest symphony." Subsequently, he called on her, but she refused to see him. He arranged a special performance of his music to win her notice, but she remained unaware. He wrote letters, but she did not reply.

In February 1830, the frustrated Berlioz told his friend poet Humbert Ferrand that he had worked out in his head "my great symphony, in which the development of my infernal passion is to be portrayed." While setting the notes down on paper, Berlioz heard rumors—later proven false—that Harriet was involved in some opprobrious behavior. The ugly gossip led the heartsick composer to depict his beloved as a witch in the last movement of the *Fantastic Symphony.*

Berlioz completed the symphony on April 16, 1830, and the premiere was given in Paris on December 5, 1830, with François Habeneck conducting. Harriet, who was performing at the time, did not attend. Some years later, however, Berlioz finally met the object of his obsession, after Smithson attended a performance and learned of her pivotal role in the symphony's creation. In 1833, he and Harriet were married, but the union failed, and the couple separated in 1840.

Three important features characterize the *Fantastic Symphony;* they constitute a marked advance in the development of the Romantic style in music and also help to make this one of the best-liked compositions in the repertoire. First, the symphony follows an incredibly explicit and specific programmatic form—that is, the music refers directly to events, feelings, and scenes, which Berlioz describes in abstract musical tones. Berlioz even suggested that members of the concert audience receive the literary program before hearing the work, though he wrote: "There is absolutely no question of the program reproducing (as some people seem to have thought) what the composer is trying to communicate through the orchestra. He knows perfectly well that music cannot substitute for either words or pictures." Also, he later said: "The Symphony can (the composer hopes) offer musical interest independent of any dramatic purpose." More confounding is evidence that Berlioz borrowed much of the music in this programmatic symphony from earlier works, where he used it to depict completely different situations.

Second, Berlioz employed the idée fixe, a concept he borrowed from the newly developing science of psychology. In music, idée fixe refers to a brief melody that the composer identifies with a particular idea or character (in this case Harriet) and uses in various transformations throughout the piece. In the *Fantastic Symphony,* the idée fixe appears initially at the end of the slow introduction to the first movement.

Finally, Berlioz displayed exceptional skill and imagination by drawing from the orchestra an amazing kaleidoscope of tonal effects. The resulting legacy was an increased palette of tones and colors available to later composers.

Here, then, is the program that Berlioz supplied for his *Fantastic Symphony:*

I. *Reveries—Passions: Largo; Allegro agitato.* The author imagines that a young musician, afflicted by the disease of the spirit which a famous writer has referred to as the "surge of the passions," sees for the first time a woman who combines all the charms of the ideal being of whom he has for so long dreamed, and becomes hopelessly taken with her. By a strange turn of fate, the cherished image only presents itself to the artist's spirit in connection with a musical idea, in which he discovers a character impassioned, but at the same time noble and timid, similar to that which he attributes to the object of his affection.

This melodic reflection with its model follow him incessantly like a double obsession. This is the reason for the constant appearance, in all the movements of the symphony, of the melody with which the first Allegro begins. The passage from this state of melancholy reverie, interrupted by several outbursts of groundless joy, to a state of delirious passion, with movements of anger, jealousy, reversions to tenderness, tears, religious consolation, is the subject of this first piece.

II. *A Ball: Valse: Allegro non troppo.* The artist finds himself in the most varied circumstances of life, in the middle of the "bustle of a festival," in the quiet contemplation of the beauties of nature; but everywhere, in the town, in the fields, the beloved image presents itself to him and throws him into disquiet.

III. *Scene in the Meadows: Adagio.* Finding himself one evening in the countryside, he hears from afar two herdsmen singing a pastoral melody; this pastoral duo, the site, the light rustling of the trees gently shaken by the wind, some reason for hope that he has just conceived, all combine to give his heart an unaccustomed sense of calm, and to give a more cheerful color to his thoughts. He reflects on his loneliness; he hopes that he will not be alone much longer. . . . But if she were to deceive him! . . . This mixture of hope and fear, these thoughts of happiness, troubled by black forebodings, form the subject of the Adagio. At the end, one of the herdsmen begins singing the pastoral melody once again; the other no longer responds. . . . The sound of thunder in the distance—loneliness—silence.

IV. *March to the Scaffold: Allegretto non troppo.* Having become certain that his love is unrecognized, the artist poisons himself with opium. The dose of the narcotic, too slight to kill him, plunges him into a deep sleep accompanied by horrible visions. He dreams that he has killed the one he loves, that he has been condemned, led to the scaffold, and that he is present at his own execution. The procession advances to the sound of a march both dark and cruel, both brilliant and solemn, in which the sound of muffled footsteps gives way without transition to the most resounding outbursts. At the end of the march, the first four measures of the obsession reappear as a final thought of love interrupted by the fatal blow.

V. *Dream of a Witches' Sabbath.* He sees himself at a witches' Sabbath, in the middle of a horrendous band of ghosts, witches, monsters of all kinds, gathered for his funeral. Weird noises, groans, laughter, distant cries to which other cries seem to respond. The beloved melody appears once again, but it has lost its noble and timid character; it is merely a base, trivial, and grotesque dance tune; it is she who is coming to the Sabbath. . . . A howl of joy at her arrival. . . . She joins in the diabolical orgy. . . . The funereal knell, a burlesque parody of the *Dies Irae* [a hymn sung at funeral ceremonies of the Catholic Church], a Sabbath round. The Sabbath round and the *Dies Irae* come together.

Overture to *Benvenuto Cellini,* Op. 23
(10 minutes)

Fiery, impetuous, headstrong, and reckless are words that describe the hero of Berlioz's opera *Benvenuto Cellini* as aptly as they describe the composer himself, whose personality strongly resembled that of the legendary 16th century Italian sculptor, goldsmith, and all-around roué. At the premiere of the opera at the Paris Opera on September 10, 1838, the overture (also fiery, impetuous, headstrong, and reckless) was, in Berlioz's words, "greeted with exaggerated applause, but the rest was hissed with admirable energy and unanimity." The same assessment holds today; the overture is cheered while the opera has virtually disappeared from the stage.

After the overture's rash opening, there is a sudden long silence, followed by a slower, more quiet section. Here Berlioz introduces various themes from the opera, in particular the music of the Cardinal's absolution of Cellini's sins and Cellini's love duet with Teresa, before another silence leads to a brief but brilliant conclusion.

Overture to *The Corsair,* Op. 21
(9 minutes)

"I followed the 'Corsair,' " wrote Berlioz, referring to Lord Byron's poem "The Corsair," "in his desperate adventures; I adored that inexorably yet tender nature—pitiful, yet generous—a strange combination of apparently contradictory feelings: love of woman and hatred of his kind." The story's appeal for Berlioz had no doubt to do with his disappointing love affair. In 1831, the headstrong young composer even attempted suicide after a failed romance. The doctors suggested a rest in Nice, and it was there that he began working on the overture that came to be named *Corsair.* Thirteen years later, he returned to Nice, where he finished the overture in August 1844. He named it *The Tower of Nice,* after the well-known Martello tower.

Berlioz conducted the premiere in Paris on January 19, 1845, but was dissatisfied with the results. He took about six years, until 1851 and 1852, to start revising the work, at the same time changing the title to *Le Corsaire rouge (The Red Corsair),* from a book by James Fenimore Cooper. Berlioz subsequently shortened the title to *Le Corsaire,* the title of Byron's poem.

The overture starts with two shotlike chords that unleash a furious cascade of notes in the violins. This fast section soon gives way to a brief slow interlude with a particularly appealing melody. The tempo quickens and leads to the main body of the overture, where Berlioz introduces a jaunty new theme that he treats contrapuntally in both canon and inversion. Reminders of both the fast and slow opening parts come to the fore as this fiery piece races to an exciting conclusion.

Overture, *The Roman Carnival,* Op. 9
(9 minutes)

Six years after the premiere of his opera *Benvenuto Cellini,* Berlioz composed an overture to the second act, which is set at the carnival in Rome. He conducted the first performance of only the overture at an orchestra concert in Paris on February 3, 1844, and thus began the tradition of playing the work on concert programs.

Berlioz based the stirring outburst that opens the overture on the fast, wild saltarello, a dance that takes place at the second act's festivities. The dancelike tune quickly gives way to the tender English horn melody, which Berlioz derived from Cellini's first act love song. Rapid surging up-and-down scales introduce the third subject, based on a choral selection from the opera, before the energetic and exuberant saltarello returns in an extended treatment. As the music quiets, the dance rhythm continues as the accompaniment to the love song. But the power of the dance prevails, and soon the saltarello reemerges, to conclude the overture.

Johannes Brahms

Born May 7, 1833, in Hamburg
Died April 3, 1897, in Vienna

BRAHMS'S MUSICAL TALENT was recognized early by his father, a theater and nightclub bass player, who arranged for piano lessons when the youngster was seven years old. Within a few years the teenaged Brahms was able to get jobs playing piano in Hamburg's taverns and brothels. Later, Brahms commented that his early experiences with the ladies of the night ("those who turned me against marriage") were responsible for his lifelong inability to sustain normal relationships with women.

At age 20, he met three musical figures who were to figure importantly in his life: Joseph Joachim, noted Hungarian violinist, on whom Brahms depended for reactions to his new compositions and for technical advice on writing for the violin; Robert Schumann, already an established composer and essayist, who helped Brahms by interceding on his behalf with publishers and by advancing his name with the public; and Clara Schumann, Robert's wife and an outstanding pianist and composer, who proved to be the abiding love of Brahms's life and a trusted musical confidante.

Brahms gained early acceptance as one of the leading composers of the time. His music was performed widely and the public demanded his appearances both as a conductor and as a pianist. As his fame grew, though, so did his penchant for making nasty or sarcastic remarks. In one instance, after spending several minutes studying music brought to him by young Max Bruch, Brahms had only a single reaction: "Tell me, where did you get this splendid music paper?" And on leaving a party one evening, he proclaimed: "If there is anybody here I have not insulted, I apologize!"

But under this sometimes gruff exterior, Brahms had an equally strong bent for kindness and good deeds. He befriended a number of younger composers, including Dvořák and Grieg, and championed their music. In the pockets of his too short, usually stained trousers he carried candies that he distributed to children he met on the street.

Conductor Hans von Bülow coined the phrase "the three B's"—Bach, Beethoven, and Brahms. The combination is a valid one because Brahms, to a very large extent, carried on the tradition and style of the two older composers. While he utilized the vocabulary and infused his music with the expressivity, emotional content, and individuality of 19th century Romanticism, he preserved the bonds that connected him to the Baroque practices of Bach and to the Classical style of Beethoven. By joining Brahms to Bach and Beethoven, von Bülow also rightfully asserts Brahms's place in that Olympian company.

One of the distinguishing characteristics of the music of Brahms, among the many that justify its consideration in this book, is its staying power. One can listen to a Brahms symphony or concerto over and over again and always find something new and intriguing to catch one's interest and attention.

Concerto for Piano and Orchestra No. 1 in D minor, Op. 15
(46 minutes)

In a letter to violinist Joseph Joachim in 1853, Brahms mentions that he had written a three-movement Sonata for Two Pianos. The following year, encouraged by the confidence of his dear friends Robert and Clara Schumann, Brahms decided to expand the sonata into a symphony, his First.

For several months, Brahms struggled to score the sonata for orchestra. While he felt it required a symphony orchestra to provide a sufficient range of sonorities and tone colors, aspects of the compositional style could only be realized with a piano. For some time he considered making it a symphony with an obbligato piano part. But he finally decided to cast the work as a piano concerto, his Piano Concerto No. 1. (His First Symphony was not completed until 1876, some 20 years later.)

Brahms began the actual composition of the piano concerto in 1857, after Robert Schumann's death. As was his wont, he relied heavily on advice from Clara Schumann and Joseph Joachim, his two most trusted musical friends. Brahms retained two movements from the original sonata, and wrote a new third movement. (He used the melody of the original third movement in the "Behold All Flesh" section of his *Ein deutsches Requiem.*) By March 1858 the composer felt ready to schedule a private run-through performance. Brahms played the solo piano part and Joachim conducted the Hanover orchestra.

The results met with the performers' approbation, and the first scheduled performance took place on January 22, 1859. Five days later the work was given in Leipzig, and proved to be "a brilliant and decisive failure," as

Brahms later wrote. According to his account, three people tried to applaud, but they were dissuaded by the hisses of the others in the audience. Nevertheless, despite this hostile initial reaction, the concerto went on to win a devoted following and score many successes that more than fulfilled Brahms's faith in its worth and value.

I. *Maestoso.* The first movement begins with a powerful, tragic theme in the orchestra. Many commentators hold that this melody expresses Brahms's reactions to the suicide attempt, confinement in a mental hospital, and subsequent death of Robert Schumann. In time the theme gives way to several wonderfully warm, lyrical contrasting themes, some introduced by the orchestra, some by the solo piano. The subsequent development is mostly concerned with working out the ideas presented in the orchestral opening. It is not until the recapitulation that we hear the piano in the main theme of the movement. A brilliant coda brings the movement to a conclusion.

II. *Adagio.* On the original manuscript of this choralelike movement Brahms wrote *"Benedictus qui venit in nomine Domini"* ("Blessed is he who comes in the name of the Lord"). This suggests a double dedication: to the memory of Robert Schumann, whom Brahms had nicknamed *"Mynheer Domini,"* and to Clara Schumann, to whom Brahms wrote: "I am also painting a gentle portrait of you; it is to be the Adagio."

No matter the extramusical connotations, the Adagio is an exceptionally tender and lovely contrast to the dramatic intensity of the preceding movement. It follows a simple ternary form: the deeply felt opening theme heard in the strings and bassoon and then in the solo piano; the middle section introduced by two clarinets; and the return of the opening, slightly modified, but in all its calmness and tranquillity.

III. *Rondo: Allegro non troppo.* The final Rondo presents a slightly lighter mood. The unaccompanied piano states the jaunty main theme. The piano also introduces the first contrasting interlude—a soaring lyrical melody. After some development and a return of the opening theme, the violins announce the second contrast, which Brahms treats as a fugato. Returns of the first and second themes, altered in color and heightened in intensity, follow, leading to a cadenza for the soloist. The listener hears one more quiet, pensive statement of the principal theme before the vivid, exuberant coda brings the movement, and concerto, to an end.

Concerto for Piano and Orchestra No. 2 in B flat major, Op. 83
(50 minutes)

Brahms often adopted a disparaging tone in discussing his own compositions. On the day he completed his monumental Second Piano Concerto he wrote to a friend: "I don't mind telling you that I have written a tiny, tiny piano concerto with a tiny, tiny wisp of a Scherzo. It is in B flat, and I have reason to fear that I have worked this udder, which has yielded good milk before, too often and too vigorously." When he sent a copy of the concerto to another friend a few days later, the accompanying note read: "I am sending you some little piano pieces."

Despite his censorious and belittling comments, this piano concerto has earned the respect and admiration of musicians and audiences everywhere; Vladimir Horowitz considered it *the* greatest of all works for piano and orchestra. Brahms began the composition in May 1878 on returning from an extended trip to Italy, and completed it on July 7, 1881, after having spent March and April touring that Mediterranean land. Some critics suggest that the concerto benefited from the tempering of Brahms's North German heritage by the sunny warmth of Italy.

I. *Allegro non troppo.* The concerto opens with a hauntingly lovely solo horn call. This is followed by an abundance of themes and motifs that project a wide range of different characters within the single movement. The melodic burden here, and throughout the concerto, is so equally shared by the soloist and orchestra that critic Eduard Hanslick once called the piece a "symphony with piano obbligato."

II. *Allegro appassionato.* Most concertos contain only three movements—fast, slow, fast. Brahms added his "wisp of a Scherzo," really a full-scaled movement of great vigor and passion, between what he called the "simple" first and third movements of this concerto. This interlude bursts forth with a forceful, agitated piano theme that yields to a plaintive violin melody. A restless middle section follows before the movement concludes with a freely varied return of the opening.

III. *Andante.* Brahms entrusts the main theme here to a solo cello playing over a murmured orchestral accompaniment. The meltingly soulful melody so appealed to Brahms that he later used it in his song "Immer leiser wird mein Schlummer." After a stormy interlude, Brahms brings back the solo cello and allows the movement quietly to fade away.

IV. *Allegretto grazioso.* The finale, like the opening movement, presents the listener with a plethora of themes, many of which seem derived from the rhythmic, bounding opening melody. Although the overall effect is bright and sparkling, the individual sections explore a variety of moods and feelings, from effervescent, passionate, and buoyant to plaintive and contemplative.

Although the solo piano part exhibits few of the virtuosic tricks associated with the big Romantic concertos, the technical demands are nevertheless extremely great on the performer. The November 9, 1881, premiere performance in Budapest, with Brahms as soloist and Alexander Erkel conducting, was not particularly well received. Many suspect that the composer's piano technique was just not up to the music's considerable difficulties. Supporting this view is the evidence that as other full-time piano soloists began performing the concerto it quickly won widespread acceptance and admiration.

Concerto for Violin and Orchestra in D major, Op. 77
(38 minutes)

According to an oft-repeated story, Brahms was asked one evening how he had spent the day. "I was working on my symphony all day," the composer replied. "In the morning I added a note. In the afternoon I took it out."

Spurious as this anecdote may be, it does provide some insight into the slow, careful way Brahms fashioned his music. A ruthless critic of his own works, Brahms frequently submitted new compositions to musician friends for their reactions.

Brahms's correspondence during the creation of his only violin concerto is a good example. He began the composition during the summer of 1878 in the tiny resort village of Pörtschach on Lake Wörth, Austria. On August 22 he sent sections of the solo part to his trusted friend violinist Joseph Joachim, asking him to "mark the music: difficult, awkward, impossible, etc."

On October 23 Brahms noted: "I do not like haste in writing and performing—and for good reasons, too! I have stumbled in the Adagio and Scherzo." Subsequently he discarded the Scherzo movement completely and made considerable revisions in the Adagio.

By mid-December, Brahms felt that the concerto was ready for public performance and arranged for the premiere in Leipzig on January 1, 1879, with Joachim as soloist and the composer conducting.

Three weeks after the premiere Brahms wrote to Joachim: "I should be grateful for any alternative versions"; and in March asked: "Is the piece really good and practicable enough to have it printed?" After studying the correspondence and scores connected to the work, musicologist Karl Geiringer wrote: "Brahms conscientiously asked his friend's advice on all technical questions and then hardly ever followed it." As a matter of fact, in this piece

Brahms more readily accepted Joachim's suggestions on musical, rather than on technical, matters.

Despite the labored and extended period of revision, the concerto sounds as fresh and spontaneous as if it had been written in a single burst of creative energy. And despite the close involvement with Joachim, there is not a single note that lacks the imprint of Brahms's distinctive style and musical personality.

I. *Allegro non troppo.* The first movement overflows with melodic invention. The principal thematic group includes both the poised, serene opening and the wildly leaping following section, while the subsidiary group features two gently floating, expressive cantabile melodies. After the first exposition ends with a brusque, explosive outburst in the strings, the soloist makes a dramatic entrance and freely reviews what has been heard, in addition to adding some new material here and in the following development section. After the much varied recapitulation the soloist has a long cadenza that leads to a quiet restatement of the opening theme, which grows louder and faster as it approaches the climactic ending.

II. *Adagio.* A solo oboe ushers in the tranquil theme of the second movement, accompanied by a wind band. The melody—delicate, ethereal, fragile—is then taken up and elaborated on by the solo violin. A more vigorous middle section, with the solo violin securely in the lead, offers a contrast before the return of the first theme, this time with the oboe and violin sharing in its presentation.

III. *Allegro giocoso, ma non troppo vivace.* After two movements in which cantilena melodies predominate, Brahms abruptly changes the character with a brisk, energetic finale that sparkles with Hungarian- and Gypsy-inspired dance rhythms, presumably as a tribute to Hungarian-born Joachim. The solo part, with its virtuosic and technically demanding claims on the violinist, features a brief cadenza before the coda, in which Brahms cleverly reorders the rhythm of the movement's opening theme into an energetic march.

Concerto for Violin, Cello, and Orchestra in A minor, Op. 102, "Double Concerto"
(35 minutes)

After a warm and close relationship of nearly thirty years, Brahms and the eminent violinist Joseph Joachim had a falling-out that left them out of touch with each other for over four years. The altercation resulted from Brahms's decision to support Joachim's wife in a divorce suit against her husband. Brahms wrote a letter, which was later introduced in court as evidence, that disputed the charges of her infidelity.

During the summer of 1887, probably as a way of winning back Joachim's friendship, Brahms began writing a concerto for violin and cello. The intended soloists were Joachim and the esteemed cellist of the Joachim Quartet, Robert Hausmann. While working on the concerto, the composer sent Joachim a very tentative card telling him of the new work and asking for an expression of interest. Joachim responded very warmly and then, as though nothing had interrupted the very close relationship they had previously enjoyed, the two men began corresponding about this new project.

Brahms found it difficult to write for the novel combination of violin and cello soloists. His letters speak of the entire idea as a "strange notion," of its being his "latest piece of folly," as a work better left "to someone who understands fiddles better than I do." But persevere he did, subjecting it to countless revisions and finishing in time for a private tryout performance in September 1887. The official premiere on October 18, 1887, was played by Joachim and Hausmann with Brahms on the podium. The piece proved to be Brahms's last concerto and, indeed, his final work for orchestra.

I. *Allegro.* The introduction is a sort of preview, a "coming attraction," of what is to follow. The orchestra starts the first theme, which the solo cello picks up and extends in a free cadenza; then the woodwinds give a variant of the second theme, which the solo violin, later joined by the cello, expands in a cadenza. The movement proper then begins, structured in sonata allegro form, with the two soloists and the orchestra alternately playing the leading roles.

II. *Andante.* Brahms imparts a melancholy tinge to the slow movement, which opens, after a two-note signal, with the violin and cello playing a flowing theme in octaves. A contrasting middle section begins with a more sedate theme in the winds, which gives way in time to a dialogue between the soloists. A varied return of the opening ends the movement.

III. *Vivace non troppo.* As though eager not to break the mood cast by the slow movement, Brahms starts the finale quietly with the cello's subdued statement of the principal theme with its Hungarian or Gypsy flavor. Soon enough, though, the orchestra loudly proclaims the glorious theme. New melodies, and reworkings of melodies already heard, pour out in joyful abundance as the movement unfolds with the three distinctive voices—the two soloists and the orchestra—joining in the ebullient good fun.

OVERTURES

Brahms fashioned two concert overtures—*Academic Festival* and *Tragic.* They were conceived to stand on their own and not serve as preludes to anything else. He composed both in the summer of 1880 while on holiday at the resort of Bad Ischl. The overtures reflect Brahms's penchant for creating pairs of works in the same genre that are complementary rather than similar; his first two symphonies, string quartets, and piano quartets are other examples. These two works, the short, light *Academic Festival* and the longer, more serious *Tragic,* are both in the same form, but differ considerably in scope and character.

Academic Festival Overture, Op. 80
(10 minutes)

Brahms responded strangely to two offers of honorary degrees from prestigious universities. He refused one from Cambridge University in 1876 because he dreaded sailing across the English Channel to receive the degree. When the University of Breslau made him a similar offer in 1879, Brahms accepted the honor, but with his response written on a postcard! On being informed that the recipient usually acknowledges the award with a serious musical composition befitting the occasion, Brahms composed the *Academic Festival Overture,* based on four German student drinking songs. Despite its lightness of tone, this overture is a delightful gem. The reaction of the very stuffy Rector of the University to Brahms's choice of melodies and the way the students spontaneously joined in, singing the songs with off-color lyrics, has not been recorded.

The first song Brahms quoted, "Wir hatten gebaut ein staatliches Haus" ("We Had Built a Stately House"), recalls the liberal fraternities that had been repressed by the reactionary German government earlier in the 19th century. The trumpets and horns play its choralelike melody after the orchestra presents some introductory material.

The following "Hochfeierlicher Landesvater" ("Most Solemn Song to the Father of the Country") comes from a patriotic ceremony in which each student pierces his fraternity cap with a sword point as he pledges loyalty to the nation. The second violins launch this lyrical melody.

Brahms lightens the mood by quoting from "Fuchsenritt" ("Ride of the

Freshmen"). The first line, *"Was kommt dort von Hoh?"* ("What comes from on high?"), refers to an initiation ceremony in which the freshmen ride around on chairs and benches. The composer strikes the proper comic note by assigning this tune to a pair of chattering bassoons.

Finally, after briefly developing and restating the themes, Brahms brings the overture to a rousing climax with the most familiar of all student songs, "Gaudeamus Igitur" ("Let Us Now Enjoy Ourselves").

Brahms conducted the premiere at Breslau on January 4, 1881; the program also included the *Tragic Overture*.

Tragic Overture, Op. 81
(15 minutes)

Explaining why he composed the *Tragic Overture* during the summer of 1880, while also working on the *Academic Festival Overture*, Brahms wrote: "I could not refuse my melancholy nature the satisfaction of composing an overture for a tragedy," even though there is no evidence that he had any particular tragedy—literary or personal—in mind. In another letter from that time, Brahms said of the two overtures: "One of them weeps *{Tragic}*, the other laughs *{Academic Festival}*."

Brahms organized the "weeping" overture into much modified sonata allegro form. After two stark, dramatic chords, the strings play the first theme, a somewhat oppressive melody that works its way up from the lowest to the highest notes of the violin and takes on strength and rhythmic verve as it continues. Brahms adds subsidiary themes and leisurely works through this material before introducing the second theme, a warm, cantabile melody in the violins. A development section initiated by two oboes in a slightly slower tempo, a free and foreshortened recapitulation, and a substantial coda complete the work.

Hans Richter led the premiere in Vienna on December 26, 1880.

Symphony No. 1 in C minor, Op. 68
(52 minutes)

Brahms was regarded as the musical heir of Beethoven—a burden he did not bear lightly. As he wrote in 1870: "You have no idea how one of us feels when he hears a giant like him [Beethoven] striding behind him." Although Beethoven composed in every form, except opera, Brahms felt the greatest pressure to measure up to his ideal in the symphony, the form in which Beethoven had so superbly distinguished himself.

Brahms began sketching the symphony in 1855. But it took seven years before he sent the opening movement to Clara Schumann, his dear friend and trusted musical adviser. Six years afterward he told Clara that he was finally working on the last movement. But it was not until September 1876—when he was 43 years old and after more than 20 years of deliberation—that Brahms completed this noble, poetic work. It received its first performance at Karlsruhe on November 4, 1876, led by Otto Dessoff. Perhaps Brahms summed up his two decades of travail best when he said: "Composing a symphony is no laughing matter."

I. *Un poco sostenuto; Allegro.* The slow introduction begins with a mighty unison C played by the entire orchestra over a relentless pulsing timpani beat. An ascending chromatic motif and other phrases emerge; they are all important precursors of the movement's major themes. The faster body of the movement offers up extended passages of great intensity and passion, occasionally relieved by sections of deep tenderness, but informed throughout by the melodic material first revealed in the introduction.

II. *Andante sostenuto.* The relaxed Andante sostenuto provides a needed respite from the surging power of the first movement. The opening theme projects a feeling of resignation, perhaps of melancholy. The oboe presents the more positive second subject over an ostinato rhythmic figure in the strings. After building to a climax, Brahms brings back the first theme, brilliantly joining the concertmaster's solo violin to the oboe in the second part of the theme to lend an aura of ethereal loveliness to the concluding measures.

III. *Un poco allegretto e grazioso.* Instead of placing a lively scherzo next, as the tradition of the Beethoven symphonies would seem to dictate, Brahms inserted a slow, gentle intermezzo. The woodwind tone predominates, starting with the clarinet's statement of the open-faced principal theme. It is of interest that the second phrase of the clarinet melody is a literal inversion of the first! A contrasting middle portion, which has a motif of three repeated notes running throughout, comes next and leads to a shortened, free repeat of the opening.

IV. *Adagio; Allegro non troppo ma con brio.* The finale starts with an extremely lengthy slow prologue with themes anticipatory of those that will follow. Perhaps the most arresting moment of this section is the ringing melody sounded by the French horns and accompanied by the trombones, who play here for the first time in the symphony. The melody derives from a mountaineer's Alpine horn call that Brahms heard in Switzerland. In an 1868 letter to Clara Schumann he wrote out the notes with the words "High in the mountain, deep in the valley, I greet you a thousand times." A rich singing melody in the strings starts the main part of the movement, which is followed by subsidiary themes—one sweet and tender, the other agitated and aggressive—that set off the majesty of the principal subject all the more clearly. Treating this material quite freely, Brahms crafts a movement of great sweep and grandeur.

Symphony No. 2 in D major, Op. 73
(48 minutes)

After struggling for about 20 years to complete his monumental First Symphony, one guesses that Brahms probably hesitated about quickly undertaking another such gargantuan enterprise. Perhaps that is why his musical thoughts turned to creating a smaller-scaled, engaging work, such as the Second Symphony.

Another factor that may have influenced the genial, sunny character of the Second Symphony was Brahms's immediate surroundings during the summer months of 1877. Brahms worked on the composition in the charming village of Pörtschach, on Lake Wörth near the Austrian-Italian border, which Brahms described in his letters as an "exquisite spot" and where he felt completely at ease. Pörtschach was so filled with melodies, he wrote, that one "must be careful not to tread on them."

While the Second Symphony surely forms a contrast to the First, the opening three-note motto recalls the beginning of the principal theme of the earlier work's finale—starting note/lower note/starting note. Actually, Brahms infuses the entire Second Symphony with this brief figure; it appears in almost every melody of every movement, either in its original form or inverted.

I. *Allegro non troppo.* After the initial appearance of the motto in the cellos and basses, the French horns quietly sing the principal theme of the first movement. The violins soon add their voice, with the three-note motto very much in evidence. After a striking transition theme played by the violins, the violas and cellos introduce the second theme, which bears some resemblance to the well-known Brahms "Wiegenlied" ("Lullaby"). Following the working out of both themes, Brahms brings them back for the recapitulation—but omits the motto with which the symphony began.

II. *Adagio non troppo.* Brahms was probably referring to this movement when he wrote to his publisher: "The new symphony is so melancholy that you will not be able to bear it." Although rich and complex in musical content, the movement is structured in simple three-part form, with a middle section that somewhat lightens the temper of the outer two parts.

III. *Allegretto grazioso (quasi andantino); Presto ma non assai.* The third movement sounds like an amalgam of a moderately paced intermezzo

—light and casual in tone—and a fast scherzo—spry and mischievous. The five-part form is organized as: intermezzo; scherzo (starting as a speeded-up version of the intermezzo); abbreviated repeat of the intermezzo; new, but related scherzo; intermezzo and coda.

IV. *Allegro con spirito.* Although the overall character of the finale is vibrant and powerful, the opening is hushed and dramatic. All the melodies are new and distinctive, yet the same motto that was heard in the previous movements appears here as well (albeit with considerably changed rhythms), which serves to unify the symphony. The Allegro con spirito provides a joyous and virile cap to the entire work.

The premiere was given in Vienna on December 30, 1877, with Hans Richter conducting.

Symphony No. 3 in F major, Op. 90
(33 minutes)

Two major influences probably affected the composition of Brahms's Third Symphony. The first dates from early in 1883, when the 50-year-old Brahms, who was working on his Third Symphony at the time, fell in love with the very beautiful and talented 26-year-old contralto Hermine Spiess. The affection was mutual and Brahms decided to spend the summer in her hometown of Wiesbaden, rather than go to one of his usual mountain or lakeside holiday retreats. And it was at Wiesbaden that he finished the symphony.

The second influence originated early in Brahms's career when he adopted the notes F-A-F as his musical motto. One can hear it in his A minor string quartet as well as at the very outset and throughout the Third Symphony, even though in the latter the A is lowered to A flat. The three letters stand for the words *"Frei, aber froh"* ("Free, but glad").

Scholars have long debated the significance of this quotation. One of the most likely conjectures is that F-A-F expresses Brahms's conviction that great art comes from the exercise of creative freedom within certain well-defined limitations and restraints. Thus, rather than allow himself absolute liberty when composing, Brahms adhered to certain strictures, which in his case meant obeisance to the stylistic and formal concepts of the previous Classical period. His outlook, it is worth noting, was shared by poet Johann Goethe, who wrote: "The law can only bring us freedom."

I. *Allegro con brio.* Three massive wind chords that present the F-A-F motto open the symphony and immediately bring in the impassioned, majestic principal subject in the violins. Brahms dwells on this and other themes for some time before moving on to the second theme, a gently swaying melody played by the clarinet and bassoon. An intense development ushers in a return of the thematic material, without the introductory F-A-F, and a substantial coda.

II. *Andante.* The clarinets and bassoons present the somewhat ingenuous theme of the slow movement, with the violas and cellos adding a variant of the F-A-F motto at the end of each phrase. A solo clarinet and bassoon are responsible for the second theme; the repeated notes of the accompaniment become an important element as the music progresses. Instead of ending with a return of the opening, Brahms follows with an extensive development of that section, including a few echoes of the repeated notes.

III. *Poco allegretto.* The main theme rises and falls from measure to measure, both in pitch and in dynamics, as it is stated three times in succession by the cellos, the violins, and, finally, the winds. The winds start the contrasting middle section with side comments from the strings. Brahms then brings the main theme back for three more statements, by the French horn, by the oboe, and lastly by other instruments of the orchestra, before a coda brings the movement to a quiet close.

IV. *Allegro.* After the subdued opening, the music grows more hushed as we hear a variation of the second movement's second theme. Composers use this technique of quoting themes from earlier movements, known as cyclical form, as a way of unifying a work containing several movements. Brahms soon breaks the quiet with a loud, wildly leaping motif that gives way to the second theme, a soaring melody for the French horn and cellos, followed by the rhythmic, full-voiced concluding theme and, shortly, the recapitulation. The entire movement seems to move from moments of quiet introspection to outbreaks of unbridled jubilation until the very end of the coda. Then the flute sneaks in with another statement of the F-A-F motto and the movement fades away with the violins giving a distant spectral reading of the first movement's main theme.

Hans Richter conducted the premiere in Vienna on December 2, 1883.

Symphony No. 4 in E minor, Op. 98
(45 minutes)

During Brahms's lifetime, a period characterized by rapid and pervasive change in music, many of his contemporaries dismissed him as reactionary and anachronistic. Though his music was imbued with all the fervor, emotion, and expressivity of late 19th century Romanticism, his style and forms remained rooted in the Classical and Baroque traditions. In this symphony, his final work in the form, Brahms epitomizes the Romantic spirit in music, even as he reminds us of the times of Bach, Mozart, and Beethoven.

Brahms composed his Fourth Symphony during two summers at the small

Alpine resort village of Mürzzuschlag, completing the first two movements during the summer of 1884 and the remainder the following year. Although he often experienced uncertainty about his work, the disparaging comment he made about this symphony—"I've only put together another set of polkas and waltzes"—shows that, in his typically perverse way, he viewed this symphony as uncommon and exceptional.

It is difficult to categorize the emotional content of the Fourth Symphony. On the one hand, the work expresses the strong feelings of elation and exhilaration that you might expect from a very great composer at the summit of his powers. On the other hand, a melancholy undercurrent seems to pervade the score, no matter how joyous the outward façade. The solemnity may be due to Brahms's fears about impending old age. Even though he was only in his early 50s, he had just grown an old man's beard and expressed concerns—completely unfounded—about the waning of his creative abilities.

I. *Allegro non troppo.* This splendid movement starts with a broad, vaulted theme that grows from a two-note motif and majestically spans over a flowing accompaniment in the lower strings. The composer extends the melody with a gently rocking motion as he passes the two-note fragments back and forth within the orchestra. The intensity mounts, and reaches a climax with the second theme, a stirring, fanfarelike call of the winds. The music quickly gives way to a soaring line played by cellos and horns, while elements of the fanfare persist, and a spate of varied melodic phrases brings the exposition to a close. The development is mostly concerned with the opening theme; the recapitulation is traditional, and the coda brief but powerful. Brahms's good friend Clara Schumann accurately and succinctly summarized the mood of the movement with these words: "It is as though one lay in springtime among the blossoming flowers, and joy and sorrow filled one's soul in turn."

II. *Andante moderato.* A bold horn signal heralds the second movement and grows into the tender main theme given out by the clarinets. After a transition, a luminous contrasting melody of the utmost simplicity is then played by the cellos. The rest of the movement—at times excited and agitated, at times serene and composed—is occupied with inventively working out the previously heard thematic material.

III. *Allegro giocoso.* The third movement projects the character of a scherzo. The brash and outgoing first theme crackles with wit and humor. Listen for inversions of the melody, starting in the bass instruments in the opening measures and scattered throughout the movement. Brahms introduces a quieter but equally cheerful theme in the violins, before developing and returning these two melodies. Of all the movements in Brahms's symphonies, this is the only one to use a triangle; it adds a special sparkle to the incisive rhythms.

IV. *Allegro energico e passionato.* Brahms based the finale on the Passacaglia from Bach's Cantata No. 150. (A passacaglia is a Baroque dance form characterized by a short melody, usually in triple meter, that forms the basis for a large number of continuous variations.) The composer adds three trombones to the wind band in this movement, lending grandeur and stateliness to the first statement of the glorious eight-measure passacaglia melody. Brahms then subjects the melody to over 30 variations, each unique in character, tone, rhythm, and instrumentation, yet with each one growing organically from the one before. Sometimes the ascending passacaglia melody rings out clearly; other times it is hidden within the orchestral texture or disguised by a particularly imaginative variation. Throughout, though, the bold and brilliantly constructed movement holds the listener enthralled and delighted.

The premiere was given at Meiningen on October 25, 1885. There is some confusion about the conductor for the evening; the best information seems to be that Hans von Bülow rehearsed the orchestra and that Brahms led the performance.

Variations on a Theme by Haydn, Op. 56a
(18 minutes)

In November 1870, C. F. Pohl, a friend and biographer of Brahms, showed the composer an unpublished *Feldpartita* (outdoor piece) that he believed was composed by Haydn, but is now thought perhaps to be by Haydn's student Ignaz Pleyel. The work was scored for two oboes, two horns, three bassoons, and serpent, an ancient, coiled member of the brass family. Struck by the second movement, *Chorale St. Antonii,* Brahms copied it over in his notebook for future use. According to Haydn scholar Karl Geiringer, Haydn—or Pleyel—had taken the melody from an old Austrian pilgrim tune sung on St. Anthony's Day.

Three years after he jotted down the Haydn theme, Brahms began a set of variations based on the melody. He wrote two arrangements, one for piano duet (Op. 56b) and one for orchestra (Op. 56a). Most commentators hold that Brahms conceived the theme and variations with the orchestra in mind from the start, but prepared himself for the task by writing it initially for two keyboards. The composer and Clara Schumann gave the premiere of the two-piano version in August 1873; the orchestral edition received its first performance in Vienna on November 2, 1873, under Otto Dessoff.

The work unfolds with a statement of the Haydn theme, followed by eight variations and a finale. Each variation explores a different aspect of the original melody. Some variations bear an unmistakable resemblance to the source; others are far more subtly realized.

Theme. Brahms first scored the theme for strings but subsequently changed his mind and gave it to the oboes, bassoons, and horns, in order to conform more closely to the timbre of the Haydn original.

Variation I. As the final chords of the Chorale are repeated, the strings weave a warm, lyrical tracery around material that is essentially an expansion of the basic theme.

Variation II. The theme's characteristic dotted (long/short) rhythm predominates in this radiant, brisk section.

Variation III. The long-flowing melodic line smooths out and equalizes the theme's rhythmic patterns.

Variation IV. While pleasant and amiable in sound, this variation scintillates with contrapuntal inventiveness, replete with intricate inversions and double counterpoint.

Variation V. Resembling a brilliant scherzo, the music maintains its light and saltatory character throughout.

Variation VI. This marchlike variation was obviously inspired by traditional hunting horn calls.

Variation VII. The flute and violas, playing in octaves, introduce a distinctive melody patterned in a slow, deliberate Siciliano rhythm.

Variation VIII. The fast tempo and muted strings impart a hushed, ghostly quality to this variation.

Finale. The Finale is also a set of brief variations, around 20 in number, on a solemn five-measure phrase derived from the Chorale. As the phrase repeats over and over again, mostly in the bass, Brahms spins contrapuntal lines above it, building to the final triumphant reappearance of the original melody. The form derives from the passacaglia, an old Baroque dance in which a repeated melody forms the basis for continuous variations.

Sir Benjamin Britten

Born November 22, 1913, in Lowescroft, England
Died December 4, 1976, in Aldeburgh, England

LIKE MANY outstanding composers, Benjamin Britten grew up in a musical home; his mother, an amateur singer and pianist, gave young Ben his first music lessons. There was always live music making in the Britten home; Ben's father, a dentist, did not allow a radio or phonograph in the house for fear it would interfere with the family's singing and playing. At an early age, Britten showed his talent and interest in music, writing pieces when he was only five years old that he described as "hundreds of dots all over the page connected by long lines all joined together in beautiful curves."

It was as a student that Britten began to hold the strong humanitarian and pacifist views that stayed with him for life. The young Britten argued against the bullying practices common in the English schools for the wealthy and wrote an essay denouncing hunting as organized cruelty to animals. By the late 1930s, the composer felt that world events, from the depression in England to the antidemocratic revolution in Spain to the dictatorships in Germany and Italy, were thwarting his career. Amidst rumblings of impending war, the composer came to the United States, and for a few years lived in the village of Amityville on Long Island, New York. In 1942, however, Britten returned to his beloved England, where he remained for the rest of his life.

Over the following three decades, Britten composed a number of outstanding works that established him as a leading composer of the 20th century. His best-known orchestral work, by far, is *The Young Person's Guide to the Orchestra,* which is discussed below. His other symphonic works, such as Variations on a Theme of Frank Bridge, *Sinfonia da Requiem,* and *Cello Symphony,* excellent pieces all, have not won the same broad audience acceptance.

The Young Person's Guide to the Orchestra, Op. 34
(Variations and Fugue on a Theme by Purcell)
(18 minutes)

Soon after his graduation from the Royal College of Music in 1933, Britten was engaged by the Film Unit of the British General Post Office to compose the music for their documentaries. "The film company I was working for," Britten later commented, "had very little money. I had to write scores, not for large orchestras, but for six or seven players, and to make these instruments make all the effects that each film demanded."

Composing film scores fulfilled Britten's concept of the composer's role in society, which he held should be to dedicate his talent and ability to providing the finest possible music for the public. As he put it: "I want my music to be of use to people, to please them, to 'enhance their lives' (to use Berenson's phrase)." On another occasion, he said: "As an artist I want to serve the community." Confident that a film score, or other music written for a specific purpose, was at least as worthy as music written solely in response to a composer's inspiration, Britten wrote: "Some of the greatest pieces of music in our possession were written for special occasions, grave or gay."

The four years he spent with the Film Unit helped Britten develop the economy of means and directness of expression that are the hallmarks of his music. They also prepared Britten for a Ministry of Education commission to provide the sound track for their film for young people entitled *Instruments of the Orchestra.*

In writing this score, Britten's main charge was to satisfy the film's purpose of introducing children to the instruments of the orchestra. To this end, he structured the score as a theme and variations, giving each variation to an individual instrument, topped off by a fugue that again spotlighted the various members of the orchestra. The theme he selected was by Henry Purcell, the great 17th century English composer, from his incidental music for a play entitled *Abdelazer or The Moor's Revenge.*

At the very outset of *The Young Person's Guide,* the full orchestra announces the broad, majestic Purcell theme, followed by individual statements from each family of instruments—woodwinds, brass, strings, and percussion—and a final review by the orchestra. Thirteen variations, which brilliantly capture the unique sound and character of each instrument, follow in order: flutes, oboes, clarinets, bassoons, violins, violas, cellos, double basses, harp, French horns, trumpets, trombones and tuba, and percussion (timpani, bass drum, cymbals, tambourine, triangle, snare drum, Chinese block, xylophone, castanets, gong, and whip).

After this section, Britten starts a fugue that brings in the instruments, one at a time, playing a melody loosely based on the middle part of Purcell's theme. Near the end, the brass instruments proclaim the original theme in regal, magisterial tones, while the rest of the orchestra scampers through the complexities of the fugue to bring the entire work to a stunning conclusion.

Britten composed *The Young Person's Guide to the Orchestra* early in the autumn of 1946; the first performance was given as a purely orchestral piece by Malcolm Sargent and the Liverpool Philharmonic Orchestra on October 15, 1946. The movie premiere took place the following month, with a narration written by Eric Crozier. Some modern performances include the narration, usually delivered by a celebrity, while others are restricted to the musical score without speaker.

Max Bruch

Born January 16, 1838, in Cologne
Died October 2, 1920, in Friedenau, Germany

BRUCH SHOWED HIS TALENT at an early age and got his first musical instruction from his mother, a singer. He later began studying theory and at age 14 wrote his first symphony; his first opera was produced when he was only 20! As a young man he held a number of musical posts, most for only a short period of time. Some biographers suggest that his frequent moves were due to his abrasive personality; they describe him as arrogant, humorless, and egotistical.

During his lifetime, Max Bruch figured prominently in the musical worlds of both Germany and England. A prolific composer, he completed three operas, three symphonies, three violin concertos plus many other works for soloist and orchestra, along with some 14 major choral compositions, chamber music, songs, and piano music. Performances of all his music won him wide renown, but his choral music was always particularly favored. With all this activity, Bruch still found the time to conduct (Liverpool Philharmonic and Breslau Orchestral Society) and teach (Berlin Musikhochschule).

Of Bruch's many compositions, only a few of his works for soloist and orchestra have remained central to today's repertoire: for violin and orchestra his First Violin Concerto and *Scottish Fantasy,* and for cello and orchestra his *Kol Nidrei.* (Some assume that Bruch was Jewish, since *Kol Nidrei* refers to a prayer offered on the eve of the solemn Jewish holiday of Yom Kippur. In fact, he was Protestant and wrote the piece on a commission from the Jewish community in Liverpool.)

Musicians especially value Bruch's concerted works because they are exceptionally well written for the solo instrument. They very successfully allow the performer many opportunities for virtuosic display, as well as for exploring the instrument's full range of sounds and colors. The First Violin Concerto, in particular, thrills listeners with the simple beauty and power of its melodies and its extremely polished writing for the soloist.

Concerto for Violin and Orchestra No. 1 in G minor, Op. 26
(25 minutes)

"In my youth," Bruch wrote, "I studied the violin for four or five years and, although I did not become an adept performer, I learned to know and love the instrument. The violin seemed to me even at that time the queen of instruments, and it was quite natural that I early had the inclination to write for it."

Bruch began to sketch the concerto in 1857 at age 19, but waited eight years before setting to work in earnest. He completed it in time for the premiere, given on April 24, 1866, in Coblenz, with Otto von Königslöw as soloist and the composer conducting.

Following the first performance, Bruch sent the score to the eminent violinist and composer Joseph Joachim, seeking his criticism and advice. Acting on Joachim's recommendations, Bruch extensively revised the concerto, and conducted a reading of the work with Joachim as soloist in October 1867. The new version received its formal public audition in Bremen on January 7, 1868, with Joachim playing the solo part and Karl Reinthaler leading the orchestra. When published later that year, Bruch's Violin Concerto carried a dedication to Joachim.

I. *Vorspiel: Allegro moderato.* Despite its abundance of melodic material and rich solo part, the Vorspiel, or "Prelude," serves mostly as an introduction to the second and third movements. The Vorspiel opens with two quiet woodwind phrases to which the violinist responds with short cadenzas. A solo statement of the main theme continues, bursting with passages of virtuosic bravura. The violin then brings in a more lyrical descending melody that is taken up by the orchestra violins. After working out these two ideas, Bruch brings back the opening measures and proceeds to a transition that goes directly to the second movement.

II. *Adagio.* Despite an abundance of lush, singing melody, a slightly pensive, if not melancholy, air pervades the Adagio. The sure and deft writing allows the soloist to soar effortlessly over the orchestra in clear and cogent flights of musical fantasy.

III. *Finale: Allegro energico.* The fast, insistent drumming by the violas that introduces the Finale builds in intensity until it culminates in the soloist's statement of the fiery, Gypsy-like first theme. Bruch develops this melody before giving the violinist a high-speed running passage that leads to a full-voiced statement of the expansive second theme by orchestra and an immediate repetition by violin. We hear next a brief development section, mostly based on the first theme, prior to the return of both themes and the journey to the splendid conclusion.

Anton Bruckner

Born September 4, 1824, in Ansfelden, Austria
Died October 11, 1896, in Vienna

WERNER WOLFF aptly subtitled his biography of Anton Bruckner *Rustic Genius.* In the sophisticated musical world of late 19th century Vienna, Bruckner was indeed a country bumpkin. Not especially well read or educated, Bruckner spoke with a lower-class accent and looked scruffy, given his close-shaven peasant-style hair, oversized jacket and shirt, and exceedingly short trousers.

Yet, in his music, Bruckner was neither simple nor unstudied. His compositions, which are usually classified as post-Romantic, reached deep into the human soul and overwhelmed listeners with their impressive size and scope. Although he drew much of his inspiration from Beethoven and Wagner, what he created was unique and individual; no one could mistake a piece by Bruckner for that of any other composer. Little appreciated for most of his life, Bruckner achieved recognition only in his last years. After his death, his compositions again were seldom played until the 1960s, when they were rediscovered and became an important part of the orchestral repertoire.

Bruckner's early life resembled that of Schubert. Both were born to schoolmasters and, even though they evidenced their special talent very early, began their careers as teachers. But while Schubert supported himself by living the bohemian life with several friends who shared their meager resources, Bruckner held a succession of positions, including organist at the Linz Cathedral, professor at the Vienna Conservatory and the University of Vienna, and Court Organist in Vienna.

Bruckner has the distinct and unhappy honor of suffering at the hands of both his friends and his enemies. Conductors and composers among his champions, eager to see more performances of his music, rearranged his compositions, made extensive cuts, changed the orchestration, added new melodies, and so on. Time after time, the bowdlerized versions were performed and published, despite their clear inferiority to Bruckner's original works.

Prominent among his enemies were several music critics, especially the eminent Eduard Hanslick. Hanslick believed that the mantle of Beethoven had passed to Johannes Brahms and his Classically organized, absolute music, not to Richard Wagner and his followers, such as Bruckner, who used formal freedom, powerful emotions, and extramusical associations to shape their music.

To illustrate how much anguish Bruckner suffered at the hands of his detractors, as well as his naïveté, we can cite an exchange that occurred while he was receiving an honorary award from Emperor Franz Joseph. The Emperor asked if there was some way he could help Bruckner, and the composer replied: "Perhaps Your Majesty would be so kind as to ask Mr. Hanslick not to write such nasty criticisms of my symphonies."

Symphony No. 4 in E flat major, "Romantic"
(70 minutes)

Perhaps one day psychologists will decide why Bruckner was so obsequiously grateful for even the slightest interest shown in his music. Two well-known anecdotes connected with rehearsals of his Fourth Symphony, led by the eminent conductor Hans Richter, testify to the composer's self-deprecating attitude.

At one point, Richter wasn't sure of a note in the handwritten score and asked Bruckner what note it should be. Ever eager to please, Bruckner replied: "Any note you choose." Then, at the end of a rehearsal, Bruckner rushed up to the conductor, thanked him effusively, and, pressing a thaler (a coin worth about 60 cents) into Richter's hand said: "Take this and drink a stein of beer to my health."

Bruckner's lack of self-confidence, notorious self-criticism, and apparent willingness to consider seriously all critiques of his music resulted in endless revisions. The history of the Fourth Symphony illuminates this point: Bruckner composed the original version (1) from January 2, 1874, to November 22, 1874; it was never performed. In 1878 he completely rewrote the symphony, adding the Scherzo movement that we now know, and in 1879 and 1880 made significant changes in the Finale; this is the version (2) Richter premiered on February 20, 1881, with the Vienna Philharmonic. Bruckner put in some minor changes after the performance and had the score published in this form (3). In 1886 the composer further revised the work and also published this version (4). Finally, some well-intentioned friends greatly altered the work, leading to still another printed edition (5). Today, versions 3, 4, and 5 are all available. Conductors must decide for themselves which one best represents Bruckner's vision.

After he completed the symphony, Bruckner gave it the subtitle "Romantic" at the urging of friends. He also furnished a program that describes the various images that he had in mind while composing the work. Many commentators, though, do not take this material very seriously since it might have been created just to give a more Romantic aura to the music. Every image Bruckner chose evokes some aspect of the Romantic tradition, such as the distant past, love, nature, and the common folk. Further, Bruckner's descriptions do not always conform to what one hears in the music itself. In any case, the composition is highly Romantic—that is, massive and monumental in scope and imaginative, personal, and impassioned in treatment.

I. *Ruhig bewegt.* "A citadel of the Middle Ages. Daybreak. Reveille is sounding from the tower. The gates open. Knights on proud chargers leap forth. The magic of nature surrounds them." The French horn's statement of the principal theme (perhaps representing daybreak) emerges from the mist of a string tremolo like a solemn magical incantation to the hidden forces of nature. After discoursing on this motif, Bruckner fashions the powerful second theme (perhaps the knights on chargers) from a favorite rhythmic pattern—two quarter notes followed by three quarter-note triplets (in nontechnical terms, two one-beat notes followed by three slightly faster notes, equal in total duration to the first two beats). The first violins present the third theme, a light, leaping melody that was presumably inspired by the song of the chickadee (perhaps Nature). The remainder of the movement deals amply and at great length with this thematic material in keeping with the expansive quality of the work.

II. *Andante.* "Rustic love scene. A peasant lad makes love to his sweetheart, but she scorns him." Despite the composer's suggestion of the amorous character of this movement, the first cello melody brings to mind a funeral march and the viola second theme bespeaks sorrow and loneliness. After rising to a radiant climax, Bruckner allows the music to fade into a quiet, even desolate ending.

III. *Scherzo: Bewegt.* "The Hunting of the Hare. Trio: Dance Melody During the Huntsmen's Meal." Bruckner's music suggests a distant hunting party with the ringing horn calls; the horns' rhythmic pattern resembles the one heard in the first movement's second theme. The brief middle section of the movement, the Trio, is a triple-meter peasant dance precursor to the waltz called the ländler; it is treated here slowly and without strong rhythmic impulse. An abbreviated Scherzo brings the movement to a close.

IV. *Mässig bewegt.* "Folk Festival." Rather than depicting simple peasants gamboling in the fields, the movement suggests a gathering of giants reveling in their prowess. The section includes many reminders of the first movement's rhythm. Although the mood very quickly changes and becomes tender and quiet, the composer later transforms these themes into forceful, triumphant calls. Alternating epic might with intimate contemplation, Bruckner introduces echoes of earlier movements, before providing a stunning cap to this incredible symphony.

Symphony No. 7 in E major
(70 minutes)

Contemporary audiences greeted Bruckner's first six symphonies with reactions that ranged from grudging acceptance to outright hostility. His first true success came, at age 60, with the premiere of his Seventh Symphony in Leipzig on December 30, 1884, under Arthur Nikisch's direction. Equally triumphant performances followed throughout Germany and Austria and in London, Budapest, Chicago, New York, and Amsterdam. The continuing popularity of this symphony comes, undoubtedly, from its deep and heartfelt inspirational qualities. But some part of its fame is due to the well-known second movement, which is often excerpted and played by itself on solemn occasions, leading performers and audiences to seek out the complete symphony.

I. *Allegro moderato.* According to Bruckner, the principal subject of the first movement grew from a dream in which an old friend, the *Kapellmeister* of Linz, appeared, whistled a tune, and made a prophecy: "With this theme you will make your fortune." On awakening, Bruckner quickly wrote out the melody and, considering the success of the symphony, fulfilled the prophecy. The lengthy theme, introduced at the very beginning by the cellos, moves through its wide-ranging, two-octave tessitura with great sweep and breadth, and sets the stage for many succeeding melodies and motifs in this expansive, lyrical movement.

II. *Adagio: Sehr feierlich und langsam.* Late in 1882, around the time Bruckner's model and idol Richard Wagner fell gravely ill, the composer wrote to conductor Felix Mottl: "One day I came home and felt very sad. I did not think the master would live much longer. Then I conceived the Adagio." Wagner died on February 14, 1883, when Bruckner approached the end of the movement, at precisely the second climactic point of the Adagio. According to the composer, the death of his beloved "master" engendered the final mournful epilogue. In this movement, Bruckner initiates his use of the Wagner tuba, an instrument Wagner invented for use in his music dramas because it combines the strength of the trombone with the mellowness of the French horn. Listen for the sound of the four Wagner tubas as they present the opening theme.

III. *Scherzo: Sehr schnell.* With this movement, Bruckner completely changes the musical ambiance. A repeated rhythmic figure in the strings continues and becomes the accompaniment to a stirring trumpet call that, in various guises, dominates the entire section. After a complete stop, the timpani introduces the contrasting Trio with its gently rocking melody; a repeat of the Scherzo ends the movement.

IV. *Bewegt, doch nicht schnell.* The main theme of the finale, which resembles the principal melody of the first movement, sounds gay and carefree on the surface, but with a certain unease beneath. In striking contrast, the second theme sounds serene, simple, and choralelike. After working through the two principal themes, Bruckner closes the movement and symphony with an even more forceful reminder of the "dream" melody from the first movement, concluding with a blaze of orchestral fire.

Bruckner composed the Seventh Symphony in the two years from September 1881 to September 1883.

Symphony No. 9 in D minor
(85 minutes)

Bruckner started his last symphony in September 1887, shortly after his sixty-third birthday. The composition proceeded slowly, compounded by the composer's teaching schedule at the Vienna Conservatory, lengthy interruptions to revise earlier works, and increasingly poor health, both physical and mental. Bruckner did not complete the first movement until October 1892; the second was finished in February 1893; and the third was done in October 1894. From December of that year until his death in October 1896 Bruckner toiled over the finale. Despite his fervent prayers that "death will not deprive me of my pen," he died with the last movement unwritten, leaving behind hundreds of pages of sketches, containing almost the entire movement from the opening to the start of the coda, but with five gaps probably due to lost manuscript pages.

On February 11, 1903, Bruckner's former pupil Ferdinand Löwe premiered the three movements in Vienna, using his well-intentioned, but ill-advised, massive revision of the score. In place of the fourth movement he played Bruckner's *Te Deum,* a practice that became popular with some conductors. In Munich, however, nearly thirty years later, the orchestra performed Löwe's version on the same program as Bruckner's original. The latter was so obviously superior to the substitute that since then almost every conductor uses the Bruckner score.

Since 1984, however, some orchestras perform the entire work using a reconstructed finale prepared from Bruckner's sketches by William Carragan.

Even more conductors seem to prefer using Bruckner's three movements as written, without the finale, since the Adagio makes such an excellent conclusion to the symphony and a touching postscript to Bruckner's life.

I. *Feierlich, misterioso.* "It really annoys me that the theme of my new symphony came to me in D minor, because everybody will now say, 'Of course Bruckner's Ninth must be in the same key as Beethoven's [Ninth Symphony]!' " Bruckner remarked to his biographer August Göllerich— even though Beethoven was a composer that he revered. The movement opens with a hushed, magical tremolo in the strings, out of which the first group of themes emerges. The composer builds to an overwhelming climax in which the entire orchestra in unison plays the principal herculean melody with its wild descending octave leaps. Next comes a more lyrical, introspective violin theme in a slightly slower tempo. After dwelling for some time on this melody, Bruckner moves to a group of melodies, more in the style of Brahms, which conclude the exposition. In keeping with the spacious dimensions of the thematic presentation, Bruckner works through all the material in a deliberate, grandiose manner, leading to an impressive coda.

II. *Scherzo: Bewegt, lebhaft.* The Scherzo relieves to some extent the predominantly solemn, if not gloomy mood of the first movement. Arpeggiated figures speed up and down, while an ostinato rhythmic pattern—now soft, now loud—keeps them in check with a grim stubbornness. The lighter Trio has a slightly faster tempo and much more cheerful mien, but it does not differ considerably in melodic contour from the Scherzo. After the Trio, the Scherzo returns in traditional fashion.

III. *Adagio: Langsam, feierlich.* Despite climactic moments of great force and power, the Adagio is suffused with the calm, quiet spiritual repose that Bruckner described as his "farewell to life." The opening theme, starting with the anguished interval of a rising minor ninth, gives way in time to a broadly sweeping second theme. Although written by a frail, elderly man, the score rises to youthful climaxes of fervor and vitality. After the turmoil fades away, Bruckner presents short quotations from his Seventh and Eighth symphonies and his D Minor Mass, and the music ends in peaceful acceptance and resignation.

Frédéric Chopin

Born March 1, 1810, in Zelazowa Wola, Poland
Died October 17, 1849 in Paris

CHOPIN DESCRIBED his musical purpose in a letter to his friend Countess Delphine Potocka: "Bach is like an astronomer who, with the help of ciphers, finds the most wonderful stars. Beethoven embraced the universe with the power of his spirit. I do not climb so high. A long time ago I decided that my universe will be the soul and heart of man." Thus, the highly Romantic Chopin wrote compositions characterized by strong individuality, great warmth, and persistent melancholy and longing. Frequently drawing on nationalistic melodies and rhythms, the music of Chopin requires a free, flexible style (rubato) from performers.

For all his Romanticism, though, Chopin was also a Classicist in his approach to composing and making music. While not strictly following the traditional Classical forms and organizations, Chopin did imbue his music with Classical clarity and purity. As a performer, it is said, he always kept a metronome on the piano; and in his teaching he insisted that his many students keep strict rhythms and steady tempos and play works by such Baroque and Classical masters as Bach and Mozart.

Just as we associate Verdi almost exclusively with the voice, Paganini with the violin, and Sousa with the band, so we link Chopin with the piano. In the course of writing more than 200 works for piano, Chopin created a new style, approach, and vocabulary for that instrument. Of his contributions to the development of the piano repertoire, Mendelssohn wrote: "He produces new effects . . . and accomplishes things nobody could formerly have thought practicable." More recently, critic Harold Schonberg summarized Chopin's influence on the piano in performance with these words: "For the first time the piano became a *total* instrument: a singing instrument, an instrument of infinite color, poetry, and nuance, a heroic instrument, an intimate instrument."

Born and trained in Poland, Chopin left at age 20 to build a career outside his homeland, finally settling in Paris, where he lived for the remainder of his tragically short life. Although widely acclaimed as one of the leading pianists of his day, Chopin participated in comparatively few large public concerts. His frail physique and ill health prevented him from thundering to the overwhelming climaxes that audiences expected of performers at that time. Rather, he confined most of his appearances at the keyboard to small salons and intimate halls, where he played to stunning effect.

Chopin was a master of small musical forms—études, mazurkas, polonaises, and nocturnes—and a good number of such pieces now form a significant part of the piano repertoire. But he also wrote a few works for piano and orchestra. Of these, two concertos figure prominently today. Interestingly enough, Chopin composed both of them just before leaving Poland and used them to launch his career as a composer and performer.

Concerto for Piano and Orchestra No. 1 in E minor, Op. 11
(45 minutes)

We know that Chopin was already at work on the E minor concerto at the time of his 20th birthday in March 1830. He finished the first two movements by May, but took until September 22 to complete the finale. (He actually wrote the F minor concerto earlier, but he lost the orchestra parts, and by the time they were recopied, the E minor was published as Piano Concerto No. 1.) Chopin gave the very successful premiere on October 11, 1830, in Warsaw, with Carlos Evasio Soliva conducting the orchestra. Three weeks later the young musician left on a tour of Europe and, except for some occasional travel, lived in Paris for the rest of his days.

While this concerto displays the resources of the piano to full effect, it has occasionally been criticized for lacking some of the tension and drama conventionally heard in more typically Romantic concertos. Chopin precludes, to some extent, the traditional conflict between soloist and orchestra by restricting the latter to a subsidiary role. Also, he does not always create sharp contrasts between tonalities within a movement and between movements. Nonetheless, the composer carries us along very effectively by his technique of introducing moments of great tension followed by periods of comforting relaxation, and by his brilliant exploitation of every facet of the piano's potential.

I. *Allegro maestoso.* The concerto opens with a lengthy orchestral exposition that presents the major themes of the movement at the outset—the first vigorous and bold throughout; the second, starting soft and lyrical, but gradually gaining in strength and power. To placate overeager soloists some conductors cut this section and start immediately with the piano presentation of its own, somewhat altered version of the exposition. The free development of both themes follows, replete with many bravura passages for the soloist. Both the pianist and the orchestra share in the return of the themes for the recapitulation.

II. *Romance: Larghetto.* In a letter to his closest friend, Titus Woyciechowski, Chopin described the Romance, as being ". . . of a romantic, calm and rather melancholy character. It is intended to convey the impression that one receives when the eye rests on a beloved landscape, which calls up in one's soul beautiful recollections, such as a lovely spring moonlit night."

III. *Rondo: Vivace.* Chopin introduces a Polish element in the Rondo, using the rhythms of the krakowiak, a popular folk dance from the Krakow region, as the basis for the principal theme. The movement, which bubbles along with great verve and vitality, manages to remain charming and dainty, never becoming raucous or noisy.

Concerto for Piano and Orchestra No. 2 in F minor, Op. 21
(33 minutes)

In 1829, Chopin, at age 19, wrote his F minor piano concerto, the first in order of composition, but known as the Second Concerto because of a delay that caused the E minor concerto to be published as No. 1. The composer performed the premiere as soloist in Warsaw on March 17, 1830, his formal debut in that city. The concerto was so successful that he had to give another performance five days later. Over the following months Chopin delivered a number of "farewell" concerts. He finally departed Warsaw on November 2, 1830, for Paris, determined to build his career elsewhere because he believed that opportunities in Poland were too limited.

Over the years some have criticized the concerto for being too sparsely orchestrated and have attempted to rescore the orchestra parts. But time after time the result has been a new appreciation for the original, with its perfect fit between soloist and orchestra. Berlioz once referred to the orchestral writing as a "cold and useless accompaniment," but later reversed his position in his treatise on instrumentation, citing Chopin's tremolo and pizzicato string passage in the middle of the second movement as a model.

I. *Maestoso.* The first movement starts with an orchestral statement of the thematic material, virtually the full orchestra's only substantial passage in the entire concerto. The piano enters with a freely decorated traversal of the same themes and goes on to assume, with its brilliant fioritura, the leading role in both the development and recapitulation sections. For the rest of the movement the orchestra mostly provides support and occasional transitions.

II. *Larghetto.* The tender and appealing second movement conveys Chopin's infatuation with the young singer Constantinia Gladkowska. As he wrote to a friend: "I have, perhaps to my misfortune, already found my ideal, whom I worship faithfully and sincerely. Six months have elapsed and I have not yet exchanged a syllable with her of whom I dream every night. While my thoughts were with her I composed the Adagio [generic name for a slow movement] of my Concerto." After a brief orchestral introduction the piano sings the touching and highly decorated principal melody; it very much resembles an aria from one of the Bellini operas that Chopin so admired. The theme, which is heard first in a simple cantabile presentation, precedes a section stylistically related to an operatic recitative, with moments of fiery passion over the string tremolo and pizzicato. A shortened return of the opening brings the movement to a quiet close.

III. *Allegro vivace.* Chopin drew his inspiration for the third movement from the mazurka, a popular Polish folk dance characterized by its second- or third-beat accents. The jaunty second theme, which the strings introduce playing col legno (hitting the string with the wood of the bow), comes to dominate the movement and provides the material for the coda that brings the entire composition to a coruscating conclusion.

Aaron Copland

Born November 14, 1900, in Brooklyn, New York
Died December 2, 1990, in North Tarrytown, New York

TO MANY, Aaron Copland is the true voice of the American spirit. He gained his reputation as the "dean of American music" through his many outstanding compositions, his work to advance the careers of American composers, his leadership role in several musical organizations, and his unstinting efforts, including two popular books, *What to Listen for in Music* and *The New Music, 1900–1960,* to make modern music available and understandable to the public at large.

Copland's parents, immigrants from Russia, did not, beyond piano lessons, particularly encourage young Aaron's early interest in music. Nevertheless, at age 15 he determined to become a composer and began the serious study of musical composition. Not satisfied with his progress, he left for Paris soon after high school graduation and became the first American student of the brilliant pedagogue Nadia Boulanger.

While several of Copland's early works show the influence of European music of the early 1900s, the composer soon became more concerned with writing music that was uniquely American in style and meaningful to great numbers of people. Thus, Copland infused several of his early works with the melodies, rhythms, and tone colors of jazz and popular music. From the mid-1930s to the mid-1940s, Copland incorporated folk music into his compositions and dealt with patriotic or American subjects; *Billy the Kid* (1938) and *Rodeo* (1942) are two ballets that include folk songs of the American West. In line with his desire to bring music to a wider audience, he wrote pieces specifically designed for film, for radio, or for performance by young people. In 1949 he received an Academy Award for his music for the motion picture *The Heiress* (1949). Beginning in the 1950s he returned to the more severe style of some of his earlier works, employing some of the most advanced techniques of 20th century music.

Copland's music added immeasurably to the repertoires of orchestras and chamber music groups and, perhaps most importantly, has vastly expanded the appreciation of contemporary music, and of contemporary American music in particular.

Appalachian Spring Suite
(25 minutes)

Critics often call Aaron Copland the voice of the American West and its pioneer spirit. The association is quite remarkable when you consider that Copland was born in Brooklyn, studied in Paris, and lived in or near New York City for the rest of his life!

Copland largely made his reputation as a composer of the great outdoors with his ballet scores *Billy the Kid* (1938), *Rodeo* (1942), and *Appalachian Spring* (1944), his film score for *The Red Pony* (1949), and his opera *The Tender Land* (1954). Of these, the work that made the biggest impact was *Appalachian Spring,* which Copland composed in 1943 and 1944 on commission from Martha Graham, a leading American dancer, choreographer, and pioneer of the modern dance movement.

The dance that Martha Graham created takes place in spring early in the 19th century; the setting is a celebration in a newly built farmhouse in Pennsylvania. Using dance movements to reveal their true inner feelings, a bride and her farmer husband show both joy and apprehension about their future together. A visiting neighbor enacts her dreams of the Promised Land, while a stern revivalist preacher reminds the new couple of the fearful power of fate to control events. The dance ends optimistically, with the couple portraying strength and quiet confidence in their ability to face the future.

Copland wrote his score for a chamber orchestra of thirteen players, and with that group in the pit, Martha Graham and her company first staged *Appalachian Spring* in Washington, D.C., on October 30, 1944. The following year, Copland arranged the score for full orchestra and prepared a concert suite of music from the ballet. Artur Rodzinski and the New York Philharmonic premiered the orchestral suite on October 4, 1945.

Copland prepared notes for the first performance, which are excerpted below:

> I began work on the music of the ballet in Hollywood in June 1943, but didn't complete it until a year later in June 1944 at Cambridge, Massachusetts. The title, *Appalachian Spring,* was chosen by Miss Graham. She bor-

rowed it from the heading of one of Hart Crane's poems, though the ballet bears no relation to the text of the poem itself.

The Suite arranged from the ballet contains the following sections, played without interruption:

1. Very slowly. Introduction of the characters, one by one, in suffused light.

2. Fast. Sudden burst of unison strings starts the action. A sentiment both elated and religious gives the keynote to this scene.

3. Moderate. Duo for the Bride and her Intended—scene of tenderness and passion.

4. Quite fast. The Revivalist and his flock. Folksy feelings—suggestions of square dances and country fiddlers.

5. Still faster. Solo dance of the Bride—presentiment of motherhood. Extremes of joy and fear and wonder.

6. Very slow (as at first). Transition scene to music reminiscent of the introduction.

7. Calm and flowing. Scenes of daily activity for the Bride and her Farmer-husband. There are five variations on a Shaker theme. The theme, sung by a solo clarinet, was taken from a collection of Shaker melodies published under the title *The Gift to Be Simple.*

8. Moderate. Coda. The Bride takes her place among her neighbors. At the end the couple are left in their new house. Muted strings intone a hushed, prayerlike passage. The close is reminiscent of the opening music.

Concerto for Clarinet and Orchestra
(18 minutes)

In the 1920s, as Copland sought to express the American spirit in music and to make his music more accessible to the public, he started to integrate elements of jazz and popular music into his serious compositions. Nowhere is this influence more evident than in his *Music for the Theater* and Piano Concerto. By the end of the decade, though, he wrote: "With the Piano Concerto I felt I had done all I could with the idiom, considering its limited scope. True, it was an easy way to be American in musical terms, but all American music could not possibly be confined to two dominant moods: the 'blues' and the snappy number."

For the following decades, until 1947, Aaron Copland struck out in completely different musical directions. Then the American clarinet player and bandleader Benny Goodman asked him to write a clarinet concerto. Goodman, the reigning "King of Swing" and the first jazz musician to appear as soloist with symphony orchestras, inspired Copland to return to his earlier style, blending elements of jazz with serious concert music. Copland worked on the piece during the summer of 1948 while teaching at Tanglewood, completing the work in October at his home in Sneden's Landing, New York. Scored for solo clarinet and string orchestra, harp, and piano, the Clarinet Concerto received its premiere in New York City on November 6, 1950, with Benny Goodman and the NBC Symphony under Fritz Reiner.

I. *Slowly and Expressively.* The composer describes the character of the first movement as "lyric and expressive." Over a simple accompaniment the clarinet sings the slow, languid, tenderly romantic melody. A slightly faster and somewhat hymnlike middle section does not significantly diminish the overall dreamy, poetic mood. The ending part is very similar to the opening.

II. *Cadenza: Rather fast.* Without a break the soloist goes into the Cadenza, which allows for virtuosic display and anticipates themes that appear in the second movement. "Some of this material," Copland pointed out, "represents an unconscious fusion of elements obviously related to North and South American popular music." Organized as a very free rondo, the movement sparkles with jazzy rhythms—ranging from the Charleston to boogie-woogie, from the rumba to a Brazilian pop song Copland heard while in Rio—and ends with a characteristic clarinet smear up to the top of its range.

Lincoln Portrait for Speaker and Orchestra
(17 minutes)

Early in 1942, shortly after the United States entered World War II, conductor André Kostelanetz commissioned works from three composers and asked that the pieces "mirror the magnificent spirit of our country." Copland first thought to make Walt Whitman the focus of his piece, but when Kostelanetz urged him to choose a statesman, "the choice of Lincoln as my subject seemed inevitable," the composer said.

Copland decided to cast the work for a narrator and orchestra; he drew the text from Lincoln's letters and speeches. He began writing the music in February 1942 and completed the project by the end of April. Except for free quotations of two songs from that period—"Camptown Races" and "Springfield Mountain"—all the musical material is original.

"The composition," Copland wrote, "is roughly divided into three main sections. In the opening section I wanted to suggest something of the mysterious sense of fatality that surrounds Lincoln's personality. Also, near the end of that section, something of his gentleness and simplicity of spirit. The quick middle section briefly sketches in the background of the times he lived in. This merges into the concluding section where my sole purpose was to draw a simple but impressive frame about the words of Lincoln himself."

Copland dedicated the *Lincoln Portrait* to André Kostelanetz, who conducted the first performance in Cincinnati on May 14, 1942, with William Adams as narrator.

Symphony No. 3
(45 minutes)

Copland eagerly accepted a 1943 commission from the Koussevitzky Music Foundation to compose a symphony since he had already begun developing a number of themes with the thought of using them in a large-scale work. He began the actual composition in August 1944 while staying in a small village in Mexico. Always a slow worker, he did not complete the work until September 29, 1946, near Tanglewood in Massachusetts. The parts were prepared hurriedly for the October 18 premiere, given by Serge Koussevitzky and the Boston Symphony.

In the notes that Copland readied for the first performance he examined the work's musical purpose: "I suppose if I forced myself I could invent an ideological basis for my music," he wrote. "But if I did, I'd be bluffing—or, at any rate, adding something *ex post facto,* something that might or might not be true, but which played no role at the moment of creation. In other words . . . I prefer to let the music 'speak for itself.' "

Many people feel that the symphony does indeed "speak" to them, and they enjoy its positive message. In the words of commentator K. Robert Schwartz, the Third Symphony successfully captures the "hope, conviction, and affirmation" of the American people.

I. *Molto moderato.* Copland describes the first movement as "broad and expansive in character." He states very simply the three principal themes: "the first in the strings; the second in related mood in violas and oboes; the third, of a bolder nature, in the trombones and horns." The overall structure takes an arch shape, with a slightly faster middle part and a "broadened version of the opening material" in the final section.

II. *Allegro molto.* This movement, close to the usual scherzo structure, can be diagrammed as A-B-A-B. The A theme comes after a brass introduction and occurs three times. The B section follows the climax and leads to the nonliteral repeat of A, with the piano first playing it in "somewhat disguised form," and then "a full restatement" by the orchestra. The movement ends with a full-voiced canonic treatment of B in which everyone joins forces.

III. *Andantino quasi allegretto.* Although organized into separate segments, the movement's "various sections are intended to emerge from one another in continuous flow, somewhat in the manner of a closely knit series of variations." The first violins initially play "a rhythmically transformed version of the third (trombone) theme of the first movement." The solo flute then presents the melody that becomes the subject of "the sectional metamorphoses that follow."

IV. *Molto deliberato (Fanfare); Allegro risoluto.* This movement, which includes a fanfare based on Copland's well-known *Fanfare for the Common Man,* is the longest section of the symphony. It also comes closest to standard sonata allegro form: Copland builds the first theme of fast animated notes, but then introduces the second theme—which he describes as "broader and more songlike"—in the development section, rather than within the exposition. The symphony "concludes on a massive restatement of the opening phrase with which the entire work began."

John Corigliano

Born February 16, 1938, in New York City

JOHN CORIGLIANO came to music naturally: his father was concertmaster of the New York Philharmonic and his mother was an accomplished pianist. Yet both parents tried to dissuade John from pursuing a career in music composition. Nevertheless, he persisted, studying music at Columbia University and the Manhattan School of Music, and then supporting himself with a series of jobs at various music radio stations and record companies. The young Corigliano further honed his composing skills by writing orchestrations for pop music albums.

Recognition as a serious composer first came with a prize at the Festival of Two Worlds in Spoleto, Italy, in 1964 for his Violin and Piano Sonata. Numerous honors followed over the next decades, including an opera commission from the Metropolitan Opera that resulted in *Ghosts of Versailles,* along with many performances and recordings of his music.

In 1991, the American Academy and Institute of Arts and Sciences elected Corigliano to their ranks and the following year *Musical America* named him "Composer of the Year." Corigliano currently teaches at both the Juilliard School and Lehman College of the City University of New York.

Symphony No. 1
(45 minutes)

"A few years ago, I was extremely moved when I first saw 'The Quilt,' an ambitious interweaving of several thousand fabric panels, each memorializing a person who had died of AIDS, and, most importantly, each designed and constructed by his or her loved ones. This made me want to memorialize in music those I have lost, and reflect on those I am losing. I decided to relate the three movements of the symphony to three lifelong musician friends."

So wrote John Corigliano about the motivation and inspiration for his First Symphony. Commissioned by the Chicago Symphony and Meet the Composer and written in 1988 and 1989, the First Symphony quickly became one of the most honored of modern symphonies, having received the Grawemeyer Award for musical composition, the Horblir Award for "Distinguished Composition by an American Composer," two Grammy awards, and the *Stereo Review* Record of the Year Award for the recording, as well as remaining on top of the *Billboard* charts for an amazing 69 weeks. The First Symphony also ranks very high in number of performances, from the premiere by the Chicago Symphony under Daniel Barenboim on March 15, 1990, to over 100 performances by orchestras throughout the United States and the rest of the world within just the first four years.

Corigliano's First Symphony affects audiences immediately and powerfully. Its impact is so great that some criticize it as "poster art," created more to excite and inflame the audience than to touch and stir them. In any case, the music evokes a full spectrum of emotions, from sharing the anguish and suffering endured by victims of AIDS to experiencing the frightful feelings of loss and sorrow of the survivors.

I. *Apologue: Of Rage and Remembrance.* Corigliano dedicated this highly charged movement to pianist Sheldon Shkolnik, whose memory the composer evokes with the offstage piano. The music, in Corigliano's words, "alternates between the tension of anger and the bittersweet nostalgia of remembering."

II. *Tarantella.* Corigliano describes the tarantella as a "South Italian dance played at a continually increasing speed, and by means of dancing it a strange kind of insanity—attributable to a tarantula bite—could be cured." Here the subject is an unidentified executive in the music industry who suffered a mental breakdown as the result of AIDS. Corigliano subjects a slight tarantella tune to increasing disfigurement and distortion until it reaches an ending that "can only be described as a brutal scream."

III. *Chaconne: Giulio's Song.* This movement is structured as a chaconne, a musical form made up of slow, continuous variations over a repeated succession of chords. The first part memorializes Giulio, an amateur cellist with whom Corigliano became acquainted in college. The remainder of the movement honors other musician victims of AIDS—Giulio's cello teacher Fortunato Arico (second cello soloist), pianist Paul Jacobs (English horn solo), and writer Robert Jacobson (oboe solo). After building to a ferocious funeral march, the symphony concludes with an Epilogue in which "waves of brass chords" serve as a background for the remembrance of previously heard melodies.

Claude Debussy

Born August 22, 1862, in Saint-Germain-en-Laye, France
Died March 25, 1918, in Paris

COMMENTATORS frequently associate Debussy with Impressionism, the art movement represented in France by Manet, Monet, Pissarro, Degas, and Renoir. The Impressionists strove to depict the effects of light, color, and atmosphere, even as they chose subjects that suggested change and impermanence. Yet, while composing *Images,* Debussy wrote to his publisher: "I am attempting to achieve something different—a kind of reality—what some imbeciles call *impressionism."*

On the other hand, at the first performance of Debussy's *Rondes de Printemps,* annotator Charles Malherbe, presumably with Debussy's approval, categorized the composer as an adherent of the Impressionist aesthetic: "These are real pictures in which the composer has endeavored to convey, aurally, impressions received by the eye. He attempts to blend the two forms of sensation in order to intensify them. The melody, with its infinitely varied rhythms, corresponds to the multiplicity of lines in a drawing; the orchestra represents a huge palette where each instrument supplies its own color. [The composer] wants us to visualize what he makes us hear, and the pen he holds in his fingers becomes a brush. This is musical impressionism of a very special kind and of a very rare quality."

While many view Debussy as an Impressionist, others, perhaps more accurately, think of him as a Symbolist. Like the Impressionists, the Symbolist poets of the 1880s, led by Baudelaire, Mallarmé, Verlaine, and Rimbaud, also wanted to appeal more to the senses than the intellect. To that end they used words more as symbols and abstractions than for their literal meanings. Mallarmé stated his artistic goal as: "To evoke in a deliberate shadow the unmentioned object by allusive words."

No matter the source of his inspiration, Debussy filled his music with light and color and sought to capture fleeting moods and fluid images. ("Music is made for the inexpressible, and I should like it to seem to rise from the shadows and indeed sometimes to return to them," he said.) To accomplish this, he had to break free of many musical conventions and traditions and completely rethink the various elements and forms of music. A most telling illustration comes from the time a harmony teacher asked why he had chosen certain chords and Debussy replied: "My pleasure." Debussy's compositions freed music from older restraints that had limited composers and set the stage for many of the 20th century innovations.

Images pour Orchestre
(37 minutes)

Debussy originally conceived *Images* in 1905 for piano duet; over the following years, though, he transformed it into a work for orchestra, his last major orchestral composition. He completed the orchestral version of the *Ibéria* movement at the end of 1908, *Rondes de Printemps* the following year, and *Gigues* in 1912, finished with the help of the composer's friend André Caplet because of Debussy's ill health. Each section of *Images* received a separate premiere; the first performance of the entire composition took place in Paris on April 26, 1913, with Caplet conducting.

I. *Gigues.* A gigue, French for "jig," is a light and lively dance, but paradoxically enough, Debussy originally entitled this section *Gigues tristes,* or "Sad Jigs." Caplet, who assisted in the orchestration, describes the movement as "a portrait of a soul in pain . . . a wounded soul, so reticent that it dreads and shuns all lyrical effusions and quickly hides its sob behind the mask and the angular gestures of a grotesque marionette." Debussy drew his inspiration for the sad character of *Gigues* from Verlaine's poem "Streets," and the melody from the traditional Scottish tune "The Keel Row," to which Verlaine's words had been set. The melody, given out by a solo flute at the very beginning, is the movement's principal theme.

II. *Ibéria.* The eminent Spanish composer Manuel de Falla wrote the following on *Ibéria,* the central and longest part of *Images:* "The intoxicating spell of Andalusian nights, the festive gaiety of a people dancing to the joyous strains of a *banda* of guitars and *bandurrias* . . . all this whirls in the air, approaches and recedes, and our imagination is continually kept awake and dazzled by the power of an expressive and richly varied music." About the same music, Debussy said: "There is no story to it"; yet he divides the score into three titled sections: *Par les rues et par les chemins* ("On the Streets and Byways"), in which the castanets and tambourines create a bright, dancelike quality; *Les Parfums de la nuit* ("Fragrances of the Night"), an exotic and wistful nocturne; and *Le Matin d'un jour de fête* ("Morning of a Festive Day"), an exciting section made more so by the pealing bells and pizzicato strings. Listeners are, of course, free to come to their own conclusions.

III. *Rondes de Printemps.* At the top of the score of this section, Debussy quoted two lines of "La Maggiolata," an old Italian May Day song:

> Welcome to May
> With its wild banner!

In these lines, the "wild banner" refers to a branch of laurel that young lovers placed on their sweethearts' doors on May 1 as they sang "La Maggiolata." Debussy derived the melody for this joyous section from an old French folk song, "Nous n'irons plus au bois" ("We Shall Go in the Woods No More").

La Mer: Three Symphonic Sketches
(23 minutes)

Debussy had only the most tenuous of connections with the sea—several holidays at seaside resorts and two crossings of the English Channel. Yet he felt a strong affinity for the ocean. When he started composing his orchestral masterpiece, *La Mer* ("The Sea") in 1903, he wrote to a friend: "You do not know, perhaps, that I was intended for the fine career of a sailor and that only the chances of life led me away from it. Nevertheless, I still have a sincere passion for her [the sea]." He chose, though, to compose *La Mer* in Paris, far from the sea, saying: "I have an endless store of memories [of the sea], and to my mind they are worth more than the reality, whose beauty often deadens thought."

In 1905, when the piece was nearly done, he wrote to his publisher: "The sea has been very good to me; she has shown me all of her moods." And after the premiere in Paris on October 15, 1905, led by Camille Chevillard, another note to his publisher said: "Here I am again with my old friend, the sea; it is always endless and beautiful. The sea that is stirred up wants to dash across the land, tear out the rocks, and has tantrums like a little girl."

In Debussy's unique depiction, the sea is indeed clouded over with mist and darkness and presents vaguely glimpsed shapes and forms. Using a collage of musical effects—ever-shifting harmonies, brief snatches of melody, and a kaleidoscope of tone colors pulsating and shimmering throughout, the composer evokes a remarkable series of watery images. His impressionistic rendering gives us fleeting, yet memorable representations of an evanescent seascape.

I. *From Dawn to Noon on the Sea.* The quiet, sustained opening suggests the immensity of the sea and its imponderability. As the light of day strikes the water, flecks of spray whirl up and the unceasing roiling begins, building to a few climactic moments before the blazing midday sun completely transforms the sea's character.

II. *The Play of the Waves.* Starting with delicate little sprays that disappear in the air, the music mounts in intensity to become mammoth waves angrily crashing down until the music quiets and again depicts tiny plumes on a calm surface.

III. *Dialogue of the Wind and the Sea.* Gusts of wind bear down on the water, whipping it into raging waves and swells. Gentle sea breezes precede the sharp outbursts of wind as the music soars to its climactic conclusion, which includes the return of themes from the first movement.

Nocturnes
(25 minutes)

Inspired by the title, though not the subject matter, of Whistler's famous series of paintings called "Nocturnes," Debussy undertook in 1893 to compose an eponymous piece for violin and orchestra. In September 1894, he wrote the eminent Belgian violinist Eugène Ysaye: "I am working on three nocturnes for violin and orchestra that are intended for you. . . . This is, in fact, an experiment in the various arrangements that can be made with a single color—what a study in gray would be in a painting."

For some reason, the work remained unperformed for three years. In 1897, however, Debussy picked up his pen again and transformed the work into its present orchestral form, with no soloist other than the small, wordless women's choir heard near the very end.

I. *Nuages* ("Clouds"). Debussy confided to his friend Pierre Poujard that he conceived *Nuages* while walking in Paris on a blustery day with thunder clouds slowly shifting across the threatening sky. *"Nuages,"* he wrote, "renders the immutable aspect of the sky and the slow solemn motion of the clouds, fading away in gray tones lightly tinged with white."

II. *Fêtes* ("Festivals"). "The idea for *Fêtes*," Debussy told Poujard, "derived from memories of public celebrations in the Bois de Boulogne, crowded with throngs of joyous, colorfully dressed Parisians; the arriving and departing march in the middle of *Fêtes* came from remembered sounds of the approaching and departing band of the Garde Nationale. *Fêtes* provides the pulsing, dancing rhythms of the atmosphere interspersed with sudden flashes of light. We also hear the episode of the procession (a dazzling and fantastic vision) that passes through the festive scene and becomes merged in it. But the background persistently remains the same; the festival with its blending of music and luminous dust participating in the cosmic rhythm."

III. *Sirènes* ("Sirens"). "This movement," in Debussy's words, "depicts the sea and its countless rhythms, and presently, among the waves silvered by the moonlight, is heard the mysterious song of the Sirens as they laugh and pass on."

Nuages and *Fêtes* were first performed in Paris on December 9, 1900, by the Lamoureux Orchestra under Camille Chevillard; the same performers, with the addition of women's voices, gave the premiere of *Sirènes* on October 27 of the following year.

Prélude à l'Après-midi d'un faune
("Prelude to the Afternoon of a Faun")
(10 minutes)

Debussy drew his inspiration for this work from a short pastoral poem, "L'Après-midi d'un faune," by the French Symbolist poet Stéphane Mallarmé. The poem describes in vague, sensuous terms how a faun—a mythological deity, half man, half goat—awakens from a deep sleep in a sunlit forest. The mystical creature recalls a vision of an encounter with two beautiful, godlike nymphs, who eluded his grasp and rebuffed his advances. While struggling to recapture the fugitive images, the faun nibbles on a bunch of grapes. Finally, unable to summon up the pleasurable memories, he surrenders once again to somnolence.

While brilliantly evocative of the general mood, the music cannot be too specifically associated with the events of the poem, since Debussy originally projected the work as a triptych, with the *Prélude* serving as the first of three sections. In addition, the composer wrote this brief description of the music: "The music of this *Prélude* is a very free illustration of the beautiful poem of Mallarmé. By no means does it claim to be a synthesis of the latter. Rather there are the successive scenes through which pass the desires and dreams of the faun in the heat of the afternoon. Then, tired of pursuing the fearful flight of the nymphs and naiads, he succumbs to intoxicating sleep, in which he can finally realize his dreams of possession in universal Nature."

There is little question, though, that Debussy associates the prominent solo flute's elusive, wispy melody with the faun. For the rest, he presents music that is highly impressionistic in style, with its varied tone colors and light, airy texture capturing the feeling of the poem's mist-filled, evanescent character. Mallarmé, delighted with Debussy's creation, told the composer: "This music prolongs the emotion of my poem and sets its scene more vividly than color."

Debussy began composing *L'Après-midi* in 1892, probably discussing his interpretation of the poem and his thoughts about the music with Mallarmé. Completed in September 1894, the piece received its premiere in Paris on December 22 of that year with Gustave Doret conducting. Audiences today find it difficult to realize how audacious and revolutionary the musical conception and orchestral writing of *L'Après-midi* seemed 100 years ago. To many, it represents the beginning of what we now consider modern music.

Antonín Dvořák

Born September 8, 1841, in Mühlhausen, Bohemia
(now Nelahozeves, Czech Republic)
Died May 1, 1904, in Prague

DVOŘÁK WAS BORN of Slavic peasant stock in the Bohemian area of what is now the Czech Republic. His father, a poor butcher and inn-keeper, played the zither at local weddings and other celebrations. Before very long young Antonín was fiddling alongside his father and learning the folk songs and dances of the area. At age 16 he was in Prague, getting a solid grounding in traditional musical practices, when he was struck by the music of Bedřich Smetana and discovered the use of the Bohemian folk idiom in original compositions.

Bohemian national music became the main source of Dvořák's own work, as well as the way he chose to express his love of country. Many Czech patriots, with whom the composer sympathized, were now struggling to break free and establish their own nation, having long been ruled by the Hapsburgs in Vienna. Although far from a rabid revolutionary, Dvořák helped to advance the cause of nationalism by infusing his music with the melodies and rhythms of the Czechs and other Slavic peoples.

The Romantic movement of the late 1800s also influenced Dvořák's music. Around 1870, after composing for about eight years, the composer was much affected by Liszt and Wagner and embraced aspects of their style. Later he contemplated moving to Vienna to devote himself to composing German operas, instead of the Czech operas he had been writing.

But perhaps the greatest stylistic change in Dvořák's music came during the three years, 1892 to 1895, that he spent in the United States. Mrs. Jeanette M. Thurber, a wealthy philanthropist, invited Dvořák to become director of the National Conservatory of Music that she had recently founded in New York City. At first Dvořák refused, but when he learned of the salary

—$15,000 a year contrasted with the $600 a year he was earning as a professor of composition at the Prague Conservatory—he accepted the new position. In America, the composer became deeply involved in various musical activities and projects, which included learning all he could about American Negro and Indian music and helping to point new directions for American composers.

Highly successful as a composer, Dvořák was always in demand and he turned out a considerable body of work. His major orchestral compositions include nine symphonies—of which the Eighth and Ninth are best known—and concertos for piano, violin, and cello; of these the cello concerto figures most prominently. Neither a trailblazer into new aesthetic realms, nor a summarizer of what had come before, Dvořák can best be described as a composer who wrote music from his heart that appeals to the hearts of the listeners.

Concerto for Cello and Orchestra in B minor, Op. 104
(39 minutes)

Hanuš Wihan, a leading cellist of Bohemia, repeatedly asked the composer to write a cello concerto for his use. Dvořák always turned aside the request, saying that he considered the cello a valuable member of the symphony orchestra and string quartet, but as a solo instrument it "mumbled" in the low register and was nasal in sound when played high.

In 1892 Dvořák left Bohemia for the United States without having written the concerto for Wihan. While living in New York he heard Victor Herbert, who was later to become a leading composer of operettas, play his own Second Cello Concerto. Inspired by Herbert's abilities as a performer, as well as his compositional skill in bringing out the cello's best features as a solo instrument, Dvořák began to write his own work in the form on November 8, 1894.

Dvořák finished the concerto on February 9, 1895, and dedicated it to Wihan. He conducted the premiere with the London Philharmonic on March 19, 1896. Although the composer had asked that Wihan be the soloist, a confusion about dates resulted in Leo Stern playing the cello part at the first performance.

I. *Allegro.* As the concerto opens, the clarinets state the first theme with its distinctive rhythmic pattern. Dvořák extends and expands this melody before the solo horn introduces the slightly slower second theme, a songlike melody rich with poignant yearning. (Dvořák later wrote that he never failed to be moved by this melody.) After introducing some more motifs, Dvořák brings in the soloist for a varied statement of the same themes. The development starts with the orchestra's brilliant—and then the solo cellist's thoughtful and reflective—treatment of the initial theme. A spectacular ascending chromatic scale in octaves leads to the resplendent recapitulation of the second theme, which Dvořák now develops, finally concluding with a glorious peroration of the opening melody.

II. *Adagio ma non troppo.* The woodwinds, led by the clarinet, announce the beguilingly simple melody of the slow movement. A fiery orchestral outburst acts as a bridge to the cantabile central section, in which the solo cello sings the melody of Dvořák's song, "Kezduch maj sam" ("Leave Me Alone"), a favorite of his sister-in-law, Josephina Kaunič, who was seriously ill at the time. The movement ends with the return of the opening melody, this time presented by the French horns.

III. *Finale: Allegro moderato.* Over a repeated note in the lower strings, the horns start a skeletal outline of the movement's marchlike theme, which Dvořák works up to a powerful climax before allowing the cello to bring forth the fully realized melody. Various episodes follow, including a striking section of extraordinary tenderness. As he approaches the conclusion, Dvořák quotes from the opening movement, as well as from Josephina's song. The composer added the latter on learning of her death after he had finished the concerto. A quick crescendo and accelerando then lead to a brilliant, climactic ending.

Symphony No. 8 in G major, Op. 88
(36 minutes)

According to the psychobiographers, Dvořák enjoyed better mental health than most other renowned composers. For proof they proffer his Eighth Symphony, one of the most sunny, genial, and optimistic of all symphonies. True, the symphony has its morose moments, but the overall tone bespeaks a composer at peace with himself and his world.

Dvořák began planning the symphony on August 26, 1889, at his country home in Vysoká; it was to be an expression of gratitude to Emperor Franz Joseph for being elected to the Bohemian Academy for the Encouragement of Art and Literature. While working out the symphony he wrote to his friend Gobl that his "head was so full of ideas" that he could not put them on paper fast enough. The symphony abounds with fresh, attractive melodies, many that echo the national music of Bohemia, though without any obvious borrowings. He finished the work on November 8 and conducted the first performance in Prague on February 2, 1890. Despite the fact that it is the eighth of Dvořák's nine symphonies in order of composition, it was long listed as the fourth, based on sequence of publication.

I. *Allegro con brio.* As though to set off the brightness of the movement, Dvořák opens with an introductory cello melody that starts in the dark minor mode but ends in the brighter major. The melody then leads to the several motifs that make up the first thematic group, which is dominated by the flute's birdlike figure. A pensive violin melody with three repetitions of its two-note opening starts the second group. Dvořák then adroitly and imaginatively works out the many themes, bringing most of them back, much changed, for the recapitulation. The movement ends with a coda drawn from the flute's birdsong melody.

II. *Adagio.* Dvořák composed the rather serious slow movement in a minor key. A fast, three-note anticipatory figure runs through most of the thematic material in the movement and characterizes the opening theme. A middle section in the major, which features an interlude for solo violin, lightens the atmosphere and builds to a climax. A very free return of the initial melody follows, along with glimpses of the central portion.

III. *Allegretto grazioso.* Dvořák launches the third movement with a most merry, captivating waltz. (Is the three-note upbeat an advertent or inadvertent link to the Adagio?) A flute and oboe tune in the style of a Bohemian folk dance introduces the contrasting central part. A return of the waltz and a quick two-step coda round off this delightful movement.

IV. *Allegro ma non troppo.* A brilliant trumpet call sets the stage for a deliberate cello theme that recalls the flute melody of the first movement. The composer then freely varies the melody, exploiting the full palette of orchestral effects. Among the more striking features are a virtuosic section for solo flute and the high trills of the French horns.

Symphony No. 9 in E minor, Op. 95, "From the New World"
(43 minutes)

Growing fame and the success of his works in the United States brought Dvořák an invitation to come to New York and serve as director of the National Conservatory of Music in New York City. The composer held this position from his arrival in September 1892 until his departure three years later. During that period, Dvořák learned a great deal about American music and searched for ways to make some original contribution. He became familiar with Negro spirituals and plantation songs by asking blacks at the Conservatory to sing for him; he also studied transcriptions of American Indian melodies. At the same time, he visited Czech and other Slavic settlements in the Midwest.

Among the original projects he considered, and dropped, were a new national anthem and an opera based on Longfellow's "Hiawatha." In his notebook dated December 1892, though, we find some preliminary sketches for a new symphony, which he completed on May 24, 1893. In November of that year he added the subtitle "From the New World."

In a newspaper interview just before the December 16, 1893, premiere of the symphony by Anton Seidl and the New York Philharmonic, Dvořák expounded his ideas on the direction he felt American music should take: "I am convinced that the future music of this country must be founded on what are called Negro melodies. They are the folk songs of America, and your composers must turn to them."

Dvořák, however, did not follow his own dictum in the "New World" Symphony. In a letter to Oskar Nedbal, who conducted the German premiere of the symphony, Dvořák denied using any spirituals or plantation songs, writing: "Leave out that nonsense about my having made use of original American melodies. I have only composed in the spirit of such American national melodies." On another occasion he claimed that he wrote only "genuine Bohemian music." While one can dispute the source of inspiration for the "New World" Symphony, Dvořák's final essay in this form, the work remains a first-rate composition and among the most popular of all symphonies.

I. *Adagio; Allegro molto.* After a slow introduction, a stirring horn call rings out the first of the movement's three themes. A charming little tune, given out by flute and oboe, continues. The third theme, bearing an unmistakable similarity to the spiritual "Swing Low, Sweet Chariot," is played first by the flute in its lowest register and is then taken up by the violins. Dvořák then develops and brings back these themes, leading to a triumphant conclusion.

II. *Largo.* The notable English horn theme of the popular Largo very closely resembles a spiritual in character. In fact, when William Fischer later set words to the melody, many mistakenly assumed that Dvořák based the movement on an existing spiritual known as "Goin' Home."

III. *Scherzo: Molto vivace.* Now forceful and fiery, now light and delicate, the Scherzo races along with great energy and rhythmic drive. The melody, which Dvořák derived from music planned for his opera *Hiawatha,* describes, in the composer's words, "a feast in the wood where the Indians dance." A slower, more legato trio section offers some contrast, but we're soon back to the fervor and excitement of the opening. A coda, with echoes of the first movement's horn call, ends the movement.

IV. *Allegro con fuoco.* After an explosive opening, the trumpet and French horn proclaim the finale's exultant first theme. A cymbal stroke signals the end of the furor and sets the stage for the clarinet to introduce the tender, soulful second theme. Dvořák works out this material, and also recalls themes from earlier movements, before he allows the powerful final chord to slowly fade away.

A wonderful anecdote attached to this last chord concerns Leopold Stokowski, who was known to change elements of music he was conducting. Stokowski had just finished a performance of the "New World" when critic Irving Kolodin rushed backstage. "Maestro," he demanded, "am I crazy or did I hear a cymbal crash on the last chord?" Stokowski stared balefully at him and slowly replied: "Yes—and yes!"

Sir Edward Elgar

Born June 2, 1857, in Broadheath, England
Died February 23, 1934, in Worcester

ALWAYS DRESSED in well-tailored, tweedy clothes over his tall, ram-rod-straight frame, Elgar was the very picture of an English gentleman at the peak of his country's imperial glory. Even his hobbies—golf, hunting, and kite flying—fit this staid, conservative image. Yet, despite his stodgy, even stuffy outward appearance, Elgar's music showed great vitality and a strong affinity for the lush harmonies and expanded musical forms of the Romantic era. Given his musical imagination, melodic gifts, and grasp of compositional technique, he created a number of outstanding works. In addition, his work led to the flowering of 20th century British music, with such composers as Benjamin Britten, William Walton, Michael Tippett, and Ralph Vaughan Williams.

Elgar received only minimal instruction on piano and violin, and was largely self-taught in composition. As a young man he participated in a broad range of musical activities in the city of Worcester, England, near where he was born. In addition to conducting the Worcester Glee Club and the band at the County Lunatic Asylum, playing concertmaster with the Worcester Philharmonic, leading the Worcester Amateur Instrumental Society, serving as organist of St. George's Roman Catholic Church, and giving private music lessons, he turned out a large number of mostly short, sentimental pieces.

By the 1890s, though, Elgar started to be taken more seriously as a composer and was able to devote more time to his creative efforts. The "Enigma" Variations (1899) and *Dream of Gerontius* (1900) established him as England's leading composer, a position he maintained for the rest of his life. He was by most accounts, though, bitter, cynical, and disillusioned, and did little composing after the death of his wife in 1920.

Two of Elgar's most frequently heard orchestral compositions today are the Cello Concerto and "Enigma" Variations; his two symphonies and Violin Concerto appear less often on concert programs. But there is little question that his best-known work by far is the march *Pomp and Circumstance,* the musical mainstay of virtually every graduation ceremony.

Concerto for Cello and Orchestra in E minor, Op. 85
(30 minutes)

The Cello Concerto, Elgar's last major work, was written in 1918 and 1919, during a period when the composer was distressed over his wife's failing health, his own chronic laryngitis and vertigo, and his straitened financial condition. Whether or not these circumstances contributed to the strain of despondency that seems to run throughout the concerto is a matter of speculation.

I. *Adagio; Moderato.* The concerto opens with a dramatic outcry for the solo cello in the form of a bold, challenging recitative. The orchestra echoes the initial measures before the violas introduce the principal theme of the movement, a rocking melody that keeps the same rhythmic pattern throughout. The clarinets and bassoons next introduce a lighter, rhythmically more piquant second theme, but the first, agitated melody easily dominates the movement, much as the cello continues to tower over the orchestra.

II. *Allegro molto.* Elgar breaks with the accepted tradition in solo concertos and makes the second movement a scherzo, albeit not as gay and frolicsome as is usual for the form. After some introductory material, the cello presents the main subject of the movement—a fast scurrying figure with many repeated notes that starts several times, but runs wearily out of energy before appearing in its entirety. At times the movement sounds like a perpetual motion, but with several extended interruptions, including the introduction of a more lyrical theme, which Elgar later combines with the rapid figuration.

III. *Adagio.* The cello sings throughout the Adagio, the movement in which the melancholy cast of the concerto emerges most clearly. One beautifully crafted, highly expressive melody runs throughout this appealing movement.

IV. *Allegro; Moderato; Allegro ma non troppo.* A few measures of cadenzalike introduction, reminiscent of the first movement opening, precede the rousing good tune that makes up the subject of the final movement. Elgar generally maintains the jolly nature of the theme, despite many changes of tempo and echoes of less joyful melodies from earlier movements, before ending the concerto with a final ebullient outburst.

Variations on an Original Theme, "Enigma," Op. 36
(30 minutes)

Elgar explained his "Enigma" Variations in this way: "In this music I have sketched, for their amusement and mine, the idiosyncrasies of 14 of my friends, not necessarily musicians." Later, he elaborated on how the piece came to be written: "One evening, after a long and tiresome day's teaching, aided by a cigar, I musingly played on the piano the theme as it now stands. The voice of C.A.E. [Lady Elgar] asked with a sound of approval, 'What was that?' I answered, 'Nothing—but something might be made of it.' " Then, to Lady Elgar's great delight, the composer proceeded to use the theme as the basis for improvised musical sketches of several friends.

In time, Elgar expanded the concept into a theme and variations for orchestra, mysteriously marking each variation with initials, a nickname, or asterisks. By now, the identities have been exposed, and we can use Elgar's descriptions or what is known of these individuals to enhance our listening pleasure:

C.A.E.—Caroline Alice Elgar, his wife; "a prolongation of the theme with what I wished to be romantic and delicate additions."

H.D.S.-P.—H. David Stuart-Powell, a pianist with whom Elgar played chamber music: "His characteristic diatonic run over the keys before beginning to play is here travestied in the semiquaver [sixteenth note] passages."

R.B.T.—Richard Baxter Townshend, an actor, famous for playing the roles of old men, with their "low voices flying off occasionally into 'soprano' timbre," as heard in the dialogue between the bassoon and the higher woodwinds.

W.M.B.—William M. Baker, a fiery and vigorous country squire who one time "forcibly read out the arrangements for the day and hurriedly left the music-room with an inadvertent bang of the door."

R.P.A.—Richard P. Arnold, a self-taught amateur pianist about whom Elgar noted: "His serious conversation was continually broken up by whimsical and witty remarks."

Ysobel—Isabel Fitton was an amateur violist, which explains the prominent viola part, and she was very tall, which may explain the huge upward leaps in the melody. Elgar described her music as "pensive and, for a moment, romantic."

Troyte—Arthur Troyte Griffith, a truculent and argumentative architect and amateur pianist. According to the composer, "the strong rhythm suggests the attempts of the instructor (E.E.) to make something like order out of chaos."

W.N.—Winifred Norbury and her sister Florence were elegant and patrician friends. About this section Elgar commented: "The gracious personalities of the ladies are shown . . . a little suggestion of a characteristic laugh is given."

Nimrod—August Jaeger, music publisher and critic, inspired this movement; Nimrod is the hunter from the Book of Genesis and *Jaeger* is German for "hunter." The music, Elgar stated, "is the record of a long summer evening talk, when my friend discoursed eloquently on the slow movements of Beethoven." The opening actually brings to mind the slow movement of Beethoven's Piano Sonata No. 8, the "Pathétique."

Dorabella—Dora Penny, a close friend who spoke hesitatingly, is characterized by separations between the phrases of the music. "The movement suggests a dancelike lightness," explained Elgar.

G.R.S.—Dr. George Robinson Sinclair was organist at Hereford Cathedral. The music, however, has "nothing to do with organs or cathedrals. . . . The first few bars were suggested by his great bulldog Dan . . . falling down the steep bank into the River Wye . . . and his rejoicing bark on landing. G.R.S. said, 'Set that to music.' I did; here it is."

B.G.N.—Basil G. Nevinson, amateur cellist, which explains the leading role given to the cellos. "A tribute to a very dear friend," wrote the composer.

***—Lady Mary Lygon. "The asterisks take the place of the name of a lady who was, at the time of composition, on a sea voyage [and hence could not be asked for permission to use her initials]. The drums suggest the distant throb of the engine over which the clarinet quotes a phrase from Mendelssohn's *Calm Sea and Prosperous Voyage.*"

E.D.U.—"Edoo," Lady Elgar's nickname for Sir Edward; the music is "bold and vigorous in general style."

The true enigma of this work, though, lies not in discovering the identities of the people portrayed; Elgar felt "this is a personal matter and need not have been mentioned publicly." The real puzzle is the original theme. "The enigma I will not explain," wrote Elgar, "its 'dark saying' must be left unguessed. . . . Further, through and over the whole set another and larger theme 'goes' but is not played."

Despite Elgar's caution that "the variations should stand simply as a piece of music," musicians have sought for nearly 100 years this "larger theme" that "goes" with Elgar's theme and the variations. While proposed solutions have ranged from "Auld Lang Syne" to a theme from Wagner's *Parsifal,* British pianist Joseph Cooper might have come closest with his 1991 discovery that the first 10 notes of Elgar's theme are identical with or very close to 10 notes in Mozart's Symphony No. 38, "Prague" (starting at measure 122 of the Andante).

Elgar began composing the "Enigma" Variations in the fall of 1898 and finished it on February 2, 1899. Hans Richter led the premiere in London on June 19, 1899. The composer subsequently revised the work and conducted the first performance of the final version in Worcester on September 13, 1899.

César Franck

Born December 10, 1822, in Liège, Belgium
Died November 8, 1890, in Paris

CÉSAR FRANCK received his musical training first at the Royal Conservatory in Liège and then at the Paris Conservatory, where he captured several prizes for piano, organ, and composing. Following graduation he remained in Paris, composing, teaching, and performing recitals as pianist or organist—but winning little recognition.

Franck's fortunes began to change in 1858, when he was appointed organist at Sainte-Clotilde and improved further in 1872 when, in addition, he began teaching at the Paris Conservatory. Paris at that time was dominated by opera and training at the Conservatory emphasized the operatic tradition. It was largely through Franck's influence as a teacher and composer that instrumental composition won a new respect and inspired other composers.

Famous for his placid, serene personality (his students adoringly called him "Pater Seraphicus"), Franck was little suited to do battle with the musical establishment in Paris. Many of his works were criticized harshly by fellow musicians and in the press. But his personal vision and the great appeal of his music won out. He left posterity a small but treasured legacy of innovative compositions that combine formal structures that grow from the melodic material with rich, highly chromatic harmonies, and frequent modulations from key to key.

Symphonic Variations for Piano and Orchestra
(16 minutes)

Franck achieved great success with Symphonic Variations, a work in which audiences find great immediacy of appeal. Yet formally it is a complex, intricate composition that causes experts to differ considerably in their analyses.

Basically, the piece consists of freely organized variations on a few related themes. The work opens with a terse, aggressive motif in the strings followed by a dreamy, somewhat despondent motif in the piano. Franck briefly works through these two subjects before the piano states a new melody, a distant relative of the opening string figure. He devotes the main body of the work to putting this new melody through several variations. After a long trill in the piano he appends a concluding section that is really a miniature piano concerto movement—with its own exposition, development, and recapitulation.

Franck composed the Symphonic Variations in Paris in 1885. Pianist Louis Diémer was soloist for the first performance in Paris on May 1, 1886.

Symphony in D minor
(43 minutes)

Franck's search for musical unity and synthesis, which extends through all his music, reached its fullest and most satisfying realization in his Symphony in D minor, completed in 1888 at age 65. His most frequently performed piece, the symphony is fully integrated by the use of two germinal motifs that appear in each of the three movements. This technique is known as cyclic form; that is, either quotes from earlier movements appear in later movements or themes used in later movements are derived from themes heard earlier. In this symphony Franck uses both kinds of cyclic form to excellent advantage.

The immense appeal of this symphony comes largely from the alternation of the two predominant moods—the calm, otherworldly, reverential sections and the impassioned, intense, climactic moments.

I. *Lento; Allegro non troppo.* The first motif turns up immediately, played by cellos and basses; it can be described as a note, a second note one step lower, and a third note several steps higher. The theme bears a strong resemblance to similar themes in at least three other major works and projects the same tone of uncertainty and wonder. In Beethoven's String Quartet, Op. 135, he wrote the question *"Muss es sein?"* ("Must it be?") over the motif's three notes; Liszt used the notes in his tone poem *Les Préludes,* the program of which starts: "What is life but a series of preludes to that unknown song whose first solemn note is sounded by Death?"; and you hear the same motif as the Fate theme in the music dramas that make up Wagner's *Ring of the Nibelung.*

The symphony's second motif also contains three notes—a note, a higher note, and the return of the original note. This motif, sometimes called the "faith motif" because of its strong spiritual component, comes in the second theme of the first movement. Sung out in full splendor by the violins, trumpets, and woodwinds, the motif refers back to the *torculus,* a medieval neume that was used to notate Gregorian chant. After presenting the two motifs, Franck devotes the rest of the movement to working out the conflicts between them in relatively strict sonata allegro form.

II. *Allegretto.* The Allegretto telescopes what is usually two separate movements—a slow movement and a scherzo—into a single section. Franck hints at a program for this movement when he said: "I did think—oh so vaguely—of a procession in the olden times." After a few measures of introduction, the English horn plays the main, doleful melody of the movement. Careful listening to the melody reveals the first motif in a new guise. A return of the English horn theme brings this section to a close. The faster scherzo begins without any pause. Its two themes—a running figure for the violins and a jaunty little tune played by the clarinets—contain within them skeletal outlines of the two motifs. Franck finally unifies the entire movement by using the scherzo theme to accompany a restatement of the opening melody.

III. *Allegro non troppo.* The finale offers Franck's positive, affirmative response to the tentative question with which he opened the symphony. Two new themes, both closely and obviously related to the basic motifs, and several recurring quotes from earlier movements serve to unify the whole symphony. Franck concludes the work on a triumphant, uplifting note.

The premiere of this symphony, Franck's only effort in the form, was given in Paris on February 17, 1889, with Jules Garcin conducting.

George Gershwin

Born September 25, 1898, in Brooklyn, New York
Died July 11, 1937, in Hollywood, California

BORN IN BROOKLYN, New York, of Russian immigrant parents, George Gershwin exhibited an early love for music: "One of my first definite memories goes back to the age of six. I stood outside a penny arcade listening to an automatic piano leaping through Rubinstein's *Melody in F.*" But his musical training was extremely circumscribed—piano lessons as a child and occasional periods of study of harmony and orchestration later. His academic training was even more lacking—he never even graduated from high school.

By age 15 Gershwin began writing popular songs and one year later got a job playing piano in a music publishing house, trying to convince performers to include his publisher's songs in their shows and acts. In 1919, at age 21, he wrote "Swanee," one of America's enduring song classics. Over the following two decades he rose to fame with a succession of immensely successful popular songs, Broadway musicals, and Hollywood films.

While winning accolades as a leading composer of popular music, Gershwin also began to move into the concert hall and opera house. The first step came in 1924 when conductor Paul Whiteman featured his *Rhapsody in Blue* in an experimental concert that combined what was then called jazz with classical music. Two commissions from the New York Symphony (now the New York Philharmonic) followed—Concerto in F and *An American in Paris*. With his reputation firmly established the composer produced other symphonic works—*Rhapsody No. 2, Cuban Overture,* and Variations for Piano and Orchestra on "I Got Rhythm"—but none approached the level of his earlier efforts. Finally, in 1935, Gershwin completed his last major work, the opera *Porgy and Bess,* which became the most popular opera written by an American and capped his career as a synthesizer of popular and serious music.

Perhaps Gershwin best summed up his music when he wrote: "Music must reflect the thoughts and aspirations of the people and the time. My people are American. My time is today." His compositions bespeak a hopeful, vital, and energetic nation, tempered by love, warmth, and a broad streak of sentimentality—attributes that strike a most responsive chord in modern audiences.

An American in Paris
(20 minutes)

In 1926, having scored immense successes with his symphonic scores as well as his Broadway musicals, Gershwin was asked by Walter Damrosch, conductor of the New York Symphony (now the New York Philharmonic), to compose a major orchestral work. It is quite fitting that he wrote most of the piece during a holiday in Paris in the spring of 1928.

The composer clearly stated his goal: "My purpose here is to portray the impression of an American visitor in Paris, as he strolls about the city, and listens to various street noises and absorbs the French atmosphere. As in my other orchestral compositions, I've not endeavored to represent any definite scenes in this music . . . so that the individual listener can read into the music such as his imagination pictures for him."

Gershwin completed the piano score back in New York on August 1, 1928, and by November 18 had finished the orchestration, calling for a number of instruments not usually found in a symphony orchestra—three saxophones, four French taxi horns, and several percussion instruments more closely associated with dance bands. Damrosch conducted the premiere on December 13, 1928.

For the premiere, program annotator Deems Taylor, with Gershwin's approval, presented a detailed and specific list of incidents portrayed in the music. From Gershwin's writings and Taylor's notes one can fashion a scenario to serve as a guide: The music opens with an American walking down a Paris boulevard on a beautiful spring day, with the sounds of Paris, particularly the taxi horns, in the background; his footsteps hesitate as he passes a church (English horn), but he soon resumes his sprightly pace. The change to American pop style signals that the hero crosses to the Left Bank, where Americans tend to congregate; the solo violin represents a conversation with a pretty Parisian girl. Now, though, homesickness strikes, as evidenced by the slower blues section, but a meeting with another American (Charleston rhythm) cheers him up. The return of the walking music and sounds of Paris suggest that being in Paris is not so bad after all.

Some might argue that *An American in Paris* is too frivolous to be considered a masterpiece. Yet there can be no question of Gershwin's mastery in bringing together incredibly diverse musical elements. Telling a story while creating a logical and satisfying musical form, combining pop with serious musical styles, and displaying a superb sense of melody with an amazing musical sensitivity, make this an enduring work of exceptional quality.

Concerto in F for Piano and Orchestra
(25 minutes)

In the distinguished audience at the premiere of Gershwin's *Rhapsody in Blue* on February 12, 1924, was Walter Damrosch, conductor of the New York Symphony (later the New York Philharmonic). Damrosch joined in the enthusiastic praise for the preeminent composer of Broadway musicals who had so successfully adapted his popular music style to the very different demands of the concert hall.

Damrosch put the imprimatur of the musical establishment on Gershwin by commissioning him to compose a piano concerto that he would perform in Carnegie Hall and on tour with the orchestra.

Gershwin eagerly accepted. The story, probably apocryphal, is that Gershwin's first act after signing the contract was to rush out and buy a book on how to write a concerto. More probable is that Gershwin knew full well how to compose a concerto, but studied several outstanding piano concertos to learn what he could from the masters. Gershwin wanted to surpass the success of *Rhapsody in Blue*. "Many persons had thought that the *Rhapsody* was only a happy accident," he later wrote. "Well, I went out, for one thing, to show them that there was plenty more where that had come from. I made up my mind to do a piece of 'absolute' music."

The Concerto in F sparkles with energy and excitement; its jaunty air reflects the widely accepted optimism of the times. The music also speaks of New York City and all the burgeoning American cities at their height in the 1920s, with an innocence and affectionate warmth rarely found in art today.

Gershwin himself prepared a brief description of the concerto:

[**I. *Allegro molto moderato.***] "The first movement employs the Charleston rhythm. It is quick and pulsating, representing the young enthusiastic spirit of American life. It begins with a rhythmic motif given out by the kettle-drums, supported by other percussion instruments and with a Charleston motif introduced by bassoon, horns, clarinets, and violas. The principal theme is announced by the bassoon." After the full orchestra takes up and expands this arch-shaped melody, the piano enters with the quiet, nostalgic second theme. Gershwin works over the thematic material in an extended development section before bringing back the two principal themes in a grandiose coda.

[II. *Adagio; Andante con moto.*] "The second movement has a poetic nocturnal atmosphere which has come to be referred to as the American blues, but in a purer form than that in which they are usually treated." The movement is in three parts: the bluesy opening section with the dominant trumpet, the new melody that comes with the piano entrance in the middle part, and the loosely realized return of the trumpet melody at the end.

[III. *Allegro agitato.*] "The third movement reverts to the style of the first. It is an orgy of rhythms, starting violently and keeping the same pace throughout." This rondolike movement separates returns of the high-voltage subject with interludes based on themes from the earlier movements—a frequently used device known as cyclic form.

Gershwin began preparing sketches for the concerto in London in May 1925, using the title *New York Concerto.* He began full-time work in July of that year, finished the actual composition in September, and completed the orchestration on November 10. Gershwin played the solo piano part at the premiere of what he now simply called Concerto in F in Carnegie Hall on December 3, 1925, with Damrosch conducting the orchestra.

Rhapsody in Blue
(15 minutes)

Late in 1923, pop bandleader Paul Whiteman asked George Gershwin to compose a piece for piano and jazz band for a concert Whiteman was presenting at New York City's Aeolian Hall, a distinguished home of classical music. As Gershwin later wrote: "Suddenly an idea occurred to me. There had been so much chatter about the limitations of jazz . . . I resolved, if possible, to kill that misconception with one blow. The rhapsody, as you see, began as a purpose not a plan."

Although he did some preliminary work on a piece he planned to call *American Rhapsody,* Gershwin soon set it aside to prepare his musical *Sweet Little Devil* for its Boston tryouts. It was only in January 1924, when he read in a newspaper that Gershwin's "jazz concerto" was being featured on the upcoming Whiteman concert, that the composer realized the premiere was a scant five weeks away. "It was on the train [to Boston for the *Sweet Little Devil* opening]," Gershwin later wrote, "with its steely rhythms, its rattlety-bang, that is often so stimulating to a composer, [that] I suddenly heard—and even saw on paper—the complete construction of the rhapsody, from beginning to end. I heard it as a sort of musical kaleidoscope of America—of our vast melting pot, of our unduplicated national pep, of our blues, our metropolitan madness. By the time I reached Boston I had a definite plot of the piece, as distinguished from its actual substance."

In only three weeks, Gershwin finished a two-piano version of the rhapsody and Ferde Grofé, Whiteman's arranger, orchestrated the second piano part for the band. Gershwin's brother Ira suggested the title *Rhapsody in Blue,* inspired by an exhibition of Whistler's paintings, featuring the famous *Arrangement in Gray and Black* (better known as *Whistler's Mother).*

Gershwin composed the opening of the rhapsody as a trill, low in the clarinet's register, followed by a 17-note articulated ascending run. At a rehearsal, Ross Gorman, Whiteman's clarinetist, exhausted from hours of playing, substituted a glissando, a smooth slide up the entire scale. The composer was so delighted with the sound that it has now become the traditional performance style.

Rhapsody in Blue appeared next to last in Whiteman's concert—which was called "Experiment in Modern Music"—on February 12, 1924. The preceding works had already convinced the many musical luminaries in the audience that the experiment was a failure. But when Gorman started slithering and sliding up the scale and the solo piano, played by Gershwin, made its quiet entrance, the concert came to life. The audience raptly listened as the melodies poured forth in rhapsodic profusion—from the jazzy, syncopated dance tunes of the opening to the slower, richly sentimental melody of the middle section, to the up-tempo transformation of the sentimental theme. A reminder of the opening melody brought the piece to its stunning conclusion —and brought the audience to its feet, cheering.

Edvard Grieg

Born June 15, 1843, in Bergen, Norway
Died September 4, 1907, in Bergen

FROM 1814 UNTIL 1905, Norway was under the rule of the Swedish king. Norwegian patriots struggled for independence during all those years, and many leading artists of Grieg's time, including playwright Henrik Ibsen and world-famous violin virtuoso Ole Bull, enthusiastically joined the nationalistic movement.

At about age 21, primarily influenced by Ibsen and Bull, Grieg committed himself to expressing the Norwegian spirit in music. He wrote much of his music in the style of Norwegian folk songs and folk dances and chose as his subjects Norwegian heroes, legends, and landscapes. He also encouraged others to create art related to Norway's national heritage.

Grieg trained at the Leipzig Conservatory, with some further study in Copenhagen. He returned to Norway in 1866 and immediately became deeply involved in the musical life of the country, composing, conducting, performing as pianist, and directing the Norwegian Academy of Music, which he founded in 1867. Over the years the government, recognizing Grieg as its leading musical figure, showered him with honors and in 1874 bestowed on the composer an annual stipend for life that freed him from financial concerns. As Grieg modestly said: "Orders and medals are most useful to me in the top layer of my trunk. The customs officials are always so kind to me at the sight of them."

Of all of Grieg's compositions, none is more beloved today than his Piano Concerto, with its expressive melodies and original rhythms and harmonies.

Concerto for Piano and Orchestra in A minor, Op. 16
(30 minutes)

Solo piano pieces and songs make up the bulk of Grieg's oeuvre. He seldom ventured into large-form works, wrote very few pieces for orchestra, and seemed in particular to avoid composing display works for virtuoso performers—except for his Piano Concerto. An impressive composition for piano and orchestra, with a demanding part for the soloist, the concerto is by far Grieg's best-known work. Audiences and performers enjoy the fresh and attractive themes, the idiomatic writing for soloist, and the appealing integration of all the musical elements.

Grieg composed the concerto while on summer holiday in a small country cottage in Sölleröd, Denmark, in 1868. Edmund Neupert played the solo part in the first performance on April 3, 1869, in Copenhagen with the composer conducting.

I. *Allegro molto moderato.* A timpani roll and a brilliant flourish for the soloist open the concerto and lead to the woodwind statement of the movement's simple and engaging principal theme. The cellos and woodwinds introduce the second theme, a warm, soulful melody. After the orchestral presentation of each theme, the soloist enters again, adding complex ornaments and accompaniments while restating and expanding the melodies. After a short development section and a regular recapitulation, the soloist plays a long, written-out cadenza that is, in effect, a second development section. A brief coda recalls the opening phrase and concludes the movement.

II. *Adagio.* Muted violins state the sweet, sentimental theme of the slow movement. The piano enters for a brief contrasting middle section before a varied repeat of the opening, which the piano starts with a loud, blustery transformation of the initial quiet melody.

III. *Allegro moderato molto e marcato.* While traces of Norwegian melodies and rhythms appear in the first two movements, the finale—which follows without pause—truly celebrates Grieg's national identity. A few introductory measures precede the piano's statement of the vigorous main theme, characterized by the rhythm of Norway's most popular folk dance, the *halling.* The composer brings in various episodes, including a haunting melody stated by the flute, but the *halling* is never far out of earshot. A brief cadenza comes near the end of the movement, after which Grieg presents the halling tune in the pattern of a triple-meter *springdans,* another Norwegian folk dance. The concerto ends with a triumphant restatement of the earlier flute melody.

George Frideric Handel

Born February 23, 1685, in Halle, Germany
Died April 14, 1759, in London

HANDEL RECEIVED his first musical instruction on the organ in his hometown of Halle. At age 18 he left for the larger city of Hamburg, where he was soon busily occupied performing and composing. Particularly significant to his development were the next three years, from 1707 to 1710, which he spent in Rome absorbing the sunny lyricism of Italian operatic style. When he returned to Germany he entered the employ of the Elector of Hanover, but took leave just two years later for an extended visit to England.

Handel, however, decided to settle in London, where he began composing and producing operas in the Italian style. London was an amazing cultural center at that time, boasting such figures as Jonathan Swift, Alexander Pope, Joseph Addison, Richard Steele, John Gay, and Isaac Newton. But Italian opera was still quite new to the English, and these intellectuals were not impressed by the lusty, burly intruder from across the Channel. Handel, however, gradually gained popularity among the nobility and soon began attracting the middle class to his operatic productions.

Since he was enjoying such success, Handel remained in London, to the obvious displeasure of his German patron, the Elector of Hanover. Imagine Handel's dismay, then, when the Elector became King George I and succeeded Queen Anne to the British throne! But soon the two men were reconciled and George even doubled Handel's pension.

In 1741 Handel abandoned opera and turned to composing oratorios—unstaged music dramas on religious themes. Throughout his career, though, Handel composed various works for orchestra; among them are two that are especially well liked in our time—*Water Music* and *Royal Fireworks Music*.

Royal Fireworks Music
(19 minutes)

Soon after the signing of the Treaty of Aix-la-Chapelle on October 18, 1748, which put an end to the War of the Austrian Succession, King George II started to plan a giant national celebration to be held on April 27, 1749, in Green Park, London. He hired Giovanni Niccolò Servandoni to build a huge building for the fireworks display and he commissioned Handel to compose the music.

Handel completed the work early in April 1749; he scored it for a giant orchestra of 24 oboes, 12 bassoons, contrabassoon, 9 horns, 9 trumpets, and 3 pairs of timpani—but no strings. Londoners were so excited about this event that a crowd of 12,000 paid a half crown each for the privilege of attending, not a performance, but an outdoor rehearsal six days before the performance! Servandoni finished the 410-foot-long, 114-foot-high building the day before the actual happening, topping it with a 200-foot pole that held up a giant sun.

Spectators packed Green Park on the evening of the performance, which started splendidly with Handel's magnificent Ouverture, followed by a deafening salute fired by 101 cannons. As the music continued, the fireworks display started. But very quickly the fireworks developed all sorts of problems: Some were not going off at all, others were exploding at the wrong times. Workers clambered over the building to try to correct the situation. And then, suddenly, parts of the building itself burst into flame!

The crowd panicked as brisk winds blew flaming embers across the park. Adding to the confusion, the volatile Servandoni, with drawn sword and murder in his eyes, was chasing the Duke of Montague, who had been in charge of the evening's arrangements.

Handel valiantly continued conducting. But by then, of course, the audience was fighting its way out of the park and in the pandemonium nobody heard a note of the music. Since then, under infinitely better listening conditions, the spirited, dynamic music has been accepted as a cherished orchestral masterpiece, and one realizes how very successful Handel was in creating a work that is an immensely appealing popular entertainment as well as a serious composition.

I. *Ouverture.* The first movement is in the popular French overture style, with a characteristic long/short rhythmic pattern in the slow opening and a substantial section in which Handel contrasts the sonorities of different groups of instruments coming next.

II. *Bourrée.* A lively little dance serves as a relaxation after the pomp and grandiosity of the Ouverture.

III. *La Paix.* Since the music was to celebrate the coming of peace, Handel includes the gently swaying *La Paix* ("The Peace"), a section that sounds like one of the pastorals often heard in Baroque Christmas music.

IV. *La Réjouissance.* The musical exuberance of this movement, "The Rejoicing" in English, offers a celebratory paean to the end of war.

V. *Menuet.* This quiet section functions as a counterweight to the wild jubilation of *La Réjouissance.*

VI. *Menuet.* The concluding Minuet ends the work with the properly festive air.

Sometime after the fiasco of the premiere, Handel added string parts to the music for indoor performances. The work is now seldom performed with either the original or revised orchestration; most conductors favor one of the currently available arrangements for modern orchestra.

Water Music
(57 minutes)

A favorite diversion for London's aristocracy in the early 18th century was a leisurely sail down the Thames River in a luxuriously appointed barge. The nobles of highest rank indulged in the added pleasure of having another barge follow, with musicians on board, playing appropriate outdoor music for their entertainment. It was for just such outings taken by King George I that Handel composed his *Water Music.*

Handel's first biographer, the Reverend John Mainwaring, created the impression that the *Water Music* was composed to effect a reconciliation with King George I—a story now taken to be apocryphal. Recent scholarship seems to indicate that Handel supplied the music for three royal barge trips, in August 1715, July 1717, and April 1736, although some hold that all the music was intended for just one lengthy outing. While the original manuscript of the *Water Music* has been lost, most current editions divide the 20 or so pieces into three separate suites. Editions and arrangements of the *Water Music* for modern orchestras vary considerably in number of movements and in instrumentation.

SUITE 1

I. *Ouverture.* The Ouverture is a majestic and festive opening to the suite in the typically grandiose style of a French overture.

II. *Adagio e staccato.* This movement contains a cantabile melody for oboes over a quiet accompaniment of separated (staccato) chords.

III. *[Allegro.]* Although unmarked, this movement seems to be an Allegro that features virtuosic writing for a pair of French horns.

IV. *Andante.* This quiet movement contrasts woodwind and string sonorities.

V. *[Allegro.]* Another unmarked movement, probably an Allegro, which again features two horns.

VI. *Air.* Handel crafted one of his most eloquent melodies for the Air; he directs that it be played three times; in performance each repeat is usually played with different instrumentation and added ornamentation.

VII. *Minuet.* The muscular Minuet starts as a horn duet before the other instruments join in; the strings play a contrasting middle section, after which the orchestra freely repeats the opening.

VIII. *Bourrée.* Handel changes the character for the light, bouncy Bourrée, which is also played three times, by strings, winds, and finally tutti.

IX. *Hornpipe.* The Hornpipe is a vigorous old English sailors' dance; here the winds, strings, and tutti assume the three repetitions.

X. *[Allegro.]* The substantial final movement, which lacks a marking but suggests an Allegro, is rich in contrapuntal inventiveness.

SUITE 2

I. *[Allegro.]* The first marchlike movement lacks a tempo designation but is usually performed as a brisk Allegro.

II. *Alla Hornpipe.* The spirited rhythmic drive and sparkling syncopations of the Alla Hornpipe make this movement the signature tune of the entire *Water Music.*

III. *Minuet.* Trumpets and French horns in the robust Minuet impart a rugged outdoor feeling.

IV. *Lentamente.* This movement reminds us of Handel's great skill in writing singing, cantabile melodies.

V. *Bourrée.* Handel ends the suite with the delightful Bourrée, a fast, lively dance that dates back to 17th century France.

SUITE 3

Suite 3, the shortest of the three, uses the smallest orchestra by omitting the brass instruments.

I. *[Sarabande.]* Although not so designated, the first movement is a stately Sarabande, an old designated form in triple meter with an accented second beat.

II. *Rigaudon.* Two lively Rigaudons come next; most editions assume a repetition of the first after the second, creating an A-B-A pattern.

III. *Minuet.* Handel probably also intended the more elegant Minuets to be played in the same A-B-A organization as the Rigaudons.

IV. *Gigue.* Many Baroque suites end with a Gigue, the French version of the English "jig," a highly rhythmic dance with a lively, sprightly air.

Roy Harris

Born February 12, 1898, in Lincoln County, Oklahoma
Died October 1, 1979, in Santa Monica, California

ROY HARRIS won recognition during his lifetime as an American composer in close touch with his roots. His parents had arrived in Oklahoma by oxcart during the land rush and he was born in their log cabin on Lincoln's birthday. After musical studies in California, Harris went to Paris like many other American composers and studied under the world-famous teacher Nadia Boulanger from 1926 to 1929.

Roy Harris penned the following words to explain his vision of the American spirit: "The moods which seem particularly American to me are the noisy ribaldry, the sadness, a groping earnestness which amounts to suppliance toward those deepest spiritual yearnings within ourselves; there is little grace or mellowness in our midst." The quotation also points out the special qualities that contribute to Harris' distinctive style of music.

Harris often used themes from American folk music in his compositions. Famous for creating and promoting American music, Harris influenced other composers, including Aaron Copland and Walter Piston, with his use of sweeping melodies and driving rhythms. Yet he did not define himself as an American composer. "The critics are the ones who call me typically American," he once wrote. "I never say it. Serge Koussevitzky [Russian-born conductor of the Boston Symphony] used to claim I was typically Russian. Feri Roth [Hungarian-born violinist] tells everyone I am not American at all, but Hungarian."

Harris wrote 16 symphonies, 14 for orchestra and one each for band and for chorus. But only his Third Symphony has won a prominent place among contemporary masterpieces, sparked in part by Leonard Bernstein's electrifying recording with the New York Philharmonic.

Symphony No. 3 (in one movement)
(20 minutes)

In Roy Harris' Third Symphony, many hear the true voice of the American spirit. The voice speaks to us, not of the sophisticated urbanism of our cities, but of the broad expanses of our plains, our vast forest lands, and our towering mountains.

Harris used an original method that he called autogenetics to structure his Third Symphony. The method lets the musical material determine the form of the piece of music, much as the seed of a tree determines its form. Instead of a traditional three- or four-movement symphony, Harris fashioned a five-movement symphony that he combined into one extended movement.

When asked to furnish program notes for the premiere, Harris submitted an easily followed outline of the formal structure:

Section I. Tragic—low string sonorities.

Section II. Lyric—strings, horns, woodwinds.

Section III. Pastoral—woodwinds with a polytonal background.

Section IV. Fugue—Dramatic

   A. Brass and percussion predominating.

   B. Canonic development of materials from Section II constituting background for further development of fugue.

   C. Brass climax, rhythmic motive derived from fugue subject.

Section V. Dramatic—Tragic

   A. Restatement of violin theme of Section I; tutti strings in canon with tutti woodwinds against brass and percussion developing rhythmic motive from climax of Section IV.

   B. Coda—Development of materials from Sections I and II over pedal timpani.

Composed in 1938, Harris' Third Symphony received its first performance on February 24, 1939, by the Boston Symphony. The conductor, Serge Koussevitzky, called it "the first great symphony by an American composer." An unidentified critic of *Modern Music* went on to describe it in these glowing terms: "For significance of material, breadth of treatment, and depth of meaning; for tragic implication, dramatic intensity, concentration; for moving beauty, glowing sound, it can find no peer in the musical art of America."

Franz Joseph Haydn

Born March 31, 1732, in Rohrau, Austria
Died May 31, 1809, in Vienna

HAYDN WAS BORN in the small village of Rohrau in lower Austria, where he became familiar with the peasant music of the area. After some rudimentary schooling and music instruction, he was selected at age eight for the choir of St. Stephen's in Vienna, where his academic and music training continued. Although he received no formal lessons in composition, his exposure to the finest music was an education in itself.

When Haydn's voice changed at age seventeen, he was forced to leave St. Stephen's. But he stayed on in Vienna, playing violin on the streets, giving lessons, and honing his composing skills. After a couple of minor court posts, Haydn was appointed second and then first *Kapellmeister* at the sumptuous Esterházy castle some 25 miles outside of Vienna, a position he retained from 1761 until 1790.

Although he was a servant at Esterházy, Haydn held a rank that afforded him a substantial salary as well as the services of a footman and maid. His duties included composing, rehearsing, and conducting music for frequent orchestral, chamber music, and opera performances by the 25 instrumentalists, five singers, and choir on Prince Esterházy's staff, as well as writing music for the Prince, an avid amateur performer.

After Prince Esterházy died in 1790, Haydn made his permanent home in Vienna but visited England and Paris several times. He composed some of his greatest works from 1791 until his death in 1809; the twelve symphonies (numbers 93 to 104), known as his "London" symphonies, and several great masses and oratorios date from that time.

While Haydn's very early music tended to be light, charming, and elegant, he later added folk and rustic elements from his childhood memories. In his maturity, the composer developed and wove these two threads into skillfully organized, learned works that helped set the standard for musical style and taste. But even as he imbued his compositions with such hallmarks of the Classical style as proportion, symmetry, restraint, and clarity, his inventiveness and originality allowed him to satisfy his own need for untrammeled self-expression.

The works discussed below are identified in the usual way, but also with Hoboken (H.) numbers from Anthony van Hoboken's 1957 thematic catalog of Haydn's works.

Concerto for Cello and Orchestra in D major, H. VIIb:2
(24 minutes)

In 1783, while employed as *Kapellmeister* to Prince Nikolaus Esterházy, Haydn wrote this concerto for Anton Kraft, the outstanding principal cellist of the Esterházy orchestra. No record exists of the first performance, but musicologist Lionel Nowak believes it might have been at the festivities connected with Prince Esterházy's wedding on September 15, 1783.

Sometime later, Kraft's son, probably not having understood that Haydn only consulted with Anton about the technical details of the cello part, claimed that his father wrote the concerto. To complicate matters, the manuscript of the concerto disappeared right after publication in 1810, which many believed supported young Kraft's claim. It was not until 1953, when the authentic manuscript reappeared and was placed in the Austrian National Library, that Haydn was widely accepted as the composer.

I. *Allegro moderato.* The movement begins with the orchestra statement of the two themes, both sunny and genial in character, followed by the soloist's much elaborated traversal of the same melodies. The ensuing development and recapitulation sections rely heavily on brilliant, virtuosic writing for the cello. A cadenza for the soloist and a brief coda end the movement.

II. *Adagio.* The songlike second movement beguiles listeners with its great charm and simplicity. The cello states the principal theme at the outset; a contrasting theme and variations on the original melody fill out the remainder of the movement.

III. *Allegro.* The refrain for the rondo finale consists of a happy, lilting tune. Three episodes give the soloist many opportunities for bravura display, with returns of the delightful refrain coming in between.

Concerto for Trumpet and Orchestra in E flat major, H. VIIe:1

(16 minutes)

The standard trumpet in Haydn's day was a very limited instrument; as it lacked keys, its range was confined to the comparatively small number of notes performers could play by altering their lip formation and breath pressure. Trumpeters had lost the amazing technique of the earlier Baroque musicians that allowed them to play in the instrument's highest range, and the valved trumpet that enabled performers to play all the notes of the scale had not yet been invented.

Haydn's friend trumpeter, Anton Weidinger of the Court Orchestra in Vienna, attempted to improve the trumpet by developing an instrument with keys resembling those of a modern saxophone. This trumpet could play all the notes of the scale, but unfortunately had a key mechanism that deadened the instrument's usually brilliant tone. Haydn composed his Trumpet Concerto for Weidinger; one can only imagine what the concerto sounded like on his trumpet.

I. *Allegro.* In this compact movement, the orchestra states the two themes —the first quiet but jaunty, the second a chromatic descending line that Haydn may well have created to show off the capabilities of Weidinger's trumpet. Haydn structures the soloist's presentation of the themes, the working out, and the return largely as a dialogue between the soloist and the orchestra. He follows the recapitulation with a cadenza and short coda.

II. *Andante.* As we have said, Haydn may have composed the second theme of the first movement to illustrate the trumpet's range of notes. So, too, he may have chosen the character of the second movement to demonstrate its ability to play somber, dark-hued music. Gentle and tender in overall tone, the movement follows a simple three-part form, with a contrasting middle part between similar opening and closing sections.

III. *Allegro.* The joyous principal theme of the finale ushers in a truly delightful movement. Haydn gives the trumpet free rein in brilliant passages and ringing fanfares, along with lyrical portions, all enlivened with dramatic surprises in the musical line.

Haydn composed his only trumpet concerto in 1796, at the very height of his powers. Anton Weidinger gave the premiere in Vienna on March 28, 1800. No one knows why the trumpet player waited four years to perform the work.

Symphony No. 45 in F sharp minor, H. I:45, "Farewell"
(22 minutes)

Prince Nikolaus Esterházy, for whom Haydn was *Kapellmeister,* had a castle in what is now Hungary, as well as a town house in Vienna. Since the Prince preferred his country home, over the years he lengthened the time spent there and consequently spent less time in the city. The arrangement troubled many members of his orchestra, since it meant more time away from their families and friends in Vienna.

In 1772, the Prince went one step further; he extended the season at the castle so much longer that it actually cut into the musicians' vacation time. The players complained to Haydn, who asked the Prince to release them earlier. When the Prince refused, Haydn composed his "Farewell" Symphony. He added an Adagio to the last movement in which the musicians, one or two at a time, finish playing, blow out the candles on their music stands, and depart, leaving only two violins to finish the symphony. Apparently, the Prince took the hint and moved the court to Vienna the very next day.

I. *Allegro assai.* The concise first movement opens with a bold, striding first theme, followed by a more lyrical, cantabile second theme. After working through the first theme in the development section, Haydn introduces a new, light little tune and finally ends the movement with a regular recapitulation.

II. *Adagio.* Haydn creates a wonderfully tender quality by having the violins muted throughout the slow movement. To add some spice to the simple main melody he attaches little decorative upbeats to many of the notes.

III. *Menuetto: Allegretto.* The Minuet alternates soft and loud phrases with piquant offbeat rhythms. Haydn bases the theme of the middle section Trio on a Gregorian chant melody associated with the Lamentations of Jeremiah—perhaps a prophetic omen for the Prince.

IV. *Finale: Presto; Adagio.* The major part of the Finale is as brisk and bustling as most last movements by Haydn. Then the tempo, meter, and mood uncharacteristically change for what is really an extended, highly emotional coda. Gradually, as the various instruments finish their parts, starting with the oboes and second French horn, the players take their instruments and leave the stage, until two violins bring the symphony to its despondent close.

Symphony No. 83 in G minor, H. I:83, "The Hen"
(25 minutes)

During his long tenure as *Kapellmeister* at Prince Esterházy's castle, Haydn seldom ventured far afield. Yet people throughout Europe recognized and admired his music. His repute led a young French nobleman, Comte d'Ogny, in 1784, to commission Haydn to write a set of six symphonies for performance at the prestigious Concerts de la Loge Olympique in Paris. Haydn composed the pieces in 1785 and 1786; they are now known as the "Paris" symphonies, and are numbered 82 through 87.

Symphony No. 83 was first performed during the 1787 season by members of the Parisian orchestra, who dressed in sky-blue coats and elaborate lace ruffles for the occasion, with ornate ceremonial swords hanging at their sides. The audience, struck by the repeated clucking oboe figure in the first movement, dubbed the symphony "The Hen," though the barnyard connection was most likely unintended.

I. *Allegro spiritoso.* The symphony begins with a driving first theme—a series of declamatory chords followed by an assertive long/short rhythmic pattern. The restlessness subsides with the appearance of a frolicsome second theme; it is the ostinato echoing of the long/short rhythm in the oboe accompaniment to this theme that engendered the symphony's nickname. Throughout the development section, the power and spirit of the first subject dominate the skittish character of the second. Both themes return for the recapitulation and coda, which ends unexpectedly in the major mode, relieving somewhat the serious mood of the movement.

II. *Andante.* Haydn creates a certain tension in the second movement as he pits the repeated notes of the first subject against the succeeding scalelike runs. The composer heightens the drama by breaking into soft passages with loud bursts of sound, one of his favored devices.

III. *Menuetto: Allegretto.* The stately Menuetto suggests robust country steps, rather than a delicate courtly dance. Audiences find the bewitching, simple Trio section particularly delightful.

IV. *Finale: Vivace.* The dynamic and energetic rondo-form Finale, in the major mode, is a good-humored headlong dash. Near the end, though, Haydn playfully calls a few sudden halts to the forward motion. The unexpected silences add to the high spirits with which the symphony ends.

Symphony No. 88 in G major, H. I:88
(22 minutes)

Scholars have long wondered why Haydn wrote his Symphony No. 88 for Johann Tost. Tost had been a violinist in Haydn's orchestra at the Esterházy estate from 1783 to 1788. That year, he took the scores of two Haydn symphonies, numbers 88 and 89, to place with publisher Sieber in Paris. Apparently, he also brought along the score of a symphony by Adalbert Gyrowetz, which he passed off as a third Haydn symphony. To compound his dishonesty, Tost was terribly slow in forwarding the money from Sieber to Haydn. When learning of the fraud, Haydn wrote to Sieber: "Thus Herr Tost has swindled you; you may claim your damages in Vienna."

In any case, Symphony No. 88 ranks near the top of all the Haydn symphonies. As Haydn biographer H. C. Robbins Landon wrote: "Seldom did Haydn reach the pinnacle of perfection achieved in No. 88."

I. *Adagio; Allegro.* A slow, portentous introduction soon gives way to a light, frothy tune, rhythmically built on the metrical foot of the anapest (ta-ta-TA). For the loud repetition of this theme Haydn supplies the lower strings with a swirling accompaniment figure that is quickly transformed into a melodic motif. A second theme follows, with the same anapest, leading to the development, with Haydn hammering away at the metric pattern. He makes some changes for the recapitulation, and a brief coda ends the movement.

II. *Largo.* Many consider the Largo the high point of this symphony. A solo cello and two oboes put forth a theme of ineffable, songlike beauty, which the orchestra then freely varies, although never straying too far from the original melody. About halfway through the movement the full orchestra explodes in sound; curiously enough, this marks the first entrance of the trumpets and timpani in the symphony.

III. *Menuetto: Allegretto.* Haydn fashions this movement into a heavy-shoed country dance, albeit with a few moments of extreme delicacy. The central Trio section sets up a bagpipe drone in the violas and bassoons, further confirming the peasant quality of the music. A shortened Minuet comes after the Trio.

IV. *Finale: Allegro con spirito.* The gay, frolicsome Finale starts with the anapest we know so well from the first movement. Haydn keeps the movement bubbling along with many brilliant, virtuosic passages for the strings, several jolting changes from soft to loud or loud to soft, and some wonderfully comic lead-ins to return the tune. The highly complex canon he inserts midway in the movement emerges as an exciting technical display for the players as well as a good demonstration of the composer's contrapuntal skill.

Symphony No. 92 in G major, H. I:92, "Oxford"
(28 minutes)

Early in 1791, Haydn arrived in London ready to present a number of his new symphonies. While there, he learned that he was to receive an honorary Doctor of Music degree from Oxford University, for which it was customary to present a major composition to the institution. Difficulties in getting a new work ready in time, however, forced Haydn to substitute one of three symphonies he had written in 1789 on a commission from a French noble, Comte d'Ogny. (In 1790 Haydn fulfilled a commission for three symphonies from the German Kraft-Ernst, Prince of Oettingen-Wallerstein, with the selfsame works. The Prince, as one would expect, was quite upset when he learned that "his" three symphonies had originally been composed for Count d'Ogny, and one was being played in Oxford!)

Haydn conducted the premiere in Oxford on July 7, 1791. A publisher attached the "Oxford" designation to the work some years later.

I. *Adagio; Allegro spiritoso.* The first movement starts with a slow, gentle introduction that anticipates the three repeated notes in the accompaniment of the principal subject. An extended outburst of great energy and vigor immediately answers the hushed violin statement of the theme. A subsidiary theme that is almost identical to the opening theme, except for its key, and a closing theme that seems a transplant from an opera buffa, round out the exposition. In the exposition of the themes, in the following development and recapitulation sections, and indeed throughout the symphony, Haydn uses violent contrasts of loud and soft, with few gradual changes, and almost no in-between dynamics.

II. *Adagio.* Among the most radiant and moving movements Haydn ever penned is this Adagio. After the lyrical, melancholy-tinged beauty of the opening, Haydn interrupts with a stormy, blustery middle section, its violent outbreaks separated by brief whispered comments. The movement proceeds with a shortened, embellished reprise of the opening. Near the end of this section, some breaks occur when the melody hesitates and stops, expressing a particularly touching vulnerability and sensitivity.

III. *Menuetto: Allegretto.* The wonderfully robust and rhythmic Menuetto echoes with the three repeated notes from the first movement. The Trio, which features the bassoons and French horns, romps playfully with syncopations, misplaced accents, and sudden stops that defy efforts to find a clear downbeat. At the end Haydn returns a shortened Menuetto.

IV. *Presto.* Chock-full of unexpected turns of melody and harmony, the Presto coruscates along at high speed. Its witty, vivacious principal theme and frolicsome subordinate theme bring the symphony to a bright and cheery conclusion.

THE "LONDON" SYMPHONIES, NOS. 93–104

For nearly 30 years, starting in 1761, Haydn served in the position of *Kapellmeister* at the court of Prince Nikolaus Esterházy. On the death of the Prince in 1790, his successor disbanded the orchestra, and Haydn moved to Vienna. Here he received many offers to compose and conduct his music, including an invitation from impresario Johann Peter Salomon to write and direct six symphonies in London. Haydn readily agreed and spent two concert seasons in England—from January 1791 to June 1792—presenting symphonies 95, 96, and 97 the first season and symphonies 93, 94, and 98 the second.

After the highly successful first visit, Haydn was glad to return again, from February 1794 to August 1795, when he gave the premieres of symphonies 99 through 104. These last 12 of Haydn's symphonies are known collectively as the "London" or "Salomon" symphonies, in addition to the individual nicknames many of them also have.

Symphony No. 94 in G major, H. I:94, "Surprise"
(25 minutes)

Few question the origin of the subtitle "Surprise." The English flutist Andrew Ashe supplied the nickname when he programmed the symphony for a 1795 concert, later writing: "My valued friend Haydn thank'd me for giving it such an appropriate Name."

Less certain is why Haydn inserted the loud chord in the second movement—the source of the "surprise." Composer Adalbert Gyrowetz reported that before the first performance Haydn played the symphony on the piano for him and at that point said: "There the women will jump," leading to the common explanation that it was designed to wake dozing concertgoers. But when biographer Georg August Griesinger asked Haydn about the same chord, the composer replied that "it was my wish to surprise the public with something new and to make a debut in a brilliant manner."

That the subtitle has piqued people's curiosity and led to many performances of the "Surprise" Symphony is to the good. But one must quarrel with anyone who listens to a 25-minute symphony just to be startled by one loud chord. This first-rate symphony offers many joys and pleasures beyond the "big bang."

I. *Adagio; Vivace assai.* A slow, reflective introduction opens the Adagio, after which the mood lightens for the fast body of the movement; the carefree and lighthearted feeling continues throughout this delightful movement, no matter whether the orchestra is shouting or delicately whispering.

II. *Andante.* The violins state an extremely simple little tune, one that bears some kinship to "Twinkle, Twinkle, Little Star." The melody starts softly and is repeated even more softly, after which comes the famous "surprise," followed by the more smoothly articulated second part of the theme. Haydn now presents four variations on the entire melody: (1) a countermelody added to the original, (2) a change from major to minor key, (3) a repeat of each note in the tune, and (4) a forceful playing of the melody by winds with excited comment by strings. A short coda continues to vary the theme until the music quietly fades away.

III. *Menuetto: Allegro molto.* Although called Menuetto, this movement begins with a section that is closer to the ländler, an Austrian peasant dance that was precursor to the waltz. The metrical pattern consists of one heavy beat followed by two lighter beats (UM-pah-pah). Haydn presents a slightly more sedate Trio before winding up with an abbreviated repeat of the opening.

IV. *Allegro di molto.* Haydn caps the symphony with a high-speed romp based on the spunky little tune the violins introduce at the very beginning of the movement. He adds several other contrasting melodies and sends the violins racing through some extremely demanding passages. The sparkling effects contribute to the good time and extend the light tone that informed all of the preceding movements.

Haydn composed the "Surprise" Symphony in London in 1791 and conducted the premiere there on March 23, 1792.

Symphony No. 99 in E flat major, H. I:99
(25 minutes)

Haydn composed his Symphony No. 99 in Vienna during the interval between his two trips to England. The most "newsworthy" item about this symphony is that it marks the first time Haydn used the clarinet in a symphonic work. Considering the amazing amount of superb music that Haydn had already written, Symphony No. 99 can only increase our wonder at his boundless ability to grow and improve as a composer.

I. *Adagio; Vivace assai.* The slow introduction has an anticipatory air, promising that something of interest will follow. Soon enough the fast principal theme emerges, softly at first and then in a powerful full-orchestra repeat. But even more intriguing is the second theme, a meandering melody that insinuates itself into the listener's ears. Regular development, recapitulation, and coda sections follow, differing from the pedestrian only in the skill, imagination, and special intelligence that Haydn brings to bear.

II. *Adagio.* The Parisian audience at the premiere of this symphony greatly appreciated the splendid woodwind writing in this movement. Scholar H. C. Robbins Landon suggests that the elegiac quality of the Adagio might stem from Haydn's desire to make the movement a threnody on the death of his dear friend Marianne von Genzinger.

III. *Menuetto: Allegretto.* Neither courtly nobles nor lusty peasants could have danced to the sophisticated rhythmic patterns of this Menuetto, which Haydn clearly designed for concert rather than dance use. A delicate, somewhat wistful Trio appears before the shortened reprise of the Minuet.

IV. *Finale: Vivace.* The Finale exudes happiness and good cheer from the very first note to the last. Lively and energetic in tone, it does not lose its smiling countenance even when involved in complex contrapuntal passages or when concerned with a slow echo of the principal tune.

Haydn led the premiere in London on February 10, 1794.

Symphony No. 100 in G major, H. I:100, "Military"
(25 minutes)

Haydn composed his "Military" Symphony early in 1794 and conducted the premiere in London on March 31 of that year. No one quite knows the origin of the subtitle, but it probably derives from the second movement, which adds a battery of cymbals, triangle, and bass drum to the traditional timpani of Haydn's orchestra, and also includes a forceful solo trumpet call.

After the first performance, London's *Morning Chronicle* gave this description of the music: "It is the advancing to battle; and the march of men, the sounding of the charge, the thundering of the onset, the clash of arms, the groans of the wounded, and what may well be called the hellish roar of war." During the 200 years since Haydn's "Military" Symphony, so much ferocity and violence has entered our music that we have some difficulty responding in the same way as the 18th century critic.

I. *Adagio; Allegro.* The movement opens with a somewhat serious and introspective slow introduction. The principal themes of the movement's fast body are of the utmost delicacy and innocence. It is only in the development section that Haydn reveals their potential to become threatening and bombastic. After a truncated return of the themes comes a long coda that further explores the character of the melodies.

II. *Allegretto.* Instead of a slow tempo, Haydn marks this movement Allegretto (moderately fast), and rather than produce a cantabile effect, he starts with a theme as dainty and light as those of the previous movement. About one-third of the way through, however, Haydn unleashes the full fury of the entire orchestra—including the augmented percussion section—playing a reworking of the little tune in a way that completely transforms its character. Once more the quality of the opening returns before a low trumpet call signals the start of the brief "military" section of the coda.

III. *Menuetto: Moderato.* The opening and the slightly shorter closing sections of this movement consist of the same lusty, peasantlike Minuet. The contrasting middle division, or Trio, recaptures the light touch that is so important in this symphony.

IV. *Finale: Presto.* The quicksilver Finale, which glints and glitters while dashing along at top speed, is further enlivened with several sudden stops and silences. For much of the time the racing first violin part sounds like perpetual motion. Near the end Haydn brings back the battery from the second movement for a stunning finish. That Haydn could bring such imagination and originality to this symphony after completing 99 others is truly amazing.

Symphony No. 101 in D major, H. I:101, "Clock"
(30 minutes)

The "Clock" subtitle, which is not of Haydn's invention, derives from the "tick-tock" accompaniment to the second movement's principal theme. A further connection to clocks comes in the middle section of the Menuetto movement; it shares a melody with the tune played by a mechanical clock that Haydn presented to his patron, Prince Anton Esterházy, in 1793. Whether Haydn composed the clock tune and then expanded it for the symphony or whether the symphony movement came first is unclear.

Haydn wrote the "Clock" Symphony in 1793 and 1794 and conducted the first performance in London, probably on March 3, 1794.

I. *Adagio; Presto.* Haydn opens the symphony with a grave, mysterious introduction. The slowly rising scale in the first measures ties in with the rapid ascent that later starts the principal theme of the movement's main section. Haydn follows the solemn introduction with the lighthearted Presto, which includes two themes that are not significantly different, a development section that builds to a powerful climax, the return of both melodies, and a concluding coda that further develops the melodies. Its bright character makes this movement seem more like a Haydn finale than a typically more serious first movement.

II. *Andante.* The tick-tocks of the bassoons and string pizzicato accompany the theme of the second movement. Haydn then subjects the melody to three very free variations. Most striking is the first, which serves as an excellent example of *Sturm und Drang* ("Storm and Stress"), a style in all the arts that arose in late 18th century Germany, characterized by heightened intensity of expression and great fury and ferocity. Two more variations and a coda follow, but these are much closer to the original in character.

III. *Menuetto: Allegretto.* The first part of this three-part movement creates the impression of a jolly, stamping dance. In an abrupt change of temperament, the middle section features a drone bass reminiscent of bagpipes while the flute chirps its little tune, which starts with an ascending scale that may—or may not—hark back to the first movement's ascending scale. The first part returns, this time without repeats, to end the movement.

IV. *Finale: Vivace.* H. C. Robbins Landon, the outstanding Haydn expert, has termed this movement "the greatest final movement Haydn ever wrote," a judgment that few dispute. The movement opens simply—a sprightly, flowing main theme and a second theme that seems a chromatic outgrowth of the first. Then, suddenly, the key changes from D major to D minor, and we are caught up in the maelstrom of an extensive *Sturm und Drang* section. As this part ends, Haydn prepares us for a return of the innocent opening, but instead thrusts us into a highly complex double fugue —an extremely difficult musical texture to compose that in Haydn's hands sounds perfectly natural and easy. It is not until the coda that we hear the sweet little opening tune, which soon erupts into the forceful concluding measures.

Symphony No. 103 in E flat major, H. I:103, "Drumroll"
(35 minutes)

In the 1790s, with over 100 symphonies and countless other major compositions to his credit, Haydn continued to create works of the very highest quality and to experiment with innovative ways to exercise his fecund musical imagination. Working within the comparatively rigid framework of the Classical symphony, Haydn introduced numerous stylistic touches, methods of treatment, and infinitely diverse melodic material that raised his music far above the standard works of the age. No more splendid illustration of Haydn's superlative accomplishments in his latter years exists than his "Drumroll" Symphony.

I. *Adagio; Allegro con spirito.* Haydn found a new and original way to start this symphony: he opens with an ominous timpani roll (which gave the symphony its subtitle); the introduction is unrelievedly dark and gloomy, and the introduction furnishes thematic material that reappears in the following fast part of the movement. Haydn probably based the frisky principal theme on a Croatian folk song associated with the area of his birth. The transition to the second theme, an absolutely winning waltzlike tune, refers back to the introduction melody and anticipates a more obvious connection to the introduction in the middle of the development. Then, after the recapitulation, the coda starts with a repetition of the first two slow phrases of the introduction before speeding up again to conclude the movement.

II. *Andante più tosto allegretto.* A traditional theme-and-variations movement presents a melody and then varies that melody. In this movement, though, Haydn presents two themes—one in minor and a similar theme in major, and both probably Croatian in origin—which he then proceeds to vary in alternation. One variation features a solo for violin, played by the orchestra concertmaster; some speculate that it was designed for Johann Peter Salomon, the violinist-impresario who invited Haydn to London and probably served as concertmaster of the orchestra at the premiere.

III. *Menuetto.* After a heavy-footed Menuetto with many strong accents, Haydn introduces a lyrical, intimate Trio section in stark contrast. He ends the movement with a shortened reprise of the opening part.

IV. *Finale: Allegro con spirito.* Much Classical music depends on the tension created by two or more contrasting themes in one movement. In this movement, Haydn succeeds magnificently in maintaining the tension—but with only a single theme. The movement opens with a brief horn call that becomes the background to a sparkling violin melody characterized by three repeated notes. Working only with this melody, Haydn fashions an exceptionally varied and interesting movement.

Haydn composed the "Drumroll" Symphony early in 1795 and led the London premiere on March 2 of that year.

Symphony No. 104 in D major, H. I:104, "London"
(30 minutes)

Although Haydn's final twelve symphonies were, in effect, "London" symphonies, only the twelfth and closing symphony is known as *the* "London" Symphony. Most commentators assume that Haydn knew this would probably be his last symphony. They believe that he used the occasion, not to look ahead and suggest new directions for music, but rather to summarize and create his very best work in the style and manner he had developed in composing symphonies for nearly 40 years.

Haydn finished his "London" Symphony in 1795 and conducted the first performance in that city on May 4, 1795.

I. *Adagio; Allegro.* The slow introduction to this symphony issues a stark, dramatic proclamation, awesome in its power and presence. The composer relieves the tension, however, with the appearance of the warm, relaxed first subject of the movement's fast section. We hear other flashes of melody before Haydn introduces the second subject, which is essentially the same as the first, but in a different key. The following development section hovers around the four reiterated notes and two subsequent notes that appear at the end of the first phrase of the melody. After a full stop, Haydn returns the two themes, this time in the same key, and a coda hammers away to the end of the movement.

II. *Andante.* A melody of great dignity and refinement, first given out by the strings, is the main theme of the second movement. Just as the wood-winds get started on their version we hear a bombastic tutti interruption, after which the strings, with feigned innocence, continue their graceful song. The remainder of the movement, which alternates between quiet elegance and fustian outbursts, includes some brief, wistful cadenzalike passages for flute.

III. *Menuetto: Allegro.* Many offbeat accents vitalize the Menuetto and give it a somewhat Slavic character. The composer uses the exciting timpani roll to striking effect as it leads to the final statement of the Minuet theme. Thereafter, we hear a quiet, reflective Trio before the shortened repetition of the Minuet.

IV. *Allegro spiritoso.* The finale theme suggests the Croatian folk song "Oj Jelena" and various London street cries, all of which were familiar to Haydn. The drone bass beneath the tune, according to the traditions of the day, gives further evidence of its folk origins. Haydn generously provides several motifs in the first and second groups of themes; he crafts them so carefully, though, that in the development section, he can play some of the tunes simultaneously. With great verve and energy, Haydn works through the various melodies in sonata allegro form, capping with majesty and triumph a most incredible composition—and career as a symphonist.

Paul Hindemith

Born November 16, 1895, in Hanau, Germany
Died December 28, 1963, in Frankfurt

A LEADING COMPOSER and music theorist, Hindemith also performed as soloist on the violin, viola, and piano and played dozens of other instruments very well. He conducted widely, exhibited an incredible facility and technical command of musical composition, and possessed an encyclopedic knowledge of all forms and periods of music.

The early works of Paul Hindemith, dating from the 1920s, reacted against the Romantic and Neoromantic styles popular at that time. But while some other composers reverted to the preceding Classical period for their source of inspiration, Hindemith went back even further, to the Baroque. His mostly abstract and nonprogrammatic music tends to be very linear and polyphonic, and often favors dance forms that date from the 17th and 18th centuries.

Born into a poor working-class family, Hindemith began studying violin at age seven and continued his composition studies at the Frankfurt Conservatory. At first, Hindemith's music reflected his sympathy with the artistic movement known as *Neue Sachlichkeit* (New Objectivity), a form of Neoclassicism, represented in art by the German painter Max Beckmann; it emphasized the use of shocking details in merciless clarity to demonstrate belief in an orderly universe. Later, Hindemith espoused *Gebrauchsmusik,* or "utilitarian music," as opposed to "music for music's sake." "A composer," he said, "should write today only if he knows for what purpose he is writing. The days of composing for the sake of composing are perhaps gone forever."

By 1934, Hindemith was completely out of favor with the ruling Nazis in Germany—he had married a Jewish woman and insisted on playing with Jewish musicians, he collaborated with the Communist playwright Bertolt Brecht, and his opera, *Mathis der Maler,* was taken as anti-Nazi agitation.

That year, the Nazis banned his music as degenerate, depraved, and of low moral character. Hindemith fled to Turkey, and then to the United States five years later, where he taught at Yale University from 1940 to 1953. While at Yale, he organized a *Collegium Musicum,* an association of musicians devoted to performing older music. The organization was partly responsible for the widespread revival of interest in early music. In 1953 Hindemith returned to Europe, where he died ten years later.

At least two of Hindemith's many orchestral scores have been accepted as true 20th century masterpieces—*Symphonic Metamorphosis of Themes by Carl Maria von Weber* and *Symphony, Mathis der Maler.* At first, they might sound acerbic and difficult, but these are works of great concentration and expressivity, crafted with amazing skill and confidence, which amply reward careful and repeated hearings.

Symphonic Metamorphosis of Themes by Carl Maria von Weber
(20 minutes)

In 1940, Hindemith and choreographer Léonide Massine were planning a ballet, and Hindemith prepared some sketches for a score based on themes he selected from music by Carl Maria von Weber (1786–1826). Eventually the project was forsaken, in part because Massine felt the melodies were "too personal" and in part because Hindemith found Salvador Dali's stage sets "quite simply stupid."

Three years later, Hindemith's publisher encouraged him to write a pleasing and colorful orchestral piece for American audiences. The practical Hindemith worked up the Weber sketches into *Symphonic Metamorphosis,* creating a four-movement work that approximates the structure of a symphony. Hindemith discovered the themes in obscure works by Weber and hinted that they were not of the very highest quality—which, he felt, gave him the freedom to expand, alter, and elaborate the original material.

I. *Allegro.* The composer based the first movement on the fourth of Weber's *Huit pièces,* Op. 60, for piano duet; it was marked *All' Ongarese*—"In Hungarian Style." In Hindemith's treatment the piece sounds sturdy and forthright, and displays exceptional handling of the orchestra to present a dazzling succession of brilliant tone colors.

II. *Turandot Scherzo: Moderato.* Weber's Overture to the incidental music for Schiller's play *Turandot* provided the source melody here. The original theme, which is derived from an old Chinese melody, permeates the entire movement with its strongly Asian flavor. Hindemith subjects the theme to eight variations of increasing intensity, which he interrupts for a fugal interlude featuring the various families of the orchestra, before the quiet conclusion.

III. *Andantino.* The simple, winsome theme of the slow movement comes from Weber's piano duet collection, *Pièces faciles,* Op. 3, Book 2, and is announced here by the clarinet and repeated by other winds. Another theme, not considerably different in character, introduces the central portion. A highly decorated flute repeat of the opening ends this charming interlude.

IV. *March.* The theme originates in the seventh of Weber's *Huit pièces,* Op. 60. In Hindemith's very able hands the movement becomes a stirring, exciting, and very rhythmic march.

Artur Rodzinski conducted the New York Philharmonic for the premiere of *Symphonic Metamorphosis* on January 24, 1944.

Symphony, Mathis der Maler
(30 minutes)

Hindemith created the *Symphony, Mathis der Maler* ("Matthias the Painter") in 1934 from his opera of the same name. He based the opera, which explores the role of the artist in society, on the life of the great German painter Matthias Grünewald (1460–1528). The opera is set in 1524, about nine years after Grünewald finished his very famous polyptych for St. Anthony's Church in Isenheim, Alsace. The panels, which are preserved in Colmar, show Grünewald to have been a religious mystic who created paintings of extraordinary power and emotional force.

In the opera, Grünewald, court painter for Cardinal Albrecht, sympathizes with the peasants' revolt and resigns his position to enlist in their struggle. Grünewald, however, seeing the peasants' own violence, is caught between their brutality and the tyranny of the nobles. He wanders into the forest, where he dreams that he has become St. Anthony. A figure in his dream states the central thesis of the opera: "Why hast thou forsaken thy fate? In denying art, thou hast betrayed the people." After considerable soul-searching, Grünewald finally returns to his workshop and his art.

The Nazis banned the opera performance because they believed that Hindemith's depiction of the Peasants' War was a call to revolt against the new order in Germany. They also felt that Grünewald symbolized those artists whose visions of a better world were antithetical to their goals. Since they issued the edict after Hindemith had created the *Symphony, Mathis der Maler,* the premiere of the orchestral composition was given without incident on March 12, 1934, by the Berlin Philharmonic under Wilhelm Furtwängler.

Hindemith based each section of the symphony on a panel from Grünewald's Isenheim altar.

I. *Angelic Concert.* This panel shows three angels, among many others, playing their instruments for the Christ child and Mary, who are surrounded by a large, luminous, yellow, orange, and red gloriole. The music of *Angelic Concert* functions as the overture to the opera. In the slow opening section, the trombones intone the hymn "Es sungen drei Engel" ("Three Angels Sang"). After this devotional introduction comes the three more earthy sections of the faster main part of the movement: a lively theme played by flutes and violins; a second, calmer and more lyrical melody for strings; and finally these two themes combined with the trombone hymn from the opening.

II. *The Entombment.* The predella, or footpiece, of the altar consists of a horizontal rectangle, showing John supporting the recumbent body of Christ, with Mary and Magdalene mourning in the background. Hindemith drew the music from the interlude before the last scene in which Mathis bids farewell both to art and to life itself. Of the two themes in this quiet, elegiac movement, the first is stated by the muted strings and woodwinds, the second by solo woodwinds over a pizzicato accompaniment in the strings.

III. *The Temptation of St. Anthony.* This vibrant painting shows the prostrate St. Anthony being attacked from all sides by demons, beasts, and hideous monsters. Hindemith associates the music with Grünewald's dream that he has become St. Anthony. The slow opening, with its unison string melody, free rhythms, and jarring interruptions, makes clear the saint's agony as he cries out: *"Ubi eras, bone Jesu, ubi eras, quare non affuisti ut sanares vulnera mea?"* ("Where wert Thou, good Jesus, where wert Thou; why wert Thou not present that Thou might healest my wounds?") In the following fast section the strings play the demons' melody, which is sung with the words *"Dein ärgster Feind stizt in der selbst"* ("Your greatest foe is found within"). The music then builds to a series of powerful climaxes, each one denoting a particular temptation assailing the saint. Finally, Hindemith introduces the hymn melody "Lauda Sion Salvatorem" ("Praise Thy Savior, O Zion"), and a mighty Hallelujah ends the work in divine spirituality.

Charles Ives

Born October 20, 1874, in Danbury, Connecticut
Died May 19, 1954, in New York City

A FEW IMPORTANT INFLUENCES shaped the music of Charles Ives.
One was the philosophical tenets of transcendentalism, a movement led
by such men as Ralph Waldo Emerson and Henry David Thoreau. The
philosophy held that even the most ordinary things are suffused with an
essential spirit, which is the only true reality, that there is a unity, a singleness, in all that exists, and that the human mind can comprehend much that
is beyond what is seen or experienced.

In his music, Ives sought to capture what he called the "substance," which
he defined as "the highest attributes, moral and spiritual, one sees in life."
His belief in transcendentalism led him to venture beyond the traditional
laws of musical composition to allow the music itself to determine its own
shape and form. It also allowed him to quote popular songs and seemingly
unrelated material in his works, bringing them together in a transcendental
unity. More often than not, his music is highly dissonant and difficult to
follow. But as he put it: "Beauty in music is too often confused with something that lets the ears lie back in an easy chair."

Another major influence on Charles Ives was his father, George, the youn-
gest bandmaster in the Union Army and later the bandleader in the small
New England town where Charles grew up. George gave his son a firm
grounding in the music of the past long before he went to Yale University,
where he was trained in 19th century German compositional practices. But
the highly unconventional George also had Charles singing "Swanee River"
in the key of E flat while he played the piano accompaniment in the key of C
and challenged him to notate in music everything from the sound of a sneeze
to a church congregation singing out of tune.

After graduation from Yale, though, Charles did not pursue a career in music, but entered the insurance business, founded his own firm in 1909, and became one of the most successful figures in the field; he inaugurated the concept of estate planning.

Ives composed primarily during his spare time—evenings, weekends, and during holidays and vacations. Nonetheless, in addition to four symphonies, Ives left a vast body of smaller orchestral compositions, chamber works, songs, and piano and organ solos. After going decades with few or no performances, more and more of his works are entering the repertoire: the 1974 centenary celebration of his birth attracted considerable attention to his music; the improved skill of modern performers enables them to master the technically difficult parts in his music; and audiences are finally catching up to the musical vision of one of America's most innovative and original composers.

Symphony No. 3, "The Camp Meeting"
(22 minutes)

A great musical iconoclast, Charles Ives disavowed much of 19th century European musical tradition and incorporated into his music such innovations as atonality, polytonality, polyrhythms, tone clusters, and thick, painful discords—elements that were not accepted by mainstream composers until decades after Ives's pioneering efforts.

The Third Symphony's subtitle, "The Camp Meeting," relates to important communal events that the composer fondly recalls from his New England youth. In keeping with the subject, he draws all the principal themes from well-known 19th century Protestant hymns by American composers. When Ives quotes other music, as he so frequently does, he selects excerpts that not only are musically interesting but also hold special associations and connotations for him. While to some the music may at times seem irreverent, the Third Symphony effectively conveys the composer's strong spiritual beliefs and his deep religious convictions.

I. *"Old Folks Gatherin' ": Andante maestoso.* The first movement of the Third Symphony had two previous incarnations—as the later-replaced opening movement of his First String Quartet and as a prelude he performed as organist at New York City's Central Presbyterian Church. Structurally the movement loosely follows traditional symphonic form: first theme, probably original; contrasting second theme (the hymn variously known as "Coronation," "All Hail the Power of Jesus' Name," or "O For a Thousand Tongues," by Oliver Holden [1765–1834?]); development rising to a climax and a pause; free recapitulation of the opening theme (over which the flute sings the hymn "What a Friend We Have in Jesus," by Charles Crozat Converse [1832–1918]).

II. *"Children's Day": Allegro.* The second movement evolved from the composer's *Children's Day Parade,* for string quartet and organ, which he later performed as a solo organ piece at the Central Presbyterian Church in 1902. Ives wanted the music "to represent the games which little children played while their elders listened to the Lord's word." For the "Lord's word" Ives uses Lowell Mason's (1792–1872) hymn "There Is a Fountain Filled with Blood," played by the violins at the very outset. Different commentators hear the lively middle section of the movement as a children's clapping game, a Civil War march, or a reworking of the Welsh song "All Through the Night." The movement ends with a brief, much altered return of the opening.

III. *"Communion": Largo.* The final movement may also have originated at church services for which Ives performed at the organ. The music seems to flow in a freely associative manner with two main themes—the first deriving from the initial theme of the first movement, the second from the hymn "Just As I Am, Without One Plea," by William Batchelder Bradbury (1816–68). Snatches and derivations of both themes precede their full statement late in the movement. The symphony then ends quietly with Ives's representation of "distant church bells" sounding over the orchestra.

Ives was not part of the musical establishment and was so far ahead of his time that the very accessible Symphony No. 3, completed in 1904, was not performed until 1946 (forty years later!). The work, played by the New York Little Symphony under Lou Harrison, won the 1947 Pulitzer Prize, and was finally recorded in 1950.

Three Places in New England
(20 minutes)

The title of this composition, *Three Places in New England,* also called *Orchestral Set No. 1,* suggests that this is an example of program music, music with extramusical associations. In his *Essays Before a Sonata,* Ives made a trenchant observation on program music: "Does the success of program music depend more upon the program than upon the music? If it does, what is the use of the music? If it does not, what is the use of the program?"

In *Three Places,* as well as other pieces, Ives quotes widely from the popular songs, dance tunes, and marches of the day, church hymns, with snippets of Beethoven or Brahms thrown in. Some of the sources appear quite trite, leading one to wonder why Ives includes them in serious symphonic compositions. The answer lies in Ives's transcendental beliefs, which hold that reality is but a symbol of the underlying essence of all things. Thus, everything is related, or as Emerson, the famous transcendentalist writer, said: "All things are One." Elsewhere, Emerson stated the view he held in common with Ives: "I embrace the common, I explore and sit at the feet of the familiar, the low."

I. *The "Saint Gaudens" in Boston Common (Col. Shaw and His Colored Regiment).* Ives began writing *Three Places* in 1908 with sketches for a march to honor Colonel Robert Gould Shaw and the 54th Massachusetts Volunteer Infantry, the first black regiment in the Union Army. Subsequently, he expanded the march into *The "Saint Gaudens" in Boston Common,* which refers to the commemorative bas-relief by Augustus Saint-Gaudens in front of the Massachusetts State House. To explicate the program, Ives wrote on the score an original poem that begins:

> Moving—Marching—Faces of Souls!
> Marked with generations of pain.
> Part-freers of a Destiny,
> Slowly, restlessly—swaying us on with you
> Towards other Freedom!

Instead of martial rhythms and triumphant sounds of battle, Ives uses slow, melancholy music to evoke war's suffering and sorrow. He borrows three melodies—"Old Black Joe," "Marching Through Georgia," and "The Battle Cry of Freedom"—from American folk music, but disguises them in an extremely slow and free treatment.

II. *Putnam's Camp, Redding, Connecticut.* In 1903 Ives composed two pieces, *Country Band March* and *Overture and March: 1776,* as incidental music to a play by his uncle Lyman Brewster. Nine years later he combined these two works into *Putnam's Camp,* to create the second part of *Three Places.* In addition to the original 1903 selections, Ives creates a dense, highly dissonant, but very exciting musical collage by including quotes from "Hail, Columbia," "The British Grenadiers," "The Arkansas Traveler," "Massa's in de Cold, Cold Ground," "The Star-Spangled Banner," "Yankee Doodle," and the Sousa marches "Liberty Bell" and "Semper Fidelis." At the end, Ives brings about the incredible illusion of two bands playing different marches at different speeds and in different keys!

III. *The Housatonic at Stockbridge.* The last movement, Ives wrote in the program, "was suggested by a Sunday morning walk that Mrs. Ives and I took near Stockbridge the summer after we were married. We walked in the meadows along the river and heard the distant singing from the church across the river. The mist had not entirely left the riverbed, and the colors, the running water, the banks and trees were something that one would always remember." Starting softly to capture the atmosphere of the morning mists, the music gradually builds until it reaches a climax and then grows still for a hushed, magical ending. On the score, the composer also copied Robert Underwood Johnson's poem "The Housatonic at Stockbridge," with the first line: "Contented river! in thy dreamy realm—."

Completed in 1914, *Three Places* called for a large orchestra. But when afforded an opportunity for a performance by a chamber orchestra, Ives rescored the work for a 24-piece orchestra. In that form the Boston Chamber Ensemble, led by Nicolas Slonimsky, premiered the work in New York on January 10, 1931. On February 9, 1974, John Mauceri and the Yale Symphony Orchestra in New Haven, Connecticut, gave the first performance of James Sinclair's reconstruction of the original orchestration.

The Unanswered Question
(6 minutes)

Even though it is only six minutes long, highly dissonant, metrically very free, and aleatoric in places, *The Unanswered Question* resonates strongly with modern audiences. The work is shaped like a highly compressed musical drama, with three protagonists: the strings, playing softly and implacably throughout, representing "The Silences of the Druids—Who Know, See, and Hear Nothing"; a solo trumpet, asking "The Perennial Question of Existence" seven times; and four flutes, searching for "The Invisible Answer," becoming "more active, faster and louder" with each response until the end, when they leave the trumpet's question unanswered.

Ives explains on the score that the notated entrances of the trumpet and flutes are only approximate, that they may be replaced by other instruments, and that the string body of the orchestra can be of any number from string quartet size up.

Composed in 1906 and revised in 1908, *The Unanswered Question* was not published until 1940.

Leoš Janáček

Born July 3, 1854, in Hochwald, Moravia (now Hukvaldy,
Czech Republic)
Died August 12, 1928, in Moravská Ostrava, Czech Republic

IN MODERN PARLANCE, Leoš Janáček would be described as a late
bloomer. Born to a schoolmaster/organist who gave the boy his first music
lessons, young Leoš went on to study at the Augustine Monastery in Brno,
the Organ School in Prague, and the conservatories in Leipzig and Vienna.
On his return to Brno, Janáček supported himself by teaching and conducting while continuing to compose; but he achieved little fame or recognition beyond local musical circles.

It was not until the 1918 revival of his opera *Jenufa,* written fifteen years
earlier, that the 65-year-old Janáček achieved his first international renown
as a composer. He followed this triumph with a succession of outstanding
compositions—four operas, *Kate Kavanová, The Cunning Little Vixen, The
Makropoulos Affair,* and *From the House of the Dead,* and several excellent
orchestral and chamber works, earning Janáček the same high regard as his
earlier Czech compatriots, Dvořák and Smetana.

Janáček imbued many of his compositions with the folk music and flavor
of his native Moravia, though he seldom borrowed specific rhythms or melodies. "The whole life of a man," he said, "is in folk music—body, soul,
environment, everything. He who grows out of folk music makes a whole
man of himself."

In addition, Janáček's music reflected his interest in the patterns and
inflections of human speech. Often, he would transcribe into musical nota-
tion the sound of people speaking, with the thought of adapting it in one of
his compositions. A particularly poignant instance came when he wrote out
the last words of his dying daughter, right up to her final sigh. "I do not play
about with empty melodies," Janáček said, "I dip them in life and nature."

Sinfonietta
(25 minutes)

Janáček started composing *Sinfonietta,* or "little symphony," his best-known orchestral work, late in 1925, completing it on April 1, 1926.

One can say that the story of its composition dates back to 1915, when Janáček—married and 61 years old—met Kamila Stösslová, the 23-year-old wife of a businessman. Taken with this passionate woman, so very different from his cold and aloof wife, Janáček invited Kamila to accompany him to an outdoor band concert. The band made a big impression on Janáček, especially when the brass section stood up to play its fanfares.

Later, remembering that performance, Janáček accepted a commission to compose fanfares for a gymnastics festival in Prague. Janáček was so pleased with the fanfares that he decided to use them as the basis for the first movement of an expanded composition, which he originally titled *Military Sinfonietta.* In a letter to a friend he wrote that the music expressed "the contemporary free man, his spiritual beauty and joy, his strength, courage, and determination to fight for victory." The composer dedicated the entire work to the Armed Forces of the newly created state of Czechoslovakia.

Whether the high spirits and optimism of the music grew from Janáček's patriotic fervor ("I am filled with the young spirit of our republic," he wrote) or from his love for Kamila ("How many treasured experiences we have had together! Like little flames, these will light up my soul and become the most beautiful melodies") we will never know.

When the score was published, the composer simplified the title to *Sinfonietta.* He also eliminated the five descriptive titles for the movements, which referred to events and places in the city of Brno. We include the titles below, however, to clarify the composer's intentions.

I. *Allegretto {Fanfares}.* The composer described the music as "the blare of victorious trumpets" celebrating the liberation of Brno from the Germans and "the gleam of liberty spread shining over the town." Janáček originally scored this brief movement for eleven trumpets, two tubas, and timpani, although he later arranged it for a conventional brass section.

II. *Andante; Allegretto {The Castle}.* The movement expresses the people's relief at no longer living in fear of imprisonment in the old castle's dungeons. As with all subsequent movements, this one consists of many short, freely repeated sections, each with its distinctive rhythm and melody. The folk flavor and human speech rhythms enhance the thoroughly upbeat and happy mood.

III. *Moderato {The Queen's Monastery}.* The music evokes the monas-

tery's "holy peace" in the "shadows of night." After a somber, lyrical beginning, the movement gains in force and brilliance as Janáček moves the
melodic burden from the strings to the brass instruments.

IV. *Allegretto {The Street}.* The composer repeats the opening trumpet
tune 14 times in the course of this movement, albeit in ever-new guises, with
different accompaniments, and with changing interludes between its appearances. The title refers to the people's independence and freedom to walk the
streets.

V. *Andante con moto; Allegretto {The Town Hall}.* Janáček described
the finale as "a vision of the growing greatness of the town." He gains the
effect by building throughout to a recapitulation of the opening fanfare
movement, this time gloriously sung out by the entire orchestra.

Václav Talich led the Czech Philharmonic in the premiere of *Sinfonietta* in
Prague on June 26, 1926.

Zoltán Kodály

Born December 16, 1882, in Kecskemét, Hungary
Died March 6, 1967, in Budapest

ZOLTÁN KODÁLY'S GIFT for music seemingly came from his very musical parents, who started him with violin and piano lessons at an early age. He soon turned to composing and had a work performed by a high school orchestra when he was only 14 years old.

It was while attending the University of Budapest that Kodály developed an intense interest in Hungarian folk music. He and fellow composer Béla Bartók traveled throughout Hungary tracking down, recording, transcribing, and codifying the largely unknown peasant music of their native land. Although the compositional styles of both composers were rooted in Hungarian folk idioms, Kodály was more inclined to incorporate actual folk melodies in his music.

In addition to his distinguished career as a composer, Kodály revolutionized music instruction in the Hungarian schools by devising a pedagogical system that emphasized choral singing as the simplest and most effective way to teach music. His output, which included considerable vocal music along with orchestral scores and works for individual instruments, made him a leading composer of the first half of the 20th century. While his fame was international, he was especially venerated by the Hungarian people, who showered him with innumerable prizes and awards.

Dances of Galánta
(18 minutes)

When Kodály was asked, in 1933, to write a work commemorating the 80th anniversary of the Budapest Philharmonic Society, he was eager to draw on the folk music of his native Hungary as a source of inspiration. He recalled the period from 1885 to 1892—he called them the happiest years of his childhood—that he spent in Galánta, which was then in western Hungary but is now part of the Czech Republic. An especially treasured memory was hearing a wonderful Gypsy band and the "orchestral sonority" they produced. Later, he came across a book of Hungarian and Gypsy songs from Galánta and was struck by the beauty of the melodies he found there.

Kodály was also very familiar with the *verbunkos,* the traditional Magyar dance. For about a century before Kodály's birth the *verbunkos* was commonly performed in Hungarian village squares by an army officer bedecked in his colorful uniform, a group of about twelve of his men, and the regimental Gypsy band. The young men who were attracted by the music and gathered around were then urged to enlist in the army.

The simple music of the *verbunkos* displayed clearly defined symmetrical phrases in duple meter and was harmonized by no more than one or two chords. Melodically, it was improvisatory in character, with frequent use of syncopation, elaborate ornamentation, and wide, angular leaps.

Combining the remembered sounds of the Gypsy orchestra, the melodies from the song collection, and the style of the *verbunkos,* Kodály composed his *Dances of Galánta.* The dances, which he divided into the customary slow and fast sections, are played without interruption. *Dances of Galánta* received its premiere performance on October 23, 1933, with the Budapest Philharmonic under Ernö Dohnányi.

An introductory cello theme is heard first and is repeated in variation until the clarinet starts the first, rather restrained dance *(Andante maestoso).* The pace quickens for the second dance *(Allegro moderato)* led by the flute. The flowing oboe melody of dance number three *(Allegretto con moto)* relaxes the tempo a bit. With the fourth dance *(Allegro)* the Gypsy temperament begins to flare up and reaches its climax in the final, high-speed dance *(Allegro vivace).* The coda starts with tentative reminiscences of the first dance, but this is quickly cast aside as the piece surges on to its vigorous conclusion.

Háry János Suite
(25 minutes)

Háry János, the subject of Kodály's eponymous opera buffa, was presumed to have been a real person who became the legendary liar, adventurer, and spinner of tall tales of Hungarian folklore. In the opera, set in 19th century Vienna, Háry concocts an imaginary account of how Napoleon's wife, Marie Louise, falls in love with him and implores him to join her in Paris. As a result, Napoleon declares war on Austria, but is single-handedly defeated by our hero. On Háry's triumphant return to Vienna, he realizes that he loves, not Marie Louise, but his childhood sweetheart, Orze. He marries Orze and at the opera's end is recounting his fanciful tale to a group of gullible peasants in the tavern when she arrives to escort him home.

The overwhelming success of the opera at its premiere in Budapest on October 16, 1926, led Kodály to extract an orchestral suite from the score's best pages. The *Háry János Suite,* with its evocative tone painting, received its first performance on December 15, 1927; Willem Mengelberg led the New York Philharmonic.

I. *Prelude: The Fairy Tale Begins.* Hungarian superstition holds that if someone sneezes before telling a story it means that the story is true. Accordingly, the *Háry János Suite* begins with a powerful orchestral sneeze, and then proceeds to conjure up the magical, make-believe world of the erstwhile Háry.

II. *Viennese Musical Clock.* Kodály gives us the setting: "The scene is laid in the Imperial Palace in Vienna, where the ingenious Hungarian peasant is amazed and enraptured by the famous Musical Clock with its little soldier figures in their brave uniforms appearing and disappearing at every rotation of the marvelous machinery."

III. *Song.* "Háry and his sweetheart are longing for their village home, its quiet evenings, musical with love songs." Kodály bases this section on an old Hungarian song, "This Side of the Tisza, Beyond the Danube," and makes use of the cimbalom, an instrument that resembles the hammered dulcimer.

IV. *The Battle and Defeat of Napoleon.* Háry leads the Hungarian army into battle against the French and defeats them all. Finally, he is face to face with Napoleon, who, "shaking in every limb, kneels before his conqueror and pleads for mercy."

V. *Intermezzo.* This movement derives from the *verbunkos,* the traditional Hungarian recruiting dance, and symbolizes Háry János' stalwart national spirit.

VI. *Entrance of the Emperor and His Court.* Kodály describes this movement as "an ironical march of triumph, in which Háry pictures the entrance of the emperor and the imperial court at Vienna." The composer caricatures the nobles by the mocking march melodies.

Franz Liszt

Born October 22, 1811, in Raiding, Hungary (now Austria)
Died July 31, 1886, in Bayreuth, Germany

AS A COMPOSER, conductor, and pianist, Franz Liszt was one of the great polymaths of music. His first outstanding achievements were as a pianist. Taking his cue from violin virtuoso Niccolò Paganini, he developed a number of striking onstage mannerisms, such as entering with white gloves, which he ceremoniously removed, and having two pianos onstage, which he used alternately so everyone could see his hands and to have a spare if his forceful playing style broke a string in one of the pianos. Offstage, many considered his succession of mistresses and frequent affairs scandalous and shocking.

Liszt's amazing technical prowess and deeply expressive playing, coupled with his titillating behavior, made him the venerated idol of the concertgoing public. Women swooned and grown men burst into tears at his performances. So many asked for locks of his hair that he kept a dog for the sole purpose of snipping off bits of its hair to send to his fans!

Along with attending to his heavy concert schedule, Liszt produced an incredible number of solo piano compositions, which he played at his many recital appearances. He stretched the boundaries of writing for the instrument, exploiting all possible sonorities and filling the music with sweeping scales, rapid changes of register, unusual divisions of the beat, extremes of tempo and dynamics, and dense chordal textures.

Liszt toured throughout Europe as a concert pianist until 1848, when, at the very pinnacle of his career, he settled down as court music director in Weimar. In Weimar he began composing for orchestra, producing two piano concertos, about a dozen tone poems, or symphonic poems (large-scale compositions based on a program or some extramusical association), and two symphonies.

His duties at Weimar also included conducting operas and orchestra concerts. The extremely high level of these performances made Weimar an important musical center and a forum for introducing the revolutionary new scores of Richard Wagner, Hector Berlioz, and others.

Then, in another abrupt change of lifestyle, Liszt left Weimar, moved to Rome, and, in 1865, was made an Abbé of the Catholic Church. He did not, though, give up his music; he conducted, performed as a pianist, taught, and continued composing, writing more works on religious themes.

Among Liszt's many compositions—he wrote about 1,300!—a good number remain extremely popular. Two works receive universal acclaim as true orchestral masterpieces—Piano Concerto No. 1 and *Les Préludes*.

Concerto for Piano and Orchestra No. 1 in E flat major
(18 minutes)

How fitting that Franz Liszt, the most celebrated virtuoso pianist of the 1800s, should have written one of the most brilliant and technically demanding piano concertos of all time! And just as his piano playing inflamed the blood and aroused the senses of his contemporaries, so the E-flat concerto thrills and enthralls today's audiences.

Liszt began work on the concerto, the first of two that he composed, in 1830, by jotting down the melody that was to become the principal theme of the work. Apparently he did not return to the melody during the following two decades because he was too busy pursuing his extraordinary performing career.

Liszt resumed work on the concerto in 1847, completing it two years later. Over the following years, he revised the work again and again as he strove to create a piece of "chamber music for orchestra." Finally, Liszt arranged for the premiere in Weimar on February 17, 1855, playing the solo part himself, with Hector Berlioz conducting the orchestra. Still not completely satisfied, Liszt made several more changes while readying the concerto for publication; a total of five versions reside in Weimar's Liszt archives.

The concerto departs in a few ways from the traditional style. Instead of three movements—fast, slow, fast—Piano Concerto No. 1 has four movements—fast, slow, scherzo, fast. Further, the composer directs that the four movements be performed without break, except for a brief pause at the end of the first movement. Instead of limiting the percussion section to timpani, Liszt assigns a prominent part to the triangle, which led critic Eduard Hanslick to give the work the derisive nickname "Triangle Concerto." (Apparently the triangle player at the first performance, unaccustomed to such prominence, had an attack of nerves so severe that he did not play another note after the first entrance!)

I. *Allegro maestoso, tempo giusto.* The concerto opens with the dramatic, highly charged principal motto theme played by unison strings and capped off by powerful wind chords. At the premiere, Liszt could be heard singing the words *"Das versteht ihr alle nicht"* ("This none of you understand") without providing any clue to the source of the mystery. This seven-note motto unifies the entire concerto; it appears repeatedly in various transformations— from compassionate and tender to light and skittish to ominous and threatening. Liszt also presents a lyrical contrasting theme as a foil to the puissant opening motif.

II. *Quasi adagio.* The slow movement opens with a rising, cantabile melody in the lower strings that is taken over by the solo piano. The Allegretto vivace movement follows without pause.

III. *Allegretto vivace.* This light, elfin movement, really a scherzo, introduces the triangle. Its high, tinkling tone adds to the movement's delicate, gossamer texture. A piano cadenza, based on the motto theme acts as a transition to the last movement.

IV. *Allegro marziale animato.* The music takes on a marchlike quality for the last part. Careful listening, though, reveals that Liszt presents no new thematic material until the very end, but rather reworks melodies heard before, infusing each with the propulsive power of a vigorous march. With the brilliant piano part leading the way, the music speeds along, placing ever more virtuosic demands on the soloist, and accelerating at the end to reach a stunning conclusion.

Les Préludes
(17 minutes)

In 1844 Liszt wrote a work for chorus with piano accompaniment entitled *The Four Elements: Earth, Wind, Oceans, Stars.* Four years later, he made extensive revisions in the piano introduction, arranged the work for orchestra, supplied a program, and gave the new composition the title *Les Préludes.* In this form, Liszt conducted the premiere in Weimar on February 28, 1854.

Liszt himself defined a program as "any preface in intelligible language added to a piece of instrumental music, by means of which the composer intends to direct attention to the poetical idea of the whole or a particular part of it." Despite its origin as the introduction to *The Four Elements,* Liszt drew the specific program for *Les Préludes* from a poem by the French Romantic poet Alphonse de Lamartine (1790–1869), found in his *Nouvelles Méditations poétiques.*

Lamartine's poem has four sections, dealing with love, destiny, war, and the beauties of the countryside. For his musical realization, Liszt kept love as the first part, substituted a storm for war, and made it second, followed by a pastoral section, and concluded with an upbeat march representing destiny.

Some five years after composing *Les Préludes,* when Liszt was preparing the score for publication, he added the written program, which is perhaps a more accurate description of the music than a paraphrase of Lamartine: "What is life but a series of preludes to that unknown song whose first solemn note is sounded by Death? Love is the enchanted dawn of every life, but what person is there whose first delights of happiness are not dissipated by some storm, a storm whose fatal blast dispels his youthful illusions, destroying his altar as though by a stroke of lightning? And what wounded soul, after the cruel storm, does not attempt to assuage its memories in the pleasant solitude of rural life? Nevertheless, man does not long allow himself the sweet quiet offered in Nature's bosom. When the trumpet sounds the alarm, he hurries to take up his post, no matter what struggle summons him, in order that in battle he may regain full confidence in himself and his powers."

The first three notes of the unison string melody at the start of *Les Préludes* establish a germinal motif that assumes overriding importance throughout the piece. The close affinity with the three-note phrase, *"Muss es sein?"* ("Must it be?"), with which Beethoven opens the final movement of his last String Quartet, Op. 135, leads one to speculate about its extramusical, as well as musical, significance. Beethoven first used the phrase as a joke, but later assigned it a much more profound meaning concerning the possibility of triumphing over death. Liszt's use of the theme puts him in excellent company; Wagner used the same three notes as the Fate motif in his *Ring of the Nibelungen* cycle of music dramas and César Franck made it the principal theme of his Symphony in D minor.

Although played without pause, *Les Préludes* has four sections. In the first part, referring to love, the germinal motif undergoes considerable transformation in mood, character, and individual notes, growing ever more noble and impassioned.

Suddenly, the music stops and the second division starts as the cellos play the motif—this time with mysterious and forbidding overtones. Liszt whips up a frightening musical storm, with howling winds, crashing thunder, and flashing lightning, but almost always keeps the three notes within earshot.

When the storm's fury subsides, the solo wind instruments introduce the naïve pastoral melody of the third section. Liszt reminds us of the opening by giving the violins a major theme from the first part.

As the strings speed up and down in brilliant scale passages, the brass exultantly start the final portion by proclaiming a variant of the three-note motif. Liszt brings back other themes until finally a variation of the original theme ends the piece in life-affirming splendor.

Gustav Mahler

Born July 7, 1860, in Kalischt, Bohemia (now Czech Republic)
Died May 18, 1911, in Vienna

MUCH OF MAHLER'S MUSIC reflects his lifelong struggle to understand the human soul and its place in the universe. For conductor
Bruno Walter, the composer once enumerated the subjects he was exploring
in his compositions: "Whence do we come? Whither does our road take us?
Have I really willed this life, as Schopenhauer thinks, before I was even
conceived? Why am I made to feel that I am free while yet I am constrained
within my character, as in a prison? What is the object of toil and sorrow?
How am I to understand the cruelty and malice in the creations of a kind
God? Will the meaning of life be finally revealed by death?"

Mahler completed nine symphonies and was working on a tenth at the
time of his death. Each is a large-scale work that includes every human
emotion, from sadness and resignation to joy and exultation. The scores call
for a giant orchestra, even though Mahler often used the large forces to
achieve light and delicate effects. In some cases, such as symphonies Nos. 2,
3, 4, and 8, he had human voices sing texts along with the orchestra. In other
pieces he left specific programs that adumbrated his ideas. And in still
others, he provided nothing beyond the highly expressive music, leaving it
to the listeners to fathom the music's meanings.

Mahler's involvement with music began at age three when his parents
gave him a tiny accordion, to be followed a few years later with piano lessons.
At 15, Gustav entered the Vienna Conservatory, where, despite a growing
interest in composing, he enrolled as a piano major.

To earn some money in the summer of 1880, Mahler accepted a conducting position in a small, provincial theater, which set him on a lifelong
career path that combined composing and conducting. As his conducting
career flourished, he advanced to major opera houses in Leipzig, Prague,

Budapest, and Hamburg. Finally he reached the very highest level of conducting success with appointments at the Vienna Opera and the Vienna Philharmonic, and at the Metropolitan Opera and the New York Philharmonic.

Due to his heavy performing schedule, Mahler did most of his composing during summer holidays and on short breaks between conducting assignments. While his music attracted a number of loyal and enthusiastic admirers, critical reactions mostly ranged from indifference to hostility. Only late in his life did Mahler come to enjoy wide acceptance and frequent performances.

After Mahler's death in 1911, interest in his music dropped off considerably. Then, during the 1950s and 1960s—spurred by the advocacy of conductors like Bruno Walter, a protégé and disciple of Mahler, and Leonard Bernstein, who was then Music Director of the New York Philharmonic—Mahler's music finally took its rightful place in the international concert repertoire, a preeminent position it has maintained ever since.

Das Lied von der Erde ("The Song of the Earth")
(60 minutes)

Mahler found the exotic, which included Asian art and philosophy, inspiring and stimulating. Around the turn of the century, Eastern culture became better known in Europe as a result of increased contact with the Far East and in particular through the exhibits of Asian art at the Paris Expositions of 1889 and 1900. In 1907 a number of ancient Chinese poems, translated into German by Hans Bethge under the title *The Chinese Flute,* came to Mahler's attention. Mahler adapted the Bethge translations of seven of these poems as the text for *Das Lied von der Erde.* Mahler called the work a "Symphony for tenor and contralto (or baritone) and orchestra," although it is not included among his nine completed symphonies.

Both the text and the music of *Das Lied von der Erde* project a profound pessimism. Perhaps the best summary of the overall mood comes from the refrain heard several times in the opening movement: "Dark is life, is death."

I. *The Drinking Song of Earthly Woe.* The text suggests the possibility of turning to wine to deal with the pain we endure in our short time on earth.

II. *The Lonely One in Autumn.* The poet/composer offers a lament in which, as the mists of autumn cover the land, he despairs of ever seeing the sun again.

III. *Of Youth.* A more optimistic movement describes a green pavilion set in a pond that reflects its upside-down image. Friends, drinking and chatting, fill the pavilion.

IV. *Of Beauty.* The cheerful mood continues as the text and music describe youthful maidens in a beautiful, enchanted landscape. Young men approach on horseback, calling forth "glances of yearning" from the most beautiful of the maidens.

V. *The Drunken One in Springtime.* The pathos returns as the poet/composer seeks surcease from a life that he feels is no more than a dream; his hope is to find peace in drunken sleep.

VI. *The Farewell.* Mahler combines two poems here, by far the longest of the six movements. In the first part the poet/composer longs for his friend with whom he wants to share the intoxicating beauties of nature as he awaits his demise. In the second part, which follows an extended orchestral interlude, the arriving friend speaks of wandering into the mountains in preparation for his death. Here the outlook is more Eastern, displaying faith in the continuing cycles of nature—"The dear Earth blossoms in the Spring and buds anew." The contralto ends the symphony repeating the word "Forever . . . forever . . ."

Mahler composed *Das Lied von der Erde* in the summer of 1908, when he was suffering with severe heart disease. The piece was premiered in Munich on November 20, 1911, six months after the composer's death, with Bruno Walter conducting and tenor William Miller and contralto Charles Cahier (the stage name of Sarah Jane Kayton-Walker).

Symphony No. 1 in D major, "Titan"
(60 minutes)

Around 1876 Mahler started work on a huge composition that he drew, in part, from earlier pieces for voice and for piano duet. After its completion in mid-1888, Mahler called his creation a Symphonic Poem in Two Parts, without any movement titles, and conducted its premiere with the Budapest Philharmonic on November 20, 1889.

Over the following years he gave titles to the movements, which he divided into two groups: Part I, From the Days of Youth, consisting of (1) Spring Without End, (2) Collection of Flowers, and (3) Under Full Sail; Part II, Human Comedy, including (4) Funeral March in the Manner of Callot [Jacques Callot was a famous etcher of grotesque figures] and (5) From the Inferno to Paradise. Later he removed the titles, eliminated the Collection of Flowers movement, renamed the work Symphony in D, and added the subtitle "Titan" (after a favorite novel by Jean Paul). Some conductors include the

Collection of Flowers movement, which was lost until 1959, though most feel Mahler was wise in discarding it.

I. *Langsam, schleppend.* This movement conjures up a forest scene with sparkling sunlight and the various sounds of nature. The melody that emerges in the cellos comes from Mahler's song "Ging heut' morgen über Feld" ("I Crossed the Meadow at Morn"). The composer introduces many other motifs, which he combines and treats canonically, building up to a stunning climax and leading to the abrupt timpani ending.

II. *Kräftig bewegt, doch nicht zu schnell.* Mahler builds this scherzo movement of three separate parts. First is a ländler, a heavy-footed Austrian peasant dance, which the orchestra plays over a bass ostinato figure that Mahler took from his song "Hans und Grete." The motif starts with the same descending interval (a fourth) that opened the symphony and that initiated the main theme of the first movement. He completely changes the character for the middle section, which is a tender and languorous waltz. He makes the last part a much abbreviated recall of the opening.

III. *Feierlich und gemessen, ohne zu schleppen.* The ghostly sound of a single double bass playing a distorted, minor-key "Frère Jacques" provides the funeral march theme of the slow movement. Twice the composer interrupts the funeral march—first with a parody of a Hassidic-sounding song and then with an eloquent quotation from another Mahler song.

IV. *Stürmish bewegt.* Without pause, a terrifying shriek opens the massive last movement, full of excitement, dramatic contrasts, and many quotations from earlier movements. The music evokes a fearsome struggle with death, and a triumphant ending in which the nature sounds from the first movement return to celebrate the victory of the life force.

Symphony No. 2 in C minor, "Resurrection"
(90 minutes)

Mahler proclaimed the vast scope of his monumental Second Symphony, among the most overwhelming of all symphonic creations, with these words: "The greatest problems of humanity, those which I have evoked and attempted to solve in the *Second* [are]: Why do we exist? Do we continue to exist after death?"

It took Mahler over six years, from 1888 to 1894, to complete his mighty Second Symphony. He composed each movement separately, taking particularly long breaks between the first and second and the fourth and fifth movements. Careful hearing cannot fail to move and thrill every listener.

I. *Allegro maestoso.* Mahler composed this section in 1888 as a 20-minute symphonic poem entitled *Totenfeier* ("Funeral Rites"). He described the program: "We are standing beside the coffin of a man beloved. [In some of his writings, Mahler identifies the man as the hero of the First Symphony.] For the last time, his battles, his suffering, and his purpose pass before the mind's eye." When Mahler played *Totenfeier* on the piano for the eminent conductor Hans von Bülow, his response was: "If that is still music then I do not understand a single thing about music." This stinging rebuke from a man he idolized, compounded by the difficulty of finding music to follow the epic *Allegro maestoso,* led to a hiatus of about five years before Mahler attempted the second movement.

II. *Andante moderato.* The tender, waltzlike principal theme sets the character for the gentle and lyrical second movement. This movement forms such a striking contrast with the power and epic sweep of the opening movement that Mahler eventually directed that the conductor pause at least five minutes between the first and second movements. He writes that the Andante represents the thoughts that come to mind following the funeral of a loved one: "A memory of a blissful moment in the dear departed's life and a sad recollection of his youth and lost innocence—a shaft of sunlight from out of the life of this hero."

III. *In ruhig fliessender Bewegung.* This scherzo, with its peasantlike charm overlaid with grotesque caricature, seems out of character with the rest of this exalted and spiritual symphony. Musically, it is Mahler's adaptation of his cynical, satirical song "St. Anthony of Padua's Sermon to the Fishes," in which St. Anthony, finding the church empty, preaches to the fish, who ignore his message: ". . . the pike were still thieves, the eels were still lovers, the crabs still went backwards . . ." and so on. According to Mahler, when you have awakened from the dream of the second movement "and have to return to the confusion of life, it can easily happen that this ever-moving, never-resting, never-comprehensible bustle of existence becomes horrible to you."

IV. *"Urlicht": Sehr feierlich, aber schlicht.* Mahler wrote the song "Urlicht" ("Primal Light") without any thought of using it in the symphony. Only later did he decide to orchestrate and use it as the symphony's fourth movement, where it functions as the introduction to the finale. A short, simple movement, "Urlicht" features the contralto and an offstage band of trumpets, horns, and bassoons. "In 'Urlicht,' " Mahler writes, "the questions and struggles of the human soul for God, as well as its own divine nature and existence, come to the forefront. After these terrifying questions comes the answer: redemption."

V. *Im Tempo des Scherzos.* After completing four movements, Mahler still had not found the answers to the imposing questions that gave birth to the symphony. He described his frustration in a letter: "Whenever I plan a large musical structure, I always come to a point where I have to resort to 'the word' as a vehicle for my musical idea." He searched "through the whole world of literature, including the Bible," and could not find the words to express his thoughts and feelings. "Then Bülow died and I went to the memorial service. The mood in which I sat and pondered on the departed was utterly in the spirit of what I was working on at the time. Then the choir, up in the organ loft, intoned Klopstock's [German poet Friedrich Gottlieb Klopstock, 1724–1803] *Resurrection* chorale. It flashed on me like lightning, and everything became plain and clear in my mind! What I then experienced I had to shape into tones."

Apparently, Mahler rushed to his rooms and began to compose the climactic last movement to Klopstock's words. As Mahler said, the finale "is 'the voice of him that crieth in the wilderness.' The end of all living things has come. The last judgment is announced and the ultimate terror of this Day of Days has arrived. The earth quakes, the graves burst open, the dead arise and stride hither in endless procession. The 'Great Summons' resounds; the trumpets of the apocalypse call. Softly there sounds a choir of saints and heavenly creatures: 'Rise again, yes, thou shalt rise again.' And the glory of God appears."

Starting quite late in the movement, the chorus and soprano and contralto soloists enter, and the music builds to one of the most electrifying climaxes in the entire symphonic repertoire—the affirmation of resurrection in the widest possible sense, the revival of humankind and of life itself.

Mahler completed the "Resurrection" Symphony on December 18, 1894, and conducted the premiere in Berlin on December 13, 1895.

Symphony No. 3 in D minor
(100 minutes)

When Mahler was nearing the completion of his Third Symphony, he wrote to a friend: "My Symphony will be something the world has never heard before! In it Nature acquires a voice and tells secrets so profound that they are perhaps glimpsed only in dreams!" On another occasion he explained that for him nature "includes all that is terrifying, great and also lovely . . . it is precisely this that I wanted to express in the whole work. . . . I always feel it strange that when most people speak of 'Nature' what they mean is flowers, little birds, the scent of the pinewoods, etc. No one knows the god Dionysus, or great Pan."

Mahler created a program, or rather several programs, for the Third Symphony, although he suppressed them all before publication. While involved in the composition, which lasted from 1893 to 1896, he subtitled it in turn "The Happy Life," "A Summer Night's Dream," and "My Joyful Science." On completing the work in August 1896, at the holiday village of Steinbach, near Salzburg, Mahler also prepared subtitles for each movement (shown in brackets below), which he also later withdrew.

The composer conducted the premiere in the small German city of Krefeld on June 9, 1902.

The symphony contains six movements, which are organized into two groups.

Part 1

I. *Kräftig. Entschieden.* [Introduction: The awakening of Pan; Summer marches in (Procession of Bacchus).] Of the first movement, which was the last composed and is by far the longest, Mahler said: "It is hardly music anymore, just the voice of nature," and it does indeed bring to mind the rebirth of life with the ending of winter. Majestic in conception and rich in musical ideas, the *Kräftig* starts with a solemn theme, not unlike the main theme of Brahms's First Symphony finale. Mahler called the theme *Weckruf,* or "reveille," and has it boldly stated by eight French horns in unison, following with a dirgelike melody in the woodwinds and piercing trumpet interruptions. The composer then reveals an abundance of melodic material, which he elaborates and develops. Before the return of the opening flourish, an avalanche of sound jubilantly proclaims that "summer is victorious among the divergent forces of nature."

Part 2

II. *Tempo di menuetto. Sehr mässig.* [What the flowers of the meadow tell me.] Mahler describes this movement as "the most carefree piece I have ever written. It is carefree as only flowers can be. Everything hovers in the air with grace and lightness, like flowers bending on their stems and being caressed by the wind." Very delicately orchestrated, this minuet movement —ländler might be more apt—begins with an oboe solo accompanied by pizzicato strings. At one point Mahler breaks the serene mood and the music becomes dark and pleading, but he sustains the intimate character throughout.

III. *Commodo. Scherzando. Ohne Hast.* [What the animals in the forest tell us.] The third movement follows the traditional three-part scherzo form. The first part features the sounds of the nightingale and cuckoo. After this we hear an approaching mail coach, with the ringing call of the post horn. A return of the forest sounds is announced by a brilliant trumpet fanfare.

IV. *Sehr langsam. Misterioso.* [What man tells me.] An alto soloist singing Mahler's setting of the brief "Midnight Song" from Nietzsche's *Thus Spake Zarathustra* makes up the fourth movement. A sustained low bass pedal point through much of this section lends emphasis to Nietzsche's repeated use of the word *tief* ("deep"), and adds to the power of the emotional expression.

V. *Lustig im Tempo und keck im Ausdruck.* [What the angels tell me.] Following without pause, the fifth movement gives a musical setting of a poem from the medieval German collection of folk poetry, *Des Knaben Wunderhorn* ("The Boy's Magic Horn"). This movement, which tells of Jesus forgiving Peter's sins, calls for alto soloist and boys' and women's choirs. The boys start by imitating the chiming of bells, succeeded by the women singing a sweet, almost naïve, song. The violins and timpani are notably absent from the orchestral writing.

VI. *Langsam. Ruhevoll. Empfunden.* [What love tells me.] Mahler wrote the finale, which also follows without break, for orchestra alone. Many consider it the high point of the symphony and one of the most sublime musical utterances ever penned by man. Starting with a simple, serene, almost reverential melody in the violins, the movement builds, through a series of glowing climaxes, to a glorious, resplendent apotheosis. In Mahler's words: "I could almost call the movement 'What God tells me,' in the sense that God can only be understood as love."

Symphony No. 4 in G major
(55 minutes)

Mahler's Fourth, the most charming and ingratiating of his nine completed symphonies, represents no monumental outpourings, no profound wrestling with deep philosophical questions, no cosmic conceptions. Instead, Mahler gives us an unpretentious, relaxed work, moderate in length and modest in orchestral size, requiring neither trombones nor tuba.

The genesis of the Fourth Symphony dates back to 1892, when Mahler set the poem "Der Himmel hängt voll Geigen" ("Heaven is Hung with Fiddles"), from *Des Knaben Wunderhorn* ("The Boy's Magic Horn"), a collection of medieval German folk poetry that inspired several of Mahler's compositions. He originally planned to use the song as the seventh movement of his Third Symphony, calling it "What the child tells me." When he decided against that, he chose instead to make it the final movement of a new symphony, the Fourth.

On holiday during the summer of 1899, Mahler began writing the three movements that would precede the already composed finale. He found little time for composing during the following season when he was fully occupied as conductor of both the Vienna Opera and the Vienna Philharmonic. But he returned to work the following summer on vacation in Maiernigg, where he finished the symphony on August 5, 1900.

Mahler was very ambivalent about supplying a pictorial or poetic program for his Fourth Symphony. "I know the most wonderful names for the movements, but I will not betray them to the rabble of critics and listeners so they can subject them to banal misunderstandings and distortions," he said at the premiere. At a New York performance he conducted in 1910, the program bore the message: "In deference to Mr. Mahler's wishes, there shall be no attempt at an analysis or description here of the symphony."

Yet in his letters and other writings, Mahler indicated many specific images and ideas in the music. According to Willi Reich, editor of Mahler's letters, the composer summed up the symphony this way: "In the first three movements there reigns the serenity of a higher realm, a realm strange to us, oddly frightening, even terrifying. In the finale the child, which in its previous existence already belonged to this higher realm, tells us what it all means."

Mahler himself conducted the first performance in Munich on November 25, 1901. He subsequently revised the score several times and introduced the final version with the New York Philharmonic on January 17, 1911.

I. *Bedächtig, nicht eilen.* The gracious first movement is warmly light-hearted. After a brief introduction of chirping flutes and sleigh bells, Mahler delights us with a wealth of beautiful melody, at once expressive, inviting, and beguiling, which he organizes into a free sonata allegro form, using the tinkling bells as a bridge between sections.

II. *In gemächlicher Bewegung. Ohne Hast.* Mahler had originally entitled the second movement, a scherzo, *"Freund Hein spielt auf,"* a reference to the "skeletal figure of death" and the "mistuned fiddle" he played as he led departing souls to the great beyond. The orchestra's concertmaster plays the *Freund Hein* fiddle melody. Since it is written to be played on a violin tuned one step higher, the performer often has two instruments—one with the raised pitches, one in ordinary tuning. For the rest of the movement, the macabre scherzo melody alternates with a merry ländler tune.

III. *Ruhevoll.* Mahler left two descriptions of the slow movement: One tells of a vision of "church sepulchers showing a recumbent stone image of the deceased with the arms crossed in eternal sleep"; the other identifies it with "my mother's infinitely sad face, as though she were laughing through her tears." In form, the *Ruhevoll* is a rather regular set of "real and fully developed variations" on two different themes—one, the slow ascending scalelike melody with which the movement opens; the other, a beautiful undulating strain given out, with many slides between notes, by the violins.

IV. *Sehr behaglich.* The final movement, a song for soprano that Mahler had composed earlier, projects a simple innocence that masks the intuitive wisdom of childhood. The words concern a child's wonderfully fresh, ingenuous vision of paradise. Echoes of the chirping sounds from the first movement separate some of the stanzas.

Symphony No. 5 in C sharp minor
(70 minutes)

A "holiday" composer, Mahler began the Fifth Symphony during the summer of 1901 at his vacation home at Maiernigg on Lake Wörth and completed it there the following summer.

The Fifth Symphony is unique in a few ways: It was the first of his symphonies that did not add voices—as in symphonies Nos. 2, 3, and 4—and that did not quote songs extensively—as in Symphony No. 1. It was the first symphony completely divorced from any program; as he said to conductor Bruno Walter: "Not a single note points to the influence of extramusical thoughts or emotions upon the composition of the Fifth." And it was the first symphony that Mahler conceived directly for orchestra, instead of working at the piano and then orchestrating the piano score. Musically, it made the most extensive use of polyphony, combining what seem to be extremely disparate melodies; it also extended the range of instruments to obtain special tonal effects; and it included minute and exact stylistic and dynamic directions for the performers.

Mahler divides the five movements of this symphony into three parts: Part 1 contains the first two movements, which the composer unifies by giving them shared melodic material. The Scherzo stands alone in Part 2. And Part 3 contains the final two movements, starting with the brief Adagietto, which serves essentially as an introduction to the Finale.

I. *Trauermarsch.* The Funeral March starts with a stern triplet fanfare, a summons that Mahler expands into the shuddering, quaking first theme, which quickly leads to the subsidiary subject, a dark, forlorn violin melody. In the midst of working through these two themes, Mahler interjects a section that seemingly represents a cry of pain or impassioned despair. As this outburst subsides, he brings back the triplet and violin themes to end the movement.

II. *Stürmisch bewegt.* The stormy second movement grows out of the first: The first theme is melodically related to the middle episode of the previous movement and the second theme here has ties to the second theme of the *Trauermarsch.* Mahler organizes these subjects in somewhat traditional sonata allegro form.

III. *Scherzo: Kräftig, nicht zu schnell.* This movement includes a series of waltzlike dance melodies that, in general, lean more toward Richard Strauss than Johann Strauss. Although the temperament generally ranges from gay to languid, Mahler does present a few serious and a few fiery moments. We hear a prominent solo horn or trumpet throughout the movement, which helps to unify the profusion of dance tunes that Mahler presents.

IV. *Adagietto: Sehr langsam.* By far the best-known movement of all the Mahler symphonies, the Adagietto is frequently performed by itself at solemn occasions. Played by a reduced orchestra of strings and harp, the movement seems suspended in time and space and is amazingly successful in touching listeners with the depth of its emotional appeal.

V. *Rondo Finale: Allegro giocoso.* With this movement, which follows the Adagietto without pause, Mahler completes with joy and vitality the journey that started in despair and despondency. While loosely following the structure of a rondo, Mahler makes this movement a virtuosic display of polyphonic writing, including a stunning triple fugue. The movement and symphony end with a mighty, climactic chorale.

Mahler led the first performance in Cologne on October 18, 1904, where it had the subtitle "The Giant," which conductors seldom use for modern performances. The composer made extensive revisions over the following years.

Symphony No. 6 in A minor
(88 minutes)

Mahler originally subtitled his Sixth Symphony "Tragic," but dropped that sobriquet soon after the premiere. Nevertheless, the Sixth is definitely a dark, brooding work. Surprisingly enough, Mahler composed the work at a time of great personal happiness, during the summers of 1903 and 1904, at his vacation home on Lake Wörth. Mahler had married Alma Schindler, whom he idolized, had one child with another on the way, realized that his music was gaining wider acceptance, and occupied possibly the most prestigious musical post in Europe as the highly successful Director of the Vienna Opera.

Despite the apparent dichotomy between the musical content of the symphony and his happiness at the time, Mahler had a foreboding of impending tragedy. In fact, the following year he suffered three devastating blows: his firstborn daughter died of scarlet fever complicated by diphtheria; he was forced to resign from the Vienna Opera due to the machinations and politics at that institution; and he learned that he had a serious heart condition.

Alma once commented on the Sixth Symphony: "None of his works came as directly from his innermost heart as this one." Evidence of its meaningfulness to Mahler is the great fear and trepidation with which he approached the premiere, and how, after the performance, in Essen on May 27, 1906, he returned to the dressing room sobbing uncontrollably.

I. *Allegro energico ma non troppo: Heftig aber markig.* The movement opens with a grimly striding march that the composer expands to some length before allowing it to fade away. Two timpani viciously hammer out a harsh rhythmic figure—the tragic motto—beneath the trumpets' loud major chord and its resolution into a soft minor chord. After some while Mahler introduces a soaring, passionate melody in the first violins. He describes this as a musical portrait of Alma. The rest of the movement involves the subjects that have already been introduced, including the sound of cowbells, before ending with a proud restatement of the Alma melody.

II. *Scherzo: Wuchtig.* Mahler had trouble deciding where to place the Scherzo: at first he made it the second movement, then changed it to third, and finally returned it to second. Today, some conductors prefer to set it third, following the Andante moderato. The movement begins with a furious opening theme, which Mahler derived from the march of the first movement; many of the melodies have a childlike innocence, but they are made bizarre and monstrous by their treatment. Alma refers to the middle section as "unrhythmic games of children," and says of the ending: "Ominously the childish voices became more and more tragic, and at the end died out in a whimper."

III. *Andante moderato.* After the first movement's dramatic intensity and the garishness of the second, we welcome the warm quiet of the third movement, though it does build to a climax of overwhelming strength. Other than sounding the cowbells again, Mahler makes no overt connection to any other movement. He structures the Andante around two cantabile themes—the first stated by the violins at the outset and the second following immediately in the English horn.

IV. *Allegro moderato.* Alma Mahler wrote that in the last movement Mahler "describes himself and his downfall or, as he later said, that of his hero, 'the hero who undergoes three strokes of destiny, the third of which fells him like a tree.' " A bold, assertive violin theme starts this gargantuan movement, but soon gets interrupted by the first of the several reappearances of the tragic motif from the first movement. Mahler introduces other themes, and at three climactic moments in the course of working out these themes calls for great hammer blows—the first loudest, the second weaker, and the third softest. When he revised the symphony for the last time, Mahler omitted the final crash, leaving only two. The symphony ends as a dirge, fading into silence.

Symphony No. 7 in E minor
(80 minutes)

The summer holiday seasons of 1904 and 1905 afforded Mahler the time he needed to complete the bulk of the work on his Seventh Symphony. In his little composing cottage on the grounds of his vacation home in Maiernigg on Lake Wörth, Mahler created this incredible composition.

The symphony has five movements, with movements two and four titled *Nachtmusik*, literally "night music" or serenade. These two, along with movement three, a scherzo, constitute a discrete unit within the symphony. According to his wife, Alma, Mahler composed the two serenades in the summer of 1904, while under the spell of Joseph von Eichendorff (1788–1857), the German Romantic poet, who was best known for his mystical and mysterious interpretations of the natural world.

I. *Langsam; Allegro con fuoco.* Mahler assigned the spiky main theme of the slow introduction to a tenor horn, more commonly known today as a baritone horn. The character here, and throughout the movement, is marchlike, albeit with several lyrical or even sentimental interludes. The movement ends with an exultant, full-voiced recall of themes heard earlier.

II. *Nachtmusik: Allegro moderato.* The dialogue for two French horns and birdcalls in the woodwinds open this movement and lead to the principal theme, which the French horns solemnly sound. This melody, along with subsidiary subjects and reminders of themes from the first movement, dominates the movement. One can only marvel at the amazing range of emotions and moods that Mahler conjures up with this comparatively simple little tune.

III. *Schattenhaft: Fliessend aber nicht schnell.* Mahler disciple Bruno Walter called this movement "a spooklike, nocturnal piece." A drum heartbeat starts the movement and wisps of melody become the accompaniment to a lugubrious theme in the flutes and oboes. Mahler brings in other melodies, many reminiscent of dance-hall music, but interwoven into the eerie, shadowy, grotesque orchestral fabric. Near the end of the movement, Mahler calls for a "wild" character as the music rises in demonic intensity to the single timpani stroke that unexpectedly brings it all to a sudden halt.

IV. *Nachtmusik: Andante amoroso.* Here Mahler introduces two instruments closely associated with serenades—the mandolin and guitar. Mahler builds this music up out of short motivic fragments rather than fully realized themes. In keeping with the restricted dynamic range of these instruments, he maintains a delicate, intimate texture, saving the forceful climax until near the end.

V. *Rondo Finale: Allegro ordinario.* The timpani solo and fanfares that open the Finale immediately banish the shades of night that permeated the three previous movements and introduce the glorious principal theme given out by the brass. Paying obeisance to rondo form, Mahler brings this theme back several times, each time varied and coupled with another contrasting interlude. The climax comes at the end of the movement as Mahler combines and juxtaposes themes from this and earlier movements into an extremely jubilant ending, probably the most affirmative of any Mahler symphony.

Symphony No. 8 in E flat major, "Symphony of a Thousand"
(85 minutes)

Mahler initially intended the Eighth Symphony to have four movements— starting and ending with choral movements, with two orchestral movements in between—which evolved into a two-movement, entirely choral composition. For the text he used two widely different approaches to the subject of inspiration and the human spirit. The first was the Latin hymn "Veni, Creator Spiritus" ("Come, Creative Spirit"), which Mahler described as "a song of yearning, of rapturous devotion in invocation of the creative spirit, the love that moves the worlds." Written in the 9th century by Hrabanus Magnentius Maurus, Bishop of Mainz, "Veni, Creator Spiritus" traditionally belongs to the Pentecost or Whitsun liturgy, marking the Holy Spirit's descent to the apostles.

The composer found the second text in the final scene of the second part of Goethe's *Faust* (Act V, Scene 7). Here, the creative spark exists in love, as symbolized by woman, instead of God or the Holy Ghost, as in "Veni, Creator Spiritus." Mahler wrote in a letter to his wife, Alma: "The essence of it is really Goethe's idea that all love is generative, creative, and that there is a physical and spiritual generation that is the emanation of this 'Eros.' You have it in the last scene of *Faust,* presented symbolically."

Mahler completed the symphony in just eight weeks in the summer of 1906, finishing the orchestration the following year, and did not subsequently change and revise it as he did his earlier symphonies. To achieve his vision of the Eighth Symphony, Mahler required tremendous performing forces. Aware that his Eighth Symphony was not only monumental in size but also a most outstanding artistic creation, Mahler wrote conductor Willem Mengelberg a month before the premiere: "I have just finished my Eighth! It will be something the world has never heard the likes of before. All nature is endowed with a voice in it. It is the biggest thing I have done so far. Imagine the universe beginning to ring and resound. It is no longer human voices. It is planets and suns revolving in their orbits. All my other symphonies are but preludes to this one."

A good performance of Mahler's Eighth convinces most listeners that the composer did not exaggerate in his description of the work. The hour and a half spent with this amazing composition can be among the most thrilling and stirring of musical experiences.

For the premiere in Munich on September 12, 1910, which he conducted, Mahler used over 1,000 performers: an enlarged orchestra of 171, 850 choristers in two mixed choruses, a children's chorus of 350, and 8 vocal soloists. Impresario Emil Gutmann advertised the work as the "Symphony of a Thousand," a subtitle that has stuck to the work, despite Mahler's objection to the "Barnum & Bailey" atmosphere that the publicity engendered. The first performance scored an immense success and the composer/conductor was afforded a thirty-minute ovation at its conclusion.

I. *Veni, Creator Spiritus: Allegro impetuoso.* While carrying the symphonic form to its ultimate dimension in his Eighth Symphony, Mahler stayed connected to the past by casting the first movement in traditional symphonic first-movement form: theme, contrasting theme, development of the two themes, and restatement of the two themes. The two mixed choruses join together to open the symphony with a powerful statement of the principal theme. After briefly expanding the melody, Mahler uses a soprano soloist to introduce the quiet, lyrical second subject with the words *"Imple superna gratia."* He follows the exposition of the two themes with an extended far-ranging development section that reaches its climax with an impressive double fugue, followed by a brief recapitulation of the two melodies.

II. *Final Scene, Goethe's Faust, Part II: Poco adagio; Allegro appassionato.* The much longer second part falls into three sections, corresponding to the slow movement, scherzo, and finale of a traditional symphony. It opens with the longest orchestral interlude in the symphony, which Mahler based largely on themes that had been introduced in the first part. He then brings in the voices of anchorites echoing in the mountain gorges, followed by the solo voices of Pater Ecstaticus (baritone), Pater Profundus (bass), and the chorus of angels (women's voices).

The "Blessed Boys" singing "Hände verschlinget" open the second part. The final section comes at the conclusion of Dr. Marianus' song. The violins state the slow beginning theme over a murmured harp accompaniment. Mahler follows this with the chorus of penitents and various solos and choral numbers. At the end the thrilling "Chorus Mysticus" brings the symphony to its glorious, celebratory conclusion.

Symphony No. 9 in D major
(85 minutes)

The years from 1908 to 1910 were very difficult ones for Mahler. Simultaneously he held two extremely demanding and exhausting positions—principal conductor of the Metropolitan Opera *and* Music Director of the New York Philharmonic. And while ill health was sapping him of his once considerable vitality and drive, he was composing his Ninth Symphony, his last completed work in that form. The composer worked desperately hard to finish the work while his strength endured.

Strongly aware that his end was near, he conceived the symphony as a farewell, or rather two farewells. On a personal level Mahler bid adieu to life itself and to his wife, Alma. In a bigger sense, he took leave of the 19th century, the Romantic century in music, and the social and artistic stability it represented.

In the first movement, Mahler depicts death with bitterness; it frees one from the pain of life, but it also takes the departed into a frightening new realm. The second movement casts a nostalgic look at death as the legendary skeletal fiddler. Death in the third movement emerges as the enemy against whom we all must contend. Then the final movement suggests the spiritual dimensions of death.

Completed on April 1, 1910, the Ninth Symphony received its first performance under Bruno Walter in Vienna on June 26, 1912, a little more than a year after the composer's death.

I. *Andante commodo.* Bruno Walter, the conductor and disciple of Mahler, describes this movement as "tragically moving . . . [a] noble paraphrase of the farewell feeling." The second violins present the first theme, characterized by its two-note descending sighs. Later Mahler extends this figure to three notes that are virtually identical to the three-note *Lebewohl* ("Farewell") motto of Beethoven's "Les Adieux" Piano Sonata, Op. 81A. (The resemblance to "Three Blind Mice" is completely coincidental!) After the calm resignation of this melody, Mahler offers other important themes—one scholar has counted eight major themes, some railing furiously, others intensely powerful and singing. The movement ends as repetitions of the two-note sighs fade away into silence.

II. *Im Tempo eines gemächlichen Ländlers.* The surface gaiety of this scherzo movement, with its charming ländler tune, masks a tragically macabre undertone that runs throughout. While the melodies themselves are most attractive and appealing, Mahler clothes them in distorting orchestral settings. The opening clarinet melody, curiously enough, is little more than the three-note farewell motto in a completely different rhythm.

III. *Rondo. Burleske: Allegro assai.* Really another scherzo, this predominantly brutal and stormy movement also includes some sweet and sentimental episodes. Near the end, Mahler displays his amazing skill as a contrapuntalist by brilliantly combining a number of separate themes.

IV. *Adagio.* All that has come before is put aside for the last movement, which carries us into the sphere of the divine and spiritual. Mahler illuminates its peacefulness and serenity with a glow that banishes trivial and mundane cares and replaces them with the contemplation of the loftiest thoughts of which humans are capable.

Felix Mendelssohn

Born February 3, 1809, in Hamburg
Died November 4, 1847, in Leipzig

FELIX MENDELSSOHN-BARTHOLDY, to use his full name, was the son of a wealthy banker and grandson of the German-Jewish philosopher Moses Mendelssohn. He showed an amazing gift for music, and his mother, an amateur pianist, started giving him piano lessons at about age four. When he was six, young Felix's studies in piano, violin, composition, painting, and all the academic subjects were taken over by private tutors. By the time he was nine, he gave his first piano recital and that same year heard his choral setting of the Nineteenth Psalm performed by the prestigious Berlin Singakademie.

Mendelssohn performed widely during his teenage years, but became increasingly interested in composition. At only 17 years of age he wrote his splendid overture to Shakespeare's *A Midsummer Night's Dream,* and later composed additional music for the play, including the well-known *Wedding March.*

Felix Mendelssohn was one of the few composers to receive a university education. Starting almost immediately on his graduation from the University of Berlin and continuing throughout his lifetime, he scored triumph after triumph as both composer and conductor. His music, noted more for its elegance, clarity, and tastefulness than for its depth and profundity, captivated audiences. In addition to the high esteem in which he was held in his native Germany, Mendelssohn was especially admired and respected in England. He made several trips across the Channel to perform his own music and became friendly with many leading figures there, including Queen Victoria and Prince Albert.

Among Mendelssohn's many accomplishments was the part he played in reviving the music of Johann Sebastian Bach. In 1829, he conducted Bach's

St. Matthew Passion, its first performance since Bach's death. The performance generated a great renewal of interest in Bach's music. It also showed that, despite the fact that he was baptized a Lutheran at age seven and practiced that religion as an adult, Mendelssohn never completely severed his spiritual bonds to Judaism. After presenting *St. Matthew* with a popular actor singing the role of Jesus, Mendelssohn commented: "Well, it takes a clown and a Jew to reintroduce the greatest Christian music to the people."

A few notes are in order regarding Mendelssohn's symphonies: He wrote 12 string symphonies and a symphony for full orchestra (No. 1) in his youth; they are seldom performed today. Critics consider Symphony No. 2— "Lobgesang," for choir and orchestra—more a cantata than a symphony. And because of the order of publication, the numbers of his last three symphonies are in the reverse order of composition: the "Reformation," No. 5, was completed in 1830; the "Italian," No. 4, in 1833; and the "Scotch," No. 3, in 1842.

Concerto for Piano and Orchestra No. 1 in G minor, Op. 25
(20 minutes)

In June 1830, Mendelssohn was on his way to Italy when he met and fell in love with Delphine von Schauroth, a very gifted and attractive young pianist who lived in Munich. She inspired the 21-year-old Felix to write the G minor concerto in her honor. He completed the work in October of the following year and was soloist for the premiere in Munich on October 17, 1831.

The concerto proved immediately popular with audiences; "My Concerto was applauded long and loud," Mendelssohn wrote to his father. It grew to be one of the most frequently performed concertos in the entire repertoire. Its great success springs from many factors: the work's easy grace, charm, and warmth; the wide range of feelings and emotions it expresses, from scintillating bravura to poignant sentimentality; and the virtuosic, though idiomatic, writing for the solo piano.

In his 1853 book, *Evenings with the Orchestra,* Hector Berlioz offers an apocryphal anecdote attesting to its amazing popularity. According to Berlioz, the concerto was such a favorite at the Paris Conservatory that one piano kept on playing the work—even when no one was at the keyboard. A piano maker sprinkled holy water on the piano, removed the keyboard, flung it through a window, and furiously chopped the keys into small bits with an ax, all to no avail. Only when he tossed the pieces into a fire did the music finally stop!

By his example, Mendelssohn helped composers rethink the traditional structure of the first movement of a concerto. During the preceding Classical era, composers traditionally started the movement with an orchestral exposition of the two contrasting thematic groups, followed by the soloist's statement of the same material. All too often, the audience viewed the orchestral opening as an annoying delay before the soloist entered and the concerto *really* began. Mendelssohn's innovation was to bring in the piano after only a few measures of orchestral introduction. He then assigned the soloist, along with the orchestra, the task of announcing the major subjects of the movement. The success of this new organization led many composers to follow Mendelssohn's example.

I. *Molto allegro con fuoco.* After the quick whisper-to-shout introduction, the pianist leads the orchestra through the statement of the fiery first group of themes and the quiet, lyrical second subject. A brief working out of the themes and an equally short reprise make way for a fanfarelike brass passage that acts as the transition to the second movement, which follows without break.

II. *Andante.* Mendelssohn constructs the songful, soulful Andante around a sweet, almost sentimental melody. Throughout the movement, he uses a reduced orchestra—no oboes, clarinets, trumpets, or timpani—and he brings the violins in only near the end.

III. *Presto; Molto allegro e vivace.* Another fanfare, obviously derived from the earlier one, serves as a bridge to the final movement. The principal theme, perhaps the most attractive one in the concerto, bursts forth in glittering excitement. Near the conclusion, brief reminders of themes from the opening movement unify the entire work and lead to the exuberant close.

Concerto for Violin and Orchestra in E minor, Op. 64
(30 minutes)

Mendelssohn wrote his sole violin concerto for Ferdinand David, an extremely gifted violinist who, by pure coincidence, was born one year later than Mendelssohn in the same Hamburg house. The two men met in 1827, and when Mendelssohn became conductor of the Leipzig Gewandhaus Orchestra in 1835, he invited David to become concertmaster.

Mendelssohn first mentions the violin concerto in a letter to David on July 30, 1838: "I should like to write a violin concerto for you next winter. One in E minor runs through my head, the beginning of which gives me no peace."

A year passed, and one can only guess that Mendelssohn had been thinking about the concerto but had not yet set down any notes. "It is nice of you to press me for a violin concerto!" he wrote to David while on holiday that summer. "I have the liveliest desire to write one for you, and if I have a few propitious days here, I'll bring you something. But the task is not an easy one. You demand that it should be brilliant, and how is such a one as I to manage that? The whole of the first solo is to be for the E string [the highest and most brilliant string on the violin]."

In 1841, King Frederick William IV invited Mendelssohn to come to Berlin to direct the musical activities in the city, which comprised heading the Royal Academy, starting a conservatory, and conducting operas and orchestra concerts. Unable to refuse, Mendelssohn found himself terribly busy with his official duties, which he found endlessly frustrating and unsatisfying, and which left him little time for composing. Finally, in 1844, he was able to persuade the King to relieve him of his obligations. In July 1844 at Soden, a spa near Frankfurt, Mendelssohn began work on the violin concerto, completing the manuscript on September 16. From their correspondence, we know that Mendelssohn frequently consulted with David on technical aspects of the solo part and that the violinist created most of the first movement cadenza.

I. *Allegro molto appassionato.* The concerto starts with the soloist singing the soaring theme—on the E string—over an orchestral murmur. After some virtuosic expansion of this melody, the orchestra introduces a flowing transitional theme, which the soloist takes up immediately. The woodwinds bring in the tender, lyrical second theme, identifiable by its three repeated opening notes. Extended passages of brilliant writing for the solo violin follow, with the cadenza acting as a bridge to the return of the themes, the first one sneaking in via the orchestra as the violinist continues an arpeggiated figure from the cadenza. After the movement builds to a stunning climax, a sustained soft note by the solo bassoon acts as a bridge to the second movement—even though it is all too often obliterated by thoughtless applause.

II. *Andante.* The solo violin gives out the principal subject of the three-part Andante, a wonderfully poised and graceful melody. An intense, agitated middle section, characterized by several repeated notes, is heard before the movement ends with a freely realized return of the opening part.

III. *Allegretto non troppo; Allegro molto vivace.* The finale, which also follows without pause, starts with an introduction based on the central section of the previous movement. On its completion, the orchestra sounds a pattern of imperious chords that the soloist dismisses with a musical flick of the wrist. Out of this exchange emerges the sparkling elfin first theme, which goes on to dominate the spirited proceedings with its vivacious charm.

Incidental Music for *A Midsummer Night's Dream,* Opp. 21, 61

(25 minutes)

Mendelssohn wrote the overture to *A Midsummer Night's Dream* during the summer of 1826, at age 17, after being introduced to a German translation of Shakespeare's plays. He later expanded the overture, originally written for piano duet, for full orchestra. Then, in the summer of 1843, King Frederick William IV of Prussia asked Mendelssohn to compose incidental music for a performance of *A Midsummer Night's Dream* to be presented at his new theater in Potsdam. As though the 17-year hiatus were but a few days, Mendelssohn was able to maintain the same style and tone for the 12 additional numbers he wrote to go with the play. The production of the play with all the music was given in Potsdam on October 14, 1843. Mendelssohn conducted the first concert performance of the incidental music alone in London on May 27, 1844.

Of the 13 selections in the original incidental music, only five excerpts appear with any frequency.

I. *Overture.* Four magical woodwind chords call forth the spirits that inhabit the fantastic world of *A Midsummer Night's Dream.* Mendelssohn then captures the major elements of the drama in the four themes: the fairies flitting lightly about (first theme); the court of Theseus (transition theme); the young lovers (second theme); and the braying Bottom (closing theme), which he handles within the strictures of traditional sonata allegro form.

II. *Scherzo.* Heard in the play as the introduction to Act II, the scintillating Scherzo glints and glimmers as it races along. The rhythmic, dancing figure that opens the section keeps returning as a sort of refrain throughout, with a most exceptional flute solo near the end.

III. *Intermezzo.* In performance, this agitated, excited movement comes at the end of Act II when Hermia dashes off after Lysander.

IV. *Nocturne.* The Nocturne, intended for the end of Act III as Puck casts his spell over the four lovers and they fall to sleep on the forest floor, suggests this enchanting scene very successfully. Notable in this movement is the gorgeous melody for solo Franch horn.

V. *Wedding March.* What need be said about the very familiar *Wedding March?* In the play it comes at the beginning of Act V for the wedding celebration of Theseus and Hippolyta.

Overture, *The Hebrides (Fingal's Cave)*, Op. 26
(10 minutes)

Early in 1829, Mendelssohn and his friend Karl Klingemann set out on a leisurely Grand Tour of Europe, stopping first in England and then on to Scotland. On Staffa, a tiny island in the Hebrides, about 10 miles off Scotland's west coast, they visited a leading tourist attraction, Fingal's Cave. The composer was awestruck at the sight: a sea-filled grotto, about 35 feet wide, twice as high, and over 200 feet deep, lined on one side with astonishing red and brown pillars of basalt that resembled the interior of an immense pipe organ.

On the day of their visit, August 6, 1829, Mendelssohn wrote to his sister Fanny: "In order to make you understand how extraordinarily the Hebrides affected me, I send you the following, which came into my head there." Enclosed were the opening bars of what we now know as *The Hebrides* or *Fingal's Cave.* (The confusion over the title dates from the first published edition, which was marked *Fingal's Cave* on the score and *The Hebrides* on the orchestral parts!)

Mendelssohn completed the work in Rome on December 30, 1830, but he was dissatisfied, saying that it "smells more of counterpoint than of whale oil, seagulls, and salt cod." A second version followed in 1832, and the premiere was given by the London Philharmonic under Thomas Attwood on May 14, 1832. Still not completely pleased, Mendelssohn prepared the third and final version the following year.

Mendelssohn conceived *The Hebrides* as a concert overture that was complete unto itself, not as an introduction to a larger work. In form it closely resembles a symphonic first movement with two contrasting themes—the descending figure heard at the outset that suggests the roiling waves, and the singing, essentially ascending melody later introduced by the cellos and bassoons that evokes the site's soaring, primitive beauty. Despite the formal construct, the piece is an outstanding example of program music, effectively creating a brilliant seascape, with surging tides, dashing waves, bright flecks of foam, and even hints of a passing storm.

Symphony No. 3 in A minor, Op. 56, "Scotch"
(40 minutes)

How Scottish is the "Scotch" Symphony? Mendelssohn quotes no indigenous folk songs, imitates no bagpipes, and makes little use of the characteristic long/short Scotch snap rhythm. Yet we know that the symphony was inspired by the composer's travels in Scotland.

After a stay in London, Mendelssohn paid a visit to Scotland in the summer of 1829. In a July 30 letter he mentions that "we went today to the Palace of Holyrood where Queen Mary lived and loved. The chapel close to it is now roofless. . . . I believe I found today in that old chapel the beginning of my Scotch symphony"—and he enclosed several measures of the symphony's introductory melody. Incidentally, it was this same trip that spurred Mendelssohn to compose *The Hebrides*.

Despite Mendelssohn's source of inspiration, the musical connection between the "Scotch" Symphony and the country's rugged beauty and colorful history remains elusive. Even the composer Robert Schumann, an extremely musical, knowledgeable, and perspicacious listener, thought he was hearing Mendelssohn's "Italian" Symphony when, in fact, the "Scotch" Symphony was being played! Schumann wrote enthusiastically of its "beautiful Italian pictures, so beautiful as to compensate a hearer who had never been to Italy." If the symphony could fool Schumann, the "Scotch" Symphony may not be particularly Scottish after all. Our best approach, then, is just to enjoy the splendid work for what it is, without straining to attach a program to its different parts.

I. *Andante con moto; Allegro un poco agitato.* The symphony opens with a slow introduction based on the motto melody Mendelssohn jotted down in Scotland. The two chief themes of the movement's faster main part, which is organized in sonata allegro form, are derived from the introductory motto melody. The violins state the first theme, the clarinet the second. Mendelssohn projects an unease and nervousness through most of this movement until near the end, when he brings back a melancholy reprise of the introduction.

II. *Vivace non troppo.* Mendelssohn asked that the four movements be played without pause, so the light, dancelike second movement starts right on the heels of the first. Although capturing the bubbly, capricious character of a scherzo, Mendelssohn makes it a sonata allegro—the two principal subjects being the initial clarinet theme and the staccato descending scale line of the violins.

III. *Adagio.* This movement starts with a long, contemplative song for the violins. But as the movement progresses, Mendelssohn projects a variety of other personalities, from frightening and foreboding to vibrant and aggressive.

IV. *Allegro vivacissimo.* The fiery and tempestuous finale bursts upon the listener with great verve and energy. Mendelssohn divides an abundance of thematic material into the standard two groups of sonata allegro form. The first group's lead theme is the swirling violin melody heard at the very outset; the main idea of the second group is a delicate little tune introduced by the oboes, which seems related to the original motto melody. Just when the movement sounds as though it is winding down, Mendelssohn starts a broad, sonorous coda with a theme that is another transformation of the opening motto.

Mendelssohn did not complete the symphony until January 20, 1842, about thirteen years after his visit to Scotland. He conducted the premiere with his Leipzig Gewandhaus Orchestra on March 3, 1842.

Symphony No 4 in A major, Op. 90, "Italian"
(30 minutes)

As a German composer, Mendelssohn shared his countrymen's perception of Italy as a carefree land suffused with great warmth and bright sunshine. It was during a trip to Italy that lasted several months from near the end of 1830 through early 1831 that Mendelssohn wrote: "The whole country had such a festive air that I felt as if I were a young prince making his entry." As with his earlier visit to Scotland, the strong impression prompted him to write a symphony that would capture, in very general and nonspecific ways, the temperament of the land.

Mendelssohn began to compose the "Italian" Symphony while in Italy, but made little progress until November 1832, when he was spurred to finish the work quickly to fulfill a commission from the London Philharmonic for a new symphony. He finished the score in Berlin four months later and led the first performance with the London Philharmonic on May 13, 1833.

The work found an audience immediately, but Mendelssohn felt dissatisfied with the piece and made a number of changes. His revised version was performed in London in 1838. Still seeking ways to improve the composition, particularly the last movement, he planned further alterations, but made none before his death. The delay accounts for publication of the "Italian" Symphony in 1851, after the "Scotch."

I. *Allegro vivace.* The composer calls up images of the light, airy, sunny Italian landscape as the violins sing out the sparkling first theme over rapidly repeated woodwind chords. After a brief scampering transition, the clarinets introduce the second subject, a rocking melody that brings some calm after the preceding excitement. But the high spirits are not to be denied and the following development section mostly concerns itself with the initial theme. Just before he brings the melodies back for the recapitulation, Mendelssohn inserts a wonderful little fugato. The movement ends with an extended coda.

II. *Andante con moto.* Many commentators hear a pilgrim procession in the slow movement, although Mendelssohn never mentioned any such connection. The impression comes from the several simple, songlike themes that we hear over the marching steps of the pizzicato strings. There is a brief, slightly agitated interruption before the original melody returns, along with references to the interruption, to bring the movement to a tranquil conclusion.

III. *Con moto moderato.* Traditionally, one would expect this movement to be a scherzo. But this third movement lacks the sprightly good humor that we associate with that form. Perhaps it is best described as a lyrical minuet, although without the dancelike rhythms of a traditional minuet. As is usual, the movement has a contrasting section, in this case a delicate woodwind interlude introduced by a French horn signal, which the composer follows with a free return of the opening.

IV. *Saltarello: Presto.* Mendelssohn drew his inspiration in this movement from the saltarello, a 16th century moderately fast Italian peasant jumping dance; by the 19th century, though, the steps had become much faster and more rowdy. The insistent rhythm of the saltarello underpins the entire movement as Mendelssohn spins forth melody after melody, catching everyone up in its infectious good humor.

Symphony No. 5 in D minor, Op. 107, "Reformation"
(35 minutes)

In the fall of 1829, Mendelssohn began to compose a symphony to be performed at the June 1830 ceremonies honoring the 300th anniversary of the Augsburg Confession, a document that was presented to Emperor Charles V stating the fundamental beliefs of the newly evolving Protestant faith. Mendelssohn finished the piece in a timely fashion in April 1830 and subtitled it "Confession" Symphony. But an outbreak of revolutionary activity in the various independent German states at the time led the government to cancel all festivities.

The symphony's premiere was then rescheduled for Paris the following year, but the orchestral musicians were so unhappy with the music that the work was dropped from the program. The Fifth Symphony did not receive its first hearing until November 15, 1832, when Mendelssohn conducted a performance in Berlin. For this concert the work was given the sobriquet "Symphony to Commemorate the Church Revolution." In 1868, more than two decades after Mendelssohn's death, the work was finally published with the "Reformation" subtitle; no one knows who chose that name.

I. *Andante; Allegro con fuoco.* Mendelssohn begins the symphony with a dark, gloomy slow introduction. Twice near the end of the introduction he uses the so-called *Dresden Amen,* a six-note ascending phrase played softly by the violins. The *Dresden Amen* comes from the Saxon liturgy; Wagner later made extensive use of the same melodic figure in his music drama *Parsifal.* The composer builds the rest of the restless and agitated movement on themes based on those heard in the introduction.

II. *Allegro vivace.* After the highly dramatic first movement, Mendelssohn lowers the emotional temperature considerably with a delightful scherzo. The woodwind-dominated movement starts with the flutes playing the light, airy principal theme. The middle portion introduces a lyrical theme in the oboes. An altered reprise of the original melody rounds off the movement.

III. *Andante.* The violins carry the melodic burden, mostly over a pulsing accompaniment, in this extremely short movement. The Andante functions largely as an introduction to the finale, which follows directly.

IV. *Andante con moto; Allegro vivace.* The composer entrusts a solo flute with the first statement of the well-known Lutheran chorale "Ein feste Burg ist unser Gott!" ("A Mighty Fortress Is Our God!"). Having presented the chorale, Mendelssohn picks up the tempo and devotes the remainder of the movement to variations on its melody, culminating in a glorious final peroration.

Wolfgang Amadeus Mozart

Born January 27, 1756, in Salzburg
Died December 5, 1791, in Vienna

WOLFGANG AMADEUS MOZART, one of the greatest musical ge-
niuses of all time, was also one of the world's most amazing prodigies. He was composing at age five and the following year performed as
pianist before the royal court in Vienna. At age 13 Mozart entered the
employ of the Archbishop of Salzburg as concertmaster of the orchestra and
court organist, a position that took little account of his already considerable
skill as a composer; by this time, he had already written many orchestral
works, as well as a good number of smaller and shorter pieces.

Young Mozart and his father, also a musician, often quarreled with the
Archbishop because of Wolfgang's frequent requests for leave to perform in
other cities or to apply for a situation more in keeping with his abilities. The
requests so angered the Archbishop that Wolfgang was finally dismissed in
1781 with the famous kick in the backside from the Archbishop's secretary.

Mozart left Salzburg happily, hoping to find his fortune in Vienna. No
longer a child prodigy, Mozart nevertheless was in demand as a performer
and was very active as a composer. He mostly wrote in the prevailing Rococo
style, or *style galant,* with its emphasis on elegance, grace, and charm. Save
for a few outstanding exceptions, his compositions were essentially designed
to please the nobles and church officials who were the principal patrons of
music.

But the days remaining to these aristocrats were numbered. The Absolu-
tist beliefs that had kept them in power were giving way to the new ideas of
the Enlightenment; rule by authority was slowly being replaced with rule by
reason. Mozart's music, like that of other composers, was being transformed
in the process. Building on tuneful melodies, simple forms, and clear textures of the Rococo tradition, Mozart began composing works of great ex-

pressivity, drama, and significant emotional content, which also included contrapuntal writing and other "learned" techniques.

More compositions by Mozart are considered in this volume than those of any other composer. One reason is that he lived in an era when composers traditionally produced large numbers of work, which he accomplished despite his tragically short life. His output included 41 symphonies, 27 piano concertos, five violin concertos, and any number of other orchestral compositions. He created these orchestral masterpieces, along with most of his outstanding operas, church works, and chamber music in the decade between leaving the Archbishop's service in 1781 and his death in 1791.

More importantly, though, Mozart's music is informed by a creative genius and a universality of appeal that puts him in an unique position among the great composers. Listeners with little background or sophistication are charmed by his delightful melodies and the grace and lightness of touch that runs through so much of his music. Trained musicians and experienced concertgoers also worship Mozart—but for different reasons. They discover, as well, a deepness, an emotional expressiveness, in Mozart's compositions. They are also aware of a skill and a craftsmanship that seem the very essence of perfection. Mozart is indeed a complete composer—able to speak to every listener and able to convey the full gamut of human emotions.

Since Mozart did not assign opus numbers to his 600-plus compositions, scholars often found it difficult to place his works in chronological order. Then, in 1862, an Austrian musician and naturalist, Dr. Ludwig Köchel, prepared his *Chronologisch-thematisches Verzeichnis* ("Chronological Thematic Catalog"), which listed all of Mozart's music in order of composition. Today the title of each piece is followed by a K. number from Köchel's catalog.

Concerto for Clarinet and Orchestra in A major, K. 622
(30 minutes)

The clarinet is a comparative latecomer to the family of instruments; the first true clarinets were not made until the beginning of the 18th century. Mozart was the first major composer to make extensive use of this instrument and to establish a style of writing that showed off its beauty of tone, agility, and wide range.

In 1789, Mozart began composing a Concerto in G major for basset horn, a sort of alto clarinet. After composing 199 measures he put it aside; no one knows why. In October 1791, he took up the incomplete manuscript, changed the instrument to clarinet, changed the key to A major, and produced what we now know as his Clarinet Concerto, K. 622—the last major work he finished before his death a few months later.

Mozart dedicated the concerto to Anton Stadler, a close friend, fellow Mason, and clarinetist, who was famous for the beauty of his tone. From Stadler, Mozart learned the possibilities of the instrument. From Mozart, in addition to several never repaid loans, Stadler got the Clarinet Concerto, the Clarinet Quintet, and the "Kegelstatt" Trio.

Mozart actually wrote the concerto for a special clarinet that Stadler owned, which had a slightly wider range than the standard clarinet. When the concerto was published in 1801, some unknown editor revised the solo part to make it playable on a standard clarinet. Since Stadler lost the original score—some suspect he may have sold it—we are left today with only the editor's reworking. Musicologists, though, have identified 30 passages that they believe have been changed, mostly by moving the solo line an octave higher.

I. *Allegro.* The principal subject of the first movement is a warm, tender melody first stated and extended by the orchestra and then taken up by the clarinet. The clarinet then goes on to introduce the subsidiary subject, which is in the minor key and tinged with melancholy. As Mozart develops and returns these themes, he gives all sorts of brilliant runs and arpeggios to the soloist, including incredible leaps from one register to another.

II. *Adagio.* The highly expressive Adagio is quiet and pensive in character. Although the melody could well be from an opera aria, the intimate treatment makes it sound more like chamber music.

III. *Allegro.* The last movement reveals a particularly cheerful Mozart. True, some of the episodes in this rondo movement betray a slight sadness or feeling of resignation, but the good spirits prevail.

Concerto for Piano and Orchestra No. 9 in E flat major, K. 271, "Jeunehomme"
(35 minutes)

Starting when he was five years old, young Wolfgang's parents took him on extended concert tours around Europe, hoping to find a noble who would become his patron. The lad amazed the aristocrats with his preternatural feats as pianist, violinist, and composer—but none made any offer of help. Finally, at age 13, he accepted a position in the court of the Archbishop of Salzburg.

Late in 1776, while still in the Archbishop's service, Mozart was asked by a touring French pianist, a Mlle. Jeunehomme, to write a piano concerto that she could perform. Eager to break free of writing entertainment music in the *galant* style for the unappreciative Archbishop, Mozart rose to the challenge. Commentators such as Alfred Einstein and A. Hyatt King refer to the E flat concerto as Mozart's "Eroica," a sudden and major leap forward into a mature and fully developed composing style.

I. *Allegro.* In this movement, Mozart broke with the Classical tradition of having the orchestra state the two principal themes of the first movement before the soloist entered to present another exposition. In the E flat concerto, the piano comes in immediately after the orchestra plays a brief unison motif. Back and forth the melodies flow, the first theme, alternating its brusque phrases with calm rejoinders, and the subsidiary subject, a poised, graceful melody introduced by the violins. Mozart then discourses on the two themes and brings them back for the recapitulation, which includes two versions of a cadenza that he supplied.

II. *Andantino.* The Andantino provides the emotional fulcrum of this concerto. The music is as eloquent and intensely expressive as an operatic aria.

III. *Rondeau: Presto.* Mozart casts the bright and joyous last movement as a rondo; the four appearances of the principal theme are separated by three contrasting interludes. In a bold stroke, Mozart makes the last interlude a slower minuet, followed by four variations of the minuet melody, before bringing in the final statement of the tune and a brilliant wrap-up of the entire concerto.

Mlle. Jeunehomme probably premiered the concerto, which Mozart completed in January 1777, but no record of her performance survives. Mozart himself played it in Munich on October 4 of that year.

Concerto for Piano and Orchestra No. 15 in B flat major, K. 450

(25 minutes)

The Lenten season in early spring 1784 found Mozart at the height of his popularity both as a pianist and as a composer. Since Catholic Vienna forbade opera presentations, but not concerts, during that period, he found many opportunities to perform. In a letter he lists 22 *Akademien,* or subscription concerts, that he gave between February 26 and April 23. Since these concerts were expected to feature new compositions, he wrote four piano concertos for those performances. He completed the K. 450 concerto, the second of the four, on March 15 and gave the first performance at an *Akademie* two days later.

I. *Allegro.* The first movement, bursting with a profusion of melodies, follows the traditional concerto form: The orchestra presents the exposition with the two main thematic groups, and then the soloist, after some virtuosic display, presents a second exposition, but with a different second theme. The composer then develops the many motifs that he presented and brings them back to round out the movement.

II. *Andante.* What could be simpler than this gem of a movement? It consists of a wonderfully warm two-part theme, two variations on the theme, and a brief coda. Yet Mozart imbues it with a devotional quality that audiences find extremely moving.

III. *Allegro.* Cast as a joyous, energetic rondo, the final movement presents four statements of the principal theme, which calls to mind the sound of post horns and hunting horns so beloved of 18th century composers. Between the thematic statements are contrasting interludes. This beautiful and expressive cap to the concerto, so brilliantly written for the soloist, provided Mozart with the opportunities for display he needed for his 1784 performance—and gave us an enduring masterpiece.

Concerto for Piano and Orchestra No. 17 in G major, K. 453
(30 minutes)

To help support himself, Mozart gave piano lessons—albeit reluctantly. One of his most gifted students was Barbara (Babette) Ployer, daughter of the agent of Mozart's former employer, the Archbishop of Salzburg. For Barbara, Mozart wrote his Sonata for Two Pianos K. 448, Piano Concerto K. 449, and Piano Concerto K. 453. He began the latter piece in Vienna at the end of March 1784 and finished it on April 12. Barbara gave the premiere at her father's country house in Döbling, Austria, on June 10.

A charming anecdote has been passed down in connection with this concerto. On May 27, a few weeks after completing the work, Mozart heard a caged starling whistling the concerto's last movement theme with just a few different notes. He bought the bird, wrote out the notes of the bird's song, and next to the theme wrote: *"Das war schön"* ("That was beautiful"). When the bird eventually died, Mozart buried it and erected a small tombstone at the site.

I. *Allegro.* Smiles and good cheer permeate the first movement, giving only the merest hint that the world is not suffused with infinite happiness. Melodies, each one a sparkling jewel, pour from Mozart's pen, jostling one another for prominence. An especially delectable treat is the little echoes that end the various strains of melody.

II. *Andante.* Mozart scholar A. Hyatt King very aptly describes the Andante as "dramatic, profound and remarkable." In this very special movement, the tender, yet passionate principal theme seems to spring from the second theme of the first movement. Following a form that defies easy categorization—falling somewhere between sonata allegro, rondo, and theme and variations—the Andante forms the emotional peak of the entire concerto.

III. *Allegretto.* One can easily hear the birdsong quality of the theme of the last movement. The song bears a striking similarity to Papageno's melodies in Mozart's opera *The Magic Flute.* Mozart subjects the theme to five variations, each time adding complexity to the simple tune and brilliance to the solo part. Finally, he concludes with a faster section that seems to be taken from one of his own comic operas.

Concerto for Piano and Orchestra No. 19 in F major, K. 459
(28 minutes)

The F major, the last of the six concertos that Mozart composed in 1784, ranks among the most cheerful and confident of all his works in the form. Edward Downes in his comments on this concerto suggests that some of the happiness and satisfaction, along with the few touches of solemnity, relate to the fact that Mozart completed the composition on December 11, 1784, three days before his induction into the Order of Freemasons, an event of great importance for the young composer.

I. *Allegro.* The concerto opens with a marchlike theme that Mozart first presents in a gentle and quiet manner. A number of other themes follow in the orchestra and piano expositions, but the first theme with its characteristic rhythm predominates over the movement. In this and subsequent movements Mozart treats the orchestra and soloist as virtual equals.

II. *Allegretto.* By using a tempo indication of Allegretto, Mozart indicates that the "slow" movement of the concerto should not be too leisurely, only slightly slower than the opening Allegro. Lovely and graceful, this movement captivates with its apparent simplicity.

III. *Allegro assai.* The final movement unfolds in a way that makes the first two movements appear but prelude. This masterful creation shows an expressivity and control that composers rarely, if ever, achieve. The movement opens with a droll little tune that seemingly augurs a light, good-humored cap to the concerto. But before long, Mozart completely changes voice and moves very dexterously into highly complex, learned counterpoint. For the remainder of the movement he moves from the charming homophonic sections to intricate polyphonic stretches, but making sure that the last sounds are of the happy, simple tune.

Scholars believe that Mozart composed the concerto for his own use, even though they find no record of its first performance.

Concerto for Piano and Orchestra No. 20 in D minor, K. 466

(33 minutes)

Mozart's father, Leopold, a composer and violinist, was in Vienna at the time of the D minor Concerto premiere. In letters home he described the work as *"Magnifique!,"* the concert "incomparable," and the orchestra "excellent." Little could he, or anyone at the time, have imagined that this splendid work would put an end to Mozart's short period of acclaim and acceptance in Viennese music circles, and signal the start of a desperate lifelong struggle to survive.

The D minor, written in a truly Romantic style, and notable for its very deep emotion and intense feeling, did not please the nobles and middle-class concertgoers. With this concerto, Mozart entered a realm where he no longer felt obliged to clothe the expressive qualities of his music in the charming and pretty conventions of the *galant* style. Instead he wrote a serious, demanding work that was much more of a challenge to the listeners.

Disappointed by what they heard, Viennese audiences turned away from Mozart and flocked to the composers willing to provide the frivolous music they sought. Mozart, of course, could have returned to favor had he resumed more of his old style, but his integrity as an artist led him to continue in the new direction.

I. *Allegro.* The violins play a syncopated, pulsating figure, ominous and agitated in character, yet so repressed that it barely rises above a whisper. Beneath, the cellos and basses add their threatening little punctations of quick, upward runs. Out of this the first theme emerges, a tense, brooding melody. The second theme, played by the woodwinds in the major mode, lifts the gloom somewhat and lightens the oppression caused by the minor key, but the minor returns to end the orchestra exposition. The piano enters for its exposition, carrying forward some of the melodic material from the orchestra statement and bringing in some new thematic ideas. With the piano in the lead, the development section works over the themes that have been introduced and the piano and orchestra share the recapitulation. The recapitulation ends with a piano cadenza (Mozart did not write cadenzas for this concerto, but Beethoven did) and a coda that brings the movement to a quiet, unresolved conclusion.

II. *Romanze.* A Romanze usually refers to music that is slow in tempo and rich in feeling and expression. Divided into three clearly marked sections, this Romanze starts with an attractive, serene melody to which the piano appends a melody of similar character. Just when the listener becomes accustomed to the calmness, Mozart unleashes the pent-up furies in a wild, demonic middle section. The movement ends with quiet reminiscences of the opening.

III. *Allegro assai.* Mozart, in the finale, seems to be trying to dispel the pessimistic mood cast by the first movement. He creates a more cheerful atmosphere with the skyrocket that launches the Allegro assai. The composer follows with three other themes in quick order and freely repeats them to complete the movement. The last theme blossoms forth in the major mode and supplies the desired happy ending.

Mozart completed the concerto on February 10, 1785, and gave the premiere the following day. So rushed was he that he did not even have time for a complete run-through with the orchestra!

Concerto for Piano and Orchestra No. 21 in C major, K. 467
(30 minutes)

Commentators often contrast the more joyful C major Concerto, which Mozart completed on March 9, 1785, with the severer D minor Concerto, which he finished only one month earlier. Careful listening to the C major, though, particularly the first two movements, makes it clear that both works came from the depths of the same soul. Also, the bold harmonies and striking dissonances show that the composer had little concern for the popular taste of the day and was focused instead on his need for self-expression and his desire to make an important musical statement. Beneath the surface cheerfulness of the C major is a serious, stirring musical creation.

I. *Allegro maestoso.* Mozart opens the concerto with a quiet, humorous march tune that shows up many times in the course of the movement, yet remains almost exclusively the property of the orchestra and not the soloist. Other captivating melodies follow in both the orchestra and piano expositions. Mozart carries the melodies through some bold harmonic changes, adding a very special ferocity and power to the music. He exploits the full tonal palette of the orchestra, making particularly good use of the trumpets and drums to lend strength and grandeur to the movement. This is especially effective if the soloist observes Mozart's marking of maestoso, or "majestic," and doesn't turn it into a high-speed, facile display of technical virtuosity.

II. *Andante.* Mozart biographer Alfred Einstein describes the Andante as "an ideal aria freed of the limitations of the human voice." The piano does, indeed, sing throughout this dreamy, peaceful movement. Pure cantilena replaces the massive chords and figures of the first movement. Most striking and original in this movement are the advanced harmonies and unorthodox melodic lines, creating dissonances that must have shocked an 18th century audience, but that very effectively intensify the character of the music for modern listeners. When Mozart's father, also a composer, looked over the orchestral parts, he corrected several notes that he was sure were copyist's errors. Later they proved to be exactly what the composer had in mind.

III. *Allegro vivace assai.* After the profundity of the first two movements, Mozart clears the air with a charming and graceful finale. Frisky and ebullient, the last movement sparkles with the merry character of a Mozart opera buffa.

Mozart gave the premiere of the C major in Vienna on March 10, 1785, the day after he completed the score.

Concerto for Piano and Orchestra No. 22 in E flat major, K. 482
(36 minutes)

The latter months of 1785 were an incredibly busy and difficult time for Mozart. He was working on his opera *The Marriage of Figaro,* along with a number of instrumental works, including the Piano Concerto K. 482, performing frequently as pianist, and giving music lessons. At the same time, he was experiencing financial difficulties due to the loss of support from the nobles and moneyed people of Vienna who had been his enthusiastic and generous supporters. To make matters worse, his health had started a serious decline.

Perhaps, at that time, Mozart felt that he had become too personal, too serious, too Romantic in his last two piano concertos. Maybe he merely wanted to win back the affection of the fickle Viennese public. In any case, he adopted a much more accessible and popular style in the E flat Concerto, although most will agree that it was accomplished with no loss of quality. If anything, the E flat shows greater maturity and spiritual development than the two outwardly more serious earlier concertos. A major work in Mozart's oeuvre, the E flat is also large in the sense that it is longer than his other concertos and uses a sizable orchestra that includes, for the first time, two clarinets instead of oboes.

I. *Allegro.* Mozart starts with a long orchestral exposition, followed by an equally impressive piano statement, which Mozart liberally scatters with thematic gems. He devotes the rest of the movement to elaborations, explorations, and recollections of this material, with the soloist adding embellishments of sparkling scales, arpeggios, and other figurations to the proceedings.

II. *Andante.* Organized as a theme and four variations with two interludes, this sublimely beautiful movement expresses emotions that range from great pain and grief to brooding melancholy. To their credit, the audience at the first performance was so touched by the Andante that they insisted that Mozart repeat the movement.

III. *Allegro.* The concluding Allegro opens with a piano statement of a hunting-call theme that Mozart repeats several more times in the movement. Around the repetitions of this theme Mozart introduces several varied episodes. In one, near the end of the movement, Mozart changes the meter (from ⁶/₈ to ³/₄) and the tempo (from Allegro to Andantino cantabile) for a gentle, quiet minuetlike section just before the final return of the principal theme and the coda that brings the movement to an end.

Mozart finished this concerto on December 16, 1785, in preparation for performance during the Lenten season of 1786. The premiere, however, probably took place with Mozart as soloist on December 23, 1785, at a benefit concert for the widows of Vienna's musicians. It was performed as an interlude in a concert that featured an orchestra of 108 players!

Concerto for Piano and Orchestra No. 23 in A major, K. 488
(30 minutes)

Mozart's principal source of income after leaving Salzburg in 1781 and moving to Vienna was the money he earned presenting *Akademien,* or subscription concerts, for the aristocrats and wealthy burghers of that city. Lent, when all the theaters and opera houses were closed, was the very best time of the year for the *Akademien.* Since it was expected that the performer would introduce new works at these concerts, Mozart composed three piano concertos (K. 482, K. 488, and K. 491) in preparation for his 1786 Lenten appearances. He finished the K. 488 on March 2, 1786; the date of the premiere is unknown, but probably was within a few days of its completion.

The public accords the A major Concerto a position second only to the D minor in popularity. A more intense and dramatic work, Concerto No. 23 shows a closer integration between soloist and orchestra, and encompasses a wider emotional range.

I. *Allegro.* Mozart scholar Alfred Einstein writes of the first movement's "darker shadings and concealed intensities." Despite moments of good cheer, the two languid principal subjects create an overall aura of tenderness and resignation. After the orchestra states these themes, the piano and orchestra freely review the same material. The composer bases the following brief development section largely on a new melody introduced by the violins. The recapitulation gives us an opportunity to hear the original themes once more. A coda, including a cadenza for the soloist, comes at the end.

II. *Adagio.* Notwithstanding the warmth and beauty of the Adagio's cantilena melody, the tense mood of the first movement continues, except that here it is deeper and more intense. Basing it on the rhythmic pattern (long/short/long) of a 17th century Italian dance, the siciliano, Mozart uses it here as what scholar Cuthbert Girdlestone calls a *danse triste,* a "sad dance."

III. *Allegro assai.* The opening of the Allegro assai provides a rather rude, but exhilarating shock. Bursting with vigor and energy, the final movement acts as a counterweight to the severity of the Adagio. The good humor prevails, in spite of a few quiet, contemplative moments, making it very clear that life and vitality can overcome the forces of gloom.

Concerto for Piano and Orchestra No. 24 in C minor, K. 491
(35 minutes)

In the years from 1782 to 1786, a major component of Mozart's annual income came from the *Akademien,* or subscription concerts, given during Lent, when other forms of entertainment were barred. Each *Akademie* featured a new piano concerto, and for the first few years Mozart strove to make them as accessible and appealing as possible. For the 1785 Lenten concertos, though, the composer wrote darker-hued works that were more forceful and introspective than the ones he had written previously. The first two concertos for Lent 1786 (K. 482 and K. 488) seemed to signal a return, albeit on a grander scale, to the more ingratiating older style.

The third concerto for 1786, K. 491, which Mozart completed on March 24, 1786, and premiered on April 7, is a profound and extremely personal composition. Even though a shadow of grief hovers over the entire work, Mozart achieves what Eric Blom calls a "limpid euphony" in the presentation.

I. *Allegro.* Unison strings and bassoon state the quiet, but powerful principal theme of the first movement, which soon rages forth in a full-orchestra pronouncement. Other themes follow, but the first one predominates as the composer weaves soloist and orchestra together into an indissoluble whole. The original and inventive writing conforms to traditional concerto form, with separate orchestral and solo expositions, and shared development, recapitulation, and coda.

II. *Larghetto.* In the Larghetto, Mozart moves from the cloudiness of the minor key to the sunshine of the major, and caresses the listener with its pure and tranquil strains. The composer separates the statements of the simple, exquisite main subject in this rondo movement by slightly more agitated interludes that feature the woodwinds of the orchestra.

III. *Allegretto.* Instead of a light, fluffy concluding movement, Mozart treats us to a substantial theme and variations. He subjects a halting melody, with several silent interruptions, to eight variations. The first few variations merely add embellishments to the original tune. The subsequent ones change its character—now marchlike, now dancing—until the cadenza at the end of the seventh variation leads to the sprightly concluding variation transformed to $^6/_8$ meter.

Concerto for Piano and Orchestra No. 25 in C major, K. 503
(37 minutes)

Coming between his two operatic masterpieces, *The Marriage of Figaro* in 1786 and *Don Giovanni* in 1787, and two days before he finished his outstanding "Prague" Symphony on December 6, 1786, the C major Piano Concerto finds Mozart at the very height of his creative powers. Mozart wrote the K. 503 for his own use in a series of four concerts he presented in Vienna during the 1786 Advent season (the weeks just before Christmas).

A poor money manager, Mozart was now tottering on the brink of financial collapse, only to be rescued time after time by loans from his few loyal friends, who realized that chances of repayment were slight indeed. Having just lost his infant son in November, he hoped to earn enough to pay his doctor's bills as well as his back rent. No one knows the date of the performance or how much money he raised, but commentators agree that he produced one of the greatest piano concertos of all time.

I. *Allegro maestoso.* The opening immediately establishes the heroic, Olympian character of the first movement. Out of this grandiose gesture emerges a theme that starts with three rapid repeated notes; this rhythmic figure becomes, in various guises, all-pervasive as the movement unfolds. (Beethoven later found the rhythm irresistible in his Fifth Symphony.) After the orchestral statement of the thematic material, the piano sidles in and both soloist and orchestra then carry the listener along on a compelling musical journey.

II. *Andante.* Breadth, restraint, elegance are the words that best describe the Andante. Of special interest in this movement is the exquisite use Mozart makes of the unique timbres of the various wind instruments.

III. *Allegretto.* The violins open the finale with a lilting dance tune that has all the charm and appeal of a delightful folk melody. Actually, the theme closely resembles the Gavotte in the ballet music of his opera *Idomeneo,* which

Mozart wrote five years earlier. He introduces other themes in this rondo movement, but is always drawn back to the wonderful opening phrase.

Concerto for Piano and Orchestra No. 26 in D major, K. 537, "Coronation"
(32 minutes)

In the three years from February 1784 to December 1786, while at the pinnacle of his career, Mozart composed no fewer than 12 major piano concertos to perform in his own concert appearances. The concertos are among his most important and outstanding orchestral works, ranking in significance with his great final three symphonies.

Mozart finished the score of the D major Concerto on February 24, 1788, and probably hoped to perform it at a concert during Lent; his Lenten concerts in previous years were well received and earned considerable amounts of money. There is, however, no record that he performed the D major that spring.

Instead, Mozart probably gave the premiere in Dresden on April 14, 1789, en route to Berlin, to which he was traveling in the hope of gaining a court appointment. The following day, according to Mozart's letter, he "received a very handsome snuff box"—which is virtually all he got from the entire journey.

The second performance took place in Frankfurt in October 1790, where Leopold II was being crowned Holy Roman Emperor. (This explains the largely irrelevant subtitle.) The list of musicians invited to participate in the ceremonies did not include Mozart, but he went in the hope of attracting the attention of an aristocrat who might be seeking a new *Kapellmeister*. Mozart summed up the concert and his visit in a letter: ". . . a splendid success from the point of view of honor and glory, but a failure as far as money was concerned."

I. *Allegro.* Mozart provides a good number of attractive melodies in the first movement, some presented by the orchestra alone, some by piano and orchestra. In working through these themes and returning them for the recapitulation Mozart gives the soloist a dazzling succession of figures and passages in his most appealing *galant* style.

II. *Larghetto.* The simple, intimate Larghetto is the most personal movement of the concerto. After the first theme and its extensions come to a complete close, the piano introduces a second subject, which leads to a return of the opening idea. The piano writing sounds quite thin in this movement because Mozart left the piano score incomplete and subsequent editors have largely been responsible for filling in the left-hand part.

III. *Allegretto.* The rollicking last movement provides much delight; even its few sober moments are not overly serious. Mozart repeats the foot-tapping opening theme in variation throughout the Allegretto, with contrasting episodes between its appearances.

Concerto for Piano and Orchestra No. 27 in B flat major, K. 595
(35 minutes)

Mozart completed the K. 595, his final piano concerto, on January 5, 1791, eleven months to the day before his death. By this time he had neither the means nor the sponsorship to introduce the concerto at his own *Akademie,* a concert where the performer sells subscriptions and keeps the profits. Instead he had to give the premiere at the March 4, 1791, *Akademie* of clarinetist Joseph Bähr (or Beer); the concert notice lists Mozart last, after Bähr and a singer.

Many commentators, knowing of Mozart's ill health, grinding poverty, and impending death at the time, hear overtones of great sadness and tragedy in the music. One has to wonder, though, how the music would be perceived if the listener was unaware of the composer's plight. The concerto does, perhaps, have less brilliance and sparkle than many earlier works, but there is little trace of the depressed, hopeless quality that some profess to hear in the music.

I. *Allegro.* Mozart is positively profligate in the way he scatters themes— or, more accurately, brief motifs—through the double exposition, first by the orchestra alone, then by piano and orchestra. Like a juggler with multiple balls in the air, Mozart deftly varies, develops, and repeats the melodies. Casual listening may create the mistaken impression of a completely random sequence of themes. Yet an impelling underlying logic carries the music forward from first note to last in traditional sonata allegro form.

II. *Larghetto.* The simple, lyrical Larghetto conveys the utmost serenity and nobility. But under the surface, one feels an emotionality that approaches religious reverence.

III. *Allegro.* The recurrent principal subject of the last movement, an optimistic little tune, swings along with a delightful lilt. Mozart later used the same melody in his song "Sehnsucht nach dem Frühling" ("Longing for Spring"), which starts with the words "Come, sweet May, and make the trees grow green again."

Concerto for Violin and Orchestra No. 4 in D major, K. 218
(30 minutes)

Between April and December 1775, at age 19 and while concertmaster of the court orchestra of the Archbishop of Salzburg, Mozart composed five violin concertos. We have little information about this concerto, which is among the earliest of his works to win a secure place in today's repertoire, beyond the fact that he finished it in October. Scholars debate whether Mozart wrote the concerto for himself to play with the court orchestra or on his tours of Europe, or whether he wrote it for Gaetano Brunetti, his assistant and later replacement as concertmaster in Salzburg.

I. *Allegro.* The concerto begins with a stentorian, martial melody that sets a stern, military character. But within a very few measures, the mood changes completely, and the remainder of the movement mostly alternates sections of great lightness and delicacy with rich, sonorous passages for the solo violin; only occasionally are we reminded of the forceful opening. As he so often does, Mozart introduces many motifs in the orchestral and solo expositions and then seamlessly weaves together all of the various subjects.

II. *Andante cantabile.* One cannot do better in discussing the second movement than to quote Alfred Einstein, Mozart's biographer, who called the Andante cantabile "an uninterrupted song for the violin and an avowal of love."

III. *Rondeau: Andante grazioso; Allegro ma non troppo.* The principal theme of the warm, good-humored rondo movement has two parts: the first, coquettish in moderate tempo; the second, lightly tripping along at a slightly faster pace. In the middle of the faster section we even hear a brief, speeded-up version of the Andante grazioso melody. As the movement progresses, Mozart introduces a new theme in the slower tempo and in a new meter. He first treats this melody as a gavotte—a dignified old French dance, and then as a musette—an ancient French bagpipe dance with a drone bass. Mozart's audiences surely recognized these two dances as humorous interpolations and shared in Mozart's delightful little joke.

Concerto for Violin and Orchestra No. 5 in A major, K. 219, "Turkish"
(30 minutes)

Mozart completed his fifth and final violin concerto in December 1775 when he was 19 years old and employed as concertmaster in the court orchestra of the Archbishop of Salzburg. When, where, and even if he ever performed the concerto is unknown. The subtitle "Turkish" comes from a well-known section of the last movement.

I. *Allegro aperto.* Mozart fashioned a particularly witty opening for the A major Concerto. The concerto begins with the orchestra playing a series of rising arpeggios, which sound as if they constitute the main theme of the movement; as expected, subsidiary themes follow. Then the violin enters, mysteriously playing a slow, improvisatory-sounding recitative. After a full stop the violin launches an attractive bold new theme in tempo. Careful listening reveals that the orchestra is now playing the opening arpeggios; what we thought was the principal theme was but a preview of the accompaniment! Basically, Mozart follows the traditional structure of a Classical concerto, but shows exceptional originality in bringing all the melodic, harmonic, rhythmic, and structural elements together into a captivating whole.

II. *Adagio.* The Adagio illustrates Mozart's skill in concealing considerable sophistication and subtlety under a cover of utter simplicity. The arching melodic line of this movement, though heard over a bare-bones accompaniment, nevertheless manages to project deep feelings. In 1776, when Gaetano Brunetti was to perform this concerto, he asked Mozart to compose a substitute slow movement because he found the original "too studied," according to a letter written by Mozart's father. The new Adagio is published as K. 261, but all performing editions of the concerto include the far superior and more fitting original.

III. *Rondeau: Tempo di Menuetto.* Mozart starts this movement with a graceful, lilting minuet, which he continues with several ideas in essentially the same style. But then he speeds up the tempo, changes from major to minor mode and from duple to triple meter, and embarks on the extended fiery section that is usually described as "Turkish," although "Hungarian" or "Gypsy" might be more apt. Mozart borrowed the melody from the ballet music he wrote for his opera *Lucio Silla.* After bringing back the first portion of the movement, Mozart ends quietly as the soloist plays a rising figure and vanishes in a puff of air.

Eine kleine Nachtmusik ("A Little Night Music"), K. 525
(20 minutes)

Eine kleine Nachtmusik, surely Mozart's best-known composition, is a serenade, a form that originated as an evening song delivered by a lover beneath his sweetheart's window, but became a generic term for many types of light music. Mozart completed the piece on August 10, 1787, while working on his opera *Don Giovanni.*

Musicologists puzzle over why he composed the piece, when it was first played, and what happened to the extra Menuetto movement that Mozart said was in the work but has never been found. Also, no one knows whether the composer intended the work to be played by a string quintet or by an entire string orchestra. Almost everyone agrees, though, that it is a first-rate piece that works equally well in both versions.

I. *Allegro.* A very familiar, vigorous first theme, a contrasting lyrical second theme, and a piquant closing theme make up the exposition of the sonata allegro first movement. The ensuing development section provides little more than a transition to a restatement of all three themes.

II. *Romanze: Andante.* Originally a Romanze was a sentimental song; here it is a warm, expressive movement dominated by the opening theme. Only one episode in the middle insinuates some agitation into the otherwise calm, placid mood.

III. *Menuetto: Allegretto.* The sprightly though elegant minuet has a more lyrical central section that comes before an abbreviated repeat of the opening.

IV. *Rondo: Allegro.* Sparkling and effervescent, the last movement maintains its high spirits throughout, no matter whether it is lightly tripping along or forcefully exclaiming.

Overture to *Don Giovanni,* K. 527
(6 minutes)

One day before the October 29, 1787, Prague premiere (some say it was a dress rehearsal) of his opera *Don Giovanni,* Mozart still had not composed the overture. His wife, Constanza, tells us that he attended a party that evening, came home late, and started composing, asking her to read him tales from *The Arabian Nights* while he worked. By 3 A.M., Constanza suggested he take a nap, and he slept until five o'clock, when he returned to the score, which he finished at seven in the morning. The copyists worked all day and had the parts on the orchestra stands by curtain time. Only a Mozart could compose a work as magnificent as the overture to *Don Giovanni* overnight!

The opera tells of the amorous adventures of the leading libertine of fiction, Don Giovanni, or Don Juan. Briefly stated: The Don kills the father of one of his conquests while trying to defend his daughter's honor. Near the end of the opera, Giovanni is hiding in a cemetery and invites the statue of the father to dinner. The statue arrives and drags the Don off to hell.

The overture does not summarize the opera, but does use two themes from the last scene of the opera in the slow introduction: one depicts the stony tread of the avenging statue arriving at the dinner, and the second, the waves of fear his appearance arouses in Giovanni and his servant, Leporello. The faster body of the overture, in traditional sonata allegro form, could be mistaken for the first movement of a Mozart symphony. The violins play the vigorous first theme with its arched melodic line. The second theme starts as a loud, gruff question, followed at once by a soft, high staccato answer. Mozart reworks the themes in a very brief development section and restates them in the recapitulation. Since the first scene of the opera follows without pause, Mozart's contemporary Johann André wrote an ending for concert use.

Overture to *The Magic Flute (Die Zauberflöte)*, K. 620
(7 minutes)

Since both Mozart and his librettist, Emanuel Schikaneder, were Masons, it is not surprising that *The Magic Flute*, Mozart's final opera, is rife with Masonic symbolism. The opera can, however, also be enjoyed as a fairy tale or an allegorical love story. Mozart began the composition in the spring of 1791 and finished that fall, completing the overture on September 28, just two days before he conducted the premiere in Vienna.

The overture opens with three solemn, weighty chords, which recur once more in the overture and at several significant moments in the opera. The chords deal symbolically with Masonic ritual in which the number three is particularly meaningful. The slow introduction maintains its reverential tone until the second violins initiate a fast, frolicsome tune, unrelated to any theme in the opera. This melody becomes the subject of a sparkling fugato of great verve and energy. Following sonata allegro form, Mozart then introduces an effervescent second theme that contributes to the pervasive good spirits. About halfway through the overture, Mozart brings back the three ponderous chords. Finally he returns to the joyous fugal theme, working it through to a jubilant ending.

Overture to *The Marriage of Figaro (Le Nozze di Figaro),* K. 492
(4 minutes)

The quiet, fleeting opening of the overture to *The Marriage of Figaro* barely manages to contain its suppressed glee and gaiety. Very quickly, though, shouts of joy and quicksilver giggles of merriment break through and follow in an irresistible outpouring of musical delight. Mozart quotes no melodies from the opera, yet succeeds brilliantly in establishing the comic mood and character of the opera, which describes the complications that ensue from Count Almaviva's attempts to seduce Susanna, his wife's maid, and prevent her marriage to his servant, Figaro.

In his original manuscript, Mozart had written a slow, sentimental section at the climax of the overture. He later tore out that page and went directly from the climax to a return of the whispered opening melody, allowing nothing to interfere with the ebullient good humor of the piece.

The first performance of *The Marriage of Figaro* took place in Vienna on May 1, 1786, with the composer conducting.

Sinfonia Concertante for Oboe, Clarinet, Bassoon, Horn, and Orchestra in E flat major, K. 297b (Anh 9)
(32 minutes)

An intriguing mystery surrounds this work. During the 1770s in Europe, and particularly in Paris, concertos for groups of soloists were the rage. In a letter of April 5, 1778, Mozart, who had just arrived in Paris and probably wanted to take advantage of this interest, wrote that he was composing a sinfonia concertante for flute, oboe, bassoon, and horn, to be played at the end of the month at the Concerts Spirituels, led by Jean Le Gros.

On April 20, Mozart delivered the completed score to Le Gros. But in a May 1 letter Mozart complained to his father of *hickl-hackl* ("hanky-panky") and reported that an envious composer (Giovanni Cambini) had forced Le Gros to cancel Mozart's performance to avoid unfavorable comparisons. Mozart left Paris in October without the score, since Le Gros had bought the piece. "He thinks he is the only one to have it," Mozart wrote home, "but that is not true. I still have it fresh in my head and will set it down as soon as I am home."

For nearly one hundred years, neither Le Gros's original nor Mozart's copy

—if he ever made one—was ever found. Then, in 1869, among the papers of Mozart's biographer Otto Jahn, scholars discovered a sinfonia concertante for oboe, *clarinet,* bassoon, and horn, instead of the *flute,* oboe, bassoon, and horn that Mozart had described. Even though the manuscript was not in the composer's hand and the clarinet was substituted for the flute, most experts agree that the composition was by Mozart. We will probably never know why Jahn never mentioned the work, how he obtained the copy, and why the flute and clarinet were switched.

I. *Allegro.* The work opens with the orchestra announcing the two groups of themes: the first starting with a forceful unison statement, but quickly giving way to several melodies of charm and grace; the second lighter and more lyrical in character. Once the four soloists—usually the principal oboe, clarinet, bassoon, and horn players of the orchestra—enter they maintain a dominant role, working through the melodic material and bringing back all the themes for a recapitulation, with Mozart's written-out cadenza to round everything off.

II. *Adagio.* "The highest level is reached in the slow movement," writes Mozart scholar Alfred Einstein. Mozart pours out a succession of beguiling melodies. Expansive and songlike, they evoke the most characteristic tonal qualities and melodic figures of each instrument. Mozart largely relegates the orchestra to playing a supporting role, allowing the soloists to soar without impediment.

III. *Andantino con variazoni.* The final movement consists of ten connected variations on a delightful little tune. As before, the composer focuses most attention on the soloists, who have many opportunities for virtuosic display, alone or with the others.

Sinfonia Concertante for Violin, Viola, and Orchestra in E flat major, K. 364
(32 minutes)

After a lengthy trip to Mannheim and Paris in which he failed to obtain a position that would free him from the hateful post he held in the Archbishop's court, Mozart returned early in 1779 to what he called his "Salzburg slavery." That fall he completed his Sinfonia Concertante K. 364, a superb work of great depth and maturity. Since he was living at home in Salzburg at the time, we have no letters to give details on why and for whom he wrote the piece or when it was first played. Scholars conjecture that he intended the viola part for himself. Although he played violin as concertmaster of the Archbishop's orchestra and performed widely as a piano soloist, he most enjoyed playing viola in ensembles.

I. *Allegro maestoso.* Mozart appended *maestoso* ("majestic") to the tempo designation, indicating that he considered this to be a serious movement conceived on a grand scale. To be sure, the themes are symphonic in conception, yet the treatment tends to be intimate and conversational as the two soloists and the orchestra discourse eloquently as equal partners.

II. *Andante.* Seldom has Mozart, or any other composer, conceived such an emotionally powerful movement. Interrupted with many short breaks, the principal theme arches across with sustained lyricism. The middle section brings some relaxation of the intensity, but the original feeling returns to end the movement.

III. *Presto.* The opening theme sets the joyous and jubilant character of the last movement. Part of the good fun lies in the way the two soloists toss little phrases of melody back and forth. Cast as a rondo, the gay main theme returns three times separated by contrasting episodes that contribute to the overall smiling visage of the movement.

To make the darker-toned, lower-pitched solo viola the tonal equal of the violin, Mozart asks the violist to tune the strings a half step higher. While this does give the instrument more brilliance, most violists avoid this maneuver because of the already high tension of their strings. Further, Mozart divides the orchestral violas into two groups to warm and enrich the tutti sound.

Symphony No. 29 in A major, K. 201
(25 minutes)

In 1773, when the 17-year-old Mozart went from his home in Salzburg to Vienna seeking a new position, the trip failed in that purpose, but it did introduce the young composer to the new music of Haydn and other contemporaries. Mozart absorbed what he heard and saw and, on his return to Salzburg, he applied the insights to the symphonies that he turned out soon afterward. Of the several symphonies that he completed subsequent to his Vienna visit, none show greater maturity and command than Symphony No. 29. Today critics consider this work the crowning achievement of his youthful years.

I. *Allegro moderato.* What a magical opening Mozart devised for this symphony—the downward octave jumps, the many repeated notes, and the inexorable upward movement of the whole phrase. After a full stop, Mozart introduces the subsidiary theme, very different in character from the first, but making the same liberal use of repeated notes. A closing theme ends the exposition and a brief development section leads to a recapitulation of the themes and an extended forceful ending.

II. *Andante.* After the outgoing first movement, Mozart invites the listener to come closer for a wonderfully intimate and delicate slow movement, stylistically more akin to chamber music than symphony.

III. *Menuetto.* The Menuetto contrasts the grace and lyricism of the established Rococo with the strength and vigor of the emerging Viennese Classical style. At times the music seems intended for the ballroom; at other times it sounds better designed for the concert hall.

IV. *Allegro con spirito.* An energetic, zestful finale completes the symphony. The spirited principal theme of the rondo movement features octave jumps that may—or may not—echo the jumps of the first movement melody.

Mozart composed Symphony No. 29 in Salzburg early in 1774 and probably performed the work shortly thereafter.

Symphony No. 31 in D major, K. 297, "Paris"
(17 minutes)

In September 1777, Mozart and his mother left Salzburg on a slow journey that took them to Paris in March 1778. Unfortunately, neither nobles nor the public had very much interest in a wunderkind who had grown up. And those who were attracted by his incredible ability were put off by his coarseness and lack of respect for those in authority. The trip's one benefit was that it led to the creation of the so-called "Paris" Symphony, which Mozart composed at the request of Jean Le Gros, leader of the Concerts Spirituels. Mozart completed the composition early in June and Le Gros introduced it on June 18, 1778.

I. *Allegro assai.* "I have been careful," Mozart wrote, "not to neglect the *premier coup d'archet* [literally, "first bow stroke," a reference to the orchestra's pride in starting every piece with a loud note played in perfect unison]. What a fuss the donkeys here make of the trick!" Mozart does indeed start the symphony with a blast of sound, which he immediately balances with a gossamer-light response. The rest of the movement sensitively creates sharp contrasts between forceful passages and sections of incredible lightness and delicacy, as well as between the solidity of the first theme and the flickering luminosity of the second.

II. *Andante.* "But the Andante did not have the good fortune to win his [Le Gros's] approval," wrote Mozart. Eager to please, Mozart composed a new Andante. "Each one is good in its own way, for each has a different character," Mozart later commented. Scholars have long believed the current performing version to be the revision, but musicologist Hermann Beck in 1955 offered convincing evidence that it is the original.

III. *Allegro.* Mozart omits a minuet movement and proceeds directly to the finale. "Since I observed that all last, as well as first, movements begin here with all instruments playing together, I began mine with first and second violins only," Mozart wrote, ". . . followed instantly by a loud forte. The audience, as I expected, said 'hush' at the soft beginning, and when they heard the forte began immediately to applaud." Both the thematic content and the alternation of bold and dainty writing hark back to the first movement. For the first time, we hear in the finale considerable use of imitation and counterpoint.

Symphony No. 35 in D major, K. 385, "Haffner"
(20 minutes)

July 1782 found Mozart busy in Vienna with many different projects—conducting performances of his opera *The Abduction from the Seraglio,* preparing excerpts for publication, fulfilling commissions for new works, and making plans for his upcoming marriage. In the midst of all this, Mozart's father wrote a letter informing his son that the Mayor of Salzburg, Siegmund Haffner, was being elevated to the nobility and wanted a piece from Mozart, a light, not too serious work that could be performed as background music at a reception or banquet. Over the following few weeks Mozart composed a six-movement serenade that he sent to his father, movement by movement as he finished them. Speculation has it, though, that they arrived too late to be performed.

Early the next year, Mozart was preparing for some concerts, needed a symphony in a hurry, and recalled the serenade. He asked his father to return the score. Mozart reworked the music, cut the introductory march and one of the two minuets, and added flutes and clarinets to the orchestra. Thus, from the serenade he fashioned the four-movement "Haffner" Symphony.

I. *Allegro con spirito.* The opening theme, with its two-octave upward and downward leaps, immediately captures the pomp and grandiosity of the music's original purpose. As Mozart concentrates his energy on that figure—changing its character, shrinking and inverting the leaps, and treating it in imitation—the movement assumes a more serious and symphonic air, but without losing its festive, celebratory character.

II. *Andante.* Pleasant and tender, the Andante offers a quiet, lyrical respite after the intense opening movement.

III. *Menuetto.* The first section of this movement recaptures the force and power of the symphony's opening. In stark contrast, the middle part features sweet little woodwind phrases, after which Mozart brings back a shortened reprise of the opening.

IV. *Presto.* Mozart asked that this movement be played "as fast as possible," and it is indeed a high-speed, lighthearted chase, with just a few breaks to allow the performers—and the listeners—to catch their breath.

Mozart conducted the first performance in Vienna on March 23, 1783, at an *Akademie,* a subscription concert, at which he netted 1,600 gulden, a considerable amount of money at the time.

Symphony No. 36 in C major, K. 425, "Linz"
(30 minutes)

Mozart and his wife, Constanza, arrived in Linz on October 30, 1783, on their way back to their home in Vienna after an extended visit with his father and sister in Salzburg. The following day he wrote to his father: "On Thursday, November 4, I am giving a concert in the theater here and, as I have not a single symphony with me, I am writing a new one at a head-over-heels pace." He completed the so-called "Linz" Symphony three days later and conducted the premiere at the November 4 concert. The symphony proved to be a mature, confident, fully realized work that never betrays the amazing speed with which it was composed.

I. *Adagio; Allegro spiritoso.* For the first time, Mozart added a slow introduction to the opening movement of a symphony, here solemn and portentous in character. In the faster body of the movement Mozart reverses the usual character of the thematic groups by making the first group predominantly lyrical and cantabile, and giving the second a loud, forceful quality. The structure, though, is traditional: statement of the two thematic groups, brief development, recapitulation, and very short coda.

II. *Poco adagio.* Mozart establishes the gentle rocking rhythmic pattern of an old Italian dance form, the siciliano, in this movement. The principal theme, a luminous melody with perhaps a trace of melancholy, predominates. In a striking passage near the middle of the movement, Mozart gives the lower strings and bassoon a figure with a particularly ominous sound.

III. *Menuetto.* Mozart makes this minuet more a heavy-footed peasant dance than a delicate, courtly dance. He intensifies the character by introducing a sweet, quiet interlude before concluding with a shortened reprise of the opening.

IV. *Presto.* The success of this movement depends, to a very great extent, on the performance. Although marked Presto, "very quick," the players must be sure to avoid a breakneck speed or risk losing all the music's wit and subtlety. The musicians must also make the dozens of abrupt changes between loud and soft without growing louder or softer, in order to keep the surprise element in Mozart's sudden reversals of dynamic level.

Symphony No. 38 in D major, K. 504, "Prague"
(32 minutes)

In the summer of 1786, Prague saw the very successful presentation of Mozart's opera *The Marriage of Figaro;* the opera was performed daily for several months. Its melodies became the popular songs of the day and dancers twirled to opera selections arranged as dance tunes in Prague's ballrooms.

Grateful for the wonderful reception given his opera, Mozart quickly accepted an invitation from Count Johann Thun to return to Prague in January 1787 for a revival of *Figaro.* Mozart brought along a symphony he had completed on December 6, 1786, probably with the thought of performing it in Prague. Arriving on January 11, 1787, Mozart heard the *Figaro* performance six nights later, and on January 19 conducted an evening of his own music, including the new symphony. Despite the tiny size of the orchestra, with only six violins, three violas, and two basses in the strings, the audience accorded the new piece a most enthusiastic reception.

I. *Adagio; Allegro.* The symphony's attention-grabbing opening immediately makes apparent that this will not be an idle entertainment, but a serious musical discourse. The work starts with a rather long, slow introduction in the mysterious, dramatic style that Mozart usually reserved for his operas. The mood lightens somewhat in the body of the movement as he offers up a profusion of melodic fragments for the first subject and a sustained lyrical melody as the second. So intricate and complex is the counterpoint that Mozart prepared preliminary sketches, which he very rarely did.

II. *Andante.* The composer also endowed the Andante with melodic abundance and a plenitude of motifs. The mood tends to be sober and reflective, with a good deal of counterpoint and canonic writing. Mozart introduces a certain dramatic tension by contrasting diatonic passages (using only the notes of the G major scale) with chromatic passages (adding notes in addition to those in the scale, as though playing on both the white and the black keys of a piano).

III. *Presto.* Mozart omits the minuet movement that usually precedes the finale, and immediately tosses out the gay, insouciant little tune that dominates the last movement. The composer borrowed the melody from his popular opera, *The Marriage of Figaro;* it is the orchestral accompaniment to the charming duet of Cherubino and Susanna, *"Aprite presto,"* which was surely familiar to the Prague public. The music sparkles with infectious humor, sharpened by striking contrasts between the strings and the winds, as well as by abrupt changes of dynamics. The music's delectable spirit of merriment dispels any residual solemnity from earlier movements, and catches everyone up in its exuberant happiness.

Symphony No. 39 in E flat major, K. 543
(32 minutes)

Mozart's final three great symphonies, Nos. 39, 40, and 41, composed within two months during the summer of 1788, rank as one of the most remarkable achievements in the history of music, even though no one knows exactly why he composed these symphonies so hastily. Some speculate that he was hoping to perform them the next season in concerts that never materialized. Others hold that, instead of only composing for a specific purpose or occasion, Mozart wrote these last symphonies as what Alfred Einstein called "an appeal to eternity."

Equally incredible is the fact that Mozart radiated so much joy and good cheer in Symphony No. 39. His music was proving increasingly inaccessible to Viennese audiences and he had lost most of his sponsors and patrons. In addition, Mozart was encountering opposition because of the widespread prejudice against Freemasonry and because his successes in Prague riled the competing Viennese. Forced to move from Vienna to cheaper lodgings in the suburbs and to beg for loans from his friends, Mozart still managed to make Symphony No. 39 a most pleasurable work. It was completed on June 26, 1788, and the premiere took place at some unknown time after Mozart's death in 1791.

I. *Adagio; Allegro.* The symphony opens with a slow introduction that is both dramatic and anguished; some think of it as a kind of emotional catharsis. That done, Mozart embarks on a musical voyage of enchanting beauty—now filled with graceful calm, now sparkling with brilliant verve.

II. *Andante con moto.* The second movement sets the essentially stepwise movement of the quiet principal theme against the vaulting acrobatics of the louder subsidiary subject. Mozart carries us back and forth from one to the other until two powerful chords end the final statement of the main theme.

III. *Menuetto: Allegretto.* Mozart invests this movement with an overall air of robust good humor. It is cast in three-part form: the bold beginning, a quieter central part, with prominent parts for the two clarinets, and the reprise of the opening.

IV. *Finale: Allegro.* The entire Finale grows from the bright, effervescent tune with which it starts. In a brilliant display of musical inventiveness, Mozart explores every facet of the melody, creating a movement of joyous appeal and attraction.

Symphony No. 40 in G minor, K. 550
(25 minutes)

Mozart composed the G minor during the memorable summer of 1788 that saw the creation of his final three symphonies. Probably the most frequently performed of all his symphonies, No. 40 surely stands at the very apex of his work in that form. The composer finished the G minor on July 25, 1788, one month after completing Symphony No. 39; later, though, he added parts for clarinets and made slight changes in the oboe part. Some accounts hold that Antonio Salieri, Mozart's rival, gave the premiere in Vienna on April 16, 1791, with an orchestra of 180!

I. *Molto allegro.* Instead of the traditional forthright, forceful principal theme, Mozart starts with a quiet, though agitated melody that has a distinctive rhythmic pattern. Then, instead of a contrasting second theme, he follows with still another quiet melody that sighs gently with its basically descending contour. The rhythm of the first theme predominates in the development that follows the exposition. The composer returns both themes in the recapitulation and loudly hammers home the overriding rhythm of the movement in the brief coda.

II. *Andante.* Just as the rhythmic pattern prevails in the opening movement, so repeated notes reign in the second. The first phrase of the principal subject is an upbeat and six repeated notes that moves up through the string sections. The second theme is four repeated notes, each one fading and falling away from the initial note. With great originality and inventiveness, Mozart crafts these materials into a highly emotional movement.

III. *Menuetto: Allegretto.* A hemiola, a two-beat rhythmic pattern superimposed on the three-beat minuet meter, catches one's attention in the third movement. The simple and songlike middle section offers listeners some feeling of peace and solace; it is succeeded by a shortened repeat of the opening.

IV. *Allegro assai.* The upward-thrusting opening theme emerges all-important in the finale. Mozart introduces a contrasting light and charming second theme, which he largely overlooks during the development's obsessive concern with the principal subject. On the surface the movement seems high-spirited and happy, but beneath the excitement lies a substratum of some gloom and unhappiness.

Symphony No. 41 in C major, K. 551, "Jupiter"
(32 minutes)

Mozart completed the "Jupiter," his 41st and last symphony, on August 10, 1788, soon after he finished his 39th symphony (June 26, 1788) and his 40th (July 25, 1788). Alas, we have no indication that Mozart conducted or even heard any one of these symphonies over the remaining three years of his life.

The nickname "Jupiter" was not of Mozart's invention; it was probably supplied later by London music publisher J. B. Cramer. Many have argued about the appropriateness of the subtitle and have attempted to associate specific features of the score with Jupiter's power as king of the gods in Roman mythology. Often the arguments seem spurious, but who can dispute the view that this great symphony is godlike in its inspiration and realization?

I. *Allegro vivace.* Some of the special qualities of the "Jupiter" emerge at the very outset: the extensive use of terse thematic cells, each with a distinctive melodic or rhythmic character; the abundant generosity with which Mozart pours forth these short thematic units; and the sharp, consistently striking contrasts in emotional content, dynamic level, texture, and articulation.

The imperious summons at the beginning, the immediate beseeching response, and the several additional motifs that come later complete the principal subject of the first movement. A variety of motifs also make up the subsidiary subject, in turn slow-moving and sinuous, gaily dancing, and heroic. To conclude the presentation of themes, Mozart borrows the delightful melody of an aria from his *Magic Flute;* the words are: "You are a bit dense, my dear Pompeo, go and learn the ways of the world."

II. *Andante cantabile.* The expressivity and eloquence of the Andante cantabile have led many to call it the finest of all Mozart slow movements. The muted strings add a particularly poignant air to the opening theme, but before the movement ends Mozart moves the music through a succession of widely varied emotional states.

III. *Menuetto: Allegretto.* Light and charming, the Menuetto conjures up the image of a glittering ball in 18th century Vienna with the ornately dressed aristocrats daintily negotiating their way through the intricacies of the dance. Near the end of the Trio, the middle section of the Menuetto, Mozart introduces a theme that anticipates the principal subject of the finale.

IV. *Molto allegro.* The last movement or "crown" of the entire symphony opens with a serene violin melody that was a particular favorite of Mozart; he had already used it in two masses and a symphony. Mozart then makes this theme the subject of a five-voice fugue. From here on Mozart, with an ease that masks the complexity of the writing, tosses motifs about in exuberant profusion—consecutively, simultaneously, and in various other combinations —yet always maintaining the highest level of musical expressivity. The climax comes in the extended coda, where Mozart dazzlingly interweaves five of the motifs heard earlier into a breathtaking conclusion.

Modest Mussorgsky

Born March 21, 1839, in Karevo, Russia
Died March 28, 1881, in St. Petersburg

MODEST MUSSORGSKY won his important place in the history of
music largely through his operas and songs. He became one of the
world's most original and best-known composers under two very unlikely
sets of circumstances. First, Mussorgsky had a minimal amount of musical
training and remained an undisciplined composer with a rough style all his
life. Also, instead of following a career in music, Mussorgsky attended military school and entered a regiment of guards, where, it is said, he developed a
lifelong addiction to alcohol.

Soon after entering the guards, Mussorgsky met several young composers
of St. Petersburg and decided that he too wanted to become a composer. He
started his studies with composer Mily Balakirev, which mostly involved
playing four-hand piano reductions of scores by such admired composers as
Beethoven and Schumann.

When the serfs were liberated in 1861, Mussorgsky lost his position in the
guards and from then on supported himself with various low-level civil
service positions. Nevertheless, despite his lack of formal musical training, a
drinking habit, and what biographers gently refer to as a "nervous condition," Mussorgsky kept on composing.

In addition to his other problems, Mussorgsky showed a seemingly ge-
netic inability to finish projects. At the time of his death he left several
uncompleted works, including several operas. Other Russian composers, and
particularly Nikolai Rimsky-Korsakov, finished and prepared his scores for
publication and performance. Rimsky-Korsakov considered some of Mussorgsky's works so badly written that he made extensive revisions in the
harmonies and orchestration.

Only in recent years have musicologists unearthed some of Mussorgsky's original manuscripts, which have changed their opinions about his music. Many now appreciate Mussorgsky's powerful ideas and the bold and unusual features that he introduced into his compositions. What his colleagues viewed as a lack of discipline, musicologists today regard as an amazingly fertile musical imagination that went far beyond textbook rules of composition. But as the various revisions of his music have been with us so long, most players eschew the originals. Thus, more often than not, we continue to hear Mussorgsky revised and transcribed.

A Night on Bald Mountain
(11 minutes)

Mussorgsky drew the inspiration for this piece, his only orchestral work (he originally composed *Pictures at an Exhibition* for piano), from the book *Witchcraft* by Khotinsky. The particular passage tells of evil sorcerers and witches gathering on high, isolated mountains (he set his on Mount Triglav near Kiev) to perform orgiastic rituals honoring the devil. These gatherings, called sabbats, occurred throughout the year; the most sacred one was held on the night of June 23, St. John's Eve.

Mussorgsky began speaking about composing a piece on this demonic subject in 1858. It took nine more years, however, before he could write to composer Nikolai Rimsky-Korsakov: "On June 23, on the eve of St. John's Day, I finished, with God's help, *St. John's Night on Bald Mountain*—a musical picture with the following program: (1) assembly of the witches, their chatter and gossip; (2) cortege of Satan; (3) unholy glorification of Satan; and (4) witches' sabbat."

Both Rimsky-Korsakov and Mily Balakirev, composer and mentor to Mussorgsky, pointed out many faults in the score and Mussorgsky reluctantly put the piece aside. Twice, in 1872 and 1874, Mussorgsky started to rework the composition for inclusion in an opera, but neither project came to fruition.

On Mussorgsky's death in 1881, Rimsky-Korsakov prepared the work in its present form, probably using music that had been incorporated into a much earlier opera, and correcting what he considered errors in structure and orchestration. No one knows where Mussorgsky leaves off and Rimsky-Korsakov begins, but the chilling work continues very effectively to evoke a wild and wicked witches' frenzy.

Pictures at an Exhibition
(Transcribed for orchestra by Maurice Ravel)
(35 minutes)

In 1873, Mussorgsky's close friend, the Russian painter and architect Victor Hartmann, died at age 39. Early the next year a memorial exhibit of 400 Hartmann drawings, watercolors, and stage designs was held in St. Petersburg. Mussorgsky was so affected by the show that he composed a piano suite, *Pictures at an Exhibition,* based on ten of the artworks.

Pictures quickly became extremely popular in its original version for piano. But transcriptions for orchestra, by Nikolai Rimsky-Korsakov, Maurice Ravel, Lucien Caillet, Leopold Stokowski, and many others, have earned the piece an even wider audience. The version prepared by the French composer Ravel, which he orchestrated in 1922, has become the standard. The work received its premiere in Paris under the direction of Serge Koussevitzky on May 3, 1923.

Promenade. In the publication of the original piano suite Vladimir Stassov, a critic and writer to whom Mussorgsky dedicated the work, wrote: "The composer here portrays himself walking, now right, now left, now as an idle person, now urged to go near a picture; at times his joyous appearance is dampened, he thinks in sadness of his dead friend."

Gnomus. Stassov describes the subject as a "child's plaything . . . something in the style of the fabled Nutcracker, the nuts being inserted in the gnome's mouth. The gnome accompanies his droll movements with savage shrieks."

Promenade. As above.

Il Vecchio castello. The music portrays a troubadour performing in front of a medieval Italian castle. The composer represents the player by a saxophone.

Promenade. As above.

Tuileries. Mussorgsky gave the subtitle "Dispute of the Children After Play" to this scene set in the famous Paris park.

Bydlo. Mussorgsky based the music on a watercolor showing an old-fashioned oxcart (*bydlo* means "cattle" in Polish) lumbering along on its large wooden wheels as the driver sings a "folksong in the Aeolian mode."

Promenade. As above.

Ballet of Chicks in Their Shells. "In 1870, Hartmann designed the costumes for the staging of the ballet *Trilby.* In the cast were a number of boy and girl pupils . . . dressed up as eggs." The costumes looked like large eggs, with the dancer's head, arms, and legs protruding.

Samuel Goldenberg and Schmuyle. Inspired by two Hartmann drawings of Jews from a Polish ghetto, Mussorgsky originally called this section *Two*

Jews, One Rich, the Other Poor, a title that Stassov subsequently changed. The composer characterizes the wealthy man with a pompous theme and uses a supplicating response for the less fortunate companion.

The Marketplace at Limoges. The sketch, which Hartmann did on the spot, pictures a group of animated, gossiping market women.

Catacombae Sepulchrum Romanum. In this work Hartmann portrays himself and a friend exploring the Paris catacombs. Following without pause is *Cum mortis in lingua mortua* ("With the dead in a dead language"). Mussorgsky wrote on the piano score: "Hartmann's creative spirit leads us to the place of skulls and calls to them—the skulls begin to glow faintly from within."

The Hut on Fowl's Legs. This fanciful drawing represents the home of the Russian witch Baba-Yaga, a hut in the form of a giant clock resting on fowl's legs.

The Great Gate at Kiev. Hartmann's design for a giant new gate to the city, which was never built. The design "conceived in the massive old Russian style had a cupola in the shape of a Slavonic helmet."

Sergei Prokofiev

Born April 23, 1891, in Sontsovka, Russia
Died March 5, 1953, in Moscow

EXTREMELY PRECOCIOUS, Prokofiev was only 12 when he entered the St. Petersburg Conservatory to study piano, composition, and conducting. After graduation with high honors, he performed widely as a pianist and had many of his compositions published. Fearful, though, that the Russian Revolution and the incoming Communist regime would limit his opportunities, Prokofiev moved to New York City in 1918 and then settled in Paris in 1923, where he lived for the next ten years.

The composer sorely missed his homeland and returned in stages starting in 1933; in 1936 he settled permanently in Moscow, where he was hailed as the leading composer of the Soviet Union.

Then, in 1948 Premier Joseph Stalin and the Soviet authorities expressed great displeasure with the direction Prokofiev's music was taking and denounced him soundly. In response, he wrote a humble letter of apology and promised to write in the desired style of "Socialist Realism." An oratorio, *On Guard for Peace,* and a vocal-symphonic suite, *Winter Bonfire,* satisfied the authorities, but not the public, since both have disappeared from the repertoire. However, shortly before his death in 1953 (ironically on the same day as Stalin), Prokofiev wrote two outstanding works in keeping with his artistic aims, the Symphony-Concerto for Cello and Orchestra and the Seventh Symphony.

In his autobiography, Prokofiev identifies five trends in his music: "The first is *classical,* whose origin lies in my early infancy when I heard my mother play Beethoven sonatas. The second is *innovation,* whose inception I trace to my meeting with Taneyev, when he taunted me for my rather 'elementary harmony.' The third is the element of the toccata, or *motor element,* probably influenced by Schumann's *Toccata,* which impressed me greatly at one time. The fourth element is the *lyrical*. I should like to . . . regard the fifth element, that of the *grotesque*, . . . as merely a variation of the other characteristics."

Prokofiev had one of the most distinctive of 20th century compositional voices. There is a sharpness, a clarity, a very special sparkle that is uniquely his. For wit, sardonic humor, and biting satire he has few equals. Yet, he is also capable of plumbing emotional depths in his music, not by expressing himself in a highly personal way, but by conjuring up these feelings objectively and, as it were, from a distance.

Concerto for Piano and Orchestra No. 2 in G minor, Op. 16

(35 minutes)

Prokofiev composed this concerto, the second of five, from December 1912 to April 1913, while still a student at the St. Petersburg Conservatory. He gave the premiere at Pavlovsk, a resort near St. Petersburg, on September 5, 1913, with A. P. Aslanov conducting the orchestra. The concertgoers objected vociferously; someone was heard mumbling: "Music like this is enough to drive one out of one's mind!" According to a newspaper account: "The audience was scandalized and most of them hissed. With a mocking bow, Prokofiev sat down again and at once played an encore."

A few years later, during the Russian Revolution, Soviet police purportedly raided Prokofiev's home and confiscated the single manuscript copy of the Second Piano Concerto. They did not, however, find the complete sketches from which he had composed the work, and in 1923 he used them to reconstruct the concerto.

The character of the Second Piano Concerto resembles that of its creator— brash, irreverent, and somewhat outlandish. In the many decades since its premiere, listeners have become accustomed to the dissonant and wildly barbaric sounds heard in this concerto. Today most consider it a valuable contribution to the music of the early 1900s.

I. *Andantino; Allegretto; Andantino.* Prokofiev marked the quiet, somewhat angular piano theme that opens and comes to dominate the movement *narrante* ("in the style of a narration"). The composer introduces other subsidiary melodies, all of which he treats with a good deal of dissonance. A major part of the movement consists of an extremely difficult, written-out piano cadenza that essentially functions as the development section. Recollections of the principal theme bring the movement to a quiet, pensive close.

II. *Scherzo: Vivace.* This tour de force illustrates Prokofiev's motoric style. Like perpetual motion, the solo piano never departs from its rapid, running sixteenth notes. The piano plays in octaves without chords and without rests, against which the orchestra flings out brief melodic fragments.

III. *Intermezzo: Allegro moderato.* A heavy, plodding ostinato figure with harsh brass comments opens the movement. The piano joins in, maintaining the marchlike character. We hear some moments of delicacy and charm, but the brutal forward motion always returns, propelling the music ever onward.

IV. *Allegro tempestoso.* Sparks fly in the electrifying opening of this finale as the pianist dashes over the keyboard and the orchestra joins in the high-voltage display. With a sudden and abrupt volte-face, Prokofiev brings in the slow, spare second theme. After a development section and a cadenza, Prokofiev recalls the opening and the movement surges to a bravura conclusion.

Concerto for Piano and Orchestra No. 3 in C major, Op. 26
(30 minutes)

The public considers Prokofiev's Third Piano Concerto the most approachable of his five piano concertos and among the century's most enduring creations in that form. Prokofiev completed the concerto while in Brittany in October 1921, basing some of the themes on melodies he had jotted down over the previous decade for various unrealized compositions. He played the ferociously difficult solo part at the very successful premiere on December 16, 1921, with the Chicago Symphony under Frederick Stock.

I. *Andante; Allegro.* A solo clarinet opens the concerto with a limpid melody that has the air of a Russian folk song. The tempo soon picks up and the piano states the bustling principal theme of the movement. After some lively discussion of this subject, the texture thins and a piquant second theme appears in the woodwinds, with castanets adding a somewhat humorous cast to the proceedings. Prokofiev then freely develops and returns the various subjects with brilliant writing for the orchestra and virtuosic display for the soloist.

II. *Tema con variazione.* This delightful movement offers a set of five variations on a sinuous theme. Prokofiev describes the movement: "The theme is announced by the orchestra alone, Andantino. In the first variation, the piano treats the opening of the theme in quasi-sentimental fashion, and resolves into a chain of trills as the orchestra repeats the closing phrase. The tempo changes to Allegro for the second and third variations, and the piano has brilliant figures, while snatches of the theme are introduced here and there in the orchestra. In Variation IV the tempo is once again Andante, and the piano and orchestra discourse on the theme in a quiet and meditative fashion. Variation V is energetic. It leads without pause into a restatement of the theme by the orchestra, with delicate chordal embroidery in the piano."

III. *Allegro ma non troppo.* The bassoon and lower strings pizzicato introduce the main theme, with its well-hidden meter. But the piano soon elbows its way in and the movement lifts off with the soloist and orchestra in a seeming struggle for ascendancy. As we careen along, Prokofiev treats us to new themes and mercurial changes of mood and character, while allowing the opening theme to pop up from time to time.

Concerto for Violin and Orchestra No. 1 in D major, Op. 18
(22 minutes)

In 1915, the year after his graduation from the St. Petersburg Conservatory, Prokofiev began work on a violin concertino, a miniature concerto. He got as far as the opening theme when he became involved with his opera *The Gambler.* By the time he returned to the violin work in 1917, he decided to use the concertino theme as the opening of a full-fledged violin concerto. With technical advice from the Polish violinist Paul Kochanski, Prokofiev finished the score in the summer of 1917. The concerto proved to be symphonic in conception; the solo violin had few passages of virtuosic display and no cadenzas and was treated as one voice in the overall texture, rather than as the leading voice with orchestral accompaniment.

The premiere, planned for November 1917 with Kochanski as soloist, was canceled due to the precarious political situation in Russia. Prokofiev left his native land the following year, finally settling in Paris in October 1923 and remaining there for about ten years, before returning home. The First Violin Concerto received its first performance in Paris on October 18, 1923, played by Marcel Darrieux, concertmaster of the Koussevitzky Orchestra, with Serge Koussevitzky conducting. At first, the reaction was quite cool, but when Joseph Szigeti began to play the concerto in various European musical centers one year later, it attracted worldwide attention and soon came to the prominence it enjoys today.

I. *Andantino.* The shimmering tremolo of the violas provides the background over which the solo violin sings the serenely lyrical opening theme. Prokofiev asked that the soloist play the theme with the utmost clarity and without sentimentality. An ostinato figure for the cellos introduces the second theme, a violin melody ornamented by a grace note or trill on virtually every note. The development begins after a pause with an echo of the opening theme played by flute and clarinet. Soon the soloist sets off on a series of rapid passages while the orchestra handles the melodic development. The violas again start a tremolo and the flute brings back the opening theme, which is decorated with a filigree woven by the soloist. The movement ends quietly without a reappearance of the second theme.

II. *Scherzo: Vivacissimo.* The mischievous second movement, a rondo, has a merry, highly rhythmic ascending figure as its principal theme. Biting, slightly sinister interludes twice shoulder aside its zesty optimism; the soloist heightens the effect by playing *sul ponticello,* with the bow near the bridge, to produce a particularly chilling and eerie sound. But the returns of the principal theme between the interludes and at the end bring back the movement's gay mood.

III. *Moderato.* After the Scherzo firestorm, the broad lyricism of the Moderato returns us to the character of the first movement. The solo violin states the somewhat languid main theme, and after some expansion of that melody the violas sing the second theme under continuing figurations by the soloist. After the development, devoted exclusively to the main theme, the recapitulation brings back both the principal theme of this movement, played by the orchestra, and the theme from the first movement, ornamented with high trills by the soloist. The movement fades away with the soloist and orchestra at the very top of their range.

Concerto for Violin and Orchestra No. 2 in G minor, Op. 63
(27 minutes)

In his Second, and last, Violin Concerto, Prokofiev, no longer the naughty enfant terrible of some of his earlier dissonant and shocking works, produced a very appealing, essentially consonant Romantic work. The many richly expressive and appealing melodies show particular grace and charm. Along with these lyrical features, Prokofiev provides the soloist with plenty of the virtuosic fireworks that listeners expect in a solo concerto. With good reason this has become a highly prized violin concerto of the 20th century.

Prokofiev composed his Second Violin Concerto during a period of transition in his life. For 15 years he had lived in self-imposed exile from the Soviet Union and, starting in 1933, he took the first tentative steps back to his homeland. In a way the concerto bridges the gap between his expatriation and repatriation. On a 1935 commission from admirers of violinist Robert Soetans, Prokofiev began composing a violin concerto in Paris, but finished it in the Soviet Union on August 16, 1935. Soetans gave the premiere in Madrid on December 1, 1935, with Enrique Arbós conducting.

I. *Allegro moderato.* The concerto opens with the solo violin statement of the first theme, a warm, cantabile melody. The second theme, also given out by the soloist over soft murmurings in the orchestral strings, is even more lyrical and Romantic than the first. Prokofiev devotes the remainder of the movement to working out these two melodies, though favoring the first, and sends the soloist off on flights of decorative and pyrotechnical fancy.

II. *Andante assai.* Waxing even more cantabile, the soloist sings the long vocal line over a staccato, steadily moving accompaniment of clarinets and pizzicato strings. The melody then passes to the orchestra, while the solo violin adds its ornaments. The tempo accelerates a bit for the first of three contrasting episodes that are interspersed among variations on the opening theme.

III. *Allegro ben marcato.* The brash, satirical Prokofiev comes to the fore in the highly rhythmic finale. Organized much as the previous movement, the solo violin plays the subject at the outset, which returns in altered form several times between the subsidiary themes that follow. The movement crackles with energy, and the fiendishly difficult writing for the soloist adds to the visceral excitement of this movement as it races to its tumultuous conclusion.

Romeo and Juliet, Suites 1 and 2, Opp. 64b, 64c
(30 minutes; 30 minutes)

At a party following the January 10, 1940, premiere of Prokofiev's ballet *Romeo and Juliet,* Galina Ulanova, who danced the role of Juliet, paraphrased the concluding lines of the original play:

> Never was a story of more woe
> Than this of Prokofiev's music for Romeo.

Prokofiev first proposed a ballet on Shakespeare's *Romeo and Juliet* to the Kirov Ballet in 1934, but the company withdrew from the negotiations. The composer then signed a contract for its production by Moscow's Bolshoi Theater and composed the score in the summer of 1935. The Bolshoi, however, rejected the music, declaring it unsuitable for dance, and questioning Prokofiev's decision to have the two lovers survive (Prokofiev later changed the ending to conform to Shakespeare). "Living people can dance," Prokofiev said by way of explanation, "the dying cannot."

An October 1935 performance of the music, without dance, did not engender much interest. But the two symphonic suites that Prokofiev extracted from the score were heartily received at their premieres—*Suite 1* in Moscow on November 24, 1936, *Suite 2* in Leningrad (now St. Petersburg) on April 15, 1937. Prokofiev subsequently created *Suite 3,* which orchestras perform less frequently.

In preparing the two suites, Prokofiev made no attempt to follow the sequence of the ballet nor was he completely faithful to the original score. As he wrote in his autobiography: "Some numbers were taken directly from the ballet without alteration, others incorporated diverse other material."

Each suite consists of seven separate sections:

SUITE 1

1. *Folk Dance.* A breezy, holiday celebration in the market that opens Act II.

2. *Scene.* The beginning of Act I as the revelers slowly drift home.

3. *Madrigal.* The Capulet ball from Act II, suggesting a tender conversation between the lovers.

4. *Minuet.* Romeo and Juliet dance together at the opening of the ballroom scene.

5. *Masks.* The masked Romeo and his two friends arrive at the Capulet ball.

6. *Balcony Scene.* The two lovers in the balcony scene.

7. *Tybalt's Death.* Several related episodes from the end of Act II: Tybalt's duel with Mercutio; Romeo's duel with Tybalt; Tybalt's death; and some newly composed transitional music leading to Tybalt's funeral.

SUITE 2

1. *Montagues and Capulets.* The slow opening comes from Act I when the Duke forbids the families to continue their feuding. The following faster section accompanies the knight's dance at the Capulet ball. The poignant flute solo in the middle section represents Juliet.

2. *Juliet, the Young Girl.* From Act I, Scene 2, at the point where her nurse is helping Juliet dress for the ball and her mother asks her to contemplate marriage to Count Paris; the music portrays the skittishness of the young girl, along with intimations of a mature woman's seriousness.

3. *Friar Laurence.* The mood in Friar Laurence's cell as Romeo awaits his beloved for the marriage ceremony.

4. *Dance of the Five Couples.* A lively dance scene in the market before the Act II ballroom scene.

5. *Romeo and Juliet Before Parting.* The mournful farewells as Romeo leaves Juliet's bedroom after their first and only night together.

6. *Dance of the Maids from the Antilles.* Prokofiev describes this quiet, elegant section: "Paris presents pearls to Juliet; slave girls dance with pearls."

7. *Romeo at Juliet's Tomb.* The final scene of the ballet, including Juliet's funeral procession, Romeo's arrival at the tomb, and finally a return of Juliet's music, which quietly fades away into silence.

Symphony No. 1 in D major, Op. 25, "Classical Symphony"
(14 minutes)

Completely modern in outlook and composing style, Prokofiev still felt an affinity for the music of the Classical era. The feeling sprang, in part, from early memories of his mother playing Beethoven piano sonatas and, in part, from the St. Petersburg Conservatory, where Prokofiev developed an appreciation for the old masters, along with his explorations of new composing techniques. The composition in which Prokofiev most successfully weds the two styles is the "Classical Symphony."

"It seemed to me," Prokofiev wrote, "that had Haydn lived in our century he would have retained his own style while absorbing something of the new at the same time. That was the kind of symphony I wanted to write: a symphony in the classical style. And when I saw that my idea was beginning to work, I called it the 'Classical Symphony': in the first place because it was simpler, and secondly, for the fun of it, to 'tease the geese,' and in the secret hope that I would prove to be right if the symphony did turn out to be a classic."

Prokofiev composed the "Classical Symphony," the first of seven in the form, during the summer of 1917, which he spent in a small village near St. Petersburg. It proved to be a work of irresistible glitter and sparkle. He completed the orchestration on September 10, 1917, and conducted the first performance in Petrograd (now St. Petersburg) on April 20, 1918.

I. *Allegro*. The symphony opens with an immediate statement of the bustling and zestful first theme. A contrasting theme quickly follows; wild two-octave leaps in the melody line belie its apparent air of reserve and restraint. A full stop signals the end of the exposition, to be succeeded by a brief development and the return of both themes for the recapitulation.

II. *Larghetto*. Over a murmured bouncy accompaniment figure the first violins sing the thin, tenuous melody of the second movement. After a repetition for flute and violin, pizzicato strings introduce a middle section. The first melody then returns, along with reminders of the chattering middle portion of the movement.

III. *Gavotte: Non troppo allegro*. For the Classical third movement minuet, Prokofiev substitutes a gavotte, a 17th century French dance form, which is in duple meter and moderate tempo, always starts on the third beat, and has a bagpipelike musette as a middle section. The composer hews to tradition with themes of buoyant grace in the dance proper and the obligatory drone for the musette.

IV. *Finale: Molto vivace.* Prokofiev imbues the Finale, a gay and lively romp, with elfin delicacy. One does not know if the composer struggled to write this movement, but orchestral players are only too aware of the incredible difficulty in performing this movement with the requisite lightness and accuracy. The compact movement features two similar themes, which Prokofiev sends racing to the climactic ending.

Symphony No. 5 in B flat major, Op. 100
(45 minutes)

In a 1945 interview, Prokofiev stated that he had worked on his Fifth Symphony "for several years [by] gathering themes for it in a special notebook. I always work that way and probably that is why I write so fast. The entire score of the Fifth was written in one month in the summer of 1944." He spent that summer at a rest home for composers where he, along with Shostakovich, Kabalevsky, Khachaturian, and other Soviet composers, had been evacuated in order to continue writing unimpeded by the dangers and turbulence of World War II.

While some of his colleagues wrote music directly related to the war, Prokofiev asserted that his Fifth Symphony was a "hymn to the freedom of the human spirit." Despite sections that evoke the fury of battle and mourning for the fallen, the work still projects an optimistic spirit. In a striking coincidence, cannons were heard firing a salute celebrating the Red Army's victory at the Vistula River just as Prokofiev raised his baton to conduct the symphony premiere in the Grand Hall of the Moscow Conservatory on January 13, 1945.

I. *Andante.* The lyrical first movement unfolds at a slightly slower tempo than is usual in a symphonic first movement, giving it a broad, spacious feeling. Following the dictates of traditional sonata allegro form, Prokofiev states two principal themes: the first, a wide-ranging melody in three-beat time played by flute and bassoon, the second, smaller and in four-beat time, given out by flute and oboe. The composer works through both themes and builds to a climax before returning the melodies in different orchestration. A coda of epic dimension ends the movement.

II. *Allegro marcato.* This three-part movement, really a scherzo, has an energetic, motoric character. The clarinet states the first section's main melody ($4/4$ meter). The "swing band" melody of the slightly slower central part ($3/4$ meter) follows, and leads to a concluding variation of the opening.

III. *Adagio.* Also structured in three parts, the Adagio starts with a distant, tragic melody that Prokofiev extends and varies. The somewhat angular and agitated middle portion precedes a free return of the opening.

IV. *Allegro giocoso.* The finale starts with an obvious reminder of the first movement's opening theme before going ahead to the jubilant, but somewhat grotesque principal subject played by the clarinet. The woodwinds are responsible for the themes that follow. Prokofiev sticks close to standard sonata allegro form in shaping these themes into a strong, positive wrap-up of the entire symphony.

Symphony No. 6 in E flat minor, Op. 111
(42 minutes)

In 1944, as the successful end to World War II seemed to be approaching, Prokofiev began planning a symphony of celebration. Yet the symphony did not prove to be the triumphant paean that the composer envisioned. First, he could not set aside his painful awareness of the exceptionally high price of the peace. As he wrote: "Yes, we are now rejoicing in our magnificent victory, but thousands of us have been left with wounds that cannot be healed—health ruined for life, loved ones gone forever. We must not forget this." At the same time, the heart attack he suffered early in 1945 left him seriously impaired, limiting his composing to two and a half hours a day.

The premiere took place in Leningrad (now St. Petersburg) on October 10, 1947, with Yevgeny Mravinsky leading the orchestra. The date was scarcely four months before the Central Committee of the Communist Party strenuously censured Prokofiev for "formalist perversions and undemocratic tendencies."

Prokofiev briefly described his Sixth Symphony: "The first movement is agitated, at times lyrical, at times austere; the second movement is brighter and more tuneful; the finale, rapid and in a major key, is close in character to my Fifth Symphony, save for reminiscences of the austere passages in the first movement."

I. *Allegro moderato.* After a very short, bitter introduction comes a flowing, whispered first theme in the violins and, in time, a somewhat modal, churchlike second theme in the oboes. As Prokofiev develops these themes he inserts sections of restlessness, marchlike striding, and growing intensity in the drive to the powerful climax. After relentlessly repeating one note, the composer goes into the recapitulation, starting with the second theme, and a concluding coda.

II. *Largo.* Prokofiev builds the Largo around contrasts between sections of uncompromising harsh violence and sections of gentle, lyrical tenderness. In one striking passage of ingenuous charm, Prokofiev creates the delicate ticking sound of a mechanical clock.

III. *Vivace.* The jaunty high spirits one expects from a piece celebrating the end of a war comes in the last movement; but the music is not completely joyful. Prokofiev inserts heavy stomping in the midst of the happy principal theme and the long-sustained notes of the second theme are heard over a tense, nervous accompaniment. Then, after an extended passage for bassoon and bass clarinet, he brings back the poignant oboe theme from the first movement, and ends the movement abruptly with what sound like anguished cries.

Sergei Rachmaninoff

Born April 1, 1873, in Oneg, Novgorod, Russia
Died March 28, 1943, in Beverly Hills, California

SERGEI RACHMANINOFF began his formal music education at age
nine at the St. Petersburg Conservatory. He was a lackluster student until
an inspiring teacher aroused his enthusiasm for music. Rachmaninoff soon
rose to the front of his class and continued his studies at the Moscow
Conservatory, where he graduated with high honors in 1892.

The young man seemed well on his way to a highly successful career in
music until the disastrous 1897 premiere of his First Symphony. Rachmaninoff came close to a mental collapse and was unable to compose for several
years. Only after a course of treatment with autosuggestion did his interest in
music return and was he able to write his immensely popular Second Piano
Concerto. For the remaining four decades of his life, Rachmaninoff returned
to his original course, building an international reputation as a composer, as
well as a pianist and conductor.

A statement to writer David Ewen summed up his purpose as a composer:
"I try to make my music speak simply and directly that which is in my heart
at the time I am composing. I compose music because I must give expression
to my feelings, just as I talk because I must give utterance to my thoughts."

Rachmaninoff left Russia in 1917 and never returned; late in 1918 he
settled in the United States.

Concerto for Piano and Orchestra No. 2 in C minor, Op. 18
(34 minutes)

Few other pieces in the entire musical repertoire have had as torturous a genesis as Rachmaninoff's Second Piano Concerto. During the 1898–99 season Rachmaninoff appeared as a pianist in London, and was invited to return the following season to play his First Piano Concerto with the London Philharmonic. Believing the work unworthy of the occasion, Rachmaninoff offered to compose a "new and better" concerto in its stead.

On his return to Russia, Rachmaninoff started to work, but made no progress. He traced this inability to compose, which had been going on for three years, back to the devastating failure of the premiere of his First Symphony in 1897. "I felt like a man who had suffered a stroke and for a long time had lost the use of his head and hands," he wrote.

Some friends arranged for Rachmaninoff to speak with Count Leo Tolstoy in an effort to remove the composing block. "It all ended very unpleasantly," Rachmaninoff later reported. "I then worshipped Tolstoy. When I approached him my knees trembled. He made me sit down beside him, and stroked my knees. He saw how nervous I was. And then, at the table, he said to me, 'You must work. Do you think that I am pleased with myself? Work. I work every day,' and similar stereotyped phrases."

Next, other friends introduced the frustrated composer to Dr. Nikolai Dahl, a specialist in internal medicine who had begun using hypnosis and autosuggestion in treating his patients. Knowing that Rachmaninoff was eager to write a piano concerto, Dr. Dahl started daily therapy sessions in January 1900. The composer lay half asleep in his study while the physician softly intoned the same words over and over again: "You will begin to write your concerto. You will work with great facility. The concerto will be of excellent quality."

After four months with Dr. Dahl, Rachmaninoff did indeed begin to compose again. "The material grew in bulk, and new musical ideas began to stir within me—far more than I needed for my concerto," he later recalled. By autumn the last two movements of the concerto were done. He completed the first on April 21, 1901, and dedicated the work to Dr. Dahl. Rachmaninoff played the piano part at the first performance with the Moscow Philharmonic, Alexander Siloti conducting, on October 27, 1901. The piece, which was always exceedingly well liked, grew even more familiar when the last movement theme became the melody of the 1946 song hit "Full Moon and

Empty Arms." It remains a concert favorite; both audiences and performers find its wealth of warm, surging, emotional melody well-nigh irresistible.

I. *Moderato.* The concerto opens mysteriously with a series of sonorous piano chords that gradually grow in volume until the orchestra enters with the passionate, though somber first theme. After exposing this broadly conceived theme and its extensions, Rachmaninoff has the piano introduce and amplify the soaring, songlike contrasting subject. Through the cantabile development section, mostly focused on the first theme, and the return of both themes, Rachmaninoff stresses the lyrical qualities of the material.

II. *Adagio sostenuto.* The second movement, an evocation of a peaceful nocturnal scene, has but one theme, which the flute initiates over piano arpeggios; the clarinet then takes over and shares it with the soloist. A brief piano cadenza introduces a bit of virtuosic display, but the quiet, relaxed character returns at the end.

III. *Allegro scherzando.* After some introductory measures the piano states the motoric first theme of the finale with its driving rhythmic vitality. The second theme, the sweeping Romantic melody adapted for the pop song, comes next, sung by the violas and oboe. Rachmaninoff discusses both themes at some length, including brilliant cadenzas for the soloist, and concludes the concerto with a magnificent reprise of the second theme.

Rhapsody on a Theme of Paganini for Piano and Orchestra, Op. 43
(23 minutes)

How fitting that a melody by the legendary 19th century violin virtuoso, Niccolò Paganini, should be the theme of a major composition by Sergei Rachmaninoff, the towering piano virtuoso of the early 20th century. The melody, from Paganini's *24th Caprice for Solo Violin,* has furnished the subject for dozens of musical compositions, including concert études by Schumann and Liszt, two books of variations by Brahms, orchestral variations by Boris Blacher, Alberto Ginastera's Violin Concerto, and, best known of all, Rachmaninoff's *Rhapsody on a Theme of Paganini.*

Entitled *Rhapsody,* the work is actually a theme and twenty-four variations that are played without break. After a few measures of introduction the orchestra states the theme in skeletal outline, labeled Variation 1 *(Precedente),* and then the violins present the theme in its entirety. In Variations 2 through 6 Rachmaninoff stays close to the melody, tempo, and character of the original theme. In Variation 7 he gives the piano the *Dies Irae* ("Day of Wrath"), the ominous melody from the Catholic Mass for the Dead, against a variant of the melody in the cellos and bassoon. Variations 8 and 9 continue as before; in Variation 10 the piano recalls the doleful *Dies Irae.*

Variation 11 is an accompanied cadenza for the piano that leads to Variation 12, a macabre minuet; the dance grows more frenetic in Variation 13 and more grandiose in Variation 14. The composer focuses Variations 15 through 17 on the virtuosic prowess of the soloist. The tempo slows for Variation 18 and the strings introduce a new, wonderfully rich melody—which proves to be a free inversion of the original melody. The original tempo returns and accelerates over the final variations with flamboyant, bravura writing for the piano and a more subservient role for the orchestra. After building to a powerful climax, Rachmaninoff ends with an insouciant little musical shrug of the shoulders.

Rachmaninoff never indicated that he had a particular program in mind while composing *Rhapsody.* Yet, in a 1937 letter to Michel Fokine, giving the choreographer permission to fashion a dance to the music, the composer wrote: "Why not resurrect the legend about Paganini, who, for perfection in his art and a woman, sold his soul to the Evil One? All the variations that have the theme of *Dies Irae* represent the Evil One. Variation 11 is a turning point into the domain of love. Variation 12—the Menuet—portrays the first appearance of the woman. Variation 19 [is] Paganini's triumph—his diabolic pizzicato."

Rachmaninoff worked on *Rhapsody* at his home on Lake Lucerne, Switzerland, from July 3 to August 24, 1934. Leopold Stokowski and the Philadelphia Orchestra gave the first performance in Baltimore on November 7, 1934, with Rachmaninoff as soloist.

Symphony No. 2 in E minor, Op. 27
(60 minutes)

For nearly a decade after the terrible reaction to the 1897 premiere of his First Symphony, Rachmaninoff did not attempt another work in the form. "There are serious illnesses and deadly blows from fate that entirely change a man's character," he wrote. "This was the effect of my own symphony on myself."

Another reason, curiously enough, was his great success as both a pianist and a conductor. As he explained: "When I am concertizing I cannot compose. When I feel like writing music I have to concentrate on that—I cannot touch the piano. When I am conducting I can neither compose nor play concerts." The need to compose, however, could not be denied, and in the fall of 1906 he canceled his performing engagements and went into seclusion in Dresden with his wife and young daughter, seeking the respite he needed as a creative artist. Soon after, he started work on his Second Symphony, by far the most successful of the three he composed, completing it in the fall of 1907. He led the premiere in St. Petersburg on January 26, 1908. The audience was completely won over by the symphony's lush, sweeping melodies and large-scaled, grand conception—a reaction that obtains to this day.

I. *Largo; Allegro moderato.* The slow, brooding introduction contains the germinal motif that serves as the principal theme of the first movement and appears in various forms throughout the symphony. The body of the movement starts with the violin statement of the surging main theme. After repetition and extension, Rachmaninoff brings in the second theme, a dialogue between woodwinds and strings. The development begins with a solo violin playing the first theme in augmentation; the orchestra soon takes over to work through the material. The composer reviews both themes for the recapitulation, which he follows with an elaborate coda.

II. *Allegro molto.* The second movement, really a scherzo, opens with a bold, dramatic statement by four French horns, which is then taken up by the violins. A sudden loud chord signals the middle section with the second violins initially playing its rapid, scurrying notes. The composer then freely recalls the opening and near the end alludes to a motif from the earlier Largo.

III. *Adagio.* The emotional peak of the symphony is the Adagio with its ecstatic, rapturous themes. At the opening, the violins give out the first theme, strongly suggesting yearning and unfulfilled desire. The clarinet follows almost immediately with its own reflective second theme. As Rachmaninoff expands on these materials, he makes prominent references to ideas from the first movement.

IV. *Allegro vivace.* The lively rhythm of a tarantella launches the energetic fourth movement, but the woodwinds interrupt for a marchlike interlude. After a brief reappearance of the tarantella, Rachmaninoff presents and expands an impassioned, lyrical second theme and recalls previously heard motifs. But the tarantella persists through the development and recapitulation sections, building to an exhilarating climax at the end.

Maurice Ravel

Born March 7, 1875, in Ciboure, France
Died December 28, 1937, in Paris

THERE HAVE BEEN a number of unfortunate pairings in music history —Bach and Handel, Haydn and Mozart, Bruckner and Mahler, and Debussy and Ravel. They are unfortunate because they bring together composers who, while having a great deal in common, have even more that sets them apart. Debussy and Ravel were both French, were born a scant thirteen years apart, and are often labeled as Impressionists. But while Debussy and Ravel share the ability to clothe their music in a sensuous mist, Ravel's music tends to be clearer and more direct, has more well-defined structures, and exhibits an overall sharper edge.

Ravel, slight of build and only about five feet tall, was an extremely natty dresser who appeared perfectly turned out for all occasions. Rather cold and distant in manner, he formed few close, emotional attachments and seemed to write music that reflected his personality: tight and economical, fastidiously and carefully put together, somewhat remote in tone. Nevertheless, Ravel captivates audiences with the brilliance of his orchestrations; the incredible palette of tone colors and effects he brings forth are virtually without peer.

Ravel, born near the Spanish border in the Basque region of France, began piano lessons at age seven; at fourteen he enrolled in the Paris Conservatory, where he was not a particularly distinguished student, although some of his music was already being published and performed.

After graduation in 1903 he joined a group of young Parisian artists, poets, musicians, and intellectuals who felt they were social outcasts; they called themselves Apaches. The figures the Apaches most admired included composers Rameau, Chopin, and Debussy, writers Mallarmé, Verlaine, and Rimbaud, and painters Cézanne, Van Gogh, and Whistler. A formidable scholar and intellectual, Ravel believed that music, painting, and literature were all part of one art and differed only in means of expression.

Ravel became a leading composer early on; he never had the need or desire to teach and did little performing as a pianist or conductor. He volunteered for the French army in World War I, but his frail health resulted in an assignment as a driver in the motor corps. During a 1928 visit to the United States to perform his own music, he came to know and admire American jazz. Because of the great care he lavished on every piece, Ravel left a comparatively small body of work. Among them are several works, including the very famous *Boléro,* that are justifiably regarded as masterpieces.

Boléro
(17 minutes)

Early in 1928, dancer Ida Rubinstein asked Ravel to compose a ballet score. At first he planned to orchestrate some piano pieces by Isaac Albéniz, but copyright laws made that impossible. Then, while on holiday at Saint-Jean-de-Luz, he played a one-finger melody on the piano for composer Gustave Samazeuilh. "Don't you think this theme has an insistent quality?" Ravel asked. "I'm going to try and repeat it a number of times without any development, gradually increasing the orchestra as best I can." Working from July to August of 1928, Ravel completed the piece, which he called *Boléro.* It consists of nearly 20 repetitions of a single theme that remains virtually the same throughout, but continuously grows louder as it is clothed in a staggering variety of instrumental tone colors.

Mme. Rubinstein gave the premiere of the ballet *Boléro* in Paris on November 22, 1928. The setting was a dimly lit Spanish tavern filled with men watching, immobile, as she quietly began to dance. Her movements grew ever more intense and she finally took to a large table. Her steps became increasingly suggestive and the onlookers showed more and more animation. Soon they were pounding their fists on the table and stamping their heels on the floor. At the furious climax they drew their knives and attacked each other in a mad frenzy.

In a 1931 letter to music critic Michel D. Calvocoressi, Ravel commented on *Boléro:* "It is an experiment in a very special and limited direction, and should not be suspected of achieving anything different from, or anything more than, it actually does achieve. [It is] a piece lasting seventeen minutes and consisting wholly of orchestral tissue without music—of one very long, very gradual crescendo. The themes are impersonal—folk tunes of the usual Spanish-Arabian kind."

It is hard to disagree with Ravel's description, yet he omits one crucial element—the powerful cumulative and hypnotic effect of the music as it builds to its overwhelming climax. The intoxicating climb literally brings concertgoers to their feet.

Ravel conducted the first concert performance in Paris on January 11, 1930. From its early success it has gone on to become an all-time favorite, including its use as background music for the films *Bolero* and *10*.

Concerto in D major for Piano (Left Hand) and Orchestra
(20 minutes)

In the summer of 1929 Ravel was working on his Piano Concerto in G when pianist Paul Wittgenstein presented the composer with a most intriguing and challenging commission: to write a piano concerto with a solo part for the left hand alone. Wittgenstein, after a very successful debut in 1913, had lost his right arm in World War I. On his recovery, he set out to resume his career, now limited to music written for one hand. To build a repertoire, Wittgenstein made transcriptions of two-hand compositions and, in addition to Ravel, commissioned works from Richard Strauss, Prokofiev, Britten, and Hindemith.

Ravel was suffering from severe insomnia and other ailments at the time, yet he was eager to take on the assignment. While continuing with the Concerto in G he began to prepare for the left-hand concerto by studying the few left-hand pieces available, by Saint-Saëns, Scriabin, Czerny, and Alkan.

It took Ravel about nine months to complete the concerto and he played it for Wittgenstein, with both hands, since the solo part was much too difficult for Ravel to manage with just one. Wittgenstein later commented: "He was not an outstanding pianist and I wasn't overwhelmed by the composition. Only much later, after I'd studied the concerto for months, did I become fascinated by it and realize what a great work it was."

Despite Wittgenstein's admiration for the composition, he and Ravel seriously disagreed about its interpretation. For this reason Wittgenstein played the solo part at the premiere in Vienna on January 5, 1932, but Robert Heger, not the composer, conducted.

Ravel wrote: "The concerto for the left hand alone is very different [from the Concerto in G]. It contains many jazz effects; the writing is not so light. In a work of this kind, it is essential to give the impression of a texture no thinner than that of a part written for both hands. For the same reason, I resorted to a style that is much nearer to that of the more solemn kind of traditional concerto. A special feature is that after a first section in the traditional style, a sudden change occurs and the jazz music begins. Only later does it become manifest that the jazz music is built on the same theme as the opening part."

Ravel divided the one-movement concerto into three sections. The "traditional style" comes in the slow, somber opening, which some scholars link to Ravel's preoccupation with death. The "jazz music," which had captivated Ravel on his 1928 visits to several Harlem and Greenwich Village nightspots in New York City, dominates the faster middle section with its wonderful blues melody for bassoon. Reminders of both the opening and jazz themes occur in the closing part. Most listeners agree that the amazing piano sonorities that Ravel elicits throughout this concerto for one hand sound like they require *at least* two hands to produce!

Concerto for Piano and Orchestra in G major
(23 minutes)

Of this work, Ravel said: "It is a concerto in the truest sense of the word, written very much in the same spirit as those of Mozart and Saint-Saëns. The music of a concerto, in my opinion, should be lighthearted and brilliant, and not aim at profundity or dramatic effects. It has been said of certain great classics that their concertos were not 'for' but 'against' the piano. I heartily agree."

Ravel wanted to compose a piece for solo piano and orchestra for his American concert tour of 1928. His original idea was to write a *Basque Rhapsody,* but along the way decided to make it a formal concerto. Not being able to complete the concerto before the tour, Ravel devoted 10 to 12 hours a day to the composition on his return to France, although he was in poor health and suffering from severe insomnia. In addition to its strong Basque flavor, the concerto also shows the influence of the jazz he heard in New York during his United States tour.

In November 1931, Ravel completed the score and Marguerite Long gave the first performance on January 14, 1932, in Paris, with the composer conducting the Lamoureux Orchestra. Ravel later said that he felt he had "expressed himself most completely" in this work.

I. *Allegramente.* While Ravel traced the concerto back to the forms of Mozart and Saint-Saëns, the influence of Gershwin and Stravinsky may be even stronger. The first of several short themes in the opening movement derives from a perky Basque folk dance, the *bransle;* the piccolo gives it the sound of a peasant playing on a fife. Parts of the second theme, introduced by piano alone, suggest both Spanish dance music and American jazz as filtered through the wit and intelligence of Ravel's special French style. The light and brittle treatment includes many idiomatic touches of *"le jazz hot."*

II. *Adagio assai.* Mozart's Clarinet Quintet presumably inspired the slow, contemplative Adagio. The movement opens with a lengthy, expressive piano solo in which the right hand plays in $3/4$ meter, while the left is in $3/8$ time. After reaching a climax with a harsh dissonance (a G sharp minor chord with a G natural!) the English horn repeats the opening monologue, while the piano weaves a delicate lacery.

III. *Presto.* The finale, strongly reminiscent of Stravinsky's *Petrouchka,* evokes the atmosphere and energy of a circus or carnival. The themes tumble forth resembling, in order, a shrieking train whistle, a syncopated folk melody, and a rough-humored march, all replete with fanfares, drumrolls, and glissandi.

Pavane pour une Infante défunte
("Pavane for a Dead Princess")
(7 minutes)

A pavane is a 16th century courtly Spanish dance that was performed with slow steps and solemn gestures. The name probably derives from the Spanish word for peacock, *pavo,* and the dance movements reflect the bird's poised, dignified demeanor.

Ravel's stately, melancholy *Pavane,* which he composed as a piano piece in 1899, catapulted the composer to instant fame. He suspected that the title captured the public's imagination because of its many interpretations. When asked about its connotations, he replied with disarming candor: "When I put together the words of the title, my only thought was the pleasure of the alliteration." In 1910, Ravel orchestrated the piano piece for two flutes, oboe, two clarinets, two bassoons, two horns, harp, and strings.

Alfredo Casella led the premiere of the orchestral arrangement in Paris on Christmas Day 1911. In this form *Pavane* achieved an even wider audience. Ravel actually felt it overshadowed his later, and better, compositions. Annoyed, he wrote in 1912 that *Pavane* is "a matter of ancient history."

Ravel left one remark regarding the interpretation of *Pavane.* After hearing a student pianist perform the work at a very slow tempo, the composer gently remonstrated: "Listen, my child, what I wrote is *Pavane for a Dead Princess,* not *Dead Pavane for a Princess!*"

Rapsodie espagnole
(15 minutes)

Rapsodie espagnole belongs to the group of "Spanish" pieces that Ravel composed. His interest in the music of Spain may be attributed, in part, to his birth in the Basque area of France near the Spanish border, his very fond memories of the Spanish folk melodies his mother sang to him as an infant, and to the predilection French composers have for writing music in the Spanish idiom, from Bizet's *Carmen* to Debussy's *Ibéria*.

Working at great speed, Ravel composed the *Rapsodie* in October 1907 and finished the orchestration in February 1908. Edouard Colonne conducted the premiere in Paris on March 15, 1908.

The audience's reaction was generally favorable, but there was some hissing from the orchestra seats at the end of the second movement. "Play it again for the people downstairs," boomed the voice of composer Florent Schmitt from the balcony, "they don't understand it!" Colonne did indeed repeat the movement, after which Schmitt again called out: "Tell them it's Wagner and they'll love it!"

Ravel's first published orchestral score, *Rapsodie* already shows the composer's incomparable skill as an orchestrator. The brilliant score shimmers with an endless succession of dazzling tonal hues and colors.

I. *Prélude à la nuit.* The muted and delicate first movement revolves around a whispered four-note descending figure. The figure spins along throughout the movement, interrupted only by occasional splashes of orchestral color or elusive snatches of melody.

II. *Malagueña.* The composer based *Malagueña* on a traditional Andalusian folk dance; it opens with the characteristic rhythm played pizzicato by the double basses. Over this ostinato a muted trumpet and then the English horn present the principal melodies. Ravel reminds us of the four-note figure from the first movement before he lets the *Malagueña* softly fade away.

III. *Habanera.* Ravel originally composed the *Habanera* in 1895 for two pianos; he orchestrated it for use here. The habanera rhythm migrated to Spain from Africa by way of Havana; it started as a dance song for men and women to perform facing each other in two lines, swaying to the music while making suggestive hand gestures. On the two-piano version Ravel copied a quotation from Baudelaire: *"Au pays parfumé que le soleil carerre"* ("In the perfumed land that the sun caresses").

IV. *Feria. Feria* or "Festival," conveys the impression of a wild, joyful celebration. In three parts, the *Feria* sets off the scintillating orchestral effects of the opening and closing sections with the quiet middle part, which features in turn the English horn and clarinet. Echoes of the four-note motto remind us of the first movement.

Le Tombeau de Couperin
(16 minutes)

In the summer of 1914, on the eve of World War I, Ravel began a piano suite entitled *Le Tombeau de Couperin,* a reference to François Couperin (1668–1733), the great French composer and harpsichord player. French composers, including Couperin, used *tombeau,* literally "tombstone," for works that memorialized composers from the past.

Before completing *Tombeau,* the frail Ravel volunteered for the army and was assigned to duties as a driver, which precluded any further work on the manuscript. After his military discharge, Ravel returned to *Tombeau,* completing it in November 1917. He added another layer of meaning to the music by dedicating each of the six movements to a companion who was killed in the war.

Ravel decided, in June 1919, to orchestrate four of the six original movements of *Tombeau.* This version got its first hearing in Paris on February 28, 1920, with Rhené-Baton leading the Pasdeloup Orchestra.

I. *Prélude.* With its flow of rapid notes, the *Prélude* creates the atmosphere of a Couperin harpsichord piece, which Ravel achieves despite his 20th century musical vocabulary.

II. *Forlane.* The *forlane,* an ancient dance of northern Italian origin, resembles a jig. Here, though, it has a quality of subdued gaiety, rather than the wild abandon of a more typical jig.

III. *Menuet.* Three parts make up this stately, elegant movement: an opening section in which the woodwinds predominate; a more legato middle part where winds and strings share the melodic responsibility and which includes the climax of the movement; and the free reprise of the opening with both choirs participating.

IV. *Rigaudon.* A *rigaudon* is an old French sailor's dance from Provence performed with many running and hopping steps. Cast in three parts, this movement comprises a lively and vibrant opening, a quiet pastoral section, and a literal return of the opening, minus the repeats indicated for the first traversal.

La Valse: poème choréographique
(13 minutes)

From the 1850s through the early years of the 20th century, the waltz dominated social dancing. With the prosperous, cultured city of Vienna as its epicenter, the waltz bespoke an elegance and stability that perfectly reflected the worldview of the time. Then the outbreak of World War I and the rise of a new political order in Europe, and the impact of such seminal thinkers as Freud (theory of the unconscious) and Einstein (theory of relativity), effectively shattered the old order. In the changed new system dances such as the tango and fox-trot came to the fore, and the waltz dropped from its prime position.

In 1906, as an homage to Johann Strauss, the "Waltz King," who had recently died, Ravel planned to paint a musical portrait of the Viennese waltz of the latter 1800s. Over the following years he wrote solo-piano and two-piano versions of the piece, which he entitled *Wien* ("Vienna"). When Sergei Diaghilev, impresario of the Ballets Russes, offered to use the score for a ballet, Ravel orchestrated the piano part, finishing in March 1920. That spring he played the two-piano version for Diaghilev, who declared the music "a masterpiece—but it's not a ballet."

History has proven Diaghilev correct. Ever since its premiere, by Camille Chevillard and the Lamoureux Orchestra, in Paris on December 12, 1920, *La Valse* has been a concert hall favorite, but has had much less success as a ballet score.

In preparing the orchestral version, Ravel changed the title from *Wien* to *La Valse* ("The Waltz") and wrote this description of the music: "I had intended this work to be a kind of apotheosis of the Viennese waltz, which I associated in my imagination with an impression of a fantastic and fatal sort of dervish's dance. I imagined this waltz being danced in an imperial palace about the year 1855."

On the score he added: "From time to time through the whirling cloud waltzing couples can be faintly distinguished. The clouds gradually scatter; one sees an immense ballroom filled with a crowd of whirling dancers. The scene gradually grows lighter. The light of the chandeliers bursts forth."

The music progresses from inchoate glimpses of the waltz to the glorious emergence of the various waltz melodies. As the waltz continues, the tension and excitement build, the movements become more and more frenetic, the dissonances grow wilder, the rhythms further distorted. Finally, the music climaxes at the very end—a four-beat measure superimposed on the three-beat waltz, signaling both the end of the piece and the close of an era.

Ottorino Respighi

Born July 9, 1879, in Bologna, Italy
Died April 18, 1936, in Rome

RESPIGHI, perhaps more than any other major composer, depended on outside sources for the stimulation to compose his own original compositions. As an example, his best-known orchestral works were variously inspired by ancient Italian music, Botticelli's paintings, the songs and dances of Brazil, stained-glass windows, and, most notably, the fountains, pines, and festivals of Rome. A consummate painter in sound, Respighi was able to combine his gift for melody with a brilliant flair for orchestration and a feeling for rich, exciting harmonies.

At age 12 Respighi entered the Bologna Liceo, where he studied viola and composition. On graduation in 1899 he went to St. Petersburg to play principal viola with the Russian Imperial Opera Orchestra and to study composition with Nikolai Rimsky-Korsakov. When he returned to Italy two years later he performed and taught, but eventually became fully occupied with composing, his main interest. His three "Roman" tone poems, *The Fountains of Rome* (1917), *The Pines of Rome* (1924), and *Roman Festivals* (1928), won him international fame and also influenced other Italian composers to write for the symphony orchestra, not just the opera house.

The Fountains of Rome
(17 minutes)

In this tone poem Respighi tried, in his words, "to give expression to the sentiments and vision suggested to him by four of Rome's fountains, contemplated at the hour in which their character is most in harmony with the surrounding landscape." Respighi composed the music in 1916 and Antonio Guarnieri conducted the first performance in Rome on March 11, 1917.

The orchestra plays the work's four sections without break.

I. *The Fountain of Valle Giulia at Dawn.* The beautiful, serene music of the first part "depicts a pastoral landscape; droves of cattle pass and disappear in the fresh, damp mists of the Roman dawn."

II. *The Triton Fountain in the Morning.* A loud horn blast introduces *The Triton Fountain* and the gay, joyous music goes on to depict naiads and tritons chasing about and "mingling in a frenzied dance between the jets of water."

III. *The Fountain of Trevi at Midday.* This section starts more solemnly, but grows increasingly triumphant as Neptune's chariot passes across the water "drawn by sea horses and followed by a train of sirens and tritons." As the procession leaves, the music quiets and distant trumpet calls ring out.

IV. *The Villa Medici Fountain at Sunset.* A "sad theme" over "subdued warbling" announces the final part. "It is the nostalgic hour of sunset, the air is full of the sound of tolling bells, birds twittering, leaves rustling. Then all dies peacefully into the silence of the night."

The Pines of Rome
(22 minutes)

After the great success of his 1917 *Fountains of Rome,* Respighi composed, in 1924, his *Pines of Rome.* He completed the trilogy on Roman subjects in 1928 with *Roman Festivals,* though the latter never achieved the success of the first two tone poems. In *Fountains,* Respighi said, he "sought to reproduce by means of tone an impression of Nature," but in *Pines* he "uses Nature as a point of departure in order to recall memories and visions. The century-old trees that dominate the Roman landscape so characteristically become testimony for the principal events of Roman life."

No better description of the music exists than the one Respighi had printed on the score:

I. *The Pines of the Villa Borghese.* Children are at play in the pine grove of the Villa Borghese, dancing the Italian equivalent of ring-around-a-rosy, mimicking marching soldiers and battles, twittering and shrieking like swallows at evening, and they disappear. Suddenly the scene shifts to:

II. *The Pines Near a Catacomb.* We see the shadows of the pines that overhang the entrance of the catacomb. From the depths rises a chant that reechoes solemnly, sonorously, like a hymn, and is then mysteriously silenced.

III. *The Pines of the Janiculum.* There is a rustling in the air. The full moon reveals the profile of the pines on the hill. A nightingale sings [usually a recording played in the orchestra].

IV. *The Pines of the Appian Way*. Misty dawn on the Appian Way. The tragic country is guarded by solitary pines. Indistinctly, incessantly, the rhythm of numberless steps. To the poet's fantasy appears a vision of past glories; trumpets blare and the army of the consul advances brilliantly in the grandeur of the newly risen sun toward the sacred way, mounting in triumph the Capitoline Hill.

Bernardino Molinari led the premiere of *The Pines of Rome* in Rome on December 14, 1924. One of the great showpieces in the orchestral repertoire, *Pines* provides many display opportunities for every section of the orchestra, and gives audiences an absolutely thrilling musical experience.

Nikolai Rimsky-Korsakov

Born March 18, 1844, in Tikhvin, Russia
Died June 21, 1908, in St. Petersburg

AS A CHILD, Rimsky-Korsakov excelled at his obligatory piano lessons, but his main interest was the sea. At age 12 he entered the Naval School in St. Petersburg, graduating in 1862. He spent the next 11 years on active service in the Russian navy, followed by 11 years as inspector of navy bands.

During his navy years, Rimsky-Korsakov managed to get some instruction in piano and composition and in 1861 met Mily Balakirev, a composer who sought to convince Russian composers that they should draw on their national Russian heritage in their music. Rimsky-Korsakov joined the group of Balakirev and like-minded composers devoted to developing a Russian style of music; they became known as "The Mighty Five" (Balakirev and Rimsky-Korsakov, plus Mussorgsky, Borodin, and Cui).

In 1871, with little background in music theory and only a few performances and publications of his own music to his credit, Rimsky-Korsakov was appointed professor of composition at the St. Petersburg Conservatory, a position he held until his death. Upon assuming the post, Rimsky-Korsakov began to teach himself counterpoint, harmony, and musical form. In time he became an excellent teacher and music theorist, exerting an enormous influence on the course of Russian music in the early 1900s. Several of his students, including Sergei Prokofiev, Igor Stravinsky, and Ottorino Respighi, became important figures in 20th century music, and his book *Principles of Orchestration* remains a classic on that subject.

During his lifetime, Rimsky-Korsakov was especially celebrated for his several operas on Russian themes, only two of which are now performed outside of Russia. Today he is represented on concert programs by a handful of imaginative, colorful, and brilliantly orchestrated scores that include *Ca-*

priccio espagnol and *Scheherazade.* The composer also enriched the orchestral repertoire by editing and revising compositions that his friends Alexander Borodin and Modest Mussorgsky had left unfinished at their deaths. His autobiography, *My Musical Life,* contains many valuable insights into his beliefs and ideas.

Capriccio espagnol, Op. 34
(16 minutes)

As a member of "The Mighty Five," a group of Russian nationalistic composers, Rimsky-Korsakov frequently adapted Russian folk songs and the melodies of the Russian Orthodox Church in his own music. But the composer found the inspiration for two of his best-known orchestral works, *Capriccio espagnol* and *Scheherazade,* much farther afield, in Spain and Arabia, respectively.

In 1886, Rimsky-Korsakov began composing "a virtuoso violin fantasy on Spanish themes," which he developed the following year into a brilliant display piece for full orchestra entitled *Capriccio espagnol.* One year later he completely revised that score; the sole reminder of the original conception was the striking violin cadenza in the fourth movement.

Of this work, Tchaikovsky wrote to Rimsky-Korsakov: "*Capriccio espagnol* is a colossal masterpiece of orchestration and you may regard yourself as the greatest master of the present day." Even though he was indeed a master of orchestral effects, Rimsky-Korsakov did not hold with the conventional view that considered orchestration the art of choosing the best instrument or combination of instruments to present the musical material. Rather, he held that the composer should conceive the music in terms of orchestral tone colors from the very beginning. As he wrote in his autobiography: "The opinion reached by both critics and the public, that the *Capriccio* is a magnificently orchestrated piece, is wrong. The *Capriccio* is a brilliant composition for the orchestra. The change of timbres, the felicitous choice of melodic designs and figuration patterns, exactly suiting each kind of instrument, brief virtuoso cadenzas for instrument solos, the rhythm of the percussion instruments, etc., constitute here the very essence of the composition and not its garb or orchestration."

Rimsky-Korsakov directs that the five parts of *Capriccio* be played without pause.

I. *Alborada.* The title literally means "dawn." Starting with a dazzling orchestral outburst, the movement devolves to a rather quiet ending.

II. *Variations.* Five connected variations follow the French horn announcement of the broad, suave theme.

III. *Alborada.* This movement offers a free repeat of the opening.

IV. *Scene and Gypsy Song.* Several solo cadenzas surround an impetuous Gypsy song.

V. *Fandango of the Asturias.* The music presents a fiery Andalusian dance performed to the rhythm of castanets. The movement ends with a return of the *Alborada* theme.

Completed on August 4, 1887, *Capriccio espagnol* was first aired in St. Petersburg on October 31 of that year, with Rimsky-Korsakov conducting.

Scheherazade, Op. 35
(45 minutes)

Rimsky-Korsakov drew his inspiration for *Scheherazade* from the collection of imaginative fairy tales known as *The Thousand and One Nights* or *The Arabian Nights.* He composed the music in 1888 and conducted the premiere in St. Petersburg the following season. In his autobiography the composer wrote: "The program that guided me in composing *Scheherazade* consisted of separate, unconnected episodes and pictures from *The Arabian Nights.*" He offered this description on the flyleaf of the score: "The Sultan of Schahriar, persuaded of the falseness and faithlessness of women, has sworn to put to death each one of his wives after the first night. But the Sultana Scheherazade saved her life by interesting him in tales that she told him during one thousand and one nights. Driven by curiosity, the Sultan put off his wife's execution from day to day, and at last gave up his bloody plan.

"Many marvels were told the Sultan by Sultana Scheherazade. For her stories the Sultana borrowed from the poets their verses, from folk songs the words, and she strung together fairy tales and adventures."

In *My Musical Life,* Rimsky-Korsakov tells more about the music: "The unifying thread consisted of the brief introductions to Movements I, II, and IV and the intermezzo in Movement III, written for solo violin, and delineating Scheherazade herself telling her wondrous tales to the stern Sultan.

"In vain do people seek in my suite leading motifs linked always and unvaryingly with the same poetic ideas and conceptions. On the contrary, in the majority of cases, all these seeming leading motifs are nothing but purely musical material or the given motifs for symphonic development.

"All I had desired was that the hearer . . . should carry away the impression that it is beyond doubt an Oriental narrative of some numerous and varied fairy-tale wonders and not merely four pieces played one after the other and composed on the basis of themes common to all four movements."

I. *Largo e maestoso; Lento; Allegro non troppo.* After the menacing opening motto, we hear the sensuous violin solo that is the voice of Scheherazade; both of these ideas reappear in subsequent movements. The third theme comes over a rocking accompaniment that suggests the roiling sea.

II. *Lento.* The second movement glitters with many themes and tone colors, starting with Scheherazade's violin solo at the very beginning, the lively tune that the bassoon introduces, and the loud, rude trombone intrusion.

III. *Andantino quasi allegretto.* Rimsky-Korsakov here supplies a simple, slow love song that he embellishes with running scales in different instruments. In the middle the snare drum signals a more rhythmic section, but the lyrical warmth of the song soon returns.

IV. *Allegro molto.* The last, summarizing movement brings back the opening motto, an expanded version of the violin solo associated with Scheherazade, and other previously heard melodies. Rimsky-Korsakov also introduces vivid, colorful new motifs that speed by in splendid profusion until Scheherazade's voice gently floats over the orchestra at the gentle ending.

Gioacchino Rossini

Born February 29, 1792, in Pesaro, Italy
Died November 13, 1868, in Passy, near Paris

GIOACCHINO ROSSINI, the most popular and important Italian opera composer of the early 1800s, probably got his talent from his parents; his father played trumpet in the pit of various provincial opera houses and his mother sang secondary roles on the stage. Young Gioacchino was composing before he was a teenager and received his advanced training at the Liceo Communale in Bologna.

The second opera he composed was produced in 1810, when he was only 18 years old. Audiences loved the work, and for the following two decades Rossini dominated the stages of Europe with a string of nearly 40 immensely successful operas. He wrote both *opera buffa* (comic opera) and opera seria (serious opera), sometimes at the rate of three or four a year. Richard Wagner said Rossini's operas were built on "naked, ear-delighting, absolutely melodic melody, that is, melody that was just melody and nothing else." But in addition to the attractive and memorable melodies, Rossini turned out music that perfectly fit the voice and the dramatic situations and expertly portrayed human emotions, from sensuous lovemaking to farcical humor.

At age 38, after completing *William Tell,* Rossini composed no more operas; for the final 39 years of his life all he wrote were several religious compositions, a few miscellaneous orchestral works, and a collection of about 180 assorted small pieces for various instruments and voices that he entitled *Péchés de vieillesse,* "Sins of Old Age." Certainly, he did not need more money; on his death his estate was valued at nearly $1.5 million dollars, a staggering sum in 1868. Also, he was often in ill health; as he put it: "I have all of women's ills. All that I lack is the uterus." Perhaps, too, he did not like the new operatic styles and decided to stay above the fray. Finally, late in life he may have preferred using his considerable intelligence, wit, and humor to entertain friends and host concerts at his city and suburban homes, and to cook his fabled gourmet meals and concoct new recipes for the French chefs he knew.

Modern opera houses present only a few of Rossini's operas with any frequency; the most popular is, of course, *The Barber of Seville.* In today's concert halls, we can hear several of his sparkling, effervescent orchestral opera overtures, which are exemplars of the form.

Overture to *The Barber of Seville*
(7 minutes)

The plot of Rossini's scintillating comic opera *The Barber of Seville* is familiar: A wealthy old bachelor plans to marry his beautiful young ward; she loves a handsome noble; a servant devises complex schemes to frustrate the older man; at the happy ending the young lovers are united and the bachelor is satisfied with the gift of money he receives.

Countless commentators have listened to the sprightly overture to *The Barber* and have diligently associated the various themes in the overture with characters and situations in the opera. But the fact is that the overture to *The Barber of Seville* has nothing at all to do with the opera! After the first performance, in Rome on February 20, 1816, Rossini's original overture was lost. For an August performance in Bologna, Rossini merely substituted an overture he had composed in 1813 for his opera *Aureliano in Palmira,* and had used again in 1815 as the overture to another opera, *Elizabeth, Queen of England.*

Even though the present overture was originally composed for a serious, not a comic, opera and contains no themes from the opera itself, the overture serves as the perfect introduction to *The Barber* and remains a concert favorite.

As in most Rossini overtures, the work includes the famous Rossini crescendo—a long, carefully paced progression from very soft to very loud. The exciting crescendo, plus the sparkling wit of the writing, makes the overture a truly delectable musical treat.

Overture to *La Gazza ladra*
(10 minutes)

"Nothing primes inspiration more than necessity," wrote Rossini. "I composed the Overture to *La Gazza ladra* the day of its opening in the theater itself, where I was imprisoned by the director and under the surveillance of the stagehands, who were instructed to throw my original text through the window, page by page, to the copyists waiting below to transcribe it. In default of pages they were ordered to throw me out of the window bodily!"

Despite the great speed and pressure of its composition, the overture to *La Gazza ladra* ("The Thieving Magpie") remains popular, while the opera languishes. The overture, which received its successful first performance at La Scala, Milan, on May 13, 1817, did not please everyone, however. One music student pursued the composer with a dagger to avenge the musical insult of starting a serious opera overture with a drumroll! Fortunately, Rossini calmed the young man by promising never again to write such offensive music.

La Gazza ladra, presumably based on a true story, tells of Ninetta, a servant girl who is sentenced to death for stealing a silver spoon that had actually been taken by a magpie. While in real life Ninetta was executed before authorities realized that she was innocent of the crime, Rossini spares her life in the opera.

After the slow, marchlike introduction, the fast main theme of the overture enters with its gay, lilting descending melodic line. In the opera, the theme accompanies a sad duet sung in Ninetta's prison cell. After some working out of this theme comes the hallmark crescendo of so many Rossini overtures, the steady, gradual increase in loudness. The composer follows with other, equally good-humored themes and works them all out in delightful fashion.

Overture to *La Scala di seta*
(7 minutes)

Critics received *La Scala di seta* ("The Silken Ladder") coolly at its premiere in Venice on May 9, 1812. Many objected to the libretto, which tells of the comic misadventures surrounding a secret marriage; the title refers to the silken ladder the husband climbs at night to reach his wife's bedroom. Rossini reacted to the captious reviews by writing to the director of the opera house: "In making me write the music for the libretto called *La Scala di seta,* you treated me like a boy, and I, in turning out a failure, only paid you back in kind. So now we're quits!"

Despite the failed premiere of the opera, the overture to *La Scala di seta* continues to delight audiences. It is probably the first overture to include the Rossini crescendo, a long, gradual, carefully paced increase in volume that became a familiar feature of his later opera overtures.

The overture to *La Scala di seta* starts with a slow introduction, which soon picks up tempo as the main theme bubbles forth. Into this gay, lively chatter, Rossini introduces a subsidiary theme of singing, lyrical beauty. The composer then playfully develops the two themes and brings them back before a final crescendo brings this fun-filled overture to an end.

Overture to *Semiramide*
(12 minutes)

Reluctant to compose an opera to be performed during the 1823 Carnival of Venice, Rossini demanded an exorbitant fee. To his surprise, the sponsors gave him the full amount and left him no choice but to write the music. Rossini boasted: "My contract allowed me 40 days, but I was not 40 days in composing it." Scholars estimate it took Rossini 33 days to write the opera and only a few hours to complete the overture. The first performance took place in Venice on February 3, 1823.

Rossini found the idea for *Semiramide* in Voltaire's tragic tale *Sémiramis.* Set in ancient Babylon, it tells of the murder of King Ninus by Queen Semiramis, resulting in her ascension to the throne. Subsequently she dies at the hand of her son, who avenges his father's death and becomes the new king.

The story is tragic, but in keeping with the operatic traditions of the day, Rossini preceded it with a light and frothy overture. In fact, Rossini adapts the gay, tripping principal theme of the overture from the solemn and mysterious final scene introduction, set in King Ninus' dark, gloomy tomb! The remainder of the overture bubbles along with a plethora of catchy tunes, interrupted by the famous Rossini crescendos that gradually work their way up from a whisper to a shout.

Overture to *William Tell*
(13 minutes)

William Tell occupies a high point in Rossini's operatic style. The last of his nearly 40 operas, *William Tell,* which he composed in 1829, is the only one Rossini wrote in French and his only grand opera (about six hours long!). The story concerns the legendary Swiss marksman, William Tell, whom soldiers arrest for refusing to bow to the hat set on a pole by the Austrian tyrant Gessler. Gessler offers Tell his freedom if he can shoot an apple off his son's head. Tell succeeds and then kills Gessler, leading to the Swiss revolt against the Austrians.

Rossini conceived the overture in the grand, epic style of the opera. Very sectional, the music forms a kind of medley, with four distinct parts. The dreamy, reflective first portion is for five solo cellos, creating the atmosphere of intimate chamber music. Then, without break, Rossini whips up a ferocious musical storm.

The frenzy clears for the third section, a duet for English horn and flute that suggests a pastoral Alpine scene. At the end, we hear the galloping finale, the only melody Rossini borrowed from the opera. He had actually composed this all too familiar tune some years earlier as a march for a military band in Venice and used it in the opera to represent the revolt of the Swiss patriots against their Austrian conquerors. Later, he removed the march from the opera, but left it in the overture.

Camille Saint-Saëns

Born October 9, 1835, in Paris
Died December 16, 1921, in Algiers

T HE HISTORY OF MUSIC does not lack for amazing child prodigies. But few match the achievements of Camille Saint-Saëns—picking out tunes on the piano at two and a half, composing at three (the manuscript is on exhibit at the Paris Conservatory), giving his first piano recital two years later, and making his official debut as pianist at the age of 10, when he offered to play any Beethoven piano sonata by memory as an encore—not to mention absolute pitch and a photographic memory for music. Perhaps Berlioz summed up the young Saint-Saëns best when he wrote: "That youngster knows everything, all he lacks is inexperience."

But Saint-Saëns's talents went far beyond music. By age seven he was reading Latin and studying botany, geology, and lepidoptery. He soon extended his studies to archaeology and the occult sciences and eventually was elected a member of the Astronomical Society of France. As a writer, he published two volumes of poetry, some plays, and a philosophical tract, *Problems and Mysteries.*

Saint-Saëns composed effortlessly; he once said that he turned out musical compositions "as an apple tree produces apples." Inspiration and emotional expression, he believed, had little to do with musical creation. As he put it: "The artist who does not feel completely satisfied by elegant lines, by harmonious colors, and by a beautiful succession of chords does not understand the art of music."

His great facility enabled Saint-Saëns to leave a considerable amount of music. All of it bears the hallmarks of his style—clarity and lucidity, an instinctive feeling for form and proportion, and an overall sense of grace and elegance. His compositions include five symphonies, five piano concertos, three violin concertos, seven operas, and vast amounts of miscellaneous orchestral works, operas, and chamber and solo music. Of these many works, a few, such as the "Organ Symphony," Cello Concerto, and Second Piano Concerto, hold a very special place in the affection of music lovers.

Concerto for Cello and Orchestra No. 1 in A minor, Op. 33
(20 minutes)

Serious music, and particularly serious symphonic and orchestral music, was in a sad state in France in 1871. French audiences were interested only in light operas and operettas. And the defeat in the Franco-Prussian War that same year was a terrible blow to French pride and cultural aspirations.

Saint-Saëns was in the forefront of those seeking to restore French music to its proper position. In 1871, he helped found the *Société Nationale de Musique* to encourage a rebirth of serious French music. Under his leadership, the group actively promoted the works of such outstanding French composers as Debussy, Fauré, Franck, Ravel, Chausson, d'Indy, Lalo, and many others.

One of the first works Saint-Saëns composed in his zeal to promote French orchestral music was the first of his two cello concertos, which he wrote in 1872 for Auguste Tolbecque, principal cellist of the Paris Conservatory Orchestra. M. Tolbecque gave the premiere with that orchestra on January 19, 1873. Performed without any breaks, the concerto clearly divides into fast, slow, fast sections, which correspond to the three movements of a traditional concerto.

I. *Allegro non troppo.* The entire concerto grows from the opening germinal theme, which the solo cello states after a single imperious chord from the orchestra. The theme itself sweeps down through the cello's range, ending with a three-note, up-and-down motif. Saint-Saëns also introduces a lovely lyrical subsidiary subject, but the principal theme, with its all-important closing motif, controls the movement.

II. *Allegretto con moto.* The distinctly archaic second movement follows without pause; the muted strings move through the deliberately measured rhythms of a rather formal dance from the past. The cellist responds with a warmly sung melody, shaped like a much expanded echo of the rising-and-falling motif that concludes the opening theme.

III. *Allegro non troppo.* The last movement arrives with the orchestral statement of the concerto's opening melody. After that the solo cello states a new theme, also derived from the closing motif of the germinal subject. For the remainder of the movement, the composer gives the soloist free rein for virtuosic display, ending the concerto in dazzling pyrotechnics.

Concerto for Piano and Orchestra No. 2 in G minor, Op. 22
(25 minutes)

"I haven't conducted an orchestra in Paris yet," the eminent Russian pianist and composer Anton Rubinstein told Saint-Saëns after they attended a concert together in April 1868. "Let's put on a concert that will give me the opportunity of taking the baton."

Saint-Saëns readily assented to compose a piano concerto for the upcoming concert, but then discovered that the only open date at Paris' Salle Pleyel was three weeks hence! Undaunted, he accepted the challenge. "In those three weeks I will write a concerto for the occasion," he said. Always a fast, facile composer, Saint-Saëns, completed the G minor concerto in only 17 days and performed as soloist at the concert on May 13, 1868, with Rubinstein conducting.

While Saint-Saëns had little difficulty in completing the composition in time, he did not fully succeed in mastering the devilishly difficult solo piano part. As he later wrote: "I played very badly, and, except for the scherzo, which was an immediate success, it did not go well." Still, Rubinstein added the concerto to his repertoire and reported that it "served me for many years as a first-rate warhorse! It has everything—dash and elegance, dazzling brilliance and temperament; it is good music, too."

I. *Andante sostenuto.* The concerto opens with a cadenza for the soloist that looks back to the keyboard style of Bach, but a very Romantic Bach. After a while the orchestra enters with a short, forceful interruption. The piano then reasserts its preeminence by presenting the broad, lyrical principal theme. The solo part retains the lead for the remainder of the movement, from singing out thematic material to dashing off flashing, virtuosic runs and arpeggios. Just before the conclusion, the energy subsides and gives way to a particularly pleasant, albeit brief, reminder of the opening cadenza.

II. *Allegro scherzando.* The piano unfurls the mercurial opening theme with the timpani setting the pace. Saint-Saëns refers to the movement as a scherzo, but formally it is more akin to a rondo. Two themes, the opening and the rollicking melody carried by the orchestra over a robust piano accompaniment, monopolize the proceedings.

III. *Presto.* The bravura finale has all the flow and sparkle of a perpetual motion wed to the rhythmic vigor of a tarantella. The writing is bright, scintillating, and is fun for everyone, except the pianist, who must tame and control the cascades of notes in the solo part.

Perhaps the late pianist-composer Sigismund Stojowski summed up the G minor concerto best with his comment: "It begins with Bach and ends with Offenbach!"

Symphony No. 3 in C minor, Op. 78, "Organ Symphony"
(35 minutes)

At the time Saint-Saëns composed his Third Symphony (actually his fifth and last symphony, since two youthful works were not numbered), he was reacting against two popular trends in late 19th century French music. For one thing, the French audiences were infatuated with the elegant frivolity and superficial expressivity of the immensely popular operas and operettas by Meyerbeer, Offenbach, and other, lesser figures. Also, many French composers had fallen under the spell of Wagner, convinced that his music suggested the future direction of musical composition.

Saint-Saëns chose to make his Third Symphony a purely instrumental work, unconnected either with the stage or with any extramusical program. The composer used a personal musical vocabulary, one that in some ways looked back to the old Classical style and in other ways made full use of the melodic, harmonic, and rhythmic advances that came with late 19th century Romanticism.

The 50-year-old Saint-Saëns wrote his Third Symphony to fulfill a commission from the London Symphony and conducted the premiere in London on May 19, 1886. When Franz Liszt died in July of that year, Saint-Saëns dedicated the work to his memory. It came to be called the "Organ Symphony" because of the novelty of including that instrument in the orchestra.

The symphony shows the very strong influence of Liszt's concept of thematic transformation. Much of the symphony grows from the nervous string theme that comes right after the slow, plaintive introduction. In the course of the work Saint-Saëns puts this motto theme through five transformations, each time modifying and varying its articulation, rhythm, and melodic contour, instead of developing it in a more traditional symphonic manner.

For the sake of unity and to "avoid interminable repetition," as Saint-Saëns put it, he organized the work into two extended movements, but provided clear divisions within each movement to suggest strongly the more traditional four-movement structure.

I. *Adagio; Allegro moderato; Poco adagio.* The first movement begins with a slow introduction, the motto theme, and a tranquil second theme. When Saint-Saëns puts the motto through its first transformation he superimposes on it the sad little oboe phrase from the introduction. The music quiets and the organ enters to start the Poco adagio section, the high point of the symphony with its wondrously expressive melody; Saint-Saëns described it as "peaceful and contemplative."

II. *Allegro moderato; Presto; Maestoso.* The second movement begins with a furious, energetic phrase, followed by the motto theme now transformed by the woodwinds. In time this leads to the faster part of the movement in which we hear the piano, also rare in an orchestra, playing "arpeggios and scales, swift as lightning." During a free repetition of previous material, Saint-Saëns introduces a new "grave, austere" theme in the low brass and string basses. The entrance of the organ announces the final Maestoso ("Majestic"), and proceeds with still another transformation of the theme by the violins. The coda exposes the final transformation of the theme, leading to a resplendent conclusion.

Curiously enough, the Third Symphony was Saint-Saëns's last major purely orchestral score; most of his production over the remaining 35 years of his life was for the stage and encompassed seven operas, a ballet, and incidental music for seven plays.

Arnold Schoenberg

Born September 13, 1874, in Vienna
Died July 13, 1951, in Los Angeles

A RNOLD SCHOENBERG, one of the greatest self-taught composers in musical history, recalled: "I began studying the violin at eight and almost immediately started composing." The music scores he read, the concerts he attended, and the amateur chamber groups in which he played were his teachers. To help support his family, Schoenberg took a job as a bank clerk at age 16; five years later he was earning his living conducting a choir of metalworkers and orchestrating popular operettas.

Schoenberg's early compositions show two major influences: Post-Romanticism, which can be described as an extension of the late 19th century Romanticism of such composers as Brahms, Wagner, Mahler, and Richard Strauss; and Expressionism, a German and Austrian art movement that flourished in the early 1900s in reaction to French Impressionism. Expressionist artists sought to find and express the essence of the world around them. They also turned inward to understand their feelings and emotions in light of the new theories advanced by Sigmund Freud and to reflect these insights in their compositions.

Verklärte Nacht, Schoenberg's best-known piece, combines the impassioned, emotional melodies, rich harmonies, and flexible rhythms of Romanticism with the harsh dissonances, fragmented themes, and disjunct melodic lines of Expressionism to create one of this century's most intense and exciting compositions.

Starting in 1908, Schoenberg began composing atonal music—that is, music without a strong tonal center, or key. The new music ended the practice, dating back hundreds of years, of writing every piece in a key, such as symphony in C major, concerto in F sharp minor, or whatever. Schoenberg's atonal compositions, the first music not in a key, are analogous to artist Wassily Kandinsky's paintings from about the same time, which were the first art that showed no real objects.

About 15 years later, Schoenberg went even further; he created a style of composition that he called "method of composing with 12 tones." This style not only did away with tonality, it also eliminated melody in the traditional sense. The composer organized the music around a tone row, a particular arrangement of the 12 tones of the chromatic scale.

The final word on Schoenberg's position in the annals of music history has not yet been written. Though he is universally recognized and respected as a seminal figure of 20th century music, Schoenberg is rarely performed today. Only his early *Verklärte Nacht* now appears with any frequency on concert programs; listeners are moved by its intense, heightened emotionalism and expressivity. Audiences, for the most part, find the rest of his oeuvre "difficult" and avoid exposure, thus never developing the familiarity necessary for enjoying these innovative works.

Verklärte Nacht, Op. 4
(30 minutes)

Schoenberg originally wrote *Verklärte Nacht* ("Transfigured Night") for string quartet. He completed the manuscript on December 1, 1899, when he was 25. Audiences first heard it in this form in Vienna on March 18, 1902. "The thematic construction," Schoenberg wrote, "is based on Wagnerian 'model and sequence' technique above a moving harmony, on the one hand, and on Brahms's technique of developing variation, as I call it, on the other." In 1917 he rescored it for string orchestra and revised that version in 1943.

Schoenberg drew his inspiration for *Verklärte Nacht* from Richard Dehmel's eponymous poem of 1896 and captured in sound its searing passion and intense emotion. Dehmel's poem tells of a man and woman walking through a bare, moonlit forest. She confesses that before she met him, overwhelmed by loneliness and loss of faith, she gave herself to a stranger and that she is now with child. The man she loves, walking at her side, speaks of the way the moonlight enwraps the universe and passes a special warmth between them as they drift on a vast, cold sea, transfiguring the unborn baby so that the child she bears will belong to him.

Schoenberg divides the music into five parts. First, he conjures up the couple's despair as they plod through the moonlit forest. The lower instruments depict the heavy trudging steps beneath a descending melody in the other instruments. In the second part, the music grows more agitated and anguished as the woman recounts her tale. The heavy tread of the opening returns for the third section. For the man's reply, Schoenberg presents new melodic material and expands on motifs from the second section; the character is warm and tender, even as the music builds to an impassioned climax. The final section depicts the magical moment, the transfiguration of the unborn child. Schoenberg accomplishes this ennobling change by transforming the descending opening figure and giving it to the first violins at the very top of their range. After this sublime moment the music quietly fades away.

Franz Schubert

Born January 31, 1797, in Lichtenthal (now part of Vienna)
Died November 19, 1828, in Vienna

SCHUBERT'S FATHER was the local schoolmaster as well as an amateur cellist; he provided his son's early schooling and musical training. At age 11 Schubert entered the choir of the Imperial Kapelle, the group known today as the Vienna Choirboys, where he received more advanced instruction in music.

In 1813, after Schubert's voice broke, he left the choir and, at his father's urging, took a course in teacher education to become an assistant teacher in his father's school. In the same year, he began his First Symphony and two years later wrote his Second and Third symphonies. For some four years Schubert taught school, hating the work, but grateful that he was able to compose in his free time.

In 1818 he moved to Vienna in the hope of launching a composing career. At the time, Vienna, still deeply involved with the music of Haydn and Mozart, who had died within the last few decades, was not particularly welcoming to new composers. An even greater obstacle to Schubert's acceptance was the presence of Beethoven, whom he admired greatly. Beethoven was at the height of his powers and widely hailed as the greatest instrumental composer of the age. While Schubert was a superb composer of songs, he lacked Beethoven's skill in sustaining his ideas in the larger musical forms.

Efforts to make his mark as an operatic composer were likewise stymied by Vienna's infatuation with the operas of Rossini, as well as by Schubert's seeming inability to select a libretto of quality. Although Schubert composed constantly and gained some recognition, he managed to get only a few of his works published or performed during his lifetime.

While in Vienna, therefore, Schubert lived in poverty. He was able to survive only because he joined a group that lived communally, sharing their living quarters and the little money they earned. In March 1828, shortly after Schubert's 31st birthday, the Vienna *Gesellschaft der Musikfreund* presented the first all-Schubert concert, which was most enthusiastically received. But it came too late. By then, Schubert's health had deteriorated badly and he died that November, probably of typhoid fever.

For inborn, native talent, few composers rival Schubert. Making music was for him a completely natural and unself-conscious act. His ability to create wonderful melodies—lyrical, expressive, infinitely varied—was unsurpassed. While some may question his tectonic skills or his ability as orchestrator, everyone must marvel at the flood of glorious themes that pervade every single composition he created.

Because so few of Schubert's works were published during his lifetime, it proved very difficult to place them in sequential order. Musicologist Otto Erich Deutsch prepared a chronological catalog of Schubert's music, published in English in 1951, that assigned a Deutsch number (D.) to each composition; they are used below.

Symphony No. 5 in B flat major, D. 485
(30 minutes)

Schubert began composing his Fifth Symphony in September 1816, while working as an assistant teacher in his father's school, and finished it in less than a month, on October 3. He wrote the symphony for an orchestra of amateur musicians that grew out of the Schubert family quartet, made up of the composer, his father, and two older brothers, all avid amateur players. Since the number of available wind players was limited, Schubert composed this symphony for a chamber-sized orchestra of one flute, two oboes, two bassoons, two horns, and strings—omitting the usual clarinets, trumpets, and timpani.

The small amateur orchestra gave a private performance of the Fifth Symphony that fall at the Vienna apartment of Otto Hatwig, who conducted. No further performances followed and the score and parts were lost after Schubert's death. In 1867, though, Sir George Grove (of Dictionary of Music fame) and Sir Arthur Sullivan (of operetta fame) came to Vienna to search for missing Schubert manuscripts and unearthed the Fifth Symphony, which led to the public premiere in London on February 1, 1873, with August Manns conducting.

I. *Allegro.* The orchestra sneaks in with soft woodwind chords that lead to the delicate, graceful violin melody, each phrase echoed by the lower strings. After a blustery transition based on the opening rhythm of the first theme, Schubert gives the strings the quiet and beautifully fluid second theme. Both themes are Classically perfect—that is, clear, balanced, symmetrical, without excesses of any kind. Schubert, the supreme melodist, seems impatient with working out the themes and hurries through the development section to reach the recapitulation and restatement of the glorious melodies he created.

II. *Andante con moto.* The principal subject of the second movement is a songlike melody. The short pauses at the end of each phrase, as though for breaths, contribute to its strong vocal quality. A subordinate theme, similar in character but with a slightly agitated accompaniment figure in the second violins and violas, comes as a contrast between appearances of the opening melody.

III. *Menuetto: Allegro molto.* The loud, unison opening brings to mind the very similar opening of the Menuetto in Mozart's Symphony No. 40 and perhaps pays homage to the earlier composer and to the Classical tradition in music. The first part of this movement alternates vigorous phrases with quiet, placating responses. For the middle section, or Trio, Schubert modulates to the major and introduces a wonderfully lyrical melody. The movement ends with a shortened repeat of the opening.

IV. *Allegro vivace.* If the ghost of Mozart hovers over the Menuetto, then Haydn's presence lurks over the Allegro vivace. Filled with delightful melodies and an impelling flow, this movement hurries along to a brilliant and very satisfying conclusion.

Symphony No. 8 in B minor, D. 759, "Unfinished"
(27 minutes)

Surely no musical mystery intrigues audiences as much as that of the "Unfinished" Symphony. Schubert began composing the work on October 30, 1822, completed two movements and preliminary sketches for the third, and nothing more. It was not death that stopped Schubert's pen; he lived and composed other pieces for six more years. Musicologist Alfred Einstein speculates that Schubert, realizing that he had created two such powerful movements, did not continue for fear of being unable to sustain this very high level of creativity. Another scholar, Martin Chusid, conjectures that Schubert ceased work because the two movements bore some resemblance to Beethoven's Second Symphony and he was afraid that people would accuse him of plagiarism.

Critic Harold Schonberg believes that Schubert did indeed complete the symphony, but that the last two movements were lost. A more romantic interpretation holds that Schubert was in love with his young piano student Countess Carolyn Esterházy, and was writing the symphony for her. Then, when she announced her engagement to someone else, Schubert set the incomplete symphony aside.

The known facts surrounding the "Unfinished," unfortunately, raise more questions than they answer. On April 6, 1823, the Styrian Music Society of Graz elected Schubert an honorary member; in his letter of acceptance he wrote: "I shall take the liberty of presenting your esteemed Society with a score of one of my symphonies shortly." In the fall of 1824, Schubert sent the two movements of the "Unfinished" to Anselm Hüttenbrenner, an old friend and director of the Styrian Society. Anselm kept the score, treated it as his personal property, and did not schedule a performance.

Many years later, on March 8, 1860, Anselm's brother, Joseph Hüttenbrenner, told conductor Johann Herbeck about the symphony. Herbeck, a great admirer of Schubert, inexplicably waited over five years before obtaining the score from Anselm. Finally, on December 17, 1865, Herbeck gave the premiere in Vienna.

I. *Allegro moderato.* The principal subject includes three distinct phrases, each laden with emotional connotations: the slightly ominous opening in the cellos and basses; the uneasy murmuring figure in the violins; and the melancholic song of the oboe and clarinet. After building this material to a climax, Schubert introduces calm and tranquillity with the cello statement of the second theme, one of the best-remembered of all symphonic melodies. After a quiet beginning, the ensuing development section whips up great excitement before quieting down for the recapitulation. The recapitulation lacks the opening cello-bass phrase, perhaps because that motif so dominated the development.

II. *Andante con moto.* Schubert starts the movement with a gentle, tender melody for the strings, which he soon transforms into a forceful, aggressive woodwind statement. In time, this gives way to a clarinet melody—a lonely tune that seems to sigh with pain and yearning. The composer unleashes a few musical thunderbolts before bringing both themes back and proceeding to a quiet ending.

Symphony No. 9 in C major, D. 944, "Great"
(50 minutes)

Many regard Schubert's "Great" C major (to distinguish it from his Symphony No. 6 in the same key) as the composer's greatest masterpiece. The work, though, did not win its preeminent position easily. Three times Vienna's Gesellschaft der Musikfreund rejected the symphony for performance because it was too long and too difficult. Later, the orchestra of the Concerts du Conservatoire in Paris refused to play beyond the first movement, and the musicians of the London Philharmonic so ridiculed the work that the performance had to be canceled.

On Schubert's death, the unperformed manuscript ended up in the possession of his brother Ferdinand. While on a trip to Vienna in 1839, Robert Schumann learned that Ferdinand had the score and convinced him to send it to Felix Mendelssohn, conductor of the Gewandhaus Orchestra in Leipzig, where, in Schumann's words, "it was performed [on March 21, 1839], its greatness recognized, performed again, and received with delight and almost universal admiration."

Schumann's review of the first performance, excerpted below, points out many special attributes of the symphony, and includes the notable comment about the work's "heavenly" length: "In Schubert's symphony, in the transparent, glowing, romantic life therein reflected, I see Vienna more clearly mirrored than ever. More than merely lovely melody, something above and beyond sorrow and joy lies concealed in this symphony—nay, more, that we are by the music transported to a region where we can never remember to have been before—to experience all this we must listen to symphonies such as this. Here we have, besides masterly power over the musical technicalities of composition, life in all its phases, color in exquisite gradations, the minutest accuracy and fitness of expression, and permeating the whole work, a spirit of romance such as we recognize in other works of Franz Schubert. And this heavenly, long-drawn-out symphony is like some thick romance of Jean Paul's . . . which can never end."

I. *Andante; Allegro ma non troppo.* Schubert establishes the character of the first movement at the very outset with a long, arching French horn melody. This melody also supplies, albeit much slower, the model for the dotted (long/short) rhythmic pattern of the rambunctious principal theme that opens the faster body of the movement. The woodwinds bring in a contrasting subject, distinguished by its sharply pointed articulation. In a brilliant stroke of orchestration and organization, near the end of the exposition Schubert introduces echoes of the slow opening softly intoned by the trombones. The spacious treatment of the rest of the movement sustains the expansive character of the thematic material.

II. *Andante con moto.* After a few introductory measures by the strings, the oboe states the somewhat jaunty, but haunting marchlike first theme of the second movement. After expanding and developing this material, Schubert entrusts the much more lyrical subsidiary theme to the second, instead of first, violins, perhaps to achieve a slightly more subdued and distant sound. The movement ends with the return of both melodic groups.

III. *Scherzo: Allegro vivace.* Like a coiled spring, the strings burst forth in the bold, rugged opening of the Scherzo, which quickly loses its energy in the wind response. Back and forth it goes, with sections hammering away at the original motif and sections relaxing in gently flowing interludes. After a

full stop, the cantabile middle section of the movement features the woodwinds, and leads to a return of the powerful first part.

IV. *Finale: Allegro vivace.* Two terse rhythmic figures make up the
fanfarelike opening of the Finale, and inform much of the rest of the movement either as melody or as accompaniment. Reportedly, the London Philharmonic musicians could not understand the second theme, characterized
by four iterated notes in the woodwinds over repeated triplets in the strings.
"Where's the tune?" they shouted. After working through the various melodies and restating them, Schubert ends the symphony in a resplendent burst
of sound.

Commentators long believed that Schubert composed the "Great" C major
in March 1828; recent scholarship, though, seems to indicate that he wrote it
earlier, perhaps in 1825 or 1826.

Robert Schumann

Born June 8, 1810, in Zwickau, Germany
Died July 29, 1856, in Endenich, Germany

IN MANY WAYS Robert Schumann embodied the spirit of Romanticism in music; he wanted his music "to send light into the human soul." Like other Romantic composers, Schumann emphasized passion and imagination over reason and logic. He strove for the full expression of his emotions and let the content, not strict rules, shape his music. At times the driven extrovert, at times the self-absorbed dreamer, Schumann represented in his music and personality the duality of the Romantic character.

The son of nonmusical parents, Schumann began piano lessons at seven and was soon composing on his own. In 1828, at his mother's urging, he entered the University of Leipzig to study law. A reluctant law student, Schumann devoted most of his time to his music and finally gave up his legal education to study piano with Friedrich Wieck. In an effort to strengthen the fourth finger of his right hand, however, Schumann used a mechanical device that permanently damaged his hand, forcing him to abandon hope for a career as pianist.

Turning his full attention to composing, Schumann became known for his brilliant piano compositions and stirring songs. His considerable output also includes chamber works, choral music, and an unsuccessful opera, along with four symphonies and a number of concertos. In 1833, Schumann helped found an influential music journal and wrote for it until 1853. His articles did much to advance the careers of composers that he admired, such as Brahms, Berlioz, and Chopin.

At 25 years of age, Schumann fell in love with Wieck's 16-year-old daughter, Clara, a brilliant pianist. Her father, believing that Clara was too young and Schumann's future too uncertain for marriage, tried to break up the relationship. But the two were deeply in love and finally married five years later; throughout their married life they enjoyed a most wonderful personal as well as musical bonding.

Unfortunately, not long after his marriage, Schumann began to show signs of mental illness. Various commentators speculate that his disease, which some now identify as manic-depressive illness, led to periods of amazing creativity. Unfortunately, the same condition also brought on bouts of profound depression and attempts to take his own life. Early in 1854, after he tried to commit suicide by jumping into the Rhine River, Schumann was confined to an insane asylum, where he died two years later.

Critics greatly admire Schumann's orchestral works for their passion and intensity, melodic invention, scope, and drama. But a number find in the same compositions blurred tone colors and indistinct, poorly defined timbres as a result of being too thickly orchestrated or having too many instruments sharing the same melodic line.

Some conductors take it upon themselves to try to improve Schumann's orchestration; others consider the scores sacrosanct and refuse to change one note. But thankfully, whether in spite of his orchestration or because of it, Schumann's works endure and have endeared themselves to generations of music lovers.

Concerto for Cello and Orchestra in A minor, Op. 129
(25 minutes)

Schumann was pleased with his appointment in September 1850 as Municipal Music Director for the city of Düsseldorf. But he was probably already suffering from what we now call manic-depressive illness. Disagreements and arguments continually erupted between Schumann, the performers, and the administrators of the city's music programs until he was forced to resign three years later.

Despite the effects of his mental condition, Schumann enjoyed some highly productive and creative periods of composing in Düsseldorf. In a fortnight, from October 10 to 24, he completed his sole cello concerto. The composer's special affection for the cello arose after he injured his hand and tried playing that instrument for a short while as a replacement for the piano.

The lyrical, warm, and intimate concerto proved to be a valuable addition to the solo cello literature. The concerto poses many difficulties for the solo cellist, but they are more in the nature of shaping the phrases and sustaining the songful melodic line than in accomplishing breathtaking technical feats. As Schumann said: "I cannot write a concerto for the virtuosos." Even though the cello avoids virtuosic excesses, it clearly takes the lead throughout the concerto. Schumann assigns the orchestra a subservient role, which tends to reduce the tension between soloist and tutti that characterizes most concertos.

I. *Nicht zu schnell.* After three introductory woodwind chords, the soloist presents the lyrical principal theme of the movement and, following a brief orchestral interruption, sings out the similar-sounding subsidiary subject. Schumann devotes the rest of the movement to developing and returning this material, but always dominated by the solo cello. At the end, a slightly slower interlude leads directly to the next movement.

II. *Langsam.* This beautiful, soulful, slow movement is little more than a quiet, pensive song for the solo cello, with the orchestra discretely in the background. Brief in length, the movement has but one melody, which the cello gives out at the very beginning. A transition recalls the principal theme of the first movement and introduces the third movement, which follows without pause.

III. *Sehr lebhaft.* The music changes character somewhat for the fast finale, which is more rhythmic and dancelike than anything that came before. For the second theme, Schumann returns to the lyrical mode, with the soloist and woodwinds engaging in a delightful dialogue. Near the end, the composer includes a written-out cadenza; a faster coda, based on the themes of the movement, brings the work to an end.

Ludwig Ebert performed as soloist at the premiere in Leipzig on June 9, 1860, some four years after the composer's death.

Concerto for Piano and Orchestra in A minor, Op. 54
(33 minutes)

The marriage of Robert Schumann and his beloved Clara Wieck on September 12, 1840, came after a long struggle to overcome her father's opposition to the union. What would be more natural than for Robert to write a piece for Clara, which he called *Fantasy for Piano and Orchestra,* some eight months after their wedding? Unfortunately, other than a run-through reading, this tender, gentle *Fantasy* languished for a long while, gaining neither performance nor publication.

Some four years later, Robert had the idea of keeping the *Fantasy* as a first movement and adding two movements to make it a proper piano concerto; he completed that task on July 31, 1845. Clara played the solo part and Ferdinand Hiller conducted the rather coolly received premiere of the complete concerto in Dresden on December 4, 1845. Clara subsequently performed the concerto widely, often with Robert conducting the orchestra, and it gradually gained acceptance. By the end of the century the A minor was being hailed as an outstanding Romantic piano concerto.

I. *Allegro affetuoso.* After a commanding flourish by the piano, the oboe sings the poetic germinal theme from which the entire concerto grows. The movement contains the regular components of sonata allegro form, but Schumann's treatment might be termed transformations of the original melody, rather than the more typical thematic development. Texturally, the piano and orchestra engage in considerable interplay, with the soloist now taking the lead, now playing a subsidiary role to the orchestra.

II. *Intermezzo: Andante grazioso.* Schumann fashions the staccato principal theme from the four-note ascending phrase heard near the beginning of the first movement theme. Following the expansion of this idea, he introduces a new, contrasting theme, a radiant, sustained melody in the cellos. Then, after bringing back the opening staccato phrase, he recalls the initial theme of the concerto in a transition to the finale, which follows directly.

III. *Allegro vivace.* The principal theme of the last movement presents a bold new transformation of the germinal melody. Schumann follows this with a distinctive second subject, a somewhat mysterious, syncopated tune that superimposes a $6/4$ pattern on the established $3/4$ meter. In concert, the listener can best appreciate the effect by watching how the conductor seemingly beats against the orchestra part. The development starts with a fugato and then mostly concerns itself with the principal theme. A somewhat free recapitulation and long coda conclude the movement.

Symphony No. 1 in B flat major, Op. 38, "Spring"
(35 minutes)

The fall and winter months of 1840 were truly the "springtime" of Schumann's life. Having just married Clara, the composer was enjoying a particularly active period as teacher, writer, and, of course, composer. In the middle of a snowy Leipzig winter, he began to compose his First Symphony, which he completed on February 20, 1841, and described to his friend Ernst Wenzel as "a Spring Symphony."

In a letter to composer Ludwig Spohr, Schumann wrote: "I composed the symphony in that flush of spring that carries a man away even in his old age, and comes over him anew every year. Description and painting were not part of my intention, but I believe that the time at which it came into existence may have influenced its shape and made it what it is." Schumann also indicated that the symphony was inspired by a poem by Adolf Böttger that speaks of the gloomy clouds obscuring the landscape, but ends with the lines: "O turn, O turn aside thy course / For the valley blooms with spring."

On the manuscript score of the symphony, Schumann gave a title to each movement: I. Spring's Awakening; II. Evening; III. Merry Companions; IV. Spring's Farewell. He removed these designations before the score was printed, probably because he did not want the music to be interpreted too literally as "description and painting."

I. *Andante un poco maestoso; Allegro molto vivace.* The slow introduction starts with what Schumann, in a letter to conductor Wilhelm Taubert, referred to as "a call to awaken." The composer continues: "In what follows of the introduction there might be a suggestion of the growing green of everything, even of a butterfly flying up, and in the subsequent Allegro of the gradual assembling of all that belongs to spring." The forthright principal theme of the movement obviously grows out of the opening brass call and is set into sharp relief by the demure little second subject. An extensive development, primarily of the principal theme, follows, and a return of the trumpet call signals the recapitulation.

II. *Larghetto.* A gorgeous, soulful melody informs the slow movement. Schumann brings in contrasting episodes between varied reappearances of this moving theme. Near the end of the movement, the trombones quietly intone a variant of the melody that suggests the theme of the next movement, which follows without break.

III. *Scherzo: Molto vivace.* This bold, vigorous movement uses an energized transformation of the Larghetto melody as its theme. Instead of a single contrasting middle trio, this movement has two trios between shortened returns of the opening Scherzo. The first trio uses repeated iambs; the second, descending and ascending scales.

IV. *Allegro animato e grazioso.* A forceful outcry opens the finale, but quickly gives way to the light, bouncy principal theme. The lusty subsidiary subject obviously derives from the initial flourish. Schumann ends the ensuing development with a striking passage for French horns and flute, which leads to the recapitulation and a fiery coda.

Felix Mendelssohn led the premiere with the Leipzig Gewandhaus Orchestra on March 31, 1841.

Symphony No. 2 in C major, Op. 61
(40 minutes)

During the first five months of 1844 Schumann accompanied his wife, Clara, on her concert tour of Russia, where he was repeatedly identified as the husband of the pianist. ("Tell me, Mr. Schumann," he was once asked, "are you at all musical?") After their return to Leipzig in May, stung by the lack of recognition and eager to be working again, Schumann enthusiastically applied himself to his musical compositions.

As the months passed, Schumann began to show the deteriorating effects of his poor mental and physical condition. Unable to sleep, tormented by phobias, nervous, depressed, and drained of all energy, he suffered a severe mental breakdown in August.

It took Schumann over a year to recover. One of the first positive signs came in a 1845 letter to Mendelssohn: "Drums and trumpets in C have been blaring in my head. I have no idea what will come of it." Gradually, the Second Symphony, with its soft but stirring opening motto for trumpets in C, started to emerge.

Working at top speed, Schumann finished the first draft in less than a week in December 1845, and then took nearly a year, until October 19, 1846, to complete the remainder. "I sketched the symphony while suffering severe physical pain," Schumann wrote. "Indeed, I may well call it the struggle of my mind that influenced this, and by which I sought to beat off my disease."

Mendelssohn conducted the Leipzig Gewandhaus Orchestra for the November 5, 1846, premiere.

I. *Sostenuto assai; Allegro ma non troppo.* Schumann described the first movement as full of his "struggle" and "very peevish and perverse in character." The symphony opens with a slow introduction that pits the trumpet motto against a sinuous, flowing string melody. In the faster main body of the movement two principal themes appear: the first characterized by repeated quirky, dotted (long/short) rhythms; the second a surging chromatic melody divided between the strings and the woodwinds. Near the end of the movement, the music reaches a climax as the trumpets sing out the opening motto phrase.

II. *Scherzo: Allegro vivace.* Instead of the expected slow movement, Schumann places the Scherzo next. The first violins whip through the headlong flight of the principal theme. Of the two contrasting trios, Schumann makes the first light and sprightly, and the second much more lyrical. After each trio he gives a shortened repetition of the Scherzo, with a brief trumpet reminder of the motto near the end.

III. *Adagio espressivo.* Suffused with tender, melancholy beauty, the Adagio may be the most perfectly realized movement of all the Schumann symphonies. It is cast in three-part form: the expressive, poignant opening melody, a short contrapuntal interlude, and a return of the melody, which Schumann now transforms into the radiant major mode.

IV. *Allegro molto vivace.* "It was only in the finale that I began to feel myself again," wrote Schumann. A robust marchlike first theme initiates this cheerful and optimistic movement; the second subject obviously refers back to the principal theme of the previous movement. Toward the end of the finale, the motto returns, gradually growing in strength to reach a proud, confident conclusion.

Symphony No. 3 in E flat major, Op. 97, "Rhenish"
(37 minutes)

Schumann and his family moved from Dresden to Düsseldorf on September 2, 1850, so he could take up his new post as conductor of the city's orchestra and chorus. Happy to be in Düsseldorf, he wanted to write a symphony that would capture the history and natural beauty of the Rhineland, or Rhenish region, the area that extends west from the Rhine River to the borders of Holland and Belgium. He started composing the "Rhenish" Symphony on November 2, 1850, finished on December 9, and conducted the Düsseldorf orchestra in the first performance on February 6, 1851.

I. *Lebhaft.* The symphony immediately launches into the buoyant theme that may well reflect Schumann's love of the Rhineland. The woodwinds present the very different second theme, with its rather sad and elegiac tone. The composer considers both themes equally in the development and recapitulation, and ends the movement with a forceful coda.

II. *Scherzo: Sehr mässig.* After the driving first movement, the Scherzo seems very tame by comparison. Schumann originally called this section "Morning on the Rhine," but later removed the title. According to critic William Foster Apthorp, the principal theme, introduced by the lower strings and bassoons, is an old German drinking song, "Rheinweinlied." In the second part of the theme, Schumann introduces fast, skipping notes, which he then combines with the legato opening melody. After a brief trio in which the winds monopolize the smoothly sung theme, Schumann brings back the Scherzo in a free repetition.

III. *Nicht schnell.* Little more than a brief intermezzo, this movement is pervaded by a quiet, gentle charm. The first melody in the clarinets and the second melody in violas and bassoons provide the thematic material.

IV. *Feierlich.* Among the pleasures of Schumann's stay in Düsseldorf were several visits to the unfinished Gothic Cathedral of Cologne. On one occasion, Schumann witnessed the elevation of Archbishop von Geissel to the position of Cardinal. Evidence that this event was significant in the creation of this movement is Schumann's note on the score: "In the character of the accompaniment to a solemn ceremony." By adding three trombones to the orchestra and creating a more polyphonic texture, Schumann succeeds in evoking the awesome sight of the huge cathedral and the inspiring ritual.

V. *Lebhaft.* The final, fast movement calls to mind a joyful folk festival and may suggest the public celebration of the Archbishop's elevation. At the end, Schumann brings back stirring echoes of the cathedral music.

Symphony No. 4 in D minor, Op. 120
(35 minutes)

Schumann began composing his Fourth Symphony in May 1841 and presented the completed work to his wife, Clara, on September 13 as a present to celebrate her twenty-second birthday and the christening of their first child, Marie, on the same day. But the composer was not pleased with the premiere on December 6, 1841, by the Leipzig Gewandhaus Orchestra under Ferdinand David, and withdrew the score.

Ten years later, in December 1851, Schumann revised the symphony, mostly by thickening and doubling the wind parts. In this new form, he introduced the symphony in Düsseldorf on March 3, 1853, conducting the orchestra himself. Since Schumann had completed his symphonies in C and E flat in the interim, the D minor is second in order of composition, but fourth in publication order and numbering. While most conductors today perform the 1851 version, some prefer the original for what they regard as its cleaner, leaner sound.

Schumann's concern from the very start was in finding a way to unify this large-scaled work. The solution he hit on involved returning themes from earlier movements in later movements, and directing the orchestra to play all four movements without break.

I. *Ziemlich langsam; Lebhaft.* At the very outset of the slow, somber introduction, the second violins, violas, and bassoons state the all-important motto with its up-and-down scalar pattern. The tempo quickens as Schumann brings in the frisky principal theme of the Lebhaft, which seems to arise from the introduction motto. Schumann presents other motifs, but focuses most attention on the principal theme; the second theme, as a matter of fact, is the principal theme transposed to another key (F major). In a sharp departure from standard sonata allegro form, Schumann ends the movement after the development, perhaps as a way of drawing listeners into the next movement.

II. *Romanze: Ziemlich langsam.* Schumann conjured up one of his most exquisite and expressive melodies for the Romanze, creating a very special tonal color by directing that it be played by an oboe and solo cello. After but a single statement of this melody, Schumann brings back the motto theme from the introduction, which he then varies and decorates with a solo violin's filigree.

III. *Scherzo: Lebhaft.* As the gentle strains of the Romanze waft away,

Schumann rudely begins the Scherzo with what proves to be a free, fast, high-powered inversion of the motto theme! The dissimilar trio in the middle has the first violins playing still another version of the motto against the dreamy woodwinds. A shortened Scherzo and a glimpse of the trio return before moving on directly to the finale.

IV. *Langsam; Lebhaft.* The slow introduction to the finale starts with the principal theme of the first movement played at about half speed. Schumann then brings the somewhat altered melody up to speed for the fast body of the movement. He gives the flutes, oboes, and first violins a slightly quieter melody as the second theme. After discussing both subjects, Schumann returns only the second theme in the recapitulation and ends with a coda that he graces with a new melody in the violas and lower woodwinds.

Dmitri Shostakovich

Born September 25, 1906, in St. Petersburg
Died August 9, 1975, in Moscow

DMITRI SHOSTAKOVICH spent his entire creative life under the repressive Communist regime of the Soviet Union. Censors judged every work by how closely it adhered to Lenin's famous dictum: "Art belongs to the people."

Shostakovich's first major work, the brash, barbed Symphony No. 1, composed some eight years after the 1917 Russian Revolution, pleased the Soviet leaders, who were still imbued with revolutionary fervor and encouraged artists to strike out in new directions. But by the early 1930s, the artistic goal had become "Socialist Realism," and only artworks glorifying the state, its heroes, and its accomplishments found favor with government officials. In 1936, the authorities denounced Shostakovich's opera *Lady Macbeth of Mtsensk* as "chaos instead of music." The next year he composed his Symphony No. 5, which brought him back into the bureaucrats' good graces.

Over the following decades, some of Shostakovich's compositions won enthusiastic governmental approval, and earned him the Stalin Prize (three times), Order of Lenin (three times), and People's Artist, Hero of Socialist Labor, and Order of the October Revolution awards. But government officials condemned other compositions with such phrases as "bourgeois decadence" and "muddle instead of music."

In 1948, Shostakovich received the most stinging rebuke of all. The Central Committee of the Communist Party accused him of "formalist perversions and antidemocratic tendencies alien to the Soviet people and its artistic tastes." As before, Shostakovich adopted an exceedingly contrite public posture. He followed the 1948 debacle with an oratorio glorifying reforestation and his Eleventh and Twelfth symphonies, which dealt with the Russian Revolution.

Spiritually, though, Shostakovich turned inward and began writing more "private" music, expressing his innermost thoughts and feelings with a strong autobiographical component. A leading work in this category is the Tenth Symphony with its prominent use of the acronym of his name.

Shostakovich's works, and particularly his symphonies and string quartets, are among the most popular 20th century compositions. Despite the strictures of totalitarianism, Shostakovich developed an original musical style that combined Russian nationalism with influences from Western music. Intimate, personal writing and contrasting flashes of wit and humor characterize his writings, all enlivened by great vitality and intensity of expression.

Symphony No. 1, Op. 10
(36 minutes)

Shostakovich entered the St. Petersburg Conservatory in 1919, when he was only 13. Six years later, while completing his studies, Shostakovich wrote his Symphony No. 1 as the graduation project. The work received its premiere on May 12, 1926, by the Leningrad Philharmonic under Nikolai Malko, which was quickly followed by performances throughout Europe and the United States. Its youthful vigor, wry wit, charming melody, and crackling rhythms made it an international favorite and officials of the still-new Communist regime approved and gave the work their blessing.

I. *Allegretto; Allegro non troppo.* Shostakovich builds the opening movement on four distinct thematic subjects. The first is a long-toned melody by muted trumpet with mocking retorts from the bassoon. Next comes a rising violin scale with many interruptions along the way. Third, the clarinet presents an arch, somewhat grotesque melody in a slightly faster tempo. And finally the flute delivers a slightly sad, slightly skewed legato waltz tune. The composer works through and combines the four groups, building to a climax, and returning the four subjects—but in reverse order—before the movement ends quietly.

II. *Allegro.* After several preliminary measures and a precipitous descent in the piano, the violins give out the light, tripping main theme of the scherzo, which the piano then repeats. The short, slower middle section features the woodwinds in an archaic-sounding, choralelike melody. Toward the end of the return of the sprightly opening section, Shostakovich uses a clever bit of contrapuntal juxtaposition to give the brass the chorale melody while the woodwinds and strings loudly insist on the bouncy scherzo theme. Three portentous piano chords promise that something of importance will follow, but they merely introduce some subdued musing on what has come before to end the movement.

III. *Lento.* The sad, almost tearful principal theme, given out at once by the oboe, derives from the clarinet tune in the first movement. As the composer extends the melody, a nervous, anxious rhythmic figure—long/short–short/long—insinuates itself into the background. The feelings of despair and gloom deepen as the oboe states the funereal, marchlike second theme. A solo violin brings back the opening melody, after which echoes of the rhythmic figure give way to a snare drum roll that connects directly with the last movement.

IV. *Allegro molto.* Following a slow introduction, the clarinet states the fleeting, puckish main theme of the finale. The orchestra grows ever more agitated, out of which emerges the subsidiary theme, forcefully presented in a powerful unison by the woodwinds and upper strings and then solo violin. Increasing excitement, with the piano playing a prominent role, leads to one of the outstanding moments of the symphony, the ominous timpani solo—with the long/short–short/long rhythm—after which the music quiets before soaring to a bold climax.

Symphony No. 5, Op. 47
(45 minutes)

In 1931, Shostakovich aligned himself foursquare with the Soviet authorities, writing: "I am a Soviet composer, and I see our epoch as something heroic, spirited, and joyous. Music cannot help having a political basis. . . . There can be no music without ideology." The following year, Shostakovich composed his opera *Lady Macbeth of Mtsensk,* which was wildly acclaimed at its premiere in 1934, leading to over one hundred performances.

Early in 1936, Premier Joseph Stalin attended a performance of the opera. Shostakovich's advanced compositional techniques distressed the dictator and the lurid sex scenes onstage and their realistic depiction in the music precipitated a devastating attack on the composer. The government-controlled press called the opera "coarse, primitive, and vulgar." Further, they said, "the music quacks, grunts, and growls, and it suffocates itself in order to express the love scenes as naturalistically as possible." Another article accused the composer of writing "pornographic music." Shostakovich was so sure that he would be arrested that he even packed a bag to take with him to prison!

For over a year Shostakovich did not put pen to paper, nor were any of his works performed. Then, in 1937, he wrote his Fifth Symphony, which he described as "a Soviet artist's reply to just criticism." Its premiere on November 21, 1937, with Yevgeny Mravinsky conducting the Leningrad Philharmonic, mollified his critics. Everyone agreed that Shostakovich had rehabilitated himself.

Staunch Soviets heard in the symphony the journey from darkness to the luminescent joy of Socialist Realism. But the composer had another interpretation: "The theme of my symphony is the development of the individual. I saw man with all his sufferings as the central idea of the work, which is lyrical in mood from start to finish. The finale resolves the tragedy and tension of the earlier movements on a joyous, optimistic note."

I. *Moderato.* The symphony opens with a forceful, jagged melody in the strings; the rhythm continues as the accompaniment to a somewhat grim, though lyrical violin line. After extensive discourse on these ideas, Shostakovich introduces the second theme, an ethereal melody in the first violins over a pulsed background. In the development section, Shostakovich explores many different moods and feelings, which probably all relate to the suffering of man. He freely recalls the various themes before allowing the movement to fade away with the sustained note of the violin solo.

II. *Allegretto.* Shostakovich displays wit, humor, and musical skill in giving this movement the character of a slightly distorted waltz, even though it is scherzolike in feeling and form. A delicious little solo violin tune ushers in the contrasting middle section before a free return of the opening and reminders of the central portion.

III. *Largo.* The profound and deeply moving Largo shows Shostakovich as a superb melodist. The complex manipulations of the several themes enhance their intense expression and carry the listener along on a stirring musical journey. While tinged with sadness, the Largo also has the "life-affirming pathos" that Shostakovich greatly admired in Shakespeare's tragedies.

IV. *Allegro non troppo.* Shostakovich launches the last movement with a boisterous theme from the brass and percussion, and continues this refrain throughout the movement, with contrasting interludes and a dark and shadowy middle section between its many appearances. The composer spoke of the symphony ending on a "joyous, optimistic note," but careful listening reveals that this may not be completely sincere. Later, Shostakovich said: "The rejoicing is forced, created under threat, as in *Boris Godunov.* It's as if someone were beating you with a stick and saying, 'Your business is rejoicing, your business is rejoicing.'"

Symphony No. 10, Op. 93
(53 minutes)

His fifteen symphonies testify to Shostakovich's lifelong struggle to reconcile the conflict between his belief that art serves a social purpose and his need for self-expression. Several of his symphonies—No. 2 (subtitled "October"), No. 3 ("May Day"), No. 7 ("Leningrad"), No. 11 ("1905"), and No. 12 ("The Year 1917")—clearly satisfied the needs of the regime. Others—Nos. 4, 8, 9, and especially 13, a setting of the poem "Babi Yar" by Yevgeny Yevtushenko —met opposition, denunciation, and repression.

Symphony No. 10, however, resists easy categorization. Some members of the Soviet Composers' Union criticized it as "nonrealistic"; others defended it as "an optimistic tragedy." The final consensus was that it expressed "pessimistic optimism," an oxymoron masquerading as wisdom.

Shostakovich did not help. Once he commented: "In this composition I wanted to portray human emotions and passions." Yet in *Testimony,* his memoirs edited by Solomon Volkov, he insisted: "It's about Stalin and the Stalin years. The second part, the scherzo, is a musical portrait, roughly speaking." And to add to the confusion, when asked about a possible program to the symphony, Shostakovich replied: "Let them listen and guess for themselves."

One clue to Shostakovich's real meaning lies hidden in the third and fourth movements. Here Shostakovich makes considerable use of an acronym of his name, the letters DSCH which, in German, are the musical notes D, E flat, C, and B. That he made these four notes his motto in several intimate works seems to suggest that this symphony is a personal testimonial, written to express his innermost thoughts, not to please the authorities.

I. *Moderato.* The long first movement opens with a six-note motif played by cellos and basses. The composer expands and develops the quiet, restrained phrase before the clarinet states a new melody. Shostakovich then introduces another theme, a rocking sort of melody first played by the flute in its lower register over a pizzicato string accompaniment. These three strands provide the melodic basis for the first movement; Shostakovich shapes this material into a giant arch form, developing, transforming, and juxtaposing the melodies and building to an impressive climax. The excitement then subsides, and the movement concludes with a free, quiet restatement of the original melodies.

II. *Allegro.* The second movement, really the first of two scherzos, proceeds with a singleness of purpose. Harsh, relentless, percussive, and crackling with rhythmic vitality, the Allegro affords the listener barely a moment of repose or relaxation.

III. *Allegretto.* This charming and genial movement presents a sharp contrast to the brutal drive of the Allegro. The composer first puts forth a rhythmically ambiguous, but poised melody in the strings. As this theme fades from view, the flutes very clearly sound out the DSCH motto. The movement continues with reminders of the six-note motif that opened the symphony, some discourse on the principal theme of this movement, a somewhat raucous interruption, and echoes of DSCH.

IV. *Andante; Allegro.* Unison strings start the quiet introduction to the final movement, followed by the oboe playing a reflective, Oriental-sounding melody. The fast main theme is bright and bouncy, but without the wild abandon of Shostakovich's more overtly joyous scores. Replete with quotations from earlier material, the body of the movement also includes themes from the second and third movements, the six-note motif, and DSCH.

Shostakovich began composing the Tenth Symphony in July 1953 and completed it on October 27. Yevgeny Mravinsky gave the premiere on December 17, 1953, conducting the Leningrad Philharmonic.

Jean Sibelius

Born December 8, 1865, at Tavastehus, Finland
Died September 20, 1957, at Järvenpää, Finland

FINLAND REGARDS Jean Sibelius as more than a leading composer; it considers him a public hero. The nation has honored him with a Sibelius Musical Institute, a Sibelius Museum, and annual festivals devoted to his music. The homage grows from his music, which, more than that of any other composer, celebrates Finland's natural beauty and expresses that nation's pride and patriotism.

The son of an army surgeon, Sibelius received an excellent early education, including instruction first in piano and then in violin. Despite his passionate interest in music, he was sent at age 19 to Helsinki to study law, but soon dropped out to enroll at the Music Institute, where he devoted himself to the violin and composition. A government grant enabled him to continue studying music from 1889 to 1892 in Berlin and Vienna.

When Sibelius returned to Finland he allied himself with the "Young Finns," a group of intellectuals and artists struggling to free Finland of Russia's domination. As the leading composer of the Finnish nationalistic movement, Sibelius wrote much music for concerts and theatrical presentations that celebrated Finnish identity. In 1918 the independence movement finally prevailed and the Russians left Finland.

While many of Sibelius' works were patriotic in nature, others were abstract with no apparent extramusical connections. His music won Sibelius a widespread reputation. In his compositions we find surging passions, cold, bleak evocations of wintery landscapes, spiritual, otherworldly qualities, and a sureness in handling the musical materials that audiences find most appealing.

Then, in 1929, Sibelius stopped composing. Some think it was because he disapproved of the new styles of musical composition. Though Sibelius produced no new works for the remaining 27 years of his life, his seven symphonies, violin concerto, and many symphonic poems continue to enjoy considerable popularity today.

Concerto for Violin and Orchestra, Op. 47
(30 minutes)

Jean Sibelius switched to the violin one year after beginning to study the piano at age nine. He devoted himself with amazing singleness of purpose to mastering that instrument, practicing, as he said, "from morning to night." His goal was "to be a celebrated violinist at any price."

At age 25 Sibelius came to the "very painful awakening when I had to admit that I had begun my training for the career of an eminent performer too late." But his musical studies had given him a solid understanding of the violin. In the summer of 1903, when he started work on his violin concerto, his 15 years of total involvement with the instrument enabled him to write an absolutely stunning solo part, one that only an affectionate composer/performer could conceive.

The violin concerto received its first performance on February 8, 1904, in Helsinki with Victor Novacek as soloist. But Sibelius found the results disappointing and asked his publisher to recall the piece. He reworked the composition in the summer of 1905 and arranged for the premiere of the new version in Berlin on October 19 of that year with Carl Haliř as soloist and Richard Strauss on the podium.

The public at the first performance seemed quite enthusiastic, but the concerto did not gain wide acceptance. Many performers probably avoided the work because of its inordinately difficult solo part and audiences rejected a composition that, when performed, was often badly played. The trouble stems from the various technical features that Sibelius considered integral to the musical texture and important in the overall musical design. They include playing on two strings at the same time (double stopping), fingering in the insecure upper reaches of the instrument, playing at high speed, negotiating huge leaps from one note to another, using a wide variety of bow strokes, and sustaining the many extended lyrical melodies of the concerto.

The concerto languished until the years after World War II, when the level of violin pedagogy and the technical achievements of players were so improved that more performers took up the concerto and played it with the required skill and understanding. Today, of course, it is a staple of the violinist's repertoire.

I. *Allegro moderato.* The concerto opens with the solo violin singing the broad, extended principal theme over the subdued murmuring of the muted strings. Sibelius introduces several subsidiary melodies that he builds around fragments of rising scales. A composed bravura cadenza works through the thematic material and leads to the restatement of the melodies and a brilliant coda that sends the violin soaring over the orchestra.

II. *Adagio di molto.* The slow movement establishes a melancholy mood as the soloist presents the long, lyrical theme. At its conclusion, the orchestral strings introduce a more forceful subject, which soloist and orchestra whip up to a passionate and dramatic climax, before returning to the melody and character of the opening.

III. *Allegro ma non tanto.* Sibelius, who was loath to discuss his music, once referred to the final movement as a *"danse macabre"* or "dance of death." Donald Tovey, the eminent British music critic, though, characterized it as a "polonaise for polar bears"! The vibrant, rhythmic movement provides a stunning display vehicle for the soloist and fittingly concludes this very exciting concerto.

Finlandia, Op. 26, No. 7
(8 minutes)

In 1892, Jean Sibelius married Aino Järnefelt, who came from a family prominent in Finland's struggle for independence from Russia. The composer became increasingly involved with the nationalistic, freedom-seeking movement as political tensions continued to rise. Events climaxed in 1899 when Czar Nicholas II issued the February Manifesto, depriving the Finns of their constitutional rights and instituting strict censorship of the press.

One way the Finns demonstrated their opposition to the restrictive new laws was through the "Press Celebrations." The most famous one, entitled *Tableaux from the Past,* took place in Helsinki on November 4, 1899. Finland's most famous poets wrote the texts, an outstanding theatrical director did the staging, and Sibelius, the most illustrious composer of the day, composed the music. From the final tableau, *Finlandia Awakes,* Sibelius drew the music for his symphonic poem *Finlandia.*

Finlandia struck a most responsive chord with the entire Finnish nation and became the anthem of its independence movement. The work so perfectly expressed the people's love for their land and their desire for freedom and self-determination that the Czar forbade any performances in Finland! While full of Finnish pride and patriotism, *Finlandia* does not quote from any Finnish folk songs. "There is a mistaken impression among the press abroad that my themes are often folk melodies," Sibelius once commented. "So far I have never used a theme that was not of my own invention. Thus the thematic material of *Finlandia* . . . is entirely my own."

Symphony No. 1 in E minor, Op. 39
(40 minutes)

Sibelius undertook the composition of his First Symphony at a relatively late age, when he was nearly 34 years old. He was already well established as a composer and the recipient of a Finnish state pension that allowed him to devote more time to composing—even though it did not make him financially independent. Sibelius completed most of the symphony during the fall of 1898, and finished it early the next year. The composer conducted the premiere at a concert devoted to his music in Helsinki on April 26, 1899, where it garnered an enthusiastic reception.

I. *Andante ma non troppo; Allegro energico.* The tension starts building from the very opening of the first movement—a lone clarinet singing its mournful melody over the gentle murmuring of a timpani roll. In the faster main body of the movement, Sibelius gradually makes full use of the large orchestral forces at his disposal. In the plethora of melodies that pour forth we can recognize some of the composer's signature devices: fragmentary melodies that start with a long-sustained note and end in a flurry of rapid notes; melodies that gently edge back and forth between two or three adjacent notes; and the extensive use of pedal tones—long-held notes, usually in the bass, which sound against changing harmonies in the other parts. Each device contributes to the visceral effect of the movement, which Sibelius structures in traditional sonata allegro form.

II. *Andante ma non troppo lento.* After the tumult and excitement of the first movement, one welcomes the quiet, poignant opening of the Andante, which Sibelius entrusts to the special timbre of the muted strings. The composer follows this section with several slightly more agitated brief episodes. Perhaps most striking is a melody for French horn. Here, and in several other places in the movement, one hears characteristics first encountered in the opening movement—a long tone followed by rapid notes, a melodic wavering between two tones, and pedal tones. The opening melody, very much altered and with some stunning climaxes, returns to end the movement.

III. *Scherzo: Allegro.* If the first movement is about drama and conflict, the third is about power and energy. Slashing drum strokes issue the principal theme, which other instruments then take up. The brusque rhythmic fragments whir around the orchestra and continue to build and surge forward throughout this section. The contrasting trio is slower in tempo and calm and placid in character. But the vigor of the opening returns once again to assert its raucous vitality.

IV. *Finale (quasi una fantasia): Andante; Allegro molto.* The Finale begins with the massed strings playing the clarinet's plaintive melody from the opening movement; implacable brass chords contribute a slightly ominous air. This introduction leads directly to the principal theme, an agitated, rhythmic melody first played by the clarinets and bassoons. After various episodes, the violins introduce the sustained, warmly lyrical second subject. Sibelius then works up the strenuous opening material and gives the second subject to the clarinet, building to a powerful, impassioned climax before the symphony ends with two quiet chords very reminiscent of those that concluded the first movement.

Symphony No. 2 in D major, Op. 43
(45 minutes)

Sibelius' Second Symphony has garnered more than its share of interpretive opinions. Early on, Finnish-born conductor Georg Schnéevoigt, a close friend of the composer, declared it to be a testament to Finnish patriotism. He suggested that the first movement depicts Finland's pastoral life, the second illustrates nationalistic fervor restrained by "timidity of soul," the stirrings of rebellion appear in the third, and the fourth holds the promise of the ultimate triumph of freedom. Echoing this view many years later, Finnish musicologist Ilmari Krohn asserted that the symphony is a vision of "Finland's struggle for political liberty."

Cecil Gray, the eminent English musical commentator, hears the symphony as an abstract composition, deeming it "a veritable revolution . . . the introduction of an entirely new principle into symphonic form." Gray contends that instead of following the orthodox procedure of introducing complete themes and then taking them apart as they are developed, Sibelius here starts with fragments that he then integrates into a climactic totality. English critic Harold Truscott scoffs at this explanation, dismissing it as an "optical illusion."

Perhaps Sibelius wants to encourage the ambiguity. In February 1901, a month after he moved to Rapallo, Italy, where he began the composition, Sibelius wrote to a friend: "I could initiate you, my understanding friend, into my work, but I do not do it from principle. To my mind it is the same with compositions as with butterflies: once you touch them, their essence is gone—they can fly, it is true, but are no longer so fair."

The composer worked on the symphony in Italy until October, when he returned to Finland. Then, having been relieved of his teaching duties at the musical academy, he devoted himself completely to the symphony, which he finished by the end of the year. Sibelius conducted the first performance in

Helsinki on March 8, 1902, as part of an entire evening of his music. The program had to be repeated three more times to satisfy the public's demand. The work is still a very well-liked 20th century symphony.

I. *Allegretto.* The symphony opens with a brief introduction and extended statement of the principal theme, both based on an emblematic motif of three consecutive conjunct notes that ascend in the introduction and descend in the main theme. Sibelius then presents subsidiary material and the second subject, a characteristic melody of the composer, with a sustained note followed by a flurry of rapid notes. Following the traditional structure of sonata allegro form, Sibelius develops the themes and brings them back for the recapitulation.

II. *Tempo andante ma rubato.* The pizzicato passage for the lower strings that starts the slow movement creates a slight air of mystery and foreboding. Finally the bassoons ease their way in with a melody that Sibelius directs be played *lugubre* ("lugubriously"). The tension builds with violent outbursts from different sections of the orchestra until the middle section, with its solemn, hymnlike theme in the violins. The composer ends the movement with a very free return of the opening section.

III. *Vivacissimo.* The first part of the third movement alternates between whispered scurrying and powerful blasts of sound. A slower, contrasting middle section features Sibelius' device of a long-sustained note (here treated as many repetitions of the same note by the oboe), followed by more rapid melodic movement. The opening section then returns, but with many alterations, and including the first hints of the three-note motif that will reign over the final movement, which follows without pause.

IV. *Allegro moderato.* Here is music of great power, with dramatic sweep and bold grandeur, all dominated by the all-important three-note motto. Building inexorably to its final glorious moments, the symphony ends radiantly as the three-note motif climbs up from the very bottom of the orchestra to reach its breathtaking conclusion.

Bedřich Smetana

Born March 2, 1824, in Litomyšl, Bohemia (now Czech Republic)
Died May 12, 1884, in Prague

IN 1843, YOUNG SMETANA came to Prague to launch his career. While he met with some musical success, he also experienced considerable political and personal difficulties. At that time the Bohemian region of Central Europe, which includes Prague, was part of the vast Austro-Hungarian Empire; Vienna was its capital and German its official language. Even though Smetana grew up speaking German, he was a fervid Czech patriot, and joined Czech nationalists in an unsuccessful attempt to establish an independent Bohemian nation. Long after the revolution failed, Smetana remained under suspicion. In the interim, his wife had become seriously ill with tuberculosis and three of his four daughters had died.

In an attempt to change his fortune, Smetana moved to Göteborg, Sweden, in 1856 and threw himself into its musical life, achieving recognition as a composer, conductor, and pianist. Over the following years, the political atmosphere in Prague started to change and Bohemian culture was beginning to reestablish itself. Smetana's thoughts turned to home and he headed back to Prague in 1862 with the idea of writing a national Bohemian opera.

In Prague, Smetana composed eight operas on Bohemian subjects, including the well-known *The Bartered Bride,* using melodies and rhythms derived from Bohemian folk songs and dances, and sung in Czech. Smetana introduced this opera at the National Theater in Prague, where he served as conductor from 1866 to 1874. Through his own compositions and the Czech operas he produced, Smetana inspired the younger generation of Czech composers, which included Antonín Dvořák and Leoš Janáček.

In 1874, just after starting work on the cycle of symphonic poems *My Country,* which includes his most popular orchestral composition, *The Moldau,* tragedy struck Smetana once again. This time the problem was a high, whistling sound in his ears, which soon led to profound deafness. Later, Smetana began suffering from serious hallucinations and his condition deteriorated until he had to be confined in a mental hospital, where he died at age 60.

Smetana is included in a book such as this for two reasons: One is his great importance in founding a nationalistic school of Bohemian music by drawing on the folk songs and dances of that region and for helping to point the way for nationalistic composers in many other lands. The other and more important reason is the freshness, verve, and bright colors that pervade so much of what he wrote.

The Moldau ("Vltava")
(15 minutes)

Most composers who are inspired by water are drawn to mighty oceans and seas; far fewer write music about lakes or rivers. Among the greatest paeans to a river is Smetana's extremely popular *The Moldau ("Vltava"* in Czech), a musical depiction of the river that passes through the Czech countryside before coursing majestically through Prague.

From 1874 to 1879, Smetana composed a cycle of six symphonic poems entitled *My Country (Má Vlast),* creating vivid musical portraits of various scenes of his beloved Bohemia. He based the principal theme of *The Moldau* on the well-known Czech nursery rhyme "Kocka leze dírou" ("The Cat Goes Through the Hole"). *The Moldau,* the second and best-known part of the cycle, was completed on November 18, 1874; the first performance took place in Prague on April 4, 1876, with Adolph Czech conducting.

Smetana wrote the following detailed description of the music on the score of *The Moldau:*

Two springs pour forth their streams in the shade of the Bohemian forest, one is warm and gushing, the other cool and tranquil. Their waves, joyfully flowing over their rocky beds, unite and sparkle in the morning sun. The forest brook, rushing on, becomes the river Moldau, which, with its waters speeding through Bohemia's valleys, grows into a mighty stream. It flows through dense woods from which come the joyous sounds of the chase, and the notes of the hunter's horn are heard ever nearer and nearer.

It flows through emerald meadows and lowlands, where a wedding feast is being celebrated with song and dancing. At night, in its shining waves, wood and water nymphs hold their revels, and in these waves are reflected many a fortress and castle—witnesses of the bygone splendor of chivalry and the vanished martial fame of days that are no more. At the Rapids of St. John the stream speeds on, winding its way through cataracts and hewing the path for its foaming waters through the rocky chasm into the broad riverbed, in which it flows on in majestic calm toward Prague, welcomed by time-honored Vysehrad, to disappear in far distance from the poet's gaze.

Richard Strauss

Born June 11, 1864, in Munich
Died September 8, 1949, in Garmisch-Partenkirchen, Germany

RICHARD STRAUSS looked like a calm, complacent businessman, but appearances are deceiving. Within lurked the heart and mind of a bold, passionate, and imaginative artist. His music portrayed the entire range of human emotions and drew forth from the orchestra sounds and effects never before heard. His music shocked turn-of-the-century audiences; some works were banned, others had to be changed before they could be performed in public.

The first major works that Strauss composed for orchestra, his two symphonies, violin concerto, and horn concerto, were in traditional forms. But he began to feel that the prevailing style had reached a dead end. In a letter to conductor Hans von Bülow, Strauss wrote: "Making music according to the rules of form as set down by Hanslick [an important critic who favored a Classical approach to music] is in any case no longer possible. From now on there will be no aimless phrase making during which the minds of both the composer and the listeners are a complete blank, and no more symphonies."

Thus it was in the mid-1880s that Strauss began composing tone poems, or symphonic poems, based on literary subjects or subjects outside the music. Franz Liszt had first used the term "symphonic poem" around 1850 to describe a large-scale, programmatic, orchestral composition that took its inspiration from a story, poem, character, place, or historical happening. "I have long recognized," Strauss once said, "that when composing I am unable to write anything without a program to guide me."

From the mid-1880s until the end of the century, Strauss wrote eight tone poems; the six most outstanding ones are discussed below. Around the year 1900, Strauss abandoned the form that had brought him much fame, and notoriety, and turned most of his attention to producing such outstanding operas as *Der Rosenkavalier, Salomé,* and *Elektra.*

In addition to his success as a composer, Strauss was also one of the outstanding conductors of his day, with stints at the Berlin Royal Opera, the Vienna State Opera, and guest conducting appearances throughout Europe. The orchestral programs he presented often featured the music of his favorite composers, Wagner and Mozart.

Also sprach Zarathustra ("Thus Spake Zarathustra"), Op. 30
(35 minutes)

Strauss frequently boasted that he could depict anything in his music. But it would seem that he accepted an impossible challenge when he took as his subject Friedrich Nietzsche's (1844–1900) monumental philosophical tract *Also sprach Zarathustra.* But the composer realized full well the futility of trying to explicate complex ideas in sound. "I did not intend to write philosophical music," said Strauss, "or portray Nietzsche's great work musically. I meant rather to convey in music an idea of the evolution of the human race from its origin, through the various phases of development, religious as well as scientific, up to Nietzsche's idea of the Superman *(Übermensch).* The whole idea of the tone poem is intended as my homage to the genius of Nietzsche, which found its greatest exemplification in his book *Also sprach Zarathustra.*"

Although it bears the same name, Nietzsche's *Also sprach Zarathustra* has little to do with the real-life Zarathustra, or Zoroaster, the 6th century B.C. Persian thinker and religious reformer. In Nietzsche's work, Zarathustra delivers some eighty discourses, or pronouncements, on various topics. The major theme concerns the glorification of the individual, along with the concepts of the perfectibility of the human race and the creation of a superior kind of being that he calls the Superman.

Strauss composed *Also sprach Zarathustra* from February 4 to August 24, 1896, and conducted the premiere in Frankfurt on November 27, 1896. He selected just eight of the many discourses of the book as titles of the sections of his composition:

I. *Of the Dwellers in the Back-World.* The work opens with a very low unison C (made familiar by its use in Stanley Kubrick's film *2001: A Space Odyssey*), after which four trumpets announce the three-rising-note theme that is associated with the Superman. Other themes follow: one in the horns has the words *Credo in unum Deum* ("I believe in one God") marked on the score. These themes presumably represent the naïve belief in God of the weak and sickly denizens of the Back-World.

II. *Of the Great Yearning.* This section expands the original three-note theme, turning it into a grand upward-thrusting melody that is thought to portray the human longing for freedom from ignorance and religious superstition.

III. *Of Joys and Passions.* A violin melody that seems to twist upon itself opens this portion. The related passage in Nietzsche discusses the necessity of strong emotions and how they are transformed into virtues: "Once hadst thou passions and calledst them evil. But now hast thou only thy virtues: they grow out of thy passions."

IV. *The Grave Song.* The tempo slows and Strauss brings back some of the themes heard earlier as Zarathustra mourns his lost youth.

V. *Of Science.* Strauss makes this part a learned fugue; he derived the subject from the initial three-note theme, but expands it here to include all twelve notes of the chromatic scale.

VI. *The Convalescent.* The joyful transformations of the fugue subject evince Zarathustra's renewed strength and vigor as he sets forth to bring his message to the people.

VII. *The Dance Song.* In this discourse, Zarathustra comes upon maidens dancing in the woods and he speaks to them of the folly of wisdom. In the music, Strauss treats us to a Viennese waltz whose melody grows out of the opening motto. It leads right into:

VIII. *Song of the Night Wanderer.* The bell tolls midnight to signal the final section, which is sometimes translated as *Song of the Sleepwalker.* The ending is quiet and unresolved, with the dissonant juxtaposition of a C chord and a B chord.

Don Juan, Tone Poem after Nikolaus Lenau, Op. 20
(17 minutes)

The dramatic poem "Don Juan" by Nikolaus Lenau (1802–50) impelled Strauss to write his eponymous tone poem. The character of Don Juan (Don Giovanni in Italian) entered the folklore of several European countries in the 16th century as a reckless libertine and seducer of women, but Lenau had a different understanding of his nature. "My Don Juan," Lenau wrote, "is no hot-blooded man eternally pursuing women. He longs to find a woman who is to him incarnate womanhood, and to enjoy, in this one, all the women on earth, whom he cannot as individuals possess. Because he does not find her, although he reels from one to another, at last disgust seizes hold of him, and this disgust is the devil that fetches him."

Strauss completed the score in September 1888, calling it a *Tondichtung,* a tone poem or symphonic poem, a programmatic work based on a literary source. Many commentators have tried to assign meanings to every musical phrase in *Don Juan,* perhaps stemming from the impression created by Strauss himself in a question he posed to conductor Anton Seidl. Strauss purportedly wanted to know if Seidl, from listening to the music, realized that the Don's second female conquest had red hair. When Seidl replied that he had not, Strauss presumably complained: "Then I have failed!"

The group of mostly ascending, agitated brief melodies that open the work set forth the vibrant, virile Don. They also function as the principal subject of the sonata allegro structure. After some development of this material, a light, frivolous section suggests a quick, flirtatious encounter. A solo violin leads to an extended episode that surges with both passion and yearning, representing the most important of Don Juan's loves, as well as providing a formal second subject and the start of the development section.

A completely new theme played by the French horns in unison loudly proclaims the heroic side of Don Juan's character. Strauss follows this very dramatic statement with a musical evocation of the masked ball described in Lenau's poem. Some of the earlier material reappears in a recapitulation before Don Juan, filled with disgust and self-loathing, allows himself to be killed in a duel with the brother of one of his victims. The composer portrays the denouement in the music by means of a soft A minor chord into which the trumpet stabs a dissonant F. As the Don fades away, so does the music.

Strauss conducted the first performance of *Don Juan* at Weimar on November 11, 1889. The audience liked the piece, but the players grumbled about the extreme difficulty of their parts. One musician was overheard praying: "Good God, in what way have we sinned that you should have sent this scourge?"

Don Quixote (Introduction, Theme with Variations and Finale), Fantastic Variations on a Theme of Knightly Character, Op. 35
(45 minutes)

"I want to be able to depict in music a glass of beer so accurately that every listener can tell whether it is a Pilsner or Kulmbacher!" So declared Richard Strauss, not entirely in jest. Given this outlook, imagine the field day he had writing a tone poem based on Cervantes' wonderful Knight of the Rueful Countenance.

Other than the title, Strauss left no specific program, no hint of the characters and events he sought to portray in the music. But so many commentators, including friends of Strauss whose interpretations are assumed to have the composer's approval, have suggested extramusical meanings that a sort of official canon has become attached to the score.

Introduction. The introduction opens with a flighty tune on the flute followed by a lyrical oboe melody (Dulcinea's theme).

Theme. The solo cello, the instrument associated with Quixote, plays his theme, and the bass clarinet, tuba, and then solo viola, which is Sancho Panza's voice in the orchestra, present the squire's melody.

Variation I. Strauss sets forth the three principal themes, those of Quixote, Sancho, and Dulcinea, in variation as the Don, imagining they are giants, tilts at the windmills.

Variation II. A flock of bleating sheep wander along, but Quixote sees them as an attacking army and charges in with lance drawn.

Variation III. A conversation between the Don (solo cello) and his squire (solo viola, bass clarinet, tuba), with occasional hints of Dulcinea's tune.

Variation IV. Quixote next attacks a band of penitent pilgrims (represented by the brass chorale) carrying a statue of the Virgin Mary. He believes they are a band of brigands who have captured a young maiden.

Variation V. As Sancho sleeps, Quixote reflects on his life and his wish to perform chivalrous deeds to win his beloved Dulcinea.

Variation VI. A coarse peasant girl comes along (a distortion of Dulcinea's theme), and Sancho tries to convince the Don that it is Dulcinea, but Quixote decides an evil magician has cast a spell on Dulcinea and he vows vengeance.

Variation VII. Quixote and Sancho imagine they are flying through the air on winged horses, even though in reality they are blindfolded and seated on toy wooden horses. In the orchestra, a percussionist plays a wind machine to help create the illusion of flight.

Variation VIII. The composer treats the Knight's theme as a barcarolle, calling to mind the two adventurers setting off in a boat. When the boat capsizes, the duo scramble to shore and offer a short prayer of thanks.

Variation IX. Two peaceful monks on mules approach, and Quixote, sure that they are evil magicians, roars loudly and scares them away.

Variation X. A neighbor, concerned for Quixote's safety, challenges him to a duel. The condition is that, if defeated, Quixote will return home for a year. The Don is trounced and sadly begins the march home with Sancho following. Echoes of music from Variation II suggest Quixote's thoughts of becoming a shepherd.

Finale. The solo cello sings a last, plaintive variant of Quixote's melody as his strength fails. He recalls his adventures as his life slowly slips away.

Ein Heldenleben ("A Hero's Life"), Op. 40
(43 minutes)

Strauss had already completed seven tone poems when he began *Ein Heldenleben,* his last work in the form, on August 8, 1898. He completed the score on December 27 of that year and led the premiere in Frankfurt on March 3, 1899.

To explain his motivation in writing the piece, Strauss wrote: "Beethoven's 'Eroica' is so little beloved of our conductors, and is on this account now only rarely performed, that to fulfill a pressing need I am composing a tone poem of substantial length entitled *Ein Heldenleben,* admittedly without a funeral march [as in the 'Eroica'], but yet in E flat, with lots of French horns, which are always a measure of heroism."

Apart from a focus on what Strauss called a "general and free ideal of great and manly heroism," he did not seem to have any specific program or story in mind for *Heldenleben.* Scholars still dispute whether the hero is Strauss ("I find myself quite as interesting as Napoleon or Alexander," he wrote to the French novelist and musicologist Romain Rolland) or an idealized figure ("It is enough to know that a hero is battling his enemies," from the same letter to Rolland). In terms of musical expression it matters little in enjoying this grandiose, utterly Romantic work.

Strauss gives titles to the six sections of the score, which the orchestra plays without break. The separate parts very neatly correspond with the six parts of a traditional symphonic first movement.

I. *The Hero.* (First subject.) The hero's bold, assertive theme is stated by horns, violas, and cellos. Various motifs within the theme point up the different facets of the hero's personality—strength, compassion, bravery, zeal, tenderness, and dignity. Strauss then introduces and repeats six times a brief new phrase, a sort of defiant challenge. Each statement ends abruptly, until the final one brings this section to a precipitous halt.

II. *The Hero's Adversaries.* (Transition.) Instead of fearsome enemies, the composer characterizes the adversaries as a sneering, snarling, mocking pack. We can recognize the carping, nitpicking music critics of his day, whom Strauss depicts with shrill, chattering woodwinds, and the pedantic academics, whom he portrays with ponderously dull and doleful tubas playing the forbidden parallel fifths.

III. *The Hero's Companion.* (Second Subject.) A solo violin represents the hero's beloved. At first she reacts coquettishly to the hero's fervent advances, but the music seems to suggest that their relationship grows increasingly intense. As the warmth and sweep of this section abate, rumbling sounds of discord and conflict are heard approaching.

IV. *The Hero's Deeds of War.* (Development.) Three offstage trumpets sound the call to arms. At first the hero resists, remaining with his companion, but as the trumpets sound again, he rushes valiantly into combat. The composer elicits some of the harshest and most raucous sounds ever summoned from an orchestra to depict the actual battle. Yet, above the mayhem, one hears the companion's theme, suggesting the source of the hero's strength and resolve. With a mighty effort, the hero triumphs, and the love theme loudly proclaims his victory. The composer also brings in a new theme, a glorious, upward-surging melody, and a quotation from Strauss's earlier tone poem *Don Juan.* As the sounds of success fade away, we hear echoes of the hero's adversaries, but the triumphant hero quickly dispatches them.

V. *The Hero's Works of Peace.* (Recapitulation.) A celebration of the hero's victory that describes the development of the spiritual side of his nature. In the course of this section, Strauss includes melodies heard earlier in *Heldenleben,* as well as 30 brief snatches of themes from previous compositions, which offer very convincing evidence that the intended hero is indeed the composer.

VI. *The Hero's Escape from the World.* (Coda.) The English horn ushers in a pastoral theme drawn from the hero's original melody in which he seems to be seeking solace in nature. Grotesque memories of his enemies intrude and disturb his solitude, but the sweet strains of his companion's melody bring him peace. A brief segment of the opening theme appears at the end, rising to a climax and then gently fading away, leaving the hero serene and fulfilled.

Till Eulenspiegels lustige Streiche ("Till Eulenspiegel's Merry Pranks"), Op. 28
(15 minutes)

Many generations of Europeans know the mischievous and adventurous folk hero Till Eulenspiegel. His legend is presumably based on the life of an actual figure from the 14th century, a German peasant whose naughty behavior and practical jokes symbolized the revolt of the common people against the ruling classes. Translated literally as "owl's mirror," his name stems from an old German proverb: "Man is as little conscious of his own faults as an owl, looking into a mirror, is aware of his ugliness."

Early in 1894, Strauss contemplated an opera based on the Till Eulenspiegel legend, but found it very difficult to create a flesh-and-blood Till, and abandoned the idea before writing any of the music. Later that year, however, he started composing a tone poem using the Till story. He finished the composition on May 6, 1895; the first performance took place in Cologne on November 5, 1895, with Franz Wüllner conducting.

Before the premiere, Wüllner asked Strauss to supply the program for *Till* to help the audience follow the story in the music. Strauss wrote back: "It is impossible for me to furnish a program . . . [it] would often seem peculiar and would possibly give offense. So let us this time leave it to the audience to crack the nuts that the rogue has prepared for them." Later, though, Wilhelm Mauke prepared a very detailed programmatic analysis of the score, and Strauss penciled short phrases from the Mauke text at relevant sections of the score.

Over the gentle opening strain Strauss wrote: "Once upon a time there was a clowning rogue." Where the French horn starts the figure that is most closely associated with Till, the phrase was ". . . whose name was Till Eulenspiegel." "That was a rascally scamp," appears on the score where the high-pitched D clarinet mocks the opening tune. A loud cymbal crash introduces the next episode, marked "Hop! On horseback straight through the market women," with its musical depiction of the clattering pots and pans being scattered about.

For the next, more solemn part Strauss noted: "Dressed as a priest he oozes unction and morality," and later: "He is seized with a horrid premonition as to the outcome of his mockery of religion." A dizzying downward swoop by the solo violin ushers in what Strauss calls "Till the cavalier exchanging courtesies with beautiful girls," followed by "Glowing with love, Till woos a girl." But he is rebuffed—"A refusal is a refusal," wrote Strauss—and Till storms off swearing vengeance.

The low-pitched mutterings of the bassoons and bass clarinet signal Till's presence among the pompous professors: "After he has posed a few theses to the philistines, he leaves them to their fate dumbfounded." At the end of this encounter Till walks away whistling a simple little tune. A "fleeting and ghostly" interlude follows.

The original Till tune returns and builds to a climax before an ominous drumroll signals his arrest—"Still whistling to himself with indifference," according to Strauss. He is, though, found guilty and sentenced to be hanged, even though the real-life Till was said to have died peacefully in his bed. And thus the tale concludes with "Up the ladder with him! Till's mortal self is finished." After the realistic sound picture of the tugs on the rope that hang Till, Strauss appends a coda that includes the gentle once-upon-a-time melody from the opening, and one last chance for the lovable rascal to thumb his nose at the world.

Tod und Verklärung ("Death and Transfiguration"), Op. 24
(25 minutes)

Strauss based most of his tone poems on works of literature or his own autobiography. He built *Tod und Verklärung,* however, around a story of his own devising. "It was six years ago [1888] when the idea came to me to write a tone poem describing the last hours of a man who had striven for the highest ideals, presumably an artist," he wrote his friend Friedrich von Hausegger. He began the composition that year, when he was only 25 years old, completed it on November 18, 1889, and conducted the premiere in Eisenach on June 21, 1890.

After finishing the music, Strauss asked another friend, Alexander Ritter, a poet-philosopher-violinist, to rewrite the program in poetic form, which the composer had printed on the flyleaf of the score. The four parts of Ritter's poem (paraphrased below) correspond to the four divisions of the music, which the orchestra plays without pause.

I. *Largo.* A sick man, near death, lies in a squalid room lit only by a flickering candle. The room is silent but for the dull ticking of the clock on the wall. A sad smile crosses the man's face; perhaps he is dreaming of his happy childhood.

II. *Allegro molto agitato.* At the end of his life, he finds no respite from the battle between his will to live and the power of death. It is a terrifying contest, but neither emerges victorious and the silence returns.

III. *Meno mosso.* In his delirious state, the dying man sees his life pass before him: the innocent childhood, the testing and gaining of strength of his youth, and the battles of manhood to transfigure all that he has experienced into a still more exalted form. Death, finally, puts an end to his quest.

IV. *Moderato.* Now, from the infinite reaches of heaven, a mighty sound of triumph rings forth, bringing the sought-after transfiguration.

An interesting footnote, perhaps apocryphal: As Strauss approached his own death in 1949, he said, obviously referring to *Tod und Verklärung:* "Dying is just as I composed it sixty years ago."

Igor Stravinsky

Born June 17, 1882, in Oranienbaum, Russia
Died April 6, 1971, in New York City

STRAVINSKY'S EARLY BALLETS, *The Firebird* (1910), *Petrouchka* (1911), and *The Rite of Spring* (1913), flashed across the musical skies like three brilliant meteors. Never before had audiences heard this kind of music, with brutal, pounding rhythms in ever-changing, irregular patterns, short bits of wild melody repeated over and over again, and harsh, grating dissonances. The new style quickly elevated Stravinsky to the role of leading apostle of musical modernism. Countless composers adopted and adapted his techniques in their own music.

After World War I, Stravinsky abandoned the revolutionary manner of the three ballets. He looked back to earlier, Classical periods of music to find the stylistic principles for his compositions, and began writing in a more restrained, austere, and tightly ordered way. Critics often identify this approach as Neoclassicism, even though Stravinsky dismissed the term as meaning "absolutely nothing."

Stravinsky's comments on his 1921 *Symphonies of Wind Instruments* apply to much of his post-*Rite of Spring* compositions: "It is futile to look in it for passionate impulse or dynamic brilliance. . . . The music is not meant to 'please' an audience, nor to arouse its passions. Nevertheless, I had hopes that it would appeal to some of those persons in whom a purely musical receptivity outweighed the desire to satisfy their sentimental cravings." His succeeding works were widely performed, but few achieved the popularity and acceptance of his earlier compositions.

Stravinsky was born to a leading singer in the St. Petersburg Opera who urged Igor to study law, even though the young man was strongly attracted to music. While still a law student, Stravinsky began studying composition privately with Nikolai Rimsky-Korsakov, and on the death of his father, dropped out of school and devoted himself full-time to composing. The five years with Rimsky-Korsakov were essentially Stravinsky's only music instruction beyond piano lessons as a child.

Soon after Rimsky-Korsakov's death in 1908, Stravinsky accepted the commissions to compose his three famous ballets. Then, in 1914, Stravinsky fled the chaos of World War I and the beginnings of the Russian Revolution to find a safe haven in Switzerland, where he remained until 1920. He followed this with an extended stay in France for the next nineteen years. Just before the outbreak of World War II, Stravinsky accepted an invitation to lecture at Harvard University. When the hostilities began, he decided to make the United States his permanent home, becoming a citizen in 1945. He died in New York City in 1971.

The Firebird Suite (L'Oiseau de feu) (Second Version, 1919)
(21 minutes)

When Serge Diaghilev, director of the Ballets Russes, decided to do a Russian folk ballet based on the legend of the Firebird, he engaged Anatol Liadov to compose the score. Some time later, Diaghilev asked Liadov how the work was progressing. The composer proudly asserted that everything was going well, he had just bought the music paper! Diaghilev, understandably, was afraid that the score would not be ready in time for the scheduled premiere. Recalling two wonderfully exciting short pieces by Stravinsky that he had recently heard, Diaghilev offered the commission to the young, unknown composer.

Stravinsky eagerly accepted, and started working on the music of *The Firebird* in November 1909, even before he received confirmation of the commission. He completed the score on May 18, 1910, and the ballet had its first performance in Paris on June 25, 1910, with Gabriel Pierné conducting. Pavlova, who had been scheduled to dance the lead, refused because of the rhythmic difficulties of the music.

The critics were impressed by the music of the ballet, even though the shocking dissonances and rhythmic complexities dismayed many in the audience. By now, though, listeners have come to accept and understand what was then perceived as outrageous, and are thrilled by the brilliance of the writing, the visceral excitement of the rhythms, and the sheer beauty of the several lyrical melodies.

In time, Stravinsky extracted three orchestral suites from the score. The first, in 1911, included much of the music of the 50-minute ballet and called for a huge orchestra, which limited the number of performances. The second, from 1919, was shorter and required a smaller orchestra; it became and remains the most popular of the three. The third, done in 1949, kept the smaller orchestra, but returned the sections that had been cut for the second version.

The composer divided the 1919 version into six sections that parallel the scenario of the dance:

I. *Introduction.* The music describes the dark, forbidding forest through which the young Czarevitch Ivan wanders and where he sees and captures the Firebird. She gives him a magic feather in return for her freedom.

II. *Dance of the Firebird.* Glittering trills and splashes of sound initiate the Firebird's dance.

III. *Dance of the Princesses.* Ivan finds himself in the garden of the castle of the evil ogre Kastchei, who keeps thirteen beautiful princesses as his prisoners. The princesses dance a simple circle dance known as a *khorovod* around a silver tree. One beautiful princess in particular catches Ivan's eye. As dawn breaks, the maidens flee into the castle.

IV. *Dance of the King Kastchei.* Ivan rushes toward the castle and out tumbles a horde of terrifying monsters and demons. The ugly, sinister Kastchei follows and leads a wild, barbaric dance.

V. *Berceuse.* Ivan waves the magic feather, which brings the Firebird to his aid. She lulls the frantically dancing monsters to sleep with this lovely lullaby.

VI. *Finale.* The Firebird shows Ivan a casket with an egg that holds Kastchei's soul. Ivan smashes the egg, the castle disappears, and all the princesses are set free. Ivan marries his beloved princess and the festive music, which grows out of the *Berceuse,* celebrates the fairy tale ending.

Petrouchka
(35 minutes)

In August 1910, Stravinsky started composing a *Conzertstück* for piano and orchestra. "In composing the music," he wrote, "I had in mind a distinct picture of a puppet, suddenly endowed with life, exasperating the patience of the orchestra with diabolical cascades of arpeggios. The orchestra in turn retaliates with menacing trumpet blasts. The outcome is a terrific noise which reaches its climax and ends in the sorrowful and querulous death of the poor puppet."

When he finished the work, Stravinsky named it *Petrouchka,* the Russian counterpart to Punch, Pierrot, or Harlequin, the "immortal and unhappy hero of every fair in all countries." Serge Diaghilev, director of the Ballets Russes, upon hearing the music immediately visualized its dance potential. He urged Stravinsky to expand the music and invent a ballet scenario. The composer accomplished these tasks in Rome on May 26, 1911, and the dance received its first performance in Paris on June 13, 1911; Pierre Monteux conducted.

The highly descriptive music falls into four sections, or tableaux, and continues without break. The setting is an 1830s fair in Admiralty Square, St. Petersburg, during Shrovetide, the three-day period before Ash Wednesday. The first tableau depicts the noisy hustle and bustle of the brightly dressed crowds at the holiday celebration. The opening theme, played by the flute, represents the carnival spirit.

The orchestra then launches a powerful rhythmic unison that announces the arrival of a group of drunken revelers. The carnival tune returns, this time giving way to an adaptation of the French music-hall ditty "Elle avait un' jambe en boise" in the woodwinds. Stravinsky brings back, in order, the carnival theme, the drunkard theme, and the carnival theme, giving this section a classically perfect rondo form. A magical cadenza for flute next rouses to life the three puppets, Petrouchka, the Blackamoor, and the Ballerina. Their high-spirited Russian dance concludes the scene.

The second tableau, set in Petrouchka's room, follows a series of rapid drumbeats and includes the music that Stravinsky originally composed for his *Conzertstück.* Two clarinets playing in different keys (one in C, the other in F sharp major) introduce Petrouchka. Furious runs in the prominent piano part and biting brass arpeggios point up Petrouchka's anger over his unrequited love for the Ballerina.

Another series of drum strokes serve as the bridge to the third tableau, which takes place in the Blackamoor's room. His theme is a confident, dignified melody played by clarinet and bass clarinet. The Ballerina enters to a pair of charming waltz tunes that Stravinsky borrowed from the Viennese waltz composer Joseph Lanner. Announced by his characteristic brass arpeggio, Petrouchka enters and soon fights the Blackamoor, who uses his superior strength to fling Petrouchka out the door.

The drumming now transports us to the final tableau. It is evening at the fair and the merrymaking is in full swing. A succession of dances follow; some are based on Russian folk songs. They are performed by Wet Nurses, a Peasant and his Bear, Gypsies and a Rake Vendor, Coachmen, and Masqueraders. Suddenly a high, sustained note in the trumpets stops the revelry; it is Petrouchka's cry as he flees the attacking Blackamoor. Petrouchka's arpeggios battle the rushing scales of the Blackamoor until a vicious chord signals the Blackamoor's fatal saber blow felling Petrouchka. Two trumpets briefly recall Petrouchka's arpeggios before the work comes to a somber conclusion.

The Rite of Spring (Le Sacre du printemps)
(33 minutes)

In his *Autobiography,* Stravinsky discusses the origins of *The Rite of Spring* in the spring of 1910: "I saw in my imagination a solemn pagan rite; sage elders, seated in a circle, watched a young girl dance herself to death. They were sacrificing her to propitiate the god spring." The musical roots of *Rite* reach back to the earliest human history, a time when people tried to control natural occurrences with ecstatic dancing and mysterious rituals and ceremonies.

Stravinsky began writing the score in the fall of 1911 in Clarens, Switzerland. "The composition of *Le Sacre,*" he later wrote, "was completed by the beginning of 1912 and the instrumentation—a mechanical job, largely, since I always compose the instrumentation when I compose the music—took me four months in the late spring."

The composer borrowed only one melody, an old Lithuanian folk song, which he adapted for the opening bassoon solo; he said it represented "the awakening of nature, the scratching, gnawing, wiggling of birds and beasts." The rest of the themes, while completely original, "tap some unconscious 'folk' memory," according to the composer. "I am the vessel through which *Le Sacre* passed."

Stravinsky treats the terse, simple, diatonic melodies, often confined to a range of no more than four notes, in very untraditional ways. Often he repeats and rearranges them, creating intricate and shifting rhythmic patterns against a background of highly dissonant, acerbic harmonies. The result is a stunning evocation of primeval ritual, alternating frenzied, barbaric passages with worshipful, ceremonial observances.

The ballet has no "plot," although the titles of the various sections indicate the content and focus of both the dance and the music. Part I, *The Adoration of the Earth,* contains *Introduction, Harbingers of Spring (Dance of the Adolescents), Game of the Abduction, Round Dance of Spring, Games of the Rival Tribes, Entrance of the Sage, Adoration of the Earth, Dance of the Earth.* Part II, *The Sacrifice,* includes *Introduction, Mysterious Circles of the Adolescents, Glorification of the Chosen One, Evocation of the Ancestors, Ritual of the Ancestors, Sacrificial Dance (The Chosen One).*

The Rite of Spring followed Stravinsky's two great ballets, *The Firebird* and *Petrouchka,* and received its premiere in Paris on May 29, 1913, with Pierre Monteux conducting. The performance occasioned one of the most notorious scandals in the history of music. Most of the audience, believing they were the victims of a monstrous joke, either laughed or booed, or gave out vicious hisses and loud catcalls. A valiant few, including Claude Debussy, tried in vain to quiet the rambunctious crowd and listen to the music. But the chaos continued, with shouting matches and fistfights erupting throughout the ornate new theater. At the end of the performance, Stravinsky, fearing for his own safety, sneaked out through a dressing-room window and escaped by joining the riotous street crowd.

Just about one year later, Stravinsky presented the same music in a Paris concert performance, but this time, in his words, "the entire audience stood up and cheered. A crowd swept backstage. I was hoisted to anonymous shoulders, carried out into the street this way, and up to the Place de la Trinité."

Many consider *The Rite of Spring* an outstanding musical expression of Primitivism in music. Drawn from the same rich sources of inspiration, and designed to produce the same magical effects, as the tribal masks and carvings of the people of Africa and Oceania, *Rite* affirms a belief in the power of art to affect and control an often perplexing and bewildering universe. Stravinsky brilliantly captures the power and vigor of these primitive times, as well as the magic of ancient shamanism. Perhaps it is this elemental appeal that makes *The Rite of Spring* one of the truly great masterpieces of 20th century music.

Symphony in Three Movements
(22 minutes)

All compositions represent the tension between the two contrasting moods of music—the Apollonian and Dionysian. Very simply stated, the Apollonian is characterized by restraint, control, and logic; the Dionysian by emotion, passion, and freedom. In his lectures *Poetics of Music,* Stravinsky discusses this dichotomy in terms of creating a work of art: "What is important for the lucid ordering of the work—for its crystallization—is that all the Dionysiac elements which set the imagination of the artist in motion and make the life sap rise must be properly subjugated before they intoxicate us, and must finally be made to submit to the law: Apollo demands it."

Symphony in Three Movements provides a fascinating paradigm of Apollonian restraint imposed on powerful Dionysian impulses. Taking his inspiration from the experiences of World War II and a film score on a religious subject, Stravinsky composed the symphony from April 4, 1942, to August 7, 1945, and conducted the premiere with the New York Philharmonic on January 24, 1946.

I. (No tempo indication.) Stravinsky composed the first movement in 1942 as a piece for solo piano and orchestra. At this earlier date, the composer tells us, the movement was inspired by a war film on the "torched-earth tactics in China." The contrasting middle section, he explains, "was conceived as a series of instrumental conversations to accompany a series of cinematographic scenes showing the Chinese people scratching and digging in their fields. The music for clarinet, piano, and strings . . . was all associated in my mind with this Chinese documentary."

II. *Andante.* Stravinsky derived the delicate, elegiac second movement from a film score that he wrote for the 1943 film version of Franz Werfel's novel *The Song of Bernadette.* The composer completed the music for the *Apparition of the Virgin* scene before abandoning the project. In it he gives a prominent part to the harp, not the piano as in the first movement. The main theme that comes at the very opening, either advertently or inadvertently, closely resembles the unctuous, mocking melody of Count Almaviva's greeting to Dr. Bartolo in Rossini's *The Barber of Seville.*

III. *Con moto.* This symphony features the piano in the first movement and the harp in the second. For the third movement, the composer uses both piano and harp in the full-orchestra passages and then gives each a significant role in the central fugue. Stravinsky's original notes furnish insights into his inspiration: "The beginning of the movement is partly . . . a reaction to the newsreels and documentaries I had seen of goose-stepping soldiers. The square march beat, the brass band instrumentation, the grotesque crescendo in the tuba, these are all related to those abhorrent pictures. In spite of contrasting episodes, such as the canon for bassoons, the march music predominates until the fugue, which is the stasis and turning point. The immobility at the beginning of this fugue is comic, I think—and so, to me, was the overturned arrogance of the Germans when their machine failed. The exposition of the fugue and the end of the Symphony are associated in my plot with the rise of the Allies."

Symphony in Three Movements bears little resemblance to a traditional composition in the form; as Stravinsky said: "Three Symphonic Movements would be a more exact title." Neither does the work easily betray the extramusical image behind each of the movements. In retrospect, the composer wrote: "This Symphony has no program, nor is it an expression of any given occasion; it would be futile to seek these in my work. But during the process of creation in this, it may be that all those repercussions have left traces in this Symphony. It is not I to judge."

Peter Ilyich Tchaikovsky

Born May 7, 1840, in Votinsk, Russia
Died November 6, 1893, in St. Petersburg

TCHAIKOVSKY'S AMAZING melodic ability, perhaps above all else, has earned him a hallowed place among the great composers of orchestral masterpieces. The melodies—emotional, expressive, often tinged with the sadness of Russian folk music, and frequently betraying the neuroticism of their creator—manage to insinuate themselves into the listener's heart.

As a youngster, Tchaikovsky showed a talent for music and received some rudimentary instruction in piano. In 1850, at his parents' behest, Tchaikovsky enrolled in the School of Jurisprudence in St. Petersburg. On graduation he took a post in the Ministry of Justice, but his interest in composing steadily grew. By 1861 he was seriously studying composition, and two years later he resigned his Ministry post to devote himself completely to music. Between 1862 and 1865 he studied with Anton Rubinstein, a Russian pianist and composer, and received Western-style training in the fundamentals of music.

In 1866, Tchaikovsky was appointed to the faculty of the Moscow Conservatory and wrote music criticism for a newspaper. Nevertheless, he found it virtually impossible to earn enough money to cover his basic needs. Then, in 1877, Nadezhda von Meck, a wealthy widow who admired his music, offered him an annual stipend so he could devote himself entirely to composing. He agreed to her request that they never meet and for years they maintained a relationship based on letters alone. His money worries now over, Tchaikovsky left the Moscow Conservatory to focus his energies on composition. He also started to travel widely and even came to the United States in 1891 to conduct the opening concerts of New York's Carnegie Hall.

Many find striking paradoxes in Tchaikovsky's music. His compositions show the influence of Russia's folk melodies and rhythms, yet Russian nationalist composers looked on him as a cosmopolite, influenced more by the music of Western Europe than that of his native land. And Tchaikovsky, the highly emotional and passionate Romantic composer, set Mozart, the purist of Classicists, as his model. "I not only like Mozart," he wrote, "I worship him." Still, even his harshest critics agree that Tchaikovsky succeeded in reconciling the conflicting elements of his musical personality and created a body of much loved music that continues to stir audiences.

Concerto for Piano and Orchestra No. 1 in B flat minor, Op. 23
(37 minutes)

Tchaikovsky began work on his First Piano Concerto in November 1874 and completed it less than two months later, on January 2, 1875. He dedicated the concerto to pianist Nicholas Rubinstein, director of the Moscow Conservatory, where Tchaikovsky himself taught.

Shortly before finishing the concerto, Tchaikovsky asked Rubinstein if he might play the concerto for him to get the older man's reactions. In a letter to his benefactor, Mme. von Meck, Tchaikovsky described what happened at the end of the play-through performance: " 'Well?' said I, as I arose. Then there burst from Rubinstein's mouth a mighty torrent of words. He spoke quietly at first, then he waxed hot, and finally he resembled Zeus hurling thunderbolts. It seems that my concerto was utterly worthless, absolutely unplayable. Certain passages were so commonplace and awkward they could not be improved, and the piece as a whole was bad, trivial, vulgar. I had stolen this from somebody and that from somebody else, so that only two or three pages were good for anything and all the rest should be wiped out or radically rewritten."

Tchaikovsky refused to change a note of the music. Instead, he rededicated the work to the German pianist Hans von Bülow, who later became the preeminent conductor of his time. Von Bülow had a completely different reaction to the concerto: "The ideas are so original, so noble, so powerful, the details are so interesting, and though there are many of them, they do not impair the clarity and the unity of the work. The form is so mature, ripe, and distinguished in style that intention and labor are everywhere concealed."

Von Bülow premiered the concerto in Boston with the Boston Symphony under Benjamin Johnson Lang on October 25, 1875, while on an American tour. The first performance caused such excitement that the pianist performed it at 139 of the 172 concerts he gave that season in the United States! Almost everyone will agree that the work is quite possibly *the* most popular and best-known of all piano concertos.

I. *Allegro non troppo e molto maestoso; Allegro con spirito.* The French horns start the concerto by singing out the first four notes of the introductory theme. This stirring, eloquent melody later became the tune of the hit song of the 1940s "Tonight We Love." Critics have long puzzled over the single statement of this theme; many regard it as an appalling waste of a wonderful tune. Eric Blom called it "one of the most baffling solecisms in the music of any great composer."

Some years ago, musicologist David Brown pointed out that the melody is a transposition of those letters in the composer's name that are musical notes —Peter *Tcha*ikovsky (in German, H is the note B natural). Thus the motto might have had some highly personal meaning to Tchaikovsky. Also, Brown suspected that, far from ignoring the opening motif, the composer used it as the source for several subsequent themes in the concerto.

Following the introduction, the composer presents the principal subject of the movement, a melody that Tchaikovsky heard while visiting in the Ukraine. "It is curious that in Little Russia [Ukraine] every blind beggar sings exactly the same tune with the same refrain," he wrote. "I have used part of this refrain in my piano concerto." Instead of the smooth melodic line of the original, though, Tchaikovsky fragments it into separate little two-note bits. A pair of songlike melodies make up the second subject and bring the exposition to a close. The rest of the movement develops and then returns the two subjects with brilliant, virtuosic writing for the piano and full exploitation of the orchestra's tonal palette.

II. *Andante semplice.* The Andante semplice, a combination of slow movement and scherzo, begins as a *notturno,* a "night song," with a simple tender flute melody. For the much faster middle section, Tchaikovsky gives us a charming French folk song, "Il faut s'amuser, danser et rire." The movement ends with a return of the *notturno.*

III. *Allegro con fuoco.* A vigorous, rhythmic Cossack dance tune, "Come, Come, Ivanka," serves as the principal melody of the finale. Tchaikovsky then introduces a soaring, broadly sung second theme. Falling between sonata allegro and rondo in form, the movement provides a felicitous conclusion to the entire concerto.

Concerto for Violin and Orchestra in D major, Op. 35
(33 minutes)

In July 1877, Tchaikovsky married his student Antonina Milyukova, partly because she pursued him so persistently and partly because he hoped the marriage would conceal his homosexuality. The marriage was short-lived, and as one terrible consequence, the composer tried to end his life in the

Moscow River. Finally, his patron, Nadezhda von Meck, gave him money to leave Russia on an extended holiday.

This trip took Tchaikovsky, along with Joseph Kotek, a young violinist and former student, to Clarens, Switzerland, early in 1878. Together they played through a great deal of violin music, including Edouard Lalo's *Symphonie espagnole,* which Tchaikovsky admired for its "freshness, lightness, and piquant rhythms."

The Lalo work inspired Tchaikovsky to compose his own violin concerto and Kotek offered the composer technical advice on the solo part. The composer began work on March 17, 1878, and finished two weeks later. Considering the slow movement as too sentimental and small in scale, Tchaikovsky created a replacement, which he inserted into the concerto on April 11.

Tchaikovsky dedicated the concerto to Leopold Auer, the famed violinist and pedagogue, teacher of such outstanding performers as Jascha Heifetz and Mischa Elman. But Auer rejected the new concerto as too difficult. At last, on December 4, 1881, violinist Adolf Brodsky gave the premiere with the Vienna Philharmonic under Hans Richter; in gratitude Tchaikovsky rededicated the work to Brodsky. Later, Auer championed the concerto, too late to play it himself, but in time to teach it to his many students.

I. *Allegro moderato.* As with his First Piano Concerto, Tchaikovsky opens with an absolutely intriguing melody, here played alone by the first violins, and also heard only one time. After the violins provide a glimpse of the first theme proper, the soloist enters for a full statement of the movement's simple, songful principal subject, and proceeds to extend the melody with some brilliant passage work. The violinist also presents the equally lyrical subsidiary theme. The following development section includes virtuosic violin writing that challenges the soloist with extremely rapid runs and acrobatic leaps covering the instrument's entire span. A solo cadenza ends this section and leads to the return of both themes.

II. *Canzonetta: Andante.* The woodwind choir sets the soulful mood of the Canzonetta, or "little song." The solo violin enters with the warm, tender theme, played in the lower part of its range; Tchaikovsky directs the soloist to play with a mute, a clamplike device attached to the bridge that darkens and veils the instrument's tone. Cast in three-part form, the movement has a middle section that is higher in tessitura and brighter and more vigorous in character than the opening. As the clarinet wanders down an arpeggio, the violin sneaks in with a shortened, varied reprise of the opening portion.

III. *Finale: Allegro vivacissimo.* Following without pause, the Finale bursts upon the scene; a fiery orchestral introduction gives way to a brief violin cadenza and the violin statement of the fleeting first subject. A slightly slower interlude ensues, starting with a stubborn emphatic melody that yields to an ingratiating little tune introduced by the oboe and clarinet. The remainder of the movement essentially concerns these two ideas as the soloist alternates dazzling technical display with meltingly beautiful cantilena. The concerto concludes with a brilliant, bravura flourish.

Nutcracker Suite, Op. 71a
(21 minutes)

Early in 1891 the Maryinski Theater of St. Petersburg asked Tchaikovsky to compose the music for a ballet based on E. T. A. Hoffmann's fanciful story "The Nutcracker and the Mouse King," as retold by Alexander Dumas the elder. The composer accepted reluctantly, objecting most to the unbelievably detailed instructions for the music given him by choreographer Marius Petipa.

In March, Tchaikovsky left on an extended tour of Europe. In Paris he discovered a new instrument, the celesta, which looks like a small upright piano, but with hammers inside that strike metal bars when activated by a keyboard. He urged his publisher to import one to Russia and eventually used it in *The Nutcracker.*

On Tchaikovsky's return to Russia on June 25 he had already finished sketches for the ballet and in February 1892 completed the orchestration. For a concert that he conducted in St. Petersburg on May 7, 1892, the composer extracted eight selections from the ballet as the *Nutcracker Suite;* the premiere of the entire ballet did not take place until December 17, 1892.

The story of the ballet is familiar: Marie receives a nutcracker for Christmas and dreams that the nutcracker becomes a handsome prince who leads the toy soldiers in a battle against the mice. The prince then takes Marie to the realm of the Sugarplum Fairy. Aside from the Overture Miniature and the March, all the selections of the *Nutcracker Suite* come from the land of the Sugarplum Fairy.

I. *Overture Miniature.* By eliminating cellos and basses from the orchestra, Tchaikovsky creates a particularly light and delicate texture.

II. *March.* The children march in for the Christmas party to this jaunty music.

III. *Dance of the Sugarplum Fairy.* Tchaikovsky introduces the twinkling tone of the celesta to represent the Sugarplum Fairy.

IV. *Russian Dance: Trepak.* The composer based this very energetic movement on an old Cossack dance. The rhythmic pattern established at the outset runs throughout.

V. *Arabian Dance.* A sultry, mysterious aura envelops this dance. Absent the brass, the muted strings and whispering woodwinds create the exotic atmosphere.

VI. *Chinese Dance.* The flutes and piccolos carry the melodic burden in this sparkling dance with bassoons and other instruments just playing an ostinato accompaniment.

VII. *Dance of the Mirlitons.* A flute trio plays the first theme, while the brass play the contrasting subject, after which the flute trio returns.

VIII. *Waltz of the Flowers.* The composer gives over the longest section of the suite to a captivating and very familiar waltz.

Overture Solennelle, "1812," Op. 49
(15 minutes)

In the spring of 1880, Tchaikovsky was asked to compose a piece to celebrate the consecration of Moscow's Cathedral of the Savior. The cathedral had been built to commemorate Napoleon's defeat in the Battle of Borodino and his subsequent retreat from Moscow. To heighten the effect, Tchaikovsky planned to hold the first performance in the large cathedral square and to incorporate salvos of real artillery at the climax, with the firing of the cannons controlled by electrical wires running from the conductor's podium.

Tchaikovsky completed the *Overture Solennelle, "1812"* in 1880 and the cathedral was dedicated in the summer of 1881, but there is no record that the *Overture* was played on that occasion. In fact, the premiere probably did not take place until August 20, 1882, at an all-Tchaikovsky concert in Moscow.

The *"1812" Overture* opens with the old Russian hymn "God, Preserve Thy People." Tchaikovsky follows with a musical depiction of the Battle of Borodino; he represents the French by the "Marseillaise" and the Russians by the hymn and some quotations of folk melodies. At the climactic moment, the roaring cannons and pealing church bells proclaim the Russian victory, and "God, Preserve Thy People" rings out in all its glory.

Romeo and Juliet Overture Fantasia
(20 minutes)

One day in May 1869, Tchaikovsky was walking with his friend and fellow composer Mily Balakirev, who suggested that Tchaikovsky write a concert overture (an orchestral composition not conceived as a prelude to anything else) on Romeo and Juliet. Balakirev even supplied an outline of the musical structure, suggesting which instruments should be used for the various themes, and the order and types of melodies.

Tchaikovsky started the overture but, despite Balakirev's detailed suggestions, or perhaps because of them, failed to make any progress for some four months. "I must confess," Tchaikovsky confided to his brother, "that his [Balakirev's] presence makes me rather uncomfortable. The narrowness of his musical opinions and his brusque manner do not please me." Nevertheless, Tchaikovsky managed to finish the work in November 1869. Nicholas Rubinstein led the first performance in Moscow on March 16, 1870. The composer wrote: "My overture had no success here at all, and was wholly ignored." That summer Tchaikovsky completely rewrote the piece, and then made further changes before the 1881 publication.

In *Romeo and Juliet,* Tchaikovsky achieves a perfect balance between program music and formal organization, in this case a traditional symphonic sonata allegro. The choralelike opening (introduction) suggests the faithful Friar Laurence. The tempo picks up for the raging strife music (first group of themes) of the feuding Montagues and Capulets. This gives way to a group of impassioned, soaring love melodies (second group), introduced by the violas and English horn. Some assert that the love themes were inspired by Tchaikovsky's infatuation at the time with actress Désirée Artôt.

Tchaikovsky then expands parts of the strife motif (development section), playing them off against the Friar Laurence melody in the background. All the themes then recur (recapitulation), although not in the original order. The epilogue (coda) mostly concerns the poignant love theme and leads to the mournful ending.

Symphony No. 2 in C minor, Op. 17, "Little Russian"
(35 minutes)

In 1865 Tchaikovsky was teaching at the Moscow Conservatory, when he became stimulated by the ideas and music of "The Mighty Five," a group of nationalistic Russian composers led by Nikolai Rimsky-Korsakov and Mily Balakirev. Even though Tchaikovsky eventually embraced a more international approach, the group's beliefs influenced his first three symphonies and some other compositions.

Tchaikovsky began work on the Second Symphony in June 1872, during a visit to his sister's estate in the Ukraine, an area known as Little Russia. A critic later subtitled the symphony "Little Russian" because Tchaikovsky derived several of its more important themes from folk songs of that area. Three of the tunes are known folk melodies; some others merely suggest folk origins.

Completed in November 1872, the symphony had a private performance at Rimsky-Korsakov's home in St. Petersburg later that year, followed by the formal public premiere on February 7, 1873, in Moscow. Tchaikovsky prepared a revision during the winter of 1879–80; K. K. Sike conducted the premiere of the final version on January 31, 1881, in St. Petersburg.

I. *Andante sostenuto; Allegro vivo.* The symphony opens with a slow introduction in which a solo French horn plays a variant of the melancholy folk song "Down by Mother Volga," which is repeated by a bassoon. The composer expands and varies the melody before leading to the faster, dancelike first theme proper of the movement, a simple, direct, folklike melody. The second subject, a rising line first stated by the oboe, plays only a small role in the thematic development. The composer focuses most interest on the contrast between the lyrical soulfulness of the opening folk melody and the first theme's staccato rhythmic drive.

II. *Andante marziale, quasi moderato.* Instead of a traditional slow movement, Tchaikovsky offers a somber march. Over a repeated two-note timpani figure, the clarinets and bassoons play the melody from the Bridal March that Tchaikovsky had salvaged from his discarded opera *Undine.* After a smooth contrasting theme stated by the violins and a return of the march section, Tchaikovsky gives the flute a variation of the folk song "Spin, O My Spinner." Both the *Undine* march and the folk-song contrast are heard again before the quiet conclusion.

III. *Scherzo: Allegro molto vivace.* In the fast, gay Scherzo, the melody rushes along from instrument to instrument. A peasantlike dance section in duple meter acts as a contrast before the return of the triple-meter opening section.

IV. *Finale: Moderato assai.* Listeners find the infectious good spirits of the fourth movement, the one that Tchaikovsky proclaimed his favorite, hard to resist. The composer bases the main theme on the folk song "The Crane," which he heard his sister's butler sing. As a foil to the rollicking abandon of this melody, Tchaikovsky throws in an insouciant second theme. After transforming and varying both melodies, the composer brings the movement to an energetic close with a fast and furious coda.

Symphony No. 4 in F minor, Op. 36
(45 minutes)

Tchaikovsky completed his Fourth Symphony, his first major success in the symphonic form, in December 1877 and dedicated it to Nadezhda von Meck, "My Best Friend." Nicholas Rubinstein gave the first performance in Moscow on March 11, 1878. Tchaikovsky wrote about the work to Mme. von Meck:

Our Symphony has a program. That is, it is possible to express its contents in words, and I will tell you—and you alone—the meaning of the entire work. Naturally, I can only do so as regards its general features.

[I. *Andante sostenuto; Moderato con anima.*] The Introduction is the kernel of the entire Symphony [the sinister motto sounded by horns and bassoons]. This is Fate, the somber power that prevents the desire for happiness from reaching its goal, a force which, like the sword of Damocles, hangs always over our heads. This force is inescapable and invincible. There is no course but to submit and inwardly lament [the descending and ascending violin theme].

The feeling of depression and hopelessness grows stronger and stronger. Would it not be better to turn away from reality and lull one's self in dreams [the wispy, evanescent clarinet melody]? A serene and radiant presence leads me on [cantabile melody in flutes and oboes as strains of the clarinet melody continue]. Deeper and deeper the soul is sunk in dreams. All that was dark and joyless is forgotten.

No. These are but dreams; roughly we are awakened by Fate. Thus we see that life is but an alternation of somber reality and fugitive dreams of happiness. This is the program of the first movement.

[II. *Andantino in modo di canzona.*] The second movement shows suffering in another stage. It is a feeling of melancholy such as fills one when sitting alone at home, exhausted by work; a swarm of reminiscences has arisen. How sad it is that so much has already been and gone! And yet it is a pleasure to think of the early years. One mourns the past and has neither the courage nor the will to begin a new life. One is rather tired of life. But these things are far away. It is sad, yet sweet, to lose one's self in the past. [Cast in three-part form, the movement opens with an extended cantabile melody, which is followed by a slightly faster, more rhythmic section and a very free, much shortened return of the beginning.]

[III. *Scherzo: Pizzicato ostinato.*] There is no determined feeling, no exact expression in the third movement. Here are capricious arabesques, vague figures that slip into the imagination when one has taken wine and is slightly intoxicated. The mood is now gay, now mournful. Suddenly there rush into the imagination the picture of a drunken peasant and a gutter song. Military music is heard passing by in the distance. There are disconnected pictures that come and go in the brain of the sleeper. They have nothing to do with reality; they are unintelligible, bizarre, "out at the elbows." [The Scherzo is in three parts: string pizzicato, woodwind central portion, string pizzicato, with a final coda.]

[IV. *Allegro con fuoco.*] If you find no pleasure in yourself, look about you. Go to the people. See how they enjoy life and give themselves up entirely to festivity. The picture of a folk holiday. Hardly have we had time to forget ourselves in the happiness of others when indefatigable Fate [the first movement Fate motto] reminds us once more of its presence. The other children of man are not concerned with us. They do not spare us a glance or stop to observe that we are lonely and sad. How merry and glad they all are. And do you still say that all the world is immersed in sorrow? There still is happiness, simple, naïve happiness. Rejoice in the happiness of others—and you can still live. [After the powerful first theme, the subsidiary subject is a simple melody based on the old Russian folk song "The Birch Tree."]

Symphony No. 5 in E minor, Op. 64
(45 minutes)

Tchaikovsky undertook his Fifth Symphony early in 1888 in a terrible state of uncertainty and self-doubt. In May he wrote to his brother that he had "no ideas, no inclination. Have I written myself out?" he asked. Nevertheless, one month later in a note to his benefactor, Nadezhda von Meck, he wrote: "The beginning was difficult, but now inspiration is coming. We shall see."

The composer completed the symphony in August 1888 and conducted the premiere in St. Petersburg on November 17. Despite the warm audience response, the critics disapproved and Tchaikovsky became depressed and melancholy. "I have come to the conclusion that it is a failure," he confided to Mme. von Meck. "There is something repellent in it, some patchiness, some exaggerated color, some insincerity that the public instinctively recognizes." A highly successful performance in Hamburg, however, dissipated some of the composer's gloom and he was able to write of the symphony: "I like it far better now, after having held a bad opinion of it for some time." Needless to say, the public has always held an excellent opinion of the symphony.

I. *Andante; Allegro con anima.* In his notebooks, Tchaikovsky wrote this enigmatic program for the first movement: "Introduction. Complete resignation before Fate, or, which is the same, before the inscrutable predestination of Providence. Allegro (I) Murmurs, doubts, plaints, reproaches against XXX. (II) Shall I throw myself in the embraces of faith???"

If the introductory motto played by two clarinets is indeed Fate, then it is a very different Fate from that depicted in Beethoven's Fifth or Tchaikovsky's Fourth, against which the individual struggles and rages. Tchaikovsky regards Fate here as inevitable human destiny, which must be accepted with resignation and quiet submission.

Scholar John Warrack suggests that "XXX" is the first theme in the fast body of the movement. Its quirky rhythms and pulsating accompaniment, says Warrack, represent Tchaikovsky's homosexuality. The warm and deeply expressive second theme derives from his religious faith. ("The intelligent man who believes in God," Tchaikovsky wrote, "has a shield against which the blows of Fate are absolutely vain.") The composer devotes the remainder of the movement to working out the thematic material and bringing it back for the recapitulation.

II. *Andante cantabile con alcuna licenza.* Surely one of the most moving and beloved of all symphonic themes appears in this movement, soulfully sung by a solo French horn over sustained strings. Before very long, though, the Fate motto violently interrupts. The tender, yearning horn theme emerges once more, this time in the violins, but again Fate intrudes. Dispirited and forlorn, the movement quietly fades away.

III. *Allegro moderato.* In this movement, Tchaikovsky treats us to a charming, albeit slightly melancholy waltz based on a street song he heard in Florence a decade earlier. As a foil to its lyricism, the composer concentrates the trio section on a rapid staccato figure that skitters through the orchestra and then becomes the accompaniment to the returning waltz tune. At the very end of the movement, Tchaikovsky brings back a hollow-sounding reminder of the Fate motto.

IV. *Andante maestoso; Allegro vivace.* The extended introduction to the finale opens with the motto now gloriously transformed into radiant major. An outpouring of themes follows, including a rhythmic remembrance of the motto. Joyous in outlook, the movement surges along until it reaches the coda, when the metamorphosed Fate motto makes its final glowing appearance.

Symphony No. 6 in B minor, Op. 74, "Pathétique"
(45 minutes)

The "Pathétique" began to take shape on Tchaikovsky's trip to Paris in December 1892: "Just as I was starting on my journey the idea came to me for a new Symphony. This time with a program, but a program of a kind that remains an enigma to all—let them guess it who can. . . . During my journey, while composing it in my mind, I frequently wept copiously. . . . There will be much that is novel as regards form in this work. For instance, the Finale will not be a loud Allegro, but a slow-moving Adagio."

Some of the themes and ideas for the new symphony came from abandoned sketches and notes for a symphony Tchaikovsky had contemplated writing earlier that year: "The ultimate essence of the plan of the Symphony is LIFE. First part—all impulsive passion, confidence, thirst for activity. Must be short. (Finale DEATH—result of collapse.) Second part, love; third, disappointments; fourth ends dying away (also short)."

By August 24, 1893, Tchaikovsky completed his Sixth (and final) Symphony and he wrote to his publisher: "I give you my word of honor that never in my life have I been so contented, so proud, so happy, in the knowledge that I have written a good piece." The composer conducted the premiere in St. Petersburg on October 28, 1893.

The next morning Tchaikovsky began to ready the score for publication. According to brother Modest's account: "He did not wish to designate it merely by a number, and had abandoned his original intention of calling it 'A Program Symphony.' I suggested 'Tragic Symphony' as an appropriate title. But this did not please him either. Suddenly the word 'pathétique' occurred to me. My brother exclaimed: 'Bravo, Modest, splendid! Pathé-tique!' Then and there, in my presence, he added to the score the title by which the Symphony has always been known." (The meaning of the subtitle, in Russian *patetichesky,* has more to do with feelings of yearning or passion than with being pathetic or pitiful.)

Of the specific program of the "Pathétique," there can be little question that the subject is death. Apparently, Tchaikovsky was bidding the world farewell, as he described in the notes for the discarded symphony. The music proved to be prophetic, since the composer died a little over a week after the premiere.

For the longest time everyone believed that the cause of Tchaikovsky's death was cholera. But recently published research findings by Alexandra Orlova, which not all scholars accept, assert that Tchaikovsky ended his life when he was forced to drink poison by a court of honor from the College of Jurisprudence after a scandalous homosexual affair with the nephew of Duke Stenbock-Thurmor.

I. *Adagio; Allegro non troppo.* The bassoon's dark, mournful introductory theme gives rise to the faster, nervous principal theme of the Adagio. After some expansion, Tchaikovsky brings the music to a complete halt and then introduces the second theme, a meltingly sweet, sad melody. This theme, along with several others in the symphony, moves in a downward direction, with occasional efforts to rise, but always falling back down again. Other themes, some of a more optimistic nature, follow. The development section begins with a startling outburst and maintains a ferocious intensity. When the pressure slackens, the brass instruments quietly quote from the Russian Orthodox Church funeral liturgy. The development then continues and a highly condensed recapitulation and a grieving coda conclude the move-ment.

II. *Allegro con grazioso.* The second movement resembles a waltz, but one that is oddly damaged. Instead of the traditional three-beat meter, the move-ment is in five, with each measure divided into unequal groups of two and three beats. The warm tune, as attractive as any Tchaikovsky melody, limps slightly because of the irregular meter. We hear a burdened, sighing middle section before the composer repeats the first part.

III. *Allegro molto vivace.* A swirl of light, fleeting triplet figures start the high-speed Allegro molto vivace until a jaunty little march tune manages to poke through the scurrying, running notes. The jolly façade is somewhat deceptive; one detects underneath a certain coldness and detachment.

IV. *Adagio lamentoso: Andante.* The surface lightness of the third movement increases the poignancy of the finale's deep gloom. Pain and despair underlie Tchaikovsky's impassioned cries of anguish. The music searchingly seeks hope or solace, but all strength and passion are spent and there is only defeat, emptiness—and death.

Variations on a Rococo Theme for Cello and Orchestra, Op. 33
(18 minutes)

Wilhelm Fitzenhagen, a leading cellist in Moscow and Tchaikovsky's colleague at the Moscow Conservatory, was invited to perform at a festival in Germany and asked the composer to write a work for the occasion. Tchaikovsky was fully aware that the Germans regarded the Russians as barbarians; he therefore composed the Variations on a Rococo Theme in a style that honored Mozart and the 18th century.

Tchaikovsky invented an original melody in the Rococo manner to serve as the basis for the Variations. The Rococo musical style, also known as the gallant style, or *style galant,* emphasized charm, elegance, and grace; the writing was usually highly ornamental, with catchy melodies and attractive rhythms designed to please and charm the listeners. The style prevailed in the middle years of the 18th century; its main flowering was from about 1725 to perhaps 1775.

After a brief orchestral introduction, the solo cello introduces the simple Rococo theme. Tchaikovsky then subjects the theme to seven connected variations that never depart too far from the source melody. The composer features the cello throughout, with passages of extreme difficulty that place tremendous demands on the soloist's technique.

Tchaikovsky composed the Variations in the latter part of 1876. Fitzenhagen, with the composer conducting, introduced the work in Wiesbaden in July 1879. Franz Liszt came backstage afterward and said to Tchaikovsky: "Ah, this is music again," an obvious reference to Tchaikovsky's First Piano Concerto, which had been played in Wiesbaden three days earlier.

Antonio Vivaldi

Born March 4, 1678, in Venice
Died July 26 (?), 1741, in Vienna

ANTONIO VIVALDI wrote more music than almost any other composer in history. His prodigious output includes nearly 50 operas, about 40 cantatas and oratorios, close to 100 orchestra works, and over 400 concertos for many different instruments.

The son of a violinist, Vivaldi studied violin and theory with his father and became a very accomplished player. He nevertheless entered the priesthood and was known as *il prete rosso* ("the red priest") because of his flaming red hair. At his first attempt to celebrate mass, though, the young priest suffered severe chest pains, either from asthma or from angina, and never officiated again. Instead, in 1704 he accepted a position as violin teacher at the Ospedale della Pietà, a charitable institution in Venice that functioned both as a conservatory and as a home for orphaned, illegitimate, and indigent girls.

For the next 35 years Vivaldi taught at the Ospedale, taking on more and more duties and rising in rank. The Ospedale was renowned throughout Europe for its extraordinarily talented young musicians and their outstanding weekly concerts; Vivaldi composed many of his works for those performances.

Vivaldi became a leading composer in the vigorous, ornate style of the Baroque. His music, and his concertos in particular, influenced later Baroque composers, especially Johann Sebastian Bach, who arranged several of Vivaldi's violin concertos as keyboard concertos.

Vivaldi's music was seldom performed for the 200 years following his death. In recent years, though, scholars have begun to unearth the huge cache of music that he had left, making many of his compositions available to modern performers. Also, the advent of the long-playing record helped to familiarize the public with the extent of Vivaldi's music. Today, of all his works, the four violin concertos known as *The Four Seasons* arouse the most enthusiasm and rank high on the "Top Ten" list of music lovers everywhere.

The RV number used to identify Vivaldi's music refers to the *Ryom Verzeichnis* ("Ryom Catalog") prepared by Danish musicologist Peter Ryom in 1974.

The Four Seasons, Op. 8, RV 269, 315, 293, 297
(40 minutes)

Of the 400 concertos that Vivaldi composed during his 35-year tenure at the Ospedale della Pietà, more than 200 were for violin. Of these, the undisputed masterpieces—for imagination, beauty of melody, and brilliance of solo writing—are the four concertos that make up *Le Quattro Stagioni* or *The Four Seasons.* They were published in Amsterdam in 1725 and were probably written some years earlier. Composed for solo violin and string orchestra, each concerto contains three separate movements—fast, slow, fast in tempo.

Philosophers in the early 18th century urged composers to make their music more "natural," which meant imitating the sounds of nature as closely as possible. Striving toward this goal, Vivaldi appended a *sonetto dimostrativo,* a "demonstration sonnet," probably of his own composition, to each concerto. To eliminate any possible misunderstanding, he correlated each line of the sonnet with a specific section of the music.

It seems clear, considering the superiority of the music to the poetry, that Vivaldi composed the music before he wrote the sonnets to conform, line by line, to the composition. To fully appreciate the representations in the music, included below is a translation of Vivaldi's sonnets.

THE SPRING

I. *Allegro*
Spring has come,
The birds greet spring with happy singing,
The streams flow in sweet murmurings, caressed by spring breezes.
The sky is veiled in black,
Lightning flashes and thunderstorms roar.
Soon it becomes quiet again; the birds return,
And again birds sing their delightful songs.

II. *Largo e pianissimo sempre*
Soon the lovely meadows are covered with flowers,
Beneath the whispering tree leaves,
The goatherd sleeps with his faithful dog at his side.

III. *Danza pastorale: Allegro*
The shepherd and nymphs dance,
To the sounds of the shepherd's pipe,
As spring enters in full resplendent beauty.

THE SUMMER

I. *Allegro non molto*
The man and his flock languish beneath the burning summer sun,
The pine tree is seared,
The cuckoo bird is calling,
And the turtledove and goldfinch are singing,
The soft zephyr winds blow.
The north wind wakes from its slumber and stirs the air,
The shepherd boy weeps in fear of the wind and its power.

II. *Adagio; Presto*
The tired shepherd cannot rest his tired limbs,
In fear of the lightning flashes and thunder roar,
And the torment of the buzzing flies and insects.

III. *Presto*
Alas, his fears are well founded,
Thunder and lightning fill the sky,
And huge hailstones pound away at the fields of grain.

THE AUTUMN

I. *Allegro*
With song and dance the peasants celebrate the harvest,
They are drunk with the nectars of Bacchus.
The festivities end as the celebrants fall asleep.

II. *Adagio*
The singing and dancing ends,
The soft, sweet breezes fan the celebrants,
Lulling everyone into peaceful slumber.

III. *Allegro*
At dawn, to the sound of horns, the hunters ride out,
They chase their fleeing prey,
In mounting fear, the wounded animal tries to escape,
Terrified, the hunted beast finally succumbs.

THE WINTER

I. *Allegro non molto*
Frozen, shivering, in the snowy cold,
In the sharp, biting winds,
You stamp your feet as your teeth chatter from the cold.

II. *Largo*
The cheer and warmth of indoors offers haven,
Against the drenching rain outside.

III. *Allegro*
With slow, cautious steps they wend their way over the ice,
Many are slipping and falling,
Once again on their feet, they move with caution,
Until the ice breaks under them,
As the winds battle in the heavens.
Such is winter—but what joy it brings!

Richard Wagner

Born May 22, 1813, in Leipzig
Died February 13, 1883, in Venice

JUST AS THE MUSIC of Beethoven dominated the first half of the 19th century, so the second half revolved around Wagner—either in imitation or in reaction. True, the public went around *whistling* the tunes of Verdi's operas, but they *talked* about Wagner's operas, or, as he called his more serious works, music dramas.

Verdi's operas were vocal operas; the primary focus was on the singer, with the orchestra furnishing support, background, and mood setting. Wagner's operas, on the other hand, were symphonic operas; the orchestra had a major role in presenting the drama that unfolded on the stage. In part, Wagner achieved this through his use of leitmotifs, short phrases of melody that represented characters, events, places, or objects in the opera. Listening carefully to the leitmotifs, how and when they appear and change, provides insights beyond what is sung by the individual characters. In addition to using the leitmotifs in the operas themselves, Wagner also used them in the overtures and preludes to the operas.

Wagner, who was largely self-taught, also brought radically new ideas to his music. In his harmonies, conception of melody, and orchestration, he pushed far beyond the traditional practices of his time.

Many have bemoaned the fact that Wagner's output was confined almost exclusively to opera; but the overtures and preludes to his operas are important works that are often performed in orchestral concerts.

Traditionally, we define an operatic overture as an orchestral introduction to an opera and an operatic prelude as the introduction to a later act of an opera. Wagner changed the definition; in his later operas he called all his instrumental introductions preludes. Since the works do not depend on the opera for their effect and since each one is a complete composition—or only needs a brief ending to be made complete—several rightfully belong among the orchestral masterpieces.

Overture to *The Flying Dutchman*
(10 minutes)

Wagner based *The Flying Dutchman* on the legend of a sailor who took a vow to sail around the Cape of Good Hope in defiance of Lucifer, or Satan. As a result, the sailor was doomed to sail the stormy seas forever. In developing his 1841 opera, Wagner specifically chose Heinrich Heine's retelling of the legend, since it contained the composer's favorite theme of redemption through love. In Heine's version, the Dutchman is allowed to come to land every seven years, and if he finds a woman who will remain faithful, can escape the curse.

Dominating the overture is the bold motif associated with the Dutchman, presented near the opening by French horns and bassoons. In contrast is the warm and compassionate theme of Senta, the woman who frees him from the curse. Surrounding these two melodies, though, are the swirling, angry sounds of the sea, effectively conjuring up the storm-tossed ship of the Dutchman.

Wagner conducted the premiere of *The Flying Dutchman* in Dresden on January 2, 1843.

Prelude to *Lohengrin*
(10 minutes)

In Wagner's romantic view of medieval life, Lohengrin, a knight of the Holy Grail, clears Elsa of the false accusation of murder and wins her hand in marriage. He sets but one condition, that she never ask his name or from whence he came. A sorceress goads Elsa into asking the fatal questions, which forces Lohengrin to leave and causes Elsa to sink lifeless to the ground. Wagner completed *Lohengrin* in 1848, and Franz Liszt conducted the premiere in Weimar on August 28, 1850.

In preparation for a performance he led in 1853, Wagner wrote a very clear description, here abridged, of the prelude: "Out of the clear blue ether of the sky there gradually emerges an angel host bearing the sacred Grail. As it approaches earth it pours out exquisite odors, like streams of gold. The vision draws nearer, and the climax is reached when at last the Grail is revealed in all its glorious reality, radiating fiery beams and shaking the soul with emotion. Then the flames gradually die away, and the angel host soars up again to the ethereal heights in tender joy, having made pure once more the hearts of men."

Wagner's description in words closely parallels the music. The theme of the Grail is first heard softly, from the violins, playing in their high register. This theme then descends from the clouds, passing through the flutes, oboes, and clarinets, to the horns, bassoons, and lower strings, reaching a climax in the majestic sound of the full brass and woodwind sections. The Grail then ascends, ending with its final whispered appearance in four solo violins.

Prelude to *Die Meistersinger von Nürnberg*
(10 minutes)

Contrary to tradition, Wagner composed the prelude to *Die Meistersinger* ("The Mastersingers") in 1862, before writing the opera, which he did not complete until 1867. It is not, therefore, a selection of themes from the opera, but actually the source of the opera's melodies. The plot of the opera involves young Walther's efforts to win the hand of Eva. Her father says he will approve only if Walther wins the song contest of the Renaissance guild of Mastersingers. Eventually Walther triumphs in the contest and wins his suit for Eva.

The prelude opens with the *Meistersinger* theme—sturdy and solid and firmly rooted in tradition. In contrast, the flute and then oboe give out a lyrical melody that the composer associates with the young, impetuous love of Walther and Eva. The stately ceremonial march that follows represents the staid guild of Mastersingers. Other material comes from the "Prize Song" with which Walther triumphs in the song contest.

To these themes the composer adds a scherzolike musical satire of Beckmesser, the bitter old fool, who vainly tries to defeat the young lovers. Some phrases bring to mind the wise cobbler-poet Hans Sachs, who holds that great art comes through a synthesis of the old and new, the traditional and novel—a position dear to Wagner's heart. Wagner expresses this reconciliation by combining the various themes in the prelude's brilliant, rousing climax.

In November 1862 in Leipzig, Wagner conducted the prelude by itself in its premiere performance.

Overture to *Rienzi*
(13 minutes)

Wagner composed *Rienzi* more in the style of French grand opera than of German opera. It received its first performance in Dresden on October 20, 1842. In the opera, Rienzi is a papal notary who tried to bring peace to 14th century Rome by leading the people in revolt against the nobles. At the end the people turn against him and he dies.

The overture starts with three trumpet notes, Rienzi's call to the people, followed by his prayer from Act V, a wistful, poignant melody that Wagner whips into a powerful brass statement surrounded by swirling string figures. The three trumpet notes usher in the faster main section of the overture. Here, after presenting a faster, lighter treatment of Rienzi's prayer, Wagner introduces several other melodies from the opera, along with echoes of the trumpet call. The overall effect is rousing and lusty.

Overture to *Tannhäuser*
(15 minutes)

Tannhäuser deals with one of Wagner's favorite themes, the conflict of sacred love and profane love set in medieval times. This time the action concerns the 13th century knight Tannhäuser, who loves the pure, beautiful Elizabeth, but is drawn to the magical grotto of the goddess Venus. In time he wearies of this life and returns to Elizabeth. The overture presents a synopsis of the opera's action: it opens with music associated with pure love, goes on to represent sensual love, and ends with an apotheosis of spiritual love.

The overture begins with the slow, solemn "Pilgrim's Chorus," which the pilgrims sing on their way to Rome in the opera. A second, upward-reaching motif, identified as "Repentance," follows before the orchestra trombones loudly play the "Pilgrim's Chorus" again, with an agitated string figure ("Pulse of Life") in the background. The "Pilgrim's Chorus" and "Repentance" fade away into the faster section of the overture, music that Wagner described as "the whirlings of a fearsomely voluptuous dance," including various motifs associated with Venus—"Bacchanale," "Sirens," "Glorification of Venus," and "Charms of Venus." After building to a climax of, in Wagner's words, "tumultuous shouts and savage cries of joy," the violins start a figure reminiscent of "Pulse of Life," under which the majestic strains of the "Pilgrim's Chorus" and "Repentance" return to bring the overture to its exalted conclusion.

Wagner composed *Tannhäuser* from 1843 to 1845 and directed the premiere in Dresden on October 19, 1845.

Prelude and Finale from *Tristan und Isolde*
(12 minutes)

Programmers almost always pair the Prelude to *Tristan und Isolde* with the finale of the music drama. Unfortunately, a misnomer creeped in when Franz Liszt prepared a piano transcription of the Finale, which he mistakenly entitled *Liebestod* ("Love Death"). The name stuck, even though in his program notes for an 1863 performance Wagner clearly listed the two excerpts as *Vorspiel (Liebestod)* ("Prelude—Love Death") and *Schluss (Verklärung)* ("Finale—Transfiguration"). Thus, the commonly seen *Prelude and Liebestod* is incorrect; it should be *Prelude and Finale* or *Love Death and Transfiguration.*

Wagner took the plot of *Tristan und Isolde* from an ancient legend. Briefly, Tristan brings Isolde to be the bride of his uncle, King Marke. But first Tristan and Isolde drink a potion and fall in love, though there is no possibility that they can stay together. The story ends with the death of the two lovers.

Following are Wagner's notes for his 1863 performance of the Prelude and Finale: "Prelude (Love Death): Tristan as bridal envoy conducts Isolde to his uncle, the King. They love each other. From the first stifled moan of quenchless longing, from the faintest tremor to the free avowal of a hopeless love, the heart goes through each phase of futile battling with its inner fever, till, swooning back upon itself, it seems extinguished as in death.

"Finale (Transfiguration): Yet, what Fate divided in this life, in death revives transfigured; the gate of union opens. Above the body of Tristan, dying Isolde sees transcendent consummation of their passionate desire, eternal union in unmeasured realms, without bond nor barrier, indivisible!"

Tristan marks an important step in music development because Wagner uses an intensely chromatic style to increase considerably the expressive nature of the couple's relationship. Wagner called this style of dealing with the inner, emotional lives of the characters more than with outside events or actions "interior drama."

Composed from 1857 to 1859, *Tristan* received its premiere on June 10, 1865, in Munich with Hans von Bülow conducting.

Carl Maria von Weber

Born November 18, 1786, in Eutin, Germany
Died June 5, 1826, in London

ASIDE FROM the three opera overtures that we discuss below, little of
Weber's music appears on modern concert programs. Yet in his short
lifetime he made an epochal impact on the development of music. In some
ways, Weber was the first of the Romantics. His colorful, powerful, and
imaginative scores were unique and personal; they often dealt with the world
of nature and the world of the supernatural. In virtually every element of his
music he went far beyond the limits accepted by the older Classical composers. His opera *Der Freischütz* created a style of German Romantic opera that
ended the monopoly of the prevalent Italian style and prepared the way for
Richard Wagner.

As the first modern conductor, Weber used a baton and podium, arranged
the players in the seating plan orchestras still follow today, and insisted on
full control of every aspect of the operas he directed. Further, he was a
brilliant virtuoso pianist who toured widely. Sad to say, the composer con-
tracted consumption, a "fashionable" disease of the Romantics, which killed
him before he reached age 40.

Weber's father, who was related to Mozart by marriage, wanted to make
his son another child prodigy and started giving him music lessons at an
early age. Indeed, by age 14, Weber had his first opera produced in Freiberg.
The following years were far less spectacular, even though he did eventually
succeed as a composer, conductor, and pianist. The 1820 production of *Der
Freischütz* brought him real prominence. In the few remaining years of his
short life he wrote two more major operas, *Euryanthe* and *Oberon,* but their
reception was limited by the poor librettos, and essentially only their overtures survive.

Overture to *Der Freischütz*
(10 minutes)

The plot of *Der Freischütz* involves Max, who has entered a shooting contest to win the hand of the beautiful Agathe. But the day before the contest he loses his skill. At the urging of Caspar, another hunter, who has already made a pact with the devil, Max goes to the terrifying Wolf's Glen to sell his soul to Samiel, the devil, for seven magic bullets. On the day of the contest, Max's aim is unerring, and he wins the contest. Samiel, unable to claim the soul of Max, takes Caspar's soul instead.

The overture opens with a slow introduction, played by strings and French horns, that evokes the magical, mystical forest. An ominous string tremolo, with foreboding pizzicato notes in the bass, represents the evil Samiel. The fast body of the overture, which starts with a bright, syncopated melody taken from the aria Max sings on his way to visit Agathe, is quickly over-whelmed by the mad pandemonium of the creatures gathered at midnight in Wolf's Glen. The second group of themes includes a passionate outburst from one of Max's second act arias and the climax of the aria Agathe sings while awaiting the visit from Max. The rest of the overture concerns the clash between good and evil and ends with a final triumphant recasting of Agathe's melody.

Weber composed the overture from February 22 to May 13, 1820, after completing the opera. He conducted the premiere in Copenhagen on October 8, 1820, before the first performance of the opera, which was given on June 18, 1821.

Overture to *Euryanthe*
(9 minutes)

After the immense success of *Der Freischütz,* the Kärntnertor Theater in Vienna commissioned Weber to compose another opera. The libretto by Wilhelmine de Chézy revolves around Count Adolar, who bets that his betrothed, Euryanthe, cannot be seduced into unfaithfulness. She remains true to Adolar, but does confide to a friend a secret that Adolar asked her never to repeat. In a rage, Adolar plans to kill Euryanthe, but finally repents and reunites with his beloved.

Weber composed *Euryanthe* from 1821 to 1823. He took themes from the completed opera for the overture, which he wrote from September 1 to October 19, 1823.

After a fierce orchestral eruption, the winds state the heroic principal theme, taken from Adolar's first act aria, in which he avows his devotion to God and to Euryanthe. After a portentous transition comes the subsidiary subject, a lyrical, flowing melody introduced by the first violins; it derives from an exceedingly joyful aria that Adolar sings in the second act. Weber then gives eight muted solo violins a wraithlike passage that suggests a ghost who figures in the opera plot. The following development and the spirited return of the themes leave little doubt that the overture as well as the opera end happily.

Overture to *Oberon*
(9 minutes)

After Weber, in 1824, received a commission for an opera from Covent Garden, he decided to base it on the story from Christoph Wieland's epic German poem *Oberon*. Oberon, king of the elves or fairies, appears in various guises in works ranging from Shakespeare's *A Midsummer Night's Dream* to Wagner's *Ring of the Nibelungen,* where he is known as Alberich.

In the opera, Oberon and Queen Titania have quarreled and will be reconciled only if they can find two earthly lovers who will remain constant to each other, no matter how their devotion is tested. Oberon meets the knight Huon of Bordeaux, who is traveling to Baghdad to win the love of the Caliph's daughter, Rezia. With the help of Oberon's magic horn, Huon overcomes the trials that test their love—a shipwreck, the kidnapping of Rezia, and an attempt to seduce him. The enduring love of Huon and Rezia reunites the fairy couple, Oberon and Titania.

The overture offers a musical representation of the opera's dramatic events. It opens with the sound of Oberon's magic horn, interspersed with other phrases that bring to mind the world of elves and spirits. A startling crash introduces the story of Huon and Rezia. Themes associated with crucial moments in the opera tell the tale: The racing string figure represents Huon and Rezia making their dangerous escape from the Caliph; a clarinet sings a love song that expresses Huon's deep affection for Rezia; and the exultant final theme in the violins, with its big upward leaps, stands for Huon's rescue of Rezia from the shipwreck. Weber then develops and expands this material and brings the melodies back for a final traversal.

Weber completed the overture on April 9, 1826, after finishing the opera. He conducted the premiere at Covent Garden three days later. Audiences received the overture with such acclaim that it had to be repeated immediately. Weber died barely two months later, at age 39.

Glossary

Arpeggio   The notes of a chord played one after another, instead of simultaneously. For example, a C chord contains the notes C-E-G; played together they form the chord, played sequentially they form an arpeggio.

Cadenza   An improvisatory section of a concerto that usually comes near the end of a movement and is played without the orchestra, giving the soloist an opportunity for virtuosic display. Most cadenzas are written by composers or by performers.

Chromatic   The use of tones in addition to those of the major or minor scale on which a passage is based. For example, the first three notes of the C major scale are C-D-E. A chromatic passage starting on C might also include C sharp (between C and D) and D sharp (between D and E).

Coda   From the Italian for "tail"; the concluding section of a movement or piece that is not usually considered part of the form. See also sonata allegro form.

Counterpoint   Playing simultaneously two or more individual lines of music. The adjective is *contrapuntal*.

Development   See Sonata allegro form.

Exposition   See Sonata allegro form.

Fugue   A form of imitative counterpoint in which one instrument states a short melody, the subject, and then others take it up in quick succession. *Fugal* means in the style of a fugue; *fugato* is a fugal section of a larger work.

Legato   Smooth articulation, in which the notes are connected without perceptible interruption.

Melody   See Theme.

Minuet   A triple-meter, dancelike movement, usually appearing third in the Classical symphony. A contrasting minuet, known as the *trio*, is played in alteration with the minuet, giving a minuet-trio-minuet form. Known as *menuetto* in German.

Motif   An identifiable fragment of music that may be no more than a rhythmic pattern or two or three notes of melody.

Ostinato   From the Italian for "obstinate"; a phrase of music that is repeated many times.

Pizzicato   Producing the sound on a string instrument by plucking the string with a finger instead of rubbing it with a bow.

Recapitulation   See Sonata allegro form.

Rondo   A popular musical form, typically diagrammed as A-B-A-C-A. A is the principal theme (or refrain), which is repeated several times; B and C are contrasting interludes that come between the repetitions of A.

Scherzo   A movement that Beethoven and later composers used to replace the minuet as the third movement in the symphony. The scherzo, which means "joke" in Italian, is usually faster than the minuet, lighter and more playful in spirit, and often includes elements of surprise and humor. The scherzo is frequently played twice, with a contrasting middle section, called a *trio,* coming between the two scherzos.

Sonata allegro form   By far the most important formal structure in orchestral music. The form has three parts: The *exposition* introduces the themes—the first or principal theme or group of themes, the second or subsidiary theme or group of themes, which is contrasting in character and in a different key, and the less important third or closing theme. Many 18th and 19th century composers ask that performers repeat the exposition, though this is not always observed in performance.

In the following *development* the composer works through the themes introduced in the exposition—extracting short fragments of melody, moving (modulating) to different keys, altering the particular notes or rhythms of the melodies, combining themes or fragments in fugatos or other contrapuntal textures, and almost always building to a climax.

The *recapitulation* brings back the themes from the exposition, usually with some modifications and with the second theme in the home key.

In addition to the standard parts of the form, the composer may sometimes include a slow introduction before the exposition, transitions between the sections, and a concluding coda.

Staccato   An articulation in which each note is short and separated from its neighbors.

Syncopation   Shifting an accent from its usual position to a normally unaccented position, which disturbs the rhythmic flow and adds a certain piquancy and tension to the music.

Theme   The basic subject matter of a piece of music. The principal theme usually appears at the very beginning of a composition or after an introduction. Also called melody, tune, or subject, although these terms have slightly different meanings.

Theme and variations   A frequently used musical form, either as a movement in a larger work or as an individual composition. It consists of a musical idea, or theme, which the composer then subjects to a number of modifications, or variations. The theme is usually a comparatively short, simple melody that is easily remembered and one that can accept increased complexity. The variations may remain close to the original, merely adding decorations or minor changes of melody or rhythm, or they may go far afield, completely changing the feeling and mood of the theme.

Three-part form A very basic formal structure, diagrammed as A-B-A, and consisting of a theme (A), a contrasting theme (B), and a return, usually changed in some ways and shorter, of the first theme (A). Sometimes called three-part song form.

Discography

Note: All recordings listed are compact discs (CDs). Each entry includes, in order, conductor, orchestra, and CD number, or soloist(s), conductor, orchestra, and CD number.

Johann Sebastian Bach

Brandenburg Concertos, Nos. 1–3, BWV 1046–1048. Leppard, English Chamber Orchestra. Philips 420345-2 PM

Brandenburg Concertos, Nos. 4–6, BWV 1049–1051. Leppard, English Chamber Orchestra. Philips 420346-2 PM

Suites for Orchestra, BWV 1066–1069. Spivakov, Moscow Virtuosi. RCA 60360-2-RC

Béla Bartók

Concerto for Orchestra. Reiner, Chicago Symphony. RCA 60175-2 RG

Concertos for Piano and Orchestra Nos. 1, 2, 3. Ashkenazy, Solti, London Philharmonic. London 2-425573-2

Concerto for Violin and Orchestra No. 2. Midori, Mehta, Berlin Philharmonic. Sony Classical 431626-2 GH

Ludwig van Beethoven

Concertos for Piano and Orchestra, Nos. 1–5, Opp. 15; 19; 37; 58; 73, "Emperor." Perahia, Haitink, Concertgebouw Orchestra. CBS 3-M3K 44575

Concerto for Violin, Cello, Piano, and Orchestra in C major, Op. 56, "Triple Concerto." Beaux Arts Trio, Haitink, London Philharmonic. Philips 420231-2 PH

Concerto for Violin and Orchestra in D major, Op. 61. Perlman, Barenboim, Berlin Philharmonic. Angel CDC 49567

Overtures (Coriolan, Op. 62; The Creatures of Prometheus, Op. 43; Egmont, Op. 84; Fidelio; Leonore Nos. 1–3, Opp. 138, 72a, 72b). Abbado, Vienna Philharmonic. Deutsche Grammophon 435617-2

342   DISCOGRAPHY

Symphonies Nos. 1–9, Opp. 21; 36; 55, "Eroica"; 60; 67; 68, "Pastoral"; 92; 93; 125, "Choral Symphony." Muti, Philadelphia. Angel 6-A26-49487

Hector Berlioz
Fantastic Symphony, Op. 14. Bernstein, New York Philharmonic. CBS MYK 38475
Overtures *(Benvenuto Cellini,* Op. 23; *The Corsair,* Op. 21; *The Roman Carnival,* Op. 9). Munch, Boston Symphony. RCA 60478-2 RV

Johannes Brahms
Concertos for Piano and Orchestra Nos. 1 and 2, Opp. 15, 83. Arrau, Haitink, Concertgebouw Orchestra. Philips 2-438320-2
Concerto for Violin and Orchestra in D major, Op. 77. Oistrakh, Klemperer, French National Radio Orchestra. EMI CDM 64632
Concerto for Violin, Cello, and Orchestra in A minor, Op. 102, "Double Concerto." Stern, Ma, Abbado, Chicago Symphony. CBS MK 42387
Overtures *(Academic Festival,* Op. 80; *Tragic,* Op. 81). Haitink, Concertgebouw Orchestra. Philips 2-438320-2
Symphony Nos. 1–4, Opp. 68, 73, 90, 98. Bernstein, Vienna Philharmonic. Deutsche Grammophon 4-415570-2 GX4
Variations on a Theme by Haydn, Op. 56a. Slatkin, St. Louis Symphony. RCA 7920-2 RC

Benjamin Britten
The Young Person's Guide to the Orchestra, Op. 34. Slatkin, London Philharmonic. RCA 09026-61226-2

Max Bruch
Concerto for Violin and Orchestra No. 1 in G minor, Op. 26. Perlman, Haitink, Concertgebouw Orchestra. Angel CDC 47074

Anton Bruckner
Symphony No. 4 in E flat major, "Romantic." Tennstedt, Berlin Philharmonic. Angel CDD 63895
Symphony No. 7 in E major. Dohnányi, Cleveland Orchestra. London 430841-2
Symphony No. 9 in D minor. Bernstein, New York Philharmonic. Sony Classical SMK 47542

Frédéric Chopin
Concertos for Piano and Orchestra Nos. 1 and 2, Opp. 11, 21. Perahia, Mehta, Israel Philharmonic. Sony Classical SK 44922

Aaron Copland

Appalachian Spring Suite. Bernstein, New York Philharmonic. CBS MK 39443

Concerto for Clarinet and Orchestra. Stoltzman, Leighton Smith, London Symphony. RCA 09026-61360-2

Lincoln Portrait for Speaker and Orchestra. Fonda, Copland, London Symphony. CBS MT 30649

Symphony No. 3. Bernstein, New York Philharmonic. Deutsche Grammophon 419170-2 GH

John Corigliano

Symphony No. 1. Barenboim, Chicago Symphony. Erato 2292-45601-2

Claude Debussy

Images pour Orchestre. Boulez, Cleveland Orchestra. Deutsche Grammophon 435766-2 GH

La Mer. Solti, Chicago Symphony. London 436468-2 LH

Nocturnes. Solti, Chicago Symphony. London 436468-2 LH

Prélude à l'Après-midi d'un faune. Boulez, Cleveland Orchestra. Deutsche Grammophon 435766-2 GH

Antonín Dvořák

Concerto for Cello and Orchestra in B minor, Op. 104. Harrell, Levine, London Symphony. RCA 6531-2 RG

Symphony No. 8 in G major, Op. 88. Munch, Boston Symphony. RCA 09026-61206-2

Symphony No. 9 in E minor, Op. 95, "From the New World." Bernstein, Israel Philharmonic. Deutsche Grammophon. 427346-2 GH

Sir Edward Elgar

Concerto for Cello and Orchestra in E minor, Op. 85. Du Pré, Barbirolli, London Symphony. EMI Classics CDC 47329

Variations on an Original Theme, "Enigma," Op. 36. Slatkin, London Philharmonic. RCA 60073-2 RC

César Franck

Symphonic Variations for Piano and Orchestra. Firkusny, Flor, Royal Philharmonic. RCA 60146-2 RC

Symphony in D minor. Flor, Royal Philharmonic. RCA 60146-2 RC

George Gershwin

An American in Paris. Levine, Chicago Symphony. Deutsche Grammophon 4316252 GH

Concerto in F for Piano and Orchestra. Wild, Fiedler, Boston Pops. RCA 6519-2 RG

Rhapsody in Blue. Levine, Chicago Symphony. Deutsche Grammophon 4316252 GH

Edvard Grieg

Concerto for Piano and Orchestra in A minor, Op. 16. Davidovich, Schwarz, Seattle Symphony. Delos DE 3091

George Frideric Handel

Royal Fireworks Music. Marriner, Academy of St. Martin in the Fields. Argo 414596-2 ZH

Water Music. Marriner, Academy of St. Martin in the Fields. Argo 414596-2 ZH

Roy Harris

Symphony No. 3. Bernstein, New York Philharmonic. Deutsche Grammophon 419780-2 GH

Franz Joseph Haydn

Concerto for Cello and Orchestra in D major, H. VIIb:2. Ma, Garcia, English Chamber Orchestra. CBS MK 39310

Concerto for Trumpet and Orchestra in E flat major, H. VIIe:1. Marsalis, Leppard, National Philharmonic of London. CBS MK 39310

Symphony No. 45 in F sharp minor, H. I:45, "Farewell." Mackerras, St. Luke's Orchestra. Telarc CD 80156

Symphony No. 83 in G minor, H. I:83, "The Hen." Wolff, St. Paul Chamber Orchestra. Teldec 2292-73133-2

Symphony No. 88 in G major, H. I:88. Bernstein, Vienna Philharmonic. Deutsche Grammophon 413777-2 GH

Symphony No. 92 in G major, H. I:92, "Oxford." Bernstein, Vienna Philharmonic. Deutsche Grammophon 413777-2 GH

Symphony No. 94 in G major, H. I:94, "Surprise." Harnoncourt, Concertgebouw Orchestra. Teldec 9031-73148-2

Symphony No. 99 in E flat major, H. I:99. Harnoncourt, Concertgebouw Orchestra. Teldec 2292-46331-2

Symphony No. 100 in G major, H. I:100, "Military." Harnoncourt, Concertgebouw Orchestra. Teldec 9031-74859-2

Symphony No. 101 in D major, H. I:101, "Clock." Brüggen, Orchestra of the 18th Century. Philips 422240-2 PH

Symphony No. 103 in E flat major, H. I:103, "Drumroll." Brüggen, Orchestra of the 18th Century. Philips 422240-2 PH

Symphony No. 104 in D major, "London." H. I:104, Harnoncourt, Concertgebouw Orchestra. Teldec 2292-43526-2

Paul Hindemith

Symphonic Metamorphosis of Themes by Carl Maria von Weber. Bernstein, Israel Philharmonic. Deutsche Grammophon 429404-2 GH

Symphony, Mathis der Maler. Bernstein, Israel Philharmonic. Deutsche Grammophon 429404-2 GH

Charles Ives

Symphony No. 3, "The Camp Meeting." Slatkin, St. Louis Symphony. RCA 09026-61222-2

Three Places in New England. Slatkin, St. Louis Symphony. RCA 09026-61222-2

The Unanswered Question. Slatkin, St. Louis Symphony. RCA 09026-61222-2

Leoš Janáček

Sinfonietta. Tilson Thomas, London Symphony. Sony Classical SK 47182

Zoltán Kodály

Dances of Galánta. Schwarz, Seattle Symphony. Delos DE 3083
Háry János Suite. Schwarz, Seattle Symphony. Delos DE 3083

Franz Liszt

Concerto for Piano and Orchestra No. 1 in E flat major. Ax, Salonen, Philharmonia Orchestra. Sony Classical SK 53289

Les Préludes. Muti, Philadelphia Orchestra. Angel CDC 47022

Gustav Mahler

Das Lied von der Erde. Forester, Lewis, Reiner, Chicago Symphony. RCA 60178-2 RG

Symphony No. 1 in D major, "Titan." Bernstein, New York Philharmonic. CBS MK 42194

Symphony No. 2 in C minor, "Resurrection." Valente, Forrester, Kaplan, London Symphony. MCA Classics 2-MCAD 11011

Symphony No. 3 in D minor. Ludwig, Bernstein, New York Philharmonic. Deutsche Grammophon 2-427328-2 GH2

Symphony No. 4 in G major. Battle, Maazel. CBS MDK 44908

Symphony No. 5 in C sharp minor. Bernstein, Vienna Philharmonic. Deutsche Grammophon 423608-2 GH

Symphony No. 6 in A minor. Bernstein, Vienna Philharmonic. Deutsche Grammophon 2-427697-2 GH2

Symphony No. 7 in E minor. Rattle, City of Birmingham Symphony. EMI Classics CDC 54344

Symphony No. 8 in E flat major, "Symphony of a Thousand." Bernstein, London Symphony. Sony Classical 3-SM3K 47581

Symphony No. 9 in D major. Bernstein, Concertgebouw Orchestra. Deutsche Grammophon 2-419208-2 GH2

Felix Mendelssohn

Concerto for Piano and Orchestra No. 1 in G minor, Op. 25. Kalichstein, Laredo, Scottish Chamber Orchestra. Nimbus NI 5112

Concerto for Violin and Orchestra in E minor, Op. 64. Perlman, Barenboim, Chicago Symphony. Erato 91732-2

Incidental Music for *A Midsummer Night's Dream,* Opp. 21, 61. Dutoit, Montreal Symphony. London 430722-2

Overture, *The Hebrides (Fingal's Cave),* Op. 26. Laredo, Scottish Chamber Orchestra. Nimbus NI 5112

Symphony No. 3 in A minor, Op. 56, "Scotch." Haitink, London Philharmonic. Philips 420884-2

Symphony No. 4 in A major, Op. 90, "Italian." Previn, London Symphony. EMI Classics CDE 67775

Symphony No. 5 in D minor, Op. 107, "Reformation." Flor, Bamberg Symphony. RCA 09026-60391-2

Wolfgang Amadeus Mozart

Concerto for Clarinet and Orchestra in A major, K. 622. Stoltzman, English Chamber Orchestra. RCA 60723-2

Concerto for Piano and Orchestra No. 9 in E flat major, K. 271, "Jeunehomme." Bilson, Gardiner, English Baroque Soloists. Deutsche Grammophon 410905-2 AH

Concerto for Piano and Orchestra No. 15 in B flat major, K. 450. Uchida, Tate, English Chamber Orchestra. Philips 426305-2 PH

Concerto for Piano and Orchestra No. 17 in G major, K. 453. Ax, Zuckerman, St. Paul Chamber Orchestra. RCA 60136-2

Concerto for Piano and Orchestra No. 19 in F major, K. 459. R. Serkin, Abbado, London Symphony. Deutsche Grammophon 410989-2

Concerto for Piano and Orchestra No. 20 in D minor, K. 466. Kissin, Spivakov, Moscow Virtuosi. RCA 09026-60400-2

Concerto for Piano and Orchestra No. 21 in C major, K. 467. De Larrocha, Tate, English Chamber Orchestra. RCA 60825-2

Concerto for Piano and Orchestra No. 22 in E flat major, K. 482. De Larrocha, Davis, English Chamber Orchestra. RCA 09026-61698-2

Concerto for Piano and Orchestra No. 23 in A major, K. 488. De Larrocha, Davis, English Chamber Orchestra. RCA 09026-60989-2

Concerto for Piano and Orchestra No. 24 in C minor, K. 491. Davis, English Chamber Orchestra. RCA 09026-60989-2

Concerto for Piano and Orchestra No. 25 in C major, K. 503. R. Serkin, Abbado, London Symphony. Deutsche Grammophon 429978-2

Concerto for Piano and Orchestra No. 26 in D major, K. 537, "Coronation." De Larrocha, Davis, English Chamber Orchestra. RCA 09026-61698-2

Concerto for Piano and Orchestra No. 27 in B flat major, K. 595. R. Serkin, Abbado, London Symphony. Deutsche Grammophon 427812-2

Concerto for Violin and Orchestra No. 4 in D major, K. 218. Oistrakh (violin and conduct), Berlin Philharmonic. Angel CDM 69064

Concerto for Violin and Orchestra No. 5 in A major, K. 219, "Turkish." Oistrakh (violin and conduct), Berlin Philharmonic. Angel CDM 69064

Eine kleine Nachtmusik, K. 525. Leinsdorf, Boston Symphony. RCA 09026-60907-2

Overtures *(Don Giovanni,* K. 527; *The Magic Flute,* K. 620; *The Marriage of Figaro,* K. 492). Marriner, Academy of St. Martin in the Fields. Angel CDC 47014

Sinfonia Concertante for Oboe, Clarinet, Bassoon, Horn, and Orchestra in E flat major, K. (297b) (Anh 9). Orpheus Chamber Orchestra. Deutsche Grammophon 429784-2

Sinfonia Concertante for Violin, Viola, and Orchestra in E flat major, K. 364. Perlman, Zuckerman, Mehta, Israel Philharmonic. Deutsche Grammophon 415486-2

Symphonies Nos. 29, K. 201; 31, K. 297, "Paris"; 35, K. 385, "Haffner"; 36, K. 425, "Linz"; 38, K. 504, "Prague"; 39, K. 543; 40, K. 550; 41, K. 551, "Jupiter." Beecham, London Philharmonic. Angel 3-CDHC 63698

Modest Mussorgsky

A Night on Bald Mountain. Bernstein, New York Philharmonic. CBS MYK 36726

Pictures at an Exhibition. Bernstein, New York Philharmonic. CBS MYK 36726

Sergei Prokofiev

Concerto for Piano and Orchestra No. 2 in G minor, Op. 16. Paik, Wit, Polish National Radio Orchestra. Naxos 8.550565

Concerto for Piano and Orchestra No. 3 in C major, Op. 26. Paik, Wit, Polish National Radio Orchestra. Naxos 8.550566

Concertos for Violin and Orchestra Nos. 1, Op. 18, and 2, Op. 63. Stern, Mehta, New York Philharmonic. CBS MK 42439

Romeo and Juliet, Suites 1 and 2, Opp. 64b, 64c. Järvi, Royal Scottish National Orchestra. Chandos CHAN 8940

Symphony No. 1 in D major, Op. 25, "Classical Symphony." Slatkin, London Philharmonic. RCA 09026-61350-2

Symphony No. 5 in B flat major, Op. 100. Slatkin, London Philharmonic. RCA 09026-61350-2

Symphony No. 6 in E flat minor, Op. 111. Järvi, Scottish National Orchestra. Chandos CHAN 8359

Sergei Rachmaninoff

Concerto for Piano and Orchestra No. 2 in C minor, Op. 18. Ashkenazy, Previn, London Symphony. London 417702-2 LM

Rhapsody on a Theme of Paganini for Piano and Orchestra, Op. 43. Ashkenazy, Previn, London Symphony. London 417702-2 LM

Symphony No. 2 in E minor, Op. 27. Litton, Royal Philharmonic. Virgin Classics CDC 59548

Maurice Ravel

Boléro. Barenboim, Chicago Symphony. Erato 2292-45766-2

Concertos in D major for Piano (Left Hand) and Orchestra and for Piano and Orchestra in G major. De Larrocha, Slatkin, St. Louis Symphony. RCA 09026-60985-2

Pavane pour une Infante défunte. Barenboim, Chicago Symphony. Erato 2292-45766-2

Rapsodie espagnole. Barenboim, Chicago Symphony. Erato 2292-45766-2

Le Tombeau de Couperin. Mata, Dallas Symphony. RCA 60485-2 RV

La Valse: poème chorégraphique. Dutoit, Montreal Symphony. London 430714-2 LM

Ottorino Respighi

The Fountains of Rome. Dutoit, Montreal Symphony. London 410145-2 LH

The Pines of Rome. Dutoit, Montreal Symphony. London 410145-2 LH

Nikolai Rimsky-Korsakov

Capriccio espagnol, Op. 34. Ormandy, Philadelphia Orchestra. Sony Classical SBK 46537

Scheherazade, Op. 35. Ormandy, Philadelphia Orchestra. Sony Classical SBK 46537

Gioacchino Rossini

Overtures (*The Barber of Seville, La Gazza ladra, La Scala di seta, Semiramide, William Tell*). Bernstein, New York Philharmonic. CBS SMK 47606

Camille Saint-Saëns

Concerto for Cello and Orchestra in A minor, Op. 33. Ma, Maazel, National Orchestra of France. Sony Classical MDK 46506

Concerto for Piano and Orchestra No. 2 in G minor, Op. 22. Davidovich, Järvi, Concertgebouw Orchestra. Philips 410052-2

Symphony No. 3 in C minor, Op. 78, "Organ Symphony." DePriest, Royal Stockholm Philharmonic. BIS CD 555

Arnold Schoenberg

Verklärte Nacht, Op. 4. Levine, Berlin Philharmonic. Deutsche Grammophon 435883-2

Franz Schubert

Symphony No. 5 in B flat major, D. 485. Bernstein, Concertgebouw Orchestra. Deutsche Grammophon 427645-2 GH

Symphony No. 8 in B minor, D. 759, "Unfinished." Bernstein, Concertgebouw Orchestra. Deutsche Grammophon 427645-2 GH

Symphony No. 9 in C major, D. 944, "Great." Bernstein, Concertgebouw. Deutsche Grammophon 427646-2 GH

Robert Schumann

Concerto for Cello and Orchestra in A minor, Op. 129. Harrell, Marriner, Cleveland Orchestra. London 430743-2 LM

Concerto for Piano and Orchestra in A minor, Op. 54. De Larrocha, Davis, London Symphony. RCA 09026-61279-2

Symphonies Nos. 1, Op. 38, "Spring"; 2, Op. 61; 3, Op. 97, "Rhenish"; 4, Op. 120. Haitink, Concertgebouw Orchestra. Philips 2-416126-2 PH2

Dmitri Shostakovich

Symphony No. 1, Op. 10. Solti, Concertgebouw Orchestra. London 436469-2 LH

Symphony No. 5, Op. 47. Inbal, Frankfurt Radio Symphony. Denon CO 74175

Symphony No. 10, Op. 93. Solti, Chicago Symphony. London 4333073-2

Jean Sibelius

Concerto for Violin and Orchestra, Op. 47. Perlman, Previn, Pittsburgh Symphony. Angel CDC 47167

Finlandia, Op. 26, No. 7. Levi, Cleveland Orchestra. Telarc CD 80095

Symphony No. 1 in E minor, Op. 39. Bernstein, Vienna Philharmonic. Deutsche Grammophon 435351-2 GH

Symphony No. 2 in D major, Op. 43. Levi, Cleveland Orchestra. Telarc CD 80095

Bedřich Smetana

The Moldau. Karajan, Vienna Philharmonic. Deutsche Grammophon 415509-2 GH

Richard Strauss

Also sprach Zarathustra, Op. 30. Solti, Chicago Symphony. London 430445-2 LM

Don Juan, Op. 20. Solti, Chicago Symphony. London 430445-2 LM

Don Quixote, Op. 35. Ozawa, Boston Symphony. Sony Classical MDK 45804

Ein Heldenleben, Op. 40. Barenboim, Chicago Symphony. Erato 2292-45621-2

Till Eulenspiegels lustige Streiche, Op. 28. Solti, Chicago Symphony. London 430445-2 LM

Tod und Verklärung, Op. 24. Previn, Vienna Philharmonic. Telarc CD80167

Igor Stravinsky

The Firebird Suite. Bernstein, Israel Philharmonic. Deutsche Grammophon 431045-2 GBE

Petrouchka. Boulez, Cleveland Orchestra. Deutsche Grammophon 435769-2 GH

The Rite of Spring. Boulez, Cleveland Orchestra. Deutsche Grammophon 435769-2 GH

Symphony in Three Movements. Tilson Thomas, London Symphony. Sony Classical 53275

Peter Ilyich Tchaikovsky

Concerto for Piano and Orchestra No. 1 in B flat minor, Op. 23. Argerich, Dutoit, Royal Philharmonic. Deutsche Grammophon 415062-2 GH

Concerto for Violin and Orchestra in D major, Op. 35. Heifetz, Reiner, Chicago Symphony. RCA 5933-2 RC

Nutcracker Suite, Op. 71A. Solti, Chicago Symphony. London 430707-2 LM

Overture Solennelle, "1812," Op. 49. Gibson, London Philharmonic. Collins Classics EC 1009-2

Romeo and Juliet Overture Fantasia. Abbado, Boston Symphony. Deutsche Grammophon 427220-2 GR

Symphonies Nos. 2, Op. 17, "Little Russian"; 4, Op. 36; 5, Op. 64; 6, Op. 74, "Pathétique." Karajan, Berlin Philharmonic. Deutsche Grammophon 429675-2 GSE4

Variations on a Rococo Theme for Cello and Orchestra, Op. 33. Rostropovich, Karajan, Berlin Philharmonic. Deutsche Grammophon 413819-2 GH

Antonio Vivaldi

The Four Seasons, Op. 8. Hogwood, Academy of Ancient Music. L'Oiseau Lyre 410126-2

Richard Wagner

Overtures and Preludes *(The Flying Dutchman, Lohengrin, Die Meistersinger von Nürnberg, Tannhäuser),* Prelude and Finale from *Tristan und Isolde.* Karajan, Berlin Philharmonic. EMI Classics CDM 64334

Overture to *Rienzi.* Mehta, New York Philharmonic. Sony Classical SK 45749

Carl Maria von Weber

Overtures *(Der Freischütz, Euryanthe, Oberon).* Järvi, Philharmonia. Chandos CHAN 9066

APPENDIX

75 More Masterpieces, with Brief Commentary

Johann Sebastian Bach
Concerto for Clavier and Orchestra in D minor, BWV 1052
Concerto for Clavier and Orchestra in F minor, BWV 1056
Concerto for Violin and Orchestra in A minor, BWV 1041
Concerto for Violin and Orchestra in E major, BWV 1042
Concerto for Two Violins and Orchestra in D minor, BWV 1043
  Concertos with rhythmically vibrant fast movements and soulful slow movements, composed by the greatest of the Baroque composers.

Béla Bartók
The Miraculous Mandarin
  A powerful suite extracted from music composed for a violent, erotic pantomime.

Alban Berg
Concerto for Violin and Orchestra
  Composed as a memorial on the death of a friend, the concerto uses the 12-tone method in a very personal and accessible way.

Hector Berlioz
Harold in Italy
  Highly Romantic recollections for viola and orchestra of scenes from Byron's poem *Childe Harold*.

Georges Bizet
Symphony in C major
  A light, delightful work by the composer of the opera *Carmen*.

Ernest Bloch

Schelomo, Hebrew Rhapsody for Cello and Orchestra

An intense, impassioned composition inspired by the biblical King Solomon (Schelomo in Hebrew).

Sir Benjamin Britten

Four Sea Interludes from *Peter Grimes*

These mostly bleak and forbidding extracts convincingly evoke the desolate scenes and tragic events in the opera.

Anton Bruckner

Symphony No. 5 in E flat major
Symphony No. 6 in A major
Symphony No. 8 in C minor

Three richly Romantic symphonies conceived on the grand scale with overwhelming climaxes.

Emmanuel Chabrier

España

Another example of a French composer brilliantly capturing the color and fire of Spanish music.

Ernest Chausson

Poème for Violin and Orchestra, Op. 25
Symphony in B flat major, Op. 20

Opulent, sensuous works that show the strong influence of Richard Wagner and César Franck.

Aaron Copland

Billy the Kid
El Salón México
Rodeo

The ballet scores *Billy the Kid* and *Rodeo* convey the spirit of the American West; *El Salón México* shapes popular Mexican folk melodies into a scintillating orchestral composition.

Manuel de Falla

El Amor brujo
Nights in the Gardens of Spain
The Three-Cornered Hat

Torrid and erotic, the Gypsy-inspired *El Amor* includes the famous *Ritual Fire Dance; Nights,* an impressionistic evocation of three nocturnal scenes, features a piano soloist; *The Three-Cornered Hat,* de Falla's best-known work, is based on traditional Spanish dances and songs.

Henryk-Mikolaj Górecki
Symphony No. 3, "Symphony of Sorrowful Songs"
A mystical, minimalist work that was a best-selling CD.

Franz Joseph Haydn
Symphony No. 22 in E flat major, H. I:22, "The Philosopher"
Symphony No. 49 in F minor, H. I:49, "La Passione"
Symphony No. 96 in D major, H. I:96, "Miracle"
Three outstanding works from the Classical period by the "Father of the Symphony."

Charles Ives
Symphony No. 2
The iconoclastic Ives combines quotes ranging from Bach and Beethoven to church hymns and patriotic songs in a highly original composition.

Edouard Lalo
Symphonie espagnole, for Violin and Orchestra, Op. 21
A Spanish-flavored, brilliant violin concerto in every sense, except the title.

Franz Liszt
Concerto for Piano and Orchestra No. 2 in A major
Tasso: Lament and Triumphant
Totentanz for Piano and Orchestra
Each of these extended works puts a single theme through many colorful, kaleidoscopic transformations.

Edward MacDowell
Concerto for Piano and Orchestra No. 2 in D minor, Op. 23
The best-known work of America's leading 19th century composer.

Wolfgang Amadeus Mozart
Concerto for Flute and Orchestra in G major, K. 313
Concerto for Flute and Orchestra in D major, K. 314
Concerto for Flute, Harp, and Orchestra in C major, K. 299
Concerto for Oboe and Orchestra in C major, K. 285D
Serenade in D major, K. 239, "Serenata Notturna"
Serenade in D major, K. 250, "Haffner"
Serenade in D major, K. 320, "Post Horn Serenade"

Serenade in B flat major, K. 361
Symphony No. 25 in G minor, K. 183, "Little G minor"
Symphony No. 28 in C major, K. 200
Symphony No. 32 in G major, K. 318
Symphony No. 33 in B flat major, K. 319
Symphony No. 34 in C major, K. 338
   A selection of important compositions that help to define the Classical
   style in music by a great creative genius.

Carl Nielsen
Symphony No. 4, Op. 29, "The Inextinguishable"
Symphony No. 5, Op. 50
   Twentieth century symphonies of great breadth and depth in the Post-
   Romantic style by Denmark's leading composer.

Niccolò Paganini
Concerto for Violin and Orchestra in D major, Op. 6
   The ultimate violin showpiece by the legendary violin virtuoso.

Sergei Prokofiev
Lieutenant Kijé Suite, Op. 60
   A suite from a comic film score spoofing the Russian bureaucracy.

Sergei Rachmaninoff
Concerto for Piano and Orchestra No. 3 in D minor, Op. 30
Symphonic Dances, Op. 45
   The Third Concerto—a worthy, important work eclipsed by the Second
   Concerto; the *Dances*—highly rhythmic and comparatively conservative
   for a 1940 composition.

Maurice Ravel
Alborada del gracioso
Daphnis and Chloé
Mother Goose Suite
   The brief *Alborada,* a jester's song to his sweetheart, suggests a guitar
   being strummed; Ravel extracted two orchestral suites (with optional
   chorus) of shimmering tone colors and orgiastic climaxes from his ballet
   Daphnis and Chloé; Mother Goose achieves a perfect balance between the
   ingenuousness of the subject and Ravel's sophisticated compositional
   style.

Arnold Schoenberg

Concerto for Piano and Orchestra, Op. 42
Five Pieces for Orchestra, Op. 16
Pelleas and Melisande, Op. 5
Variations for Orchestra, Op. 31

These four pieces trace Schoenberg's evolution from Post-Romanticism *(Pelleas),* through the breakdown of tonality (Five Pieces) and the start of 12-tone composing (Variations), to the fully 12-tone (Concerto).

Franz Schubert

Symphony No. 4 in C minor, D. 417, "Tragic"
Symphony No. 6 in C major, D. 589, "The Little C major"

There appears to be little in the music to warrant Schubert's "Tragic" subtitle for the Fourth; the Sixth is "Little" only in comparison with the "Great" C major, his Ninth Symphony.

Igor Stravinsky

Concerto for Violin and Orchestra in D major
Pulcinella
Symphony in C

While all three works are in the so-called Neoclassical style, the Violin Concerto drew its inspiration from Bach, *Pulcinella* is an adaptation and orchestration of music by Pergolesi, and Symphony in C follows in the tradition of Haydn and Mozart.

Peter Ilyich Tchaikovsky

Francesca da Rimini, Op. 32
Serenade for String Orchestra, Op. 48

Tchaikovsky summons up the demonic furies of hell in *Francesca;* he graces the Serenade with some of his most inspired melodies and an absolutely enchanting waltz.

Ralph Vaughan Williams

Fantasia on a Theme by Thomas Tallis
Symphony No. 4 in F minor

A melody by English Renaissance composer Tallis serves as the theme for Vaughan Williams' string orchestra *Fantasia;* although somewhat grim in character, the Fourth Symphony is emotionally stirring.

Carl Maria von Weber

Concerto for Clarinet and Orchestra No. 1 in F minor, Op. 73
Concerto for Clarinet and Orchestra No. 2 in E flat major, Op. 74
Conzertstück for Piano and Orchestra, Op. 52

The two clarinet concertos show Weber's affection for that instrument; the exciting *Conzertstück* mingles elements of a piano concerto with that of a narrative tone poem.

Anton Webern

Five Pieces for Orchestra, Op. 10
Passacaglia, Op. 1
Six Pieces for Orchestra, Op. 6
Variations for Orchestra, Op. 30

In Five Pieces and Six Pieces, Webern weds three elements: a strong affinity for 19th century German Romanticism, the rigorous application of his advanced compositional theories, and an obsessive concern for brevity; *Passacaglia* puts an eight-note theme through 23 continuous variations; Variations uses a tone row, the generating cell of 12-tone music, for six transformations.

ABOUT THE AUTHOR

Melvin Berger is the author of a number of books on musical subjects and is program annotator for several symphonic and chamber music organizations. He has a B.M. from the Eastman School of Music, holds an M.A. from Teachers College, Columbia University, and is an Associate of London University. He has written liner notes for RCA Records, contributed articles to *World Book,* directed music programs at Ball State University and Silvermine Guild, and taught at the City University of New York. At present, he is writing and lecturing in the New York City area.